CONTENTS

● 4 Exploring Issues in Testing and Measuring Learning   239

● 5 Defining Problems and Proposing Solutions   273

Educated in the USA

Readings on the Problems and Promise of Education

Jennie Nelson
University of Idaho

Christina Haas
Kent State University

Stuart Greene
University of Wisconsin, Madison

KENDALL/HUNT PUBLISHING COMPANY
4050 Westmark Drive   Dubuque, Iowa 52002

Copyright © 1996 by Kendall/Hunt Publishing Company

ISBN 0-7872-2472-3

All rights reserved. No part of this publication may be reproduced,
stored in a retrieval system, or transmitted, in any form or by any
means, electronic, mechanical, photocopying, recording, or otherwise,
without the prior written permission of the copyright owner.

Printed in the United States of America

10   9   8   7   6   5   4   3   2

PREFACE

In focusing on exploring the problems and promise of education in the United States, this composition reader invites students and teachers to add their voices to the wide ranging public discussion about what our schools ought to accomplish. We believe that education is an especially rich topic for investigation and reflection because, as a country, we place so much emphasis on—and faith in—the role of schooling in preparing people to be active citizens, good parents, and successful workers. Hence, when we talk about our dreams for and dissatisfactions with education, we often are also talking about broader social concerns. For, as historians David Cohen and Barbara Neufeld point out, "the schools are a great theater in which we play out [the] conflicts in the culture" (86). The varied selections in this book offer readers a chance to listen and respond to some of the conflicts in education—and American society—currently being discussed.

We chose these readings because they provide a wide range of perspectives on issues in education—including selections by Charlayne Hunter-Gault, Mike Rose, Paulo Freire, E.D. Hirsch, and the American Association of University Women. The readings also reflect a wide range of genres—from autobiography and poetry to scholarly essays and research reports. While many of these selections will be challenging for readers, we believe that the variety of genres and approaches reflected in our book not only will help students to develop the kinds of critical reading skills necessary for success in college, but will also allow them to develop a deeper understanding of what is at stake in discussions of education.

Like others, we believe that students are in a unique position to offer fresh, new perceptives about the problems and promise of education in the United States. After all, they are experts on the topic of schooling, experts who bring a wide range of experiences as learners, readers, and writers, and who understand well the complex role that schooling can play in shaping people's self images and ambitions. The selections in this book and the research topics we suggest will enable them to measure their own experiences against the words of others and to explore problems for which there are no easy solutions.

Chapter One, "Comparing Personal Narratives About Education," brings into focus some key issues in education that emerge from the lives of writers who reflect upon the factors that influenced their learning in and out of school. The stories these writers tell help us to see the important role that teachers play in education and the ways that schooling changed their understanding of themselves and the world around them. But the selections in this chapter also point to the struggle that often characterizes students' transition from home to school, to the ways that tracking, bias in standardized testing, and racial, class, or gender bias can impede learning and success in and out of school.

The selections in Chapter Two, "Stepping Inside America's Schools and Classrooms," allow readers to experience daily life inside a variety of classrooms—ranging from a one-room school near the ghost town of Polaris, Montana to an urban high school in East St. Louis, Illinois. These views of school life reveal a great deal about the variety of conditions students face in public schools and about the variety in the "formal curriculum" in America's schools—the kinds of subjects students take, the teaching practices they encounter, and the kinds of learning they are expected to demonstrate. These descriptions also reveal a great deal about what educators call the "hidden curriculum," the rules of the game that govern classroom life, rules that often are not questioned or even recognized but that have a profound effect on students and teachers.

Chapter Three, "Defining the Goals of Education and Literacy," brings together the thinking of several important educational theorists as they consider the goals of literacy education. The selections here represent a range of political positions, disciplinary backgrounds, and methods of argument, as well as deeply conflicting notions about what education "ought" to be. Readers will note too how many of these selections contain implicit, or even explicit, proposals for policy development or change.

The readings in Chapter Four, "Exploring Issues in Testing and Measuring Learning," address several issues surrounding testing within and beyond educational settings. We begin with Stephen Jay Gould's historical treatment of the complexities and contradictions in the development and early applications of the IQ text, a test Gould calls, somewhat ironically, "an American invention." The authors of these selections employ an interesting variety of authorial voices as they discuss an issue that has become a hotbed of controversy in recent years.

Finally, Chapter Five, "Defining Problems and Proposing Solutions," offers a range of perspectives on what is wrong with America's schools and what needs to be done to improve them. Excerpts from the somber and oft-cited *A Nation at Risk* (published in 1983) serve as a backdrop for more recent discussions of the problems that need to be addressed in order to improve education in the United States.

Each chapter is followed by ideas for discussion, writing, and research that ask students to analyze the readings, make connections among different selections, and to begin to articulate what they think about a given issue. In large part, these suggestions are designed to guide inquiry beyond the selections included in each chapter. For example, as students consider the experiences different authors reflect upon in their personal narratives about education, they might begin to formulate questions that they would like to ask others in both school and their community. Together, the oral histories of others' school experiences, the reading they have done, and their own experiences as learners can provide the basis for building upon, extending, or challenging the assumptions that educators and others accept as unquestioningly true. Such an inquiry is important because it can help students explore those factors that influence their learning, reading, and writing practices in a profoundly personal way.

Other questions can motivate research into such commonly accepted practices as "tracking" and the use of standardized tests to measure learning. Or they can lead to a better understanding of the relationship between democracy and education and the "hidden curriculum" that informs who speaks in the classroom and what is legitimate to talk and write about in school. In essence, the questions at the end of each chapter aim at promoting the kind of critical thinking that characterizes what it means to be an author: to understand and weigh the strengths of oftentimes conflicting points of view in order to articulate a position of one's own and, in doing so, change the way others think about the world. We envision the inquiry students do as forming the basis for essays they might write or collaborative reports they might present. In turn, these essays and presentations can become central "texts" in class, used to further the conversation about education that is at the heart of this book.

Acknowledgments

This book project had its real beginning in Mike Rose's Seminar on Literacy in the fall of 1986 at Carnegie Mellon University. It was in this seminar that all three of us were introduced to literacy studies as an area of vital personal, political, and intellectual activity, and it was Mike's research—and his teaching—that led to our interest in examining these issues in the undergraduate classroom. Thank you, Mike. We are also grateful to Steve Witte for his substantive support throughout this project—and to Jeff Walker at Penn State, as well as many colleagues at the University of Idaho, for provocative discussions on the benefits (and pitfalls) of the reading- and theme-based writing course. We would also like to thank Deborah Brandt, Steve Fox, Katherine Leake, Rebecca Schoenike, Debbie Siegel, Anne Clark, and John Duffy, whose insights helped inspire a curriculum that takes education and literacy as its focus at the University of Wisconsin-Madison.

Works Cited

Cohen, David K. and Barbara Neufeld, "The Failure of High Schools and the Progress of Education," *Daedalus*, 110 (Summer 1981).

CHAPTER 1

Comparing Personal Narratives about Education

I Just Wanna Be Average

Mike Rose

Mike Rose is on the faculty of UCLA Graduate School of Education and Information Studies and UCLA Writing Programs. The following selection is a chapter from his book *Lives on the Boundary*, 1989. In the preface to his book, Rose explains:

I've worked for twenty years with children and adults deemed slow or remedial or underprepared. And at one time in my own educational life, I was so labeled. But I was lucky. I managed to get redefined. The people I've tutored and taught and the people whose lives I've studied—working-class children, poorly educated Vietnam veterans, underprepared college students, adults in a literacy program—they, for the most part, hadn't been so fortunate. They lived for many of their years in an educational underclass. In trying to present the . . . reality of such a life—the brains as well as the heart of it—I have written a personal book.

Between 1880 and 1920, well over four million Southern Italian peasants immigrated to America. Their poverty was extreme and hopeless—twelve hours of farm labor would get you one lira, about twenty cents—so increasing numbers of desperate people booked passage for the United States, the country where, the steamship companies claimed, prosperity was a way of life. My father left Naples before the turn of the century; my mother came with her mother from Calabria in 1921. They met in Altoona, Pennsylvania at the lunch counter of Tom and Joe's, a steamy diner with twangy-voiced waitresses and graveyard stew.

For my mother, life in America was not what the promoters had told her father it would be. She grew up very poor. She slept with her parents and brothers and sisters in one room. She had to quit school in the seventh grade to care for her sickly younger brothers. When her father lost his leg in a railroad accident, she began working in a garment factory where women sat crowded at their stations, solitary as penitents in a cloister. She stayed there until her marriage. My father had found a freer route. He was closemouthed about his past, but I know that he had been a salesman, a tailor, and a gambler; he knew people in the mob and had, my uncles whisper, done time in Chicago. He went through a year or two of Italian elementary school and could write a few words—those necessary to scribble measurements for a suit—and over the years developed a quiet urbanity, a persistence, and a slowly debilitating arteriosclerosis.

When my father proposed to my mother, he decided to open a spaghetti house, a venture that lasted through the war and my early years. The restaurant collapsed in bankruptcy in 1951 when Altoona's major industry, the Pennsylvania Railroad, had to shut down its shops. My parents managed to salvage seven hundred dollars and, on the advice of the family doc-

Reprinted with the permission of The Free Press, a division of Simon & Schuster from LIVES ON THE BOUNDARY: The Struggles and Achievements of America's Underprepared by Mike Rose. Copyright © 1989 by Mike Rose.

tor, headed to California, where the winters would be mild and where I, their seven-year-old son, would have the possibility of a brighter future.

At first we lived in a seedy hotel on Spring Street in downtown Los Angeles, but my mother soon found an ad in the *Times* for cheap property on the south side of town. My parents contacted a woman named Mrs. Jolly, used my mother's engagement ring as a down payment, and moved to 9116 South Vermont Avenue, a house about one and one-half miles northwest of Watts. The neighborhood was poor, and it was in transition. Some old white folks had lived there for decades and were retired. Younger black families were moving up from Watts and settling by working-class white families newly arrived from the South and the Midwest. Immigrant Mexican families were coming in from Baja. Any such demographic mix is potentially volatile, and as the fifties wore on, the neighborhood would be marked by outbursts of violence.

I have many particular memories of this time, but in general these early years seem a peculiar mix of physical warmth and barrenness: a gnarled lemon tree, thin rugs, a dirt alley, concrete in the sun. My uncles visited a few times, and we went to the beach or to orange groves. The return home, however, left the waves and spray, the thick leaves and split pulp far in the distance. I was aware of my parents watching their money and got the sense from their conversations that things could quickly take a turn for the worse. I started taping pennies to the bottom of a shelf in the kitchen.

My father's health was bad, and he had few readily marketable skills. Poker and pinochle brought in a little money, and he tried out an idea that had worked in Altoona during the war: He started a "suit club." The few customers he could scare up would pay two dollars a week on a tailor-made suit. He would take the measurements and send them to a shop back East and hope for the best. My mother took a job at a café in downtown Los Angeles, a split shift 9:00 to 12:00 and 5:00 to 9:00, but her tips were totaling sixty cents a day, so she quit for a night shift at Coffee Dan's. This got her to the bus stop at one in the morning, waiting on the same street where drunks were urinating and hookers were catching the last of the bar crowd. She made friends with a Filipino cook who would scare off the advances of old men aflame with the closeness of taxi dancers. In a couple of years, Coffee Dan's would award her a day job at the counter. Once every few weeks my father and I would take a bus downtown and visit with her, sitting at stools by the window, watching the animated but silent mix of faces beyond the glass.

My father had moved to California with faint hopes about health and a belief in his child's future, drawn by that far edge of America where the sun descends into green water. What he found was a city that was warm, verdant, vast, and indifferent as a starlet in a sports car. Altoona receded quickly, and my parents must have felt isolated and deceived. They had fallen into the abyss of paradise—two more poor settlers trying to make a go of it in the City of the Angels.

Let me tell you about our house. If you entered the front door and turned right you'd see a small living room with a couch along the east wall and one along the west wall—one couch was purple, the other tan, both bought used and both well worn. A television set was placed at the end of the purple couch, right at arm level. An old Philco radio sat next to the TV, its speaker covered with gold lamé. There was a small coffee table in the center of the room on which sat a murky fishbowl occupied by two listless guppies. If, on entering, you turned left you would see a green Formica dinner table with four chairs, a cedar chest given as a wedding present to my mother by her mother, a painted statue of the Blessed Virgin Mary, and a black trunk. I also had a plastic chaise longue between the door and the table. I would lie on this and watch television.

A short hallway leading to the bathroom opened on one side to the kitchen and, on the other, to the bedroom. The bedroom had two beds, one for me and one for my parents, a bureau with a mirror, and a chest of drawers on which we piled old shirt boxes and stacks of folded clothes. The kitchen held a refrigerator and a stove, small older models that we got when our earlier (and newer) models were repossessed by two silent men. There was one white wooden chair in the corner beneath wall cabinets. You could walk in and through a tiny pantry to the backyard and to four one-room rentals. My father got most of our furniture from a secondhand store on the next block; he would tend the store two or three hours a day as payment on our account.

As I remember it, the house was pretty dark. My mother kept the blinds in the bedroom drawn—there were no curtains there—and the venetian blinds in the living room were, often as not, left closed. The walls were bare except for a faded picture of Jesus and a calendar from the *Altoona Mirror*. Some paper carnations bent out of a white vase on the television. There was a window on the north side of the kitchen that had no blinds or curtains, so the sink got good light. My father would methodically roll up his sleeves and show me how to prepare a sweet potato or avocado seed so it would sprout. We kept a row of them on the sill above the sink, their shoots and vines rising and curling in the morning sun.

The house was on a piece of land that rose about four feet up from heavily trafficked Vermont Avenue. The yard sloped down to the street, and three steps and a short walkway led up the middle of the grass to our front door. There was a similar house immediately to the south of us. Next to it was Carmen's Barber Shop. Carmen was a short, quiet Italian who, rumor had it, had committed his first wife to the crazy house to get her money. In the afternoons, Carmen could be found in the lot behind his shop playing solitary catch, flinging a tennis ball high into the air and running under it. One day the police arrested Carmen on charges of child molesting. He was released but became furtive and suspicious. I never saw him in the lot again. Next to Carmen's was a junk store where, one summer, I made a little money polishing brass and rewiring old lamps. Then came a dilapidated real estate office, a Mexican restaurant, an empty lot, and an appliance store owned by the father of Keith Grateful, the streetwise, chubby boy who would become my best friend.

Right to the north of us was a record shop, a barber shop presided over by old Mr. Graff, Walt's Malts, a shoe repair shop with a big Cat's Paw decal in the window, a third barber shop, and a brake shop. It's as I write this that I realize for the first time that three gray men could have had a go at your hair before you left our street.

Behind our house was an unpaved alley that passed, just to the north, a power plant the length of a city block. Massive coils atop the building hissed and cracked through the day, but the doors never opened. I used to think it was abandoned—feeding itself on its own wild arcs—until one sweltering afternoon a man was electrocuted on the roof. The air was thick and still as two firemen—the only men present—brought down a charred and limp body without saying a word.

The north and south traffic on Vermont was separated by tracks for the old yellow trolley cars, long since defunct. Across the street was a huge garage, a tiny hot dog stand run by a myopic and reclusive man named Freddie, and my dreamland, the Vermont Bowl. Distant and distorted behind thick lenses, Freddie's eyes never met yours; he would look down when he took your order and give you your change with a mumble. Freddie slept on a cot in the back of his grill and died there one night, leaving tens of thousands of dollars stuffed in the mattress.

My father would buy me a chili dog at Freddie's, and then we would walk over to the bowling alley where Dad would sit at the lunch counter and drink coffee while I had a great time with pinball machines, electric shooting galleries, and an ill-kept dispenser of cheese corn. There was a small, dark bar abutting the lanes, and it called to me. I would devise reasons to walk through it: "'Scuse me, is the bathroom in here?" or "Anyone see my dad?" though I can never remember my father having a drink. It was dark and people were drinking and I figured all sorts of mysterious things were being whispered. Next to the Vermont Bowl was a large vacant lot overgrown with foxtails and dotted with car parts, bottles, and rotting cardboard. One day Keith heard that the police had found a human head in the brush. After that we explored the lot periodically, coming home with stickers all the way up to our waists. But we didn't find a thing. Not even a kneecap.

When I wasn't with Keith or in school, I would spend most of my day with my father or with the men who were renting the one-room apartments behind our house. Dad and I whiled away the hours in the bowling alley, watching TV, or planting a vegetable garden that never seemed to take. When he was still mobile, he would walk the four blocks down to St. Regina's Grammar School to take me home to my favorite lunch of boiled wieners and chocolate milk. There I'd sit, dunking my hot dog in a jar of mayonnaise and drinking my milk while Sheriff John tuned up the calliope music on his "Lunch Brigade." Though he never complained to me, I could sense that my father's health was failing, and I began devising child's ways to make him better. We had a box of rolled cotton in the bathroom, and I would go in and peel off a long strip and tape it around my jaw. Then I'd rummage through the closet, find a sweater of my father's, put on one of his hats—and sneak around to the back door. I'd knock loudly and wait. It would take him a while to get there. Finally, he'd open the door, look down, and quietly say, "Yes, Michael?" I was disappointed. Every time. Somehow I thought I could fool him. And, I guess, if he had been fooled, I would have succeeded in redefining things; I would have been the old one, he much younger, more agile, with strength in his legs.

The men who lived in the back were either retired or didn't work that much, so one of them was usually around. They proved to be, over the years, an unusual set of companions for a young boy. Ed Gionotti was the youngest of the lot, a handsome man whose wife had run off and who spoke softly and never smiled. Bud Hall and Lee McGuire were two out-of-work plumbers who lived in adjacent units and who weekly drank themselves silly, proclaiming in front of God and everyone their undying friendship or their unequivocal hatred. Old Cheech was a lame Italian who used to hobble along grabbing his testicles and rolling his eyes while he talked about the women he claimed to have on a string. There was Lester, the toothless cabbie, who several times made overtures to me and who, when he moved, left behind a drawer full of syringes and burnt spoons. Mr. Smith was a rambunctious retiree who lost his nose to an untended skin cancer. And there was Mr. Berryman, a sweet and gentle man who eventually left for a retirement hotel only to be burned alive in an electrical fire.

Except for Keith, there were no children on my block and only one or two on the immediate side streets. Most of the people I saw day to day were over fifty. People in their twenties and thirties working in the shoe shop or the garages didn't say a lot; their work and much of what they were working for drained their spirits. There were gang members who sauntered up from Hoover Avenue, three blocks to the east, and occasionally I would get shoved around, but they had little interest in me either as member or victim. I was a skinny, bespectacled kid and had neither the coloring nor the style of dress or carriage that marked me as a rival. On the whole, the days were quiet, lazy, lonely. The heat shimmering over the asphalt had no snap to it; time drifted by. I would lie on the couch at night and listen to the music from the record store or from Walt's Malts. It was new and quick paced, exciting, a little dangerous (the church had condemned Buddy Knox's "Party Doll"), and I heard in it a deep rhythmic need to be made whole with love, or marked as special, or released in some rebellious way. Even the songs about lost love—and there were plenty of them—lifted me right out of my socks with their melodious longing:

Came the dawn,
and my heart and her love and the night
were gone.
But I know I'll never forget
her kiss in the moonlight Oooo . . .
such a kiss Oooo Oooo such a night . . .

In the midst of the heat and slow time the music brought the promise of its origins, a promise of deliverance, a promise that, if only for a moment, life could be stirring and dreamy.

But the anger and frustration of South Vermont could prove too strong for music's illusion; then it was violence that provided deliverance of a different order. One night I watched as a guy sprinted from Walt's to toss something on our lawn. The police were right behind, and a cop tackled him, smashing his face into the sidewalk. I ducked out to find the packet: a dozen glassine bags of heroin. Another night, one August midnight, an argument outside the record store ended with a man being shot to death. And the occasional gang forays brought with them some fated kid who would fumble his moves and catch a knife.

It's popular these days to claim you grew up on the streets. Men tell violent tales and romanticize the lessons violence brings. But, though it was occasionally violent, it wasn't the violence in South L.A. that marked me, for sometimes you can shake that ugliness off. What finally affected me was subtler, but more pervasive; I cannot recall a young person who was crazy in love or lost in work or one old person who was passionate about a cause or an idea. I'm not talking about an absence of energy—the street toughs and, for that fact, old Cheech had energy. And I'm not talking about an absence of decency, for my father was a thoughtful man. The people I grew up with were retired from jobs that rub away the heart or were working hard at jobs to keep their lives from caving in or were anchorless and in between jobs and spouses or were diving headlong into a barren tomorrow: junkies, alcoholics, and mean kids walking along Vermont looking to throw a punch. I developed a picture of human existence that rendered it short and brutish or sad and aimless or long and quiet with rewards like afternoon naps, the evening newspaper, walks around the block, occasional letters from children in other states. When, years later, I was introduced to humanistic psychologists like Abraham Maslow and Carl Rogers, with their visions of self-actualization, or even Freud with his sober dictum about love and work, it all sounded like a glorious fairy tale, a magical account of a world full of possibility, full of hope and empowerment. Sindbad and Cinderella couldn't have been more fanciful.

Some people who manage to write their way out of the working class describe the classroom as an oasis of possibility. It became their intellectual playground, their competitive arena. Given the richness of my memories of this time, it's funny how scant are my recollections of school. I remember the red brick building of St. Regina's itself, and the topography of the playground: the swings and basketball courts and peeling benches. There are images of a few students: Erwin Petschaur, a muscular German boy with a strong accent; Dave Sanchez, who was good in math; and Sheila Wilkes, everyone's curly-haired heartthrob. And there are two nuns: Sister Monica, the third-grade teacher with beautiful hands for whom I carried a candle and who, to my dismay, had wedded herself to Christ; and Sister Beatrice, a woman truly crazed, who would sweep into class, eyes wide, to tell us about the Apocalypse.

All the hours in class tend to blend into one long, vague stretch of time. What I remember best, strangely enough, are the two things I couldn't understand and over the years grew to hate: grammar lessons and mathematics. I would sit there watching a teacher draw her long horizontal line and her short, oblique lines and break up sentences and put adjectives here and adverbs there and just not get it, couldn't see the reason for it, turned off to it. I would hide by slumping down in my seat and page through my reader, carried along by the flow of sentences in a story. She would test us, and I would dread that, for I always got Cs and Ds. Mathematics was a bit different. For whatever reasons, I didn't learn early math very well, so when it came time for more complicated operations, I couldn't keep up and started daydreaming to avoid my inadequacy. This was a strategy I would rely on as I grew older. I fell further and further behind. A memory: The teacher is faceless and seems very far away. The voice is faint and is discussing an equation written on the board. It is raining, and I am watching the streams of water form patterns on the windows.

I realize now how consistently I defended myself against the lessons I couldn't understand and the people and events of South L.A. that were too strange to view head-on. I got very good at watching a blackboard with minimum awareness. And I drifted more and more into a variety of protective fantasies. I was lucky in that although my parents didn't read or write very much and had no more than a few books around the house, they never debunked my pursuits. And when they could, they bought me what I needed to spin my web.

One early Christmas they got me a small chemistry set. My father brought home an old card table from the secondhand store, and on that table I spread out my test tubes, my beaker, my Erlenmeyer flask, and my gas-generating apparatus. The set came equipped with chemicals, minerals, and various treated papers—all in little square bottles. You could send away to someplace in Maryland for more, and I did, saving pennies and nickels to get the substances that were too exotic for my set, the Junior Chemcraft: Congo red paper, azurite, glycerine, chrome alum, cochineal—this from female insects!—tartaric acid, chameleon paper, logwood. I would sit before my laboratory and play for hours. My father rested on the purple couch in front of me watching wrestling or *Gunsmoke* while I measured powders or heated crystals or blew into solutions that my breath would turn red or pink. I was taken by the blends of names and by the colors that swirled through the beaker. My equations were visual and phonetic. I would hold a flask up to the hall light, imagining the veils of a million atoms dancing. Sulfur and alcohol hung in the air. I wanted to shake down the house.

One day my mother came home from Coffee Dan's with an awful story. The teenage brother of one of her waitress friends was in the hospital. He had been fooling around with explosives in his garage "where his mother couldn't see him," and something happened, and "he blew away part of his throat. For God's sake, be careful," my mother said. "Remember poor Ada's brother." Wow! I thought. How neat! Why couldn't my experiments be that dangerous? I really lost heart when I realized that you could probably eat the chemicals spread across my table.

I knew what I had to do. I saved my money for a week and then walked with firm resolve past Walt's Malts, past the brake shop, across Ninetieth Street, and into Palazolla's market. I bought a little bottle of Alka-Seltzer and ran home. I chipped up the wafers and mixed them into a jar of white crystals. When my mother came home, dog tired, and sat down on the edge of the couch to tell me and Dad about her day, I gravely poured my concoction into a beaker of water, cried something about the unexpected, and ran out from behind my table. The beaker foamed ominously. My father swore in Italian. The second time I tried it, I got something milder—in English. And by my third near-miss with death, my parents were calling my behavior cute. Cute! Who wanted cute? I wanted to toy with the disaster that befell Ada Pendleton's brother. I wanted all those wonderful colors to collide in ways that could blow your voice box right off.

But I was limited by the real. The best I could do was create a toxic antacid. I loved my chemistry set—its glassware and its intriguing labels—but it wouldn't allow me to do the things I wanted to do. St. Regina's had an all-purpose room, one wall of which was lined with old books—and one of those shelves held a row of plastic-covered space novels. The sheen of their covers was gone, and their futuristic portraits were dotted with erasures and grease spots like a meteor shower of the everyday. I remember the rockets best. Long cylinders outfitted at the base with three slick fins, tapering at the other end to a perfect conical point, ready to pierce out of the stratosphere and into my imagination: X-fifteens and Mach 1, the dark side of the moon, the Red Planet, Jupiter's Great Red Spot, Saturn's rings—and beyond the solar system to swirling wisps of galaxies, to stardust.

I would check out my books two at a time and take them home to curl up with a blanket on my chaise longue, reading, sometimes, through the weekend, my back aching, my thoughts lost between galaxies. I became the hero of a thousand adventures, all with intricate plots and the triumph of good over evil, all many dimensions removed from the dim walls of the living room. We were given time to draw in school, so, before long, all this worked itself onto paper. The stories I was reading were reshaping themselves into pictures. My father got me some butcher paper from Palazolla's, and I continued to draw at home. My collected works rendered the Horsehead Nebula, goofy space cruisers, robots, and Saturn. Each had its crayon, a particular waxy pencil with mood and meaning: rust and burnt sienna for Mars, yellow for the Sun, lime and rose for Saturn's rings, and bright red for the Jovian spot. I had a little sharpener to keep the points just right. I didn't write any stories; I just read and drew. I wouldn't care much about writing until late in high school.

The summer before the sixth grade, I got a couple of jobs. The first was at a pet store a block or so away from my house. Since I was still small, I could maneuver around in breeder cages, scraping the heaps of parakeet crap from the tin floor, cleaning the water troughs and seed trays. It was pretty awful. I would go home after work and fill the tub and soak until all the fleas and bird mites came floating to the surface, little Xs in their multiple eyes. When I heard about a job selling strawberries door-to-door, I jumped at it. I went to work for a white-haired Chicano named Frank. He would carry four or five kids and dozens of crates of strawberries in his ramshackle truck up and down the avenues of the better neighborhoods: houses with mowed lawns and petunia beds. We'd work all day for seventy-five cents, Frank dropping pairs of us off with two crates each, then picking us up at preassigned corners. We spent lots of time together, bouncing around on the truck bed redolent with strawberries or sitting on a corner, cold, listening for the sputter of Frank's muffler. I started telling the other kids about my books, and soon it was my job to fill up that time with stories.

Reading opened up the world. There I was, a skinny bookworm drawing the attention of street kids who, in any other circumstances, would have had me for breakfast. Like an epic tale-teller, I developed the stories as I went along, relying on a flexible plot line and a repository of heroic events. I had a great time. I sketched out trajectories with my finger on Frank's dusty truck bed. And I stretched out each story's climax, creating cliffhangers like the ones I saw in the Saturday serials. These stories created for me a temporary community.

It was around this time that fiction started leading me circuitously to a child's version of science. In addition to the space novels, St. Regina's library also had half a dozen books on astronomy—*The Golden Book of the Planets* and stuff like that—so I checked out a few of them. I liked what I read and wheedled enough change out of my father to enable me to take the bus to the public library. I discovered star maps, maps of lunar seas, charts upon charts of the solar system and the planetary moons: Rhea, Europa, Callisto, Miranda, Io. I didn't know that most of these moons were named for women—I didn't know classical mythology—but I would say their names to myself as though they had a woman's power to protect: Europa, Miranda, Io . . . The distances between stars fascinated me, as did the sizes of the big telescopes. I sent away for catalogs. Then prices fascinated me too. I wanted to drape my arm over a thousand-dollar scope and hear its motor drive whirr. I conjured a twelve-year-old's life of the astronomer: sitting up all night with potato chips and the stars, tracking the sky for supernovas, humming "Earth Angel" with the Penguins. What was my mother to do but save her tips and buy me a telescope?!

It was a little reflecting job, and I solemnly used to carry it out to the front of the house on warm summer nights, to find Venus or Alpha Centauri or trace the stars in Orion or lock onto the moon. I would lay out my star maps on the concrete, more for their magic than anything else, for I had trouble figuring them out. I was no geometer of the constellations; I was their balladeer. Those nights were very peaceful. I was far enough away from the front door and up enough from the sidewalk to make it seem as if I rested on a mound of dark silence, a mountain in Arizona, perhaps, watching the sky alive with points of light. Poor Freddie, toothless Lester whispering promises about making me feel good, the flat days, the gang fights—all this receded, for it was now me, the star child, lost in an eyepiece focused on a reflecting mirror that cradled, in its center, a shimmering moon.

The loneliness in Los Angeles fosters strange arrangements. Lou Minton was a wiry man with gaunt, chiseled features and prematurely gray hair, combed straight back. He had gone to college in the South for a year or two and kicked around the country for many more before settling in L.A. He lived in a small downtown apartment with a single window and met my mother at the counter of Coffee Dan's. He had been alone too long and eventually came to our house and became part of the family. Lou repaired washing machines, and he had a car, and he would take me to the vast, echoing library just west of Pershing Square and to the Museum of Science and Industry in Exposition Park. He bought me astronomy books, taught me how to use tools, and helped me build model airplanes from balsa wood and rice paper. As my father's health got worse, Lou took care of him.

My rhapsodic and prescientific astronomy carried me into my teens, consumed me right up till high school, losing out finally, and only, to the siren call of pubescence—that endocrine hoodoo that transmogrifies nice boys into gawky flesh fiends. My mother used to bring home *Confidential* magazine, a peep-show rag specializing in the sins of the stars, and it beckoned me mercilessly: Jayne Mansfield's cleavage, Gina Lollobrigida's eyes, innuendos about deviant sexuality, ads for Frederick's of Hollywood—spiked heels, lacy brassieres, the epiphany of silk panties on a mannequin's hips. Along with Phil Everly, I was through with counting the stars above.

Budding manhood. Only adults talk about adolescence budding. Kids have no choice but to talk in extremes; they're being wrenched and buffeted, rabbit-punched from inside by systemic thugs. Nothing sweet and pastoral here. Kids become ridiculous and touching at one and the same time: passionate about the trivial, fixed before the mirror, yet traversing one of the most important rites of passage in their lives—liminal people, silly and profoundly human. Given my own expertise, I fantasized about concocting the fail-safe aphrodisiac that would bring Marianne Bilpusch, the cloakroom monitor, rushing into my arms or about commanding a squadron of bosomy, linguistically mysterious astronauts like Zsa Zsa Gabor. My parents used to say that their son would have the best education they could afford. Maybe I would be a doctor. There was a public school in our neighborhood and several Catholic schools to the west. They had heard that quality schooling meant private, Catholic schooling, so they somehow got the money together to send me to Our Lady of Mercy, fifteen or so miles southwest of Ninety-first and Vermont. So much for my fantasies. Most Catholic secondary schools then were separated by gender.

It took two buses to get to Our Lady of Mercy. The first started deep in South Los Angeles and caught me at midpoint. The second drifted through neighborhoods with trees, parks, big lawns, and lots of flowers. The rides were long but were livened up by a group of South L.A. veterans whose parents also thought that Hope had set up shop in the west end of the county. There was Christy Biggars, who, at sixteen, was dealing and was, according to rumor, a pimp as well. There were Bill Cobb and Johnny Gonzales, grease-pencil artists extraordinaire, who left Nembutal-enhanced swirls of "Cobb" and "Johnny" on the corrugated walls of the bus. And then there was Tyrrell Wilson. Tyrrell was the coolest kid I knew. He ran the dozens like a metric halfback, laid down a rap that outrhymed and outpointed Cobb, whose rap was good but not great—the curse of a moderately soulful kid trapped in white skin. But it was Cobb who would sneak a radio onto the bus, and thus underwrote his patter with Little Richard, Fats Domino, Chuck Berry, the Coasters, and Ernie K. Doe's mother-in-law, an awful woman who was "sent from down below." And so it was that Christy and Cobb and Johnny G. and Tyrrell and I and assorted others picked up along the way passed our days in the back of the bus, a funny mix brought together by geography and parental desire.

Entrance to school brings with it forms and releases and assessments. Mercy relied on a series of tests, mostly the Stanford-Binet, for placement, and somehow the results of my tests got confused with those of another student named Rose. The other Rose apparently didn't do very well, for I was placed in the vocational track, a euphemism for the bottom level. Neither

I nor my parents realized what this meant. We had no sense that Business Math, Typing, and English-Level D were dead ends. The current spate of reports on the schools criticizes parents for not involving themselves in the education of their children. But how would someone like Tommy Rose, with his two years of Italian schooling, know what to ask? And what sort of pressure could an exhausted waitress apply? The error went undetected, and I remained in the vocational track for two years. What a place.

My homeroom was supervised by Brother Dill, a troubled and unstable man who also taught freshman English. When his class drifted away from him, which was often, his voice would rise in paranoid accusations, and occasionally he would lose control and shake or smack us. I hadn't been there two months when one of his brisk, face-turning slaps had my glasses sliding down the aisle. Physical education was also pretty harsh. Our teacher was a stubby ex-lineman who had played old-time pro ball in the Midwest. He routinely had us grabbing our ankles to receive his stinging paddle across our butts. He did that, he said, to make men of us. "Rose," he bellowed on our first encounter; me standing geeky in line in my baggy shorts. " 'Rose'? What the hell kind of name is that?"

"Italian, sir," I squeaked.

"Italian! Ho. Rose, do you know the sound a bag of shit makes when it hits the wall?"

"No, sir."

"Wop!"

Sophomore English was taught by Mr. Mitropetros. He was a large, bejeweled man who managed the parking lot at the Shrine Auditorium. He would crow and preen and list for us the stars he'd brushed against. We'd ask questions and glance knowingly and snicker, and all that fueled the poor guy to brag some more. Parking cars was his night job. He had little training in English, so his lesson plan for his day work had us reading the district's required text, *Julius Caesar*, aloud for the semester. We'd finish the play way before the twenty weeks was up, so he'd have us switch parts again and again and start again: Dave Snyder, the fastest guy at Mercy, muscling through Caesar to the breathless squeals of Calpurnia, as interpreted by Steve Fusco, a surfer who owned the school's most envied paneled wagon. Week ten and Dave and Steve would take on new roles, as would we all, and render a water-logged Cassius and a Brutus that are beyond my powers of description.

Spanish I—taken in the second year—fell into the hands of a new recruit. Mr. Montez was a tiny man, slight, five foot six at the most, soft-spoken and delicate. Spanish was a particularly rowdy class, and Mr. Montez was as prepared for it as a doily maker at a hammer throw. He would tap his pencil to a room in which Steve Fusco was propelling spitballs from his heavy lips, in which Mike Dweetz was taunting Billy Hawk, a half-Indian, half-Spanish, reed-thin, quietly explosive boy. The vocational track at Our Lady of Mercy mixed kids traveling in from South L.A. with South Bay surfers and a few Slavs and Chicanos from the harbors of San Pedro. This was a dangerous miscellany: surfers and hodads and South-Central blacks all ablaze to the metronomic tapping of Hector Montez's pencil.

One day Billy lost it. Out of the corner of my eye I saw him strike out with his right arm and catch Dweetz across the neck. Quick as a spasm, Dweetz was out of his seat, scattering desks, cracking Billy on the side of the head, right behind the eye. Snyder and Fusco and others broke it up, but the room felt hot and close and naked. Mr. Montez's tenuous authority was finally ripped to shreds, and I think everyone felt a little strange about that. The charade was over, and when it came down to it, I don't think any of the kids really wanted it to end this way. They had pushed and pushed and bullied their way into a freedom that both scared and embarrassed them.

Students will float to the mark you set. I and the others in the vocational classes were bobbing in pretty shallow water. Vocational education has aimed at increasing the economic opportunities of students who do not do well in our schools. Some serious programs succeed in doing that, and through exceptional teachers—like Mr. Gross in *Horace's Compromise*[1]—students learn to develop hypotheses and troubleshoot, reason through a problem, and communicate effectively—the true job skills. The vocational track, however, is most often a place for those who are just not making it, a dumping ground for the disaffected. There were a few teachers who worked hard at education; young Brother Slattery, for example, combined a stern voice with weekly quizzes to try to pass along to us a skeletal outline of world history. But mostly the teachers had no idea of how to engage the imaginations of us kids who were scuttling along at the bottom of the pond.

And the teachers would have needed some inventiveness, for none of us was groomed for the classroom. It wasn't just that I didn't know things—didn't know how to simplify algebraic fractions, couldn't identify different kinds of clauses, bungled Spanish translations—but that I had developed various faulty and inadequate ways of doing algebra and making sense of Spanish. Worse yet, the years of defensive tuning out in elementary school had given me a way to escape quickly while seeming at least half alert. During my time in Voc. Ed., I developed further into a mediocre student and a somnambulant problem solver, and that affected the subjects I did have the wherewithal to handle: I detested Shakespeare; I got bored with history. My attention flitted here and there. I fooled around in class and read my books indifferently—the intellectual equivalent of playing with your food. I did what I had to do to get by, and I did it with half a mind.

But I did learn things about people and eventually came into my own socially. I liked the guys in Voc. Ed. Growing up where I did, I understood and admired physical prowess, and there was an abundance of muscle here. There was Dave Snyder, a sprinter and halfback of true quality. Dave's ability and his quick wit gave him a natural appeal, and he was welcome in any clique, though he always kept a little independent. He enjoyed acting the fool and could care less about studies, but he possessed a certain maturity and never caused the faculty much trouble. It was a testament to his independence that he included me among his friends—I eventually went out for track, but I was no jock. Owing to the Latin alphabet and a dearth of *R*s and *S*s, Snyder sat behind Rose, and we started exchanging one-liners and became friends.

There was Ted Richard, a much-touted Little League pitcher. He was chunky and had a baby face and came to Our Lady of Mercy as a seasoned street fighter. Ted was quick to laugh and he had a loud, jolly laugh, but when he got angry he'd smile a little smile, the kind that simply raises the corner of the mouth a quarter of an inch. For those who knew, it was an eerie signal. Those who didn't found themselves in big trouble, for Ted was very quick. He loved to carry on what we would come to call philosophical discussions: What is courage? Does God exist? He also loved words, enjoyed picking up big ones like *salubrious* and *equivocal* and using them in our conversations—laughing at himself as the word hit a chuckhole rolling off his tongue. Ted didn't do all that well in school—baseball and parties and testing the courage he'd speculated about took up his time. His textbooks were *Argosy* and *Field and Stream*, whatever newspapers he'd find on the bus stop—from *the Daily Worker* to pornography—conversations with uncles or hobos or businessmen he'd meet in a coffee shop, *The Old Man and the Sea*. With hindsight, I can see that Ted was developing into one of those rough-hewn intellectuals whose sources are a mix of the learned and the apocryphal, whose discussions are both assured and sad.

And then there was Ken Harvey. Ken was good-looking in a puffy way and had a full and oily ducktail and was a car enthusiast . . . a hodad. One day in religion class, he said the sentence that turned out to be one of the most memorable of the hundreds of thousands I heard in those Voc. Ed. years. We were talking about the parable of the talents, about achievement, working hard, doing the best you can do, blah-blah-blah, when the teacher called on the restive Ken Harvey for an opinion. Ken thought about it, but just for a second, and said (with studied, minimal affect), "I just wanna be average." That woke me up. Average?! Who wants to be average? Then the athletes chimed in with the clichés that make you want to laryngectomize them, and the exchange became a platitudinous melee. At the time, I thought Ken's assertion was stupid, and I wrote him off. But his sentence has stayed with me all these years, and I think I am finally coming to understand it.

Ken Harvey was gasping for air. School can be a tremendously disorienting place. No matter how bad the school, you're going to encounter notions that don't fit with the assumptions and beliefs that you grew up with—maybe you'll hear these dissonant notions from teachers, maybe from the other students, and maybe you'll read them. You'll also be thrown in with all kinds of kids from all kinds of backgrounds, and that can be unsettling—this is especially true in places of rich ethnic and linguistic mix, like the L.A. basin. You'll see a handful of students far excel you in courses that sound exotic and that are only in the curriculum of the elite: French, physics, trigonometry. And all this is happening while you're trying to shape an identity; your body is changing, and your emotions are running wild. If you're a working-class kid in the vocational track, the options you'll have to deal with this will be constrained in certain ways: You're defined by your school as "slow"; you're placed in a curriculum that isn't designed to liberate you but to occupy you, or, if you're lucky, train you, though the training is for work the society does not esteem; other students are picking up the cues from your school and your curriculum and interacting with you in particular ways. If you're a kid like Ted Richard, you turn your back on all this and let your mind roam where it may. But youngsters like Ted are rare. What Ken and so many others do is protect themselves from such suffocating madness by taking on with a vengeance the identity implied in the vocational track. Reject the confusion and frustration by openly defining yourself as the Common Joe. Champion the average. Rely on your own good sense. Fuck this bullshit. Bullshit, of course, is everything you—and the others—fear is beyond you: books, essays, tests, academic scrambling, complexity, scientific reasoning, philosophical inquiry.

The tragedy is that you have to twist the knife in your own gray matter to make this defense work. You'll have to shut down, have to reject intellectual stimuli or diffuse them with sarcasm, have to cultivate stupidity, have to convert boredom from a malady into a way of confronting the world. Keep your vocabulary simple, act stoned when you're not or act more stoned than you are, flaunt ignorance, materialize your dreams. It is a powerful and effective defense—it neutralizes the insult and the frustration of being a vocational kid and, when perfected, it drives teachers up the wall, a delightful secondary effect. But like all strong magic, it exacts a price.

My own deliverance from the Voc. Ed. world began with sophomore biology. Every student, college prep to vocational, had to take biology, and unlike the other courses, the same person taught all sections. When teaching the vocational group, Brother Clint probably slowed down a bit or omitted a little of the fundamental biochemistry, but he used the same book and more or less the same syllabus across the board. If one class got tough, he could get tougher. He was young and powerful and very handsome, and looks and physical strength were high currency. No one gave him any trouble.

I was pretty bad at the dissecting table, but the lectures and the textbook were interesting: plastic overlays that, with each turned page, peeled away skin, then veins and muscle, then organs, down to the very bones that Brother Clint, pointer in hand, would tap out on our hanging skeleton. Dave Snyder was in big trouble, for the study of life—versus the living of it—was sticking in his craw. We worked out a code for our multiple-choice exams. He'd poke me in the back: once for the answer under *A*, twice for *B*, and so on; and when he'd hit the right one, I'd look up to the ceiling as though I were lost in thought. Poke: cytoplasm. Poke, poke: methane. Poke, poke, poke: William Harvey. Poke, poke, poke, poke: islets of Langerhans. This didn't work out perfectly, but Dave passed the course, and I mastered the dreamy look of a guy on a record jacket. And something else happened. Brother Clint puzzled over this Voc. Ed. kid who was racking up 98s and 99s on his tests. He checked the school's records and discovered the error. He recommended that I begin my junior year in the College Prep program. According to all I've read since, such a shift, as one report put it, is virtually impossible. Kids at that level rarely cross tracks. The telling thing is how chancy both my placement into and exit from Voc. Ed. was; neither I nor my parents had anything to do with it. I lived in one world during spring semester, and when I came back to school in the fall, I was living in another.

Switching to College Prep was a mixed blessing. I was an erratic student. I was undisciplined. And I hadn't caught onto the rules of the game: Why work hard in a class that didn't grab my fancy? I was also hopelessly behind in math. Chemistry was hard; toying with my chemistry set years before hadn't prepared me for the chemist's equations. Fortunately, the priest who taught both chemistry and second-year algebra was also the school's athletic director. Membership on the track team covered me; I knew I wouldn't get lower than a C.U.S. history was taught pretty well, and I did okay. But civics was taken over by a football coach who had trouble reading the textbook aloud—and reading aloud was the centerpiece of his pedagogy. College Prep at Mercy was certainly an improvement over the vocational program—at least it carried some status—but the social science curriculum was weak, and the mathematics and physical sciences were simply beyond me. I had a miserable quantitative background and ended up copying some assignments and finessing the rest as best I could. Let me try to explain how it feels to see again and again material you should once have learned but didn't.

You are given a problem. It requires you to simplify algebraic fractions or to multiply expressions containing square roots. You know this is pretty basic material because you've seen it for years. Once a teacher took some time with you, and you learned how to carry out these operations. Simple versions, anyway. But that was a year or two or more in the past, and these are more complex versions, and now you're not sure. And this, you keep telling yourself, is ninth- or even eight-grade stuff.

Next it's a word problem. This is also old hat. The basic elements are as familiar as story characters: trains speeding so many miles per hour or shadows of buildings angling so many degrees. Maybe you know enough, have sat through enough explanations, to be able to begin setting up the problem: "If one train is going this fast . . ." or "This shadow is really one line of a triangle . . ." Then: "Let's see . . ." "How did Jones do this?" "Hmmmm." "No." "No, that won't work." Your attention wavers. You wonder about other things: a football game, a dance, that cute new checker at the market. You try to focus on the problem again. You scribble on paper for a while, but the tension wins out and your attention flits elsewhere. You crumple the paper and begin daydreaming to ease the frustration.

The particulars will vary, but in essence this is what a number of students go through, especially those in so-called remedial classes. They open their textbooks and see once again the familiar and impenetrable formulas and diagrams and terms that have stumped them for years. There is no excitement here. No excitement. Regardless of what the teacher says, this is not a new challenge. There is, rather, embarrassment and frustration and, not surprisingly, some anger in being reminded once again of longstanding inadequacies. No wonder so many students finally attribute their difficulties to something inborn, organic: "That part of my brain just doesn't work." Given the troubling histories many of these students have, it's miraculous that any of them can lift the shroud of hopelessness sufficiently to make deliverance from these classes possible.

Through this entire period, my father's health was deteriorating with cruel momentum. His arteriosclerosis progressed to the point where a simple nick on his shin wouldn't heal. Eventually it ulcerated and widened. Lou Minton would come by daily to change the dressing. We tried renting an oscillating bed—which we placed in the front room—to force blood through the constricted arteries in my father's legs. The bed hummed through the night, moving in place to ward off the inevitable. The ulcer continued to spread, and the doctors finally had to amputate. My grandfather had lost his leg in a stockyard accident. Now my father too was crippled. His convalescence was slow but steady, and the doctors placed him in the Santa Monica Rehabilitation Center, a sun-bleached building that opened out onto the warm spray of the Pacific. The place gave him some strength and some color and some training in walking with an artificial leg. He did pretty well for a year or so until he slipped and broke his hip. He was confined to a wheelchair after that, and the confinement contributed to the diminishing of his body and spirit.

I am holding a picture of him. He is sitting in his wheelchair and smiling at the camera. The smile appears forced, unsteady, seems to quaver, though it is frozen in silver nitrate. He is in his mid-sixties and looks eighty. Late in my junior year, he had a stroke and never came out of the resulting coma. After that, I would see him only in dreams, and to this day that is how I join him. Sometimes the dreams are sad and grisly and primal: my father lying in a bed soaked with his suppuration, holding me, rocking me. But sometimes the dreams bring him back to me healthy: him talking to me on an empty street, or buying some pictures to decorate our old house, or transformed somehow into someone strong and adept with tools and the physical.

Jack MacFarland couldn't have come into my life at a better time. My father was dead, and I had logged up too many years of scholastic indifference. Mr. MacFarland had a master's degree from Columbia and decided, at twenty-six, to find a little school and teach his heart out. He never took any credentialing courses, couldn't bear to, he said, so he had to find employment in a private system. He ended up at Our Lady of Mercy teaching five sections of senior English. He was a beatnik who was born too late. His teeth were stained, he tucked his sorry tie in between the third and fourth buttons of his shirt, and his pants were chronically wrinkled. At first, we couldn't believe this guy, thought he slept in his car. But within no time, he had us so startled with work that we didn't much worry about where he slept or if he slept at all. We wrote three or four essays a month. We read a book every two to three weeks, starting with the *Iliad* and ending up with Hemingway. He gave us a quiz on the reading every other day. He brought a prep school curriculum to Mercy High.

MacFarland's lectures were crafted, and as he delivered them he would pace the room jiggling a piece of chalk in his cupped hand, using it to scribble on the board the names of all the writers and philosophers and plays and novels he was weaving into his discussion. He asked questions often, raised everything from Zeno's paradox to the repeated last line of Frost's "Stopping by Woods on a Snowy Evening." He slowly and carefully built up our knowledge of Western intellectual history—with facts, with connections, with speculations. We learned about Greek philosophy, about Dante, the Elizabethan world view, the Age of Reason, existentialism. He analyzed poems with us, had us reading sections from John Ciardi's *How Does a Poem Mean?*, making a potentially difficult book accessible with his own explanations. We gave oral reports on poems Ciardi didn't cover. We imitated the styles of Conrad, Hemingway, and *Time* magazine. We wrote and talked, wrote and talked. The man immersed us in language.

Even MacFarland's barbs were literary. If Jim Fitzsimmons, hung over and irritable, tried to smart-ass him, he'd rejoin with a flourish that would spark the indomitable Skip Madison—who'd lost his front teeth in a hapless tackle—to flick his tongue through the gap and opine, "good chop," drawing out the single "o" in stinging indictment. Jack MacFarland, this tobacco-stained intellectual, brandished linguistic weapons of a kind I hadn't encountered before. Here was this *egghead*, for God's sake, keeping some pretty difficult people in line. And from what I heard, Mike Dweetz and Steve Fusco and all the notorious Voc. Ed. crowd settled down as well when MacFarland took the podium. Though a lot of guys groused in the schoolyard, it just seemed that giving trouble to this particular teacher was a silly thing to do. Tomfoolery, not to mention assault, had no place in the world he was trying to create for us, and instinctively everyone knew that. If nothing else, we all recognized MacFarland's considerable intelligence and respected the hours he put into his work. It came to this: The troublemaker would look foolish rather than daring. Even Jim Fitzsimmons was reading *On the Road* and turning his incipient alcoholism to literary ends.

There were some lives that were already beyond Jack MacFarland's ministrations, but mine was not. I started reading again as I hadn't since elementary school. I would go into our gloomy little bedroom or sit at the dinner table while, on the television, Danny McShane was paralyzing Mr. Moto with the atomic drop, and work slowly back through *Heart of Darkness*, trying to catch the words in Conrad's sentences. I certainly was not MacFarland's best student; most of the other guys in College Prep, even my fellow slackers, had better backgrounds than I did. But I worked very hard, for MacFarland had hooked me. He tapped my old interest in reading and creating stories. He gave me a way to feel special by using my mind. And he provided a role model that wasn't shaped on physical prowess alone, and something inside me that I wasn't quite aware of responded to that. Jack MacFarland established a literacy club, to borrow a phrase of Frank Smith's[2], and invited me—invited all of us—to join.

There's been a good deal of research and speculation suggesting that the acknowledgment of school performance with extrinsic rewards—smiling faces, stars, numbers, grades—diminishes the intrinsic satisfaction children experience by engaging in reading or writing or problem solving. While it's certainly true that we've created an educational system that encourages our best and brightest to become cynical grade collectors and, in general, have developed an obsession with evaluation and assessment, I must tell you that venal though it may have been, I loved getting good grades from MacFarland. I now know how subjective grades can be, but then they came tucked in the back of essays like bits of scientific data, some sort of spectroscopic readout that said, objectively and publicly, that I had made something of value. I suppose I'd been mediocre for too long and enjoyed a public redefinition. And I suppose the workings of my mind, such as they were, had been private for too long. My linguistic play moved into the world; like the intergalactic stories I told years before on Frank's berry-splattered truck bed, these papers with their circled, red B-pluses and A-minuses linked my mind to something outside it. I carried them around like a club emblem.

One day in the December of my senior year, Mr. MacFarland asked me where I was going to go to college. I hadn't thought much about it. Many of the students I teach today spent their last year in high school with a physics text in one hand and the Stanford catalog in the other, but I wasn't even aware of what "entrance requirements" were. My folks would say that they wanted me to go to college and be a doctor, but I don't know how seriously I ever took that; it seemed a sweet thing to say, a bit of supportive family chatter, like telling a gangly daughter she's graceful. The reality of higher education wasn't in my scheme of things: No one in the family had gone to college; only two of my uncles had completed high school. I figured I'd get a night job and go to the local junior college because I knew that Snyder and Company were going there to play ball. But I hadn't even prepared for that. When I finally said, "I don't know," MacFarland looked down at me—I was seated in his office—and said, "Listen, you can write."

My grades stank. I had A's in biology and a handful of B's in a few English and social science classes. All the rest were C's—or worse. MacFarland said I would do well in his class and laid down the law about doing well in the others. Still, the record for my first three years wouldn't have been acceptable to any four-year school. To nobody's surprise, I was turned down flat by USC and UCLA. But Jack MacFarland was on the case. He had received his bachelor's degree from Loyola University, so he made calls to old professors and talked to somebody in admissions and wrote me a strong letter. Loyola finally accepted me as a probationary student. I would be on trial for the first year, and if I did okay, I would be granted regular status. MacFarland also intervened to get me a loan, for I could never have afforded a private college without it. Four more years of religion classes and four more years of boys at one school, girls at another. But at least I was going to college. Amazing.

In my last semester of high school, I elected a special English course fashioned by Mr. MacFarland, and it was through this elective that there arose at Mercy a fledgling literati. Art Mitz, the editor of the school newspaper and a very smart guy, was the kingpin. He was joined by me and by Mark Dever, a quiet boy who wrote beautifully and who would die before he was forty. MacFarland occasionally invited us to his apartment, and those visits became the high point of our apprenticeship: We'd clamp on our training wheels and drive to his salon.

He lived in a cramped and cluttered place near the airport, tucked away in the kind of building that architectural critic Reyner Banham calls a *dingbat*. Books were all over: stacked, piled, tossed, and crated, underlined and dog eared, well worn and new. Cigarette ashes crusted with coffee in saucers or spilled over the sides of motel ashtrays. The little bedroom had, along two of its walls, bricks and boards loaded with notes, magazines, and oversized books. The kitchen joined the living room, and there was a stack of German newspapers under the sink. I had never seen anything like it: a great flophouse of language furnished by City Lights and Café le Metro. I read every title. I flipped through paperbacks and scanned jackets and memorized names: Gogol, *Finnegan's Wake*, Djuna Barnes, Jackson Pollock, *A Coney Island of the Mind*, F. O. Matthiessen's *American Renaissance*, all sorts of Freud, *Troubled Sleep*, Man Ray, *The Education of Henry Adams*, Richard Wright, *Film as Art*, William Butler Yeats, Marguerite Duras, *Redburn, A Season in Hell, Kapital*. On the cover of Alain-Fournier's *The Wanderer* was an Edward Gorey drawing of a young man on a road winding into dark trees. By the hotplate sat a strange Kafka novel called *Amerika*, in which an adolescent hero crosses the Atlantic to find the Nature Theater of Oklahoma. Art and Mark would be talking about a movie or the school newspaper, and I would be consuming my English teacher's library. It was heady stuff. I felt like a Pop Warner athlete on steroids.

Art, Mark, and I would buy stogies and triangulate from MacFarland's apartment to the Cinema, which now shows X-rated films but was then L.A.'s premiere art theater, and then to the musty Cherokee Bookstore in Hollywood to hobnob with beatnik homosexuals—smoking, drinking bourbon and coffee, and trying out awkward phrases we'd gleaned from our mentor's bookshelves. I was happy and precocious and a little scared as well, for Hollywood Boulevard was thick with a kind of decadence that was foreign to the South Side. After the Cherokee, we would head back to the security of MacFarland's apartment, slaphappy with hipness.

Let me be the first to admit that there was a good deal of adolescent passion in this embrace of the avant-garde: self-absorption, sexually charged pedantry, an elevation of the odd and abandoned. Still it was a time during which I absorbed an awful lot of information: long lists of titles, images from expressionist paintings, new wave shibboleths, snippets of philosophy, and names that read like Steve Fusco's misspellings—Goethe, Nietzsche, Kierkegaard. Now this is hardly the stuff of deep understanding. But it was an introduction, a phrase book, a Baedeker to a vocabulary of ideas, and it felt good at the time to know all these words. With hindsight I realize how layered and important that knowledge was.

It enabled me to do things in the world. I could browse bohemian bookstores in far-off, mysterious Hollywood; I could go to the Cinema and see events through the lenses of European directors; and, most of all, I could share an evening, talk that talk, with Jack MacFarland, the man I most admired at the time. Knowledge was becoming a bonding agent. Within a year or two, the persona of the disaffected hipster would prove too cynical, too alienated to last. But for a time it was new and exciting: It provided a critical perspective on society, and it allowed me to act as though I were living beyond the limiting boundaries of South Vermont.

Endnotes

1. Mr. Gross is described in Theodore Sizer, *Horace's Compromise* (Boston: Houghton Mifflin, 1985), pp. 146–148.
2. Frank Smith, *Joining the Literacy Club: Further Essays into Education* (Portsmouth, N.H.: Heinemann Educational Books, 1988).

Bootstraps: From an American Academic of Color

Victor Villanueva, Jr. _____

Victor Villanueva, Jr. is a professor of English and Director of Composition at Washington State University. The following selection contains excerpts from his book *Bootstraps: From an American Academic of Color*, 1993. The National Council of Teachers of English, which published Villanueva's book, describes it this way:

At one level it is autobiographical, detailing the life of an American of Puerto Rican extraction from his childhood in New York City, through trade school and the military, to community college, and ultimately, to an academic post at a university. Villanueva candidly offers his experiences of the inequities of American society, his struggle to succeed while maintaining his cultural identity, and his consequent doubts. . . . At this level, the book serves the valuable end of making clear the often unattended concerns of students of color or of minority ethnic backgrounds in our nation's classrooms. At another level, the book examines these same issues from a rigorously academic viewpoint.

School

All Saints, the Catholic school around the corner from Bartlett, across the street from PS 168, the public school. All Saints charges a dollar a month for tuition (three a month in the seventh and eighth grades). It is my school from kindergarten till eighth-grade graduation. There I am filled with Catholicism, "Ave Maria," and with "Jingle Bells," maxims from Poor Richard, laws from Newton, the Beaver's neighbors—Dick and Jane, the parts of speech, times tables. There I play in the melting pot.

Or maybe it was a stewpot. A stew, not the easy mixes of the salad-bowl metaphor, the static coexistence of the mosaic metaphor. The stew metaphor maintains the violence of the melting-pot metaphor while suggesting that some of the ingredients do not lose all of their original identity, though altered, taking in the juices from the other ingredients of the pot, adding to the juices; all of us this one thing, Americans, and all of us some things else; for some of us, never complete integration and never complete integrity. With the stewpot comes the sense that not all the ingredients are equally important, that the stew needs the beef of a Yankee pot roast cut more than fatback or red beans and *sofrito*.

As I saw it, prestige belonged to the Wattses, Andrew and Stephen. There were nuns and priests in their family. They lived in one of the brownstones, around the corner, not on the

From BOOTSTRAPS by Victor Villanueva, Jr., NCTE, 1993. Copyright 1993 by the National Council of Teachers of English. Reprinted with permission.

block. The kids on the block didn't look like the Wattses, didn't talk like them. I don't recall ever thinking they were better, in the sense of superior—they just had it better. And I don't recall ever thinking about what "having it better" meant; I just knew that they did.

There was something special about Jarapolk Cigash and his family too. But theirs was different from the Wattses. The Wattses were connected to All Saints, somehow, to culture, though that word—culture—only occurs to me now. Jarapolk, "Yacko," Jerry, was one of my two best friends (superlatives have no meaning for children). The Cigashes lived in the neighborhood, but there was something special about their apartment: a piano that his sister played; a stand for sheet music alongside a violin case. Jerry practiced the violin. His parents would speak of their escape from the Ukraine, explain what it meant to be a satellite country. They had accents, thick accents, but there was an air about them. They were educated, in that special sense in which *educated* is sometimes used. It was clear to me even then that Brooklyn would only be a stopover for the Cigashes. It was not their home nor would it be. That wasn't clear about the Villanuevas.

I had the sense that there was something different about Charles Bermudez. He was kind of pale, allergic to milk. There was something strange about the way Charles's father held his cigarettes: palm up, the cigarette pinched between thumb and middle finger, like a movie old-world aristocrat or a monocle-wearing fascist general. Yet I didn't see prestige in the Bermudezes, really, just difference. Now as I look back, I wonder if the Bermudezes were Latin Americans on the run. Back then, I just assumed they were portoricans. Portoricans could not be foreign, like the foreignness of the very American Wattses or the foreignness of the Eastern European Cigashes.

Marie Engells, the German girl, was another stopover. We were in school together from kindergarten through the eighth grade, yet I never knew her. Some of that was due to childish gender discrimination, no doubt, though Rose Marie, Peanuts, the Italian girl, was always a special friend, not boyfriend-girlfriend, not one of the boys, and not so as I feared being seen as a sissy, just a special friend. We'd buy each other knishes or soft, salted pretzels from the pushcart after school. But there was something about Marie Engells: an awfully erect back, the hint of a smile constantly on her lips. Maybe all this was in my imagination, but she seemed aloof to me. Marie Engells was the girl valedictorian at eighth-grade graduation. Jarapolk Cigash was the boy. They were immigrants. And something was theirs that wasn't mine. Yet I was American and so were my parents and the generation before them, full citizens since 1919.

Some fell into a grey area between the immigrants and those like me, the spies or the blacks. I knew Peanuts wasn't like us, but she wasn't like Marie Engells or Jarapolk Cigash either. And I was less sure about Frankie Thompson, the Irish kid who introduced me to my first cigarette in one of the neighborhood abandoned lots where we jumped burning Christmas trees every year. I was less sure about Paul Caesar, "the Polack." I was less sure about their advantage despite the same school, the same neighborhood.

They would have been "new immigrants," not as easily assimilable, the bad-element immigrants that prompted the latent footnote to the Statue of Liberty: "in limited numbers." In terms of ethnicity, the Cigashes should have been "new immigrants" too, but pianos and violins suggested maybe these new immigrants came from higher in the class system. Class comes into the academic's thoughts. The child only knew that Peanuts and Frankie Thompson and Paul Caesar were not in the same league as Jerry or Marie Engells, the

Wattses, maybe even Charles Bermudez. And it didn't have anything to do with brains. Yet I still believed they had something over Lana Walker and Irving Roach and me.

Irving Roach was the only African American kid I knew who didn't live on the same street I did. The African American kids went to PS 168. "You know we ain't Catholic," I was told once when Hambone said he wished he could read like I did, when I asked why his folks did-n't send him to All Saints, Irving Roach didn't live on the block, but was of the block. I had a life on the block—with Butch, the black bully (stereotypes sometimes have bases in fact—Black Butch the Badass Bully, Darnell the Dude, Lazy Leroy, Hambone with the thick glasses and bookish ways), Papo, the PR bully, Mike and Steven Figueroa and Enchi and Hershey. And I had a life at All Saints. And only Juan Torres, Johnny, my best friend from kindergarten till my family moved to California, and Irving Roach crossed over. And Irving Roach was kind, would bring his baby sister with him when he came to visit. And we would talk school things. He was smart. But I don't recall imagining him "making it."

Lana Walker might. She was as aloof as Marie Engells, as smart, too, I thought. And Lana Walker was beautiful, black and slender (but not skinny) and tall. I was short and chubby and all too insecure to do more than talk with her in passing in the nine years we were in school together. At eighth grade graduation Marie Engells would win the math award I really wanted. Lana Walker would get some special recognition, though I no longer remember what. I would get the spelling and the penmanship awards; the Merriam-Webster spelling bee champ that year. Jerry and Marie Engells went to the Catholic college-prep high school. Lana Walker made the alternate list. I never saw Irving Roach again. Juan Torres ended up in the vo-tech school in his area. I went to Alexander Hamilton Vocational-Technical High School.

So what had happened? I was an "A" student, third or fourth in the class, able with language, Saturdays spent on special classes in preparation for the entrance exam to the college prep high school. Why hadn't I made it? Mom says the Bishop's Fund, but that seems inconsistent with a dollar tuition. Cultural bias in standardized tests is the more obvious answer.

I think of cultural bias in two ways. The first is a linguistic and rhetorical bias. It has to do with the test-makers' assumption that words have fixed meanings that are not arbitrary. The psychologist Lev Vygotsky, literary critic Mikhail Bakhtin, the philosopher Jacques Derrida, the archeologist and social critic Michel Foucault, as well as the Sophists of fifth-century B.C. Greece, and a score of others, call this into question, seeing language tied to time and place and culture and even ideology. So do kids who are bilingual and bidialectical. Sociolinguist Fernando Peñalosa sees the code switcher, the bidialectal speaker, as "the skillful speaker [who] uses his knowledge of how language choices are interpreted in his community to structure the interaction so as to maximize outcomes favorable to himself" (quoted in Gilyard 31). In plain English: the code-switcher is a rhetorical power player. He knows language isn't fixed, has a relativistic perception of language, knows that words take on hues of meaning when colored by cognates; and for the bilingual there are words seeming the same in both languages, derived from the same sources, but nevertheless having undergone change through time and place. A relativistic notion of language is bound to be a problem for the standardized-test taker. A solution: English Only. One of the many problems with the solution: better writers have a heightened metalinguistic awareness, an awareness of language's multiplicity (Hartwell). So do the bidialectal and the bilingual. English Only could destroy the very metalinguistic awareness that could make for a better writer. Doomed if we teach to the test: doomed to lose the power of having a greater metalinguistic awareness. Doomed if we don't: doomed to be denied access.

The second way I think of cultural bias in standardized tests has to do with the differences between the minority and the immigrant. The immigrant seeks to take on the culture of the majority. And the majority, given certain preconditions, not the least of which is displaying the language and dialect of the majority, accepts the immigrant. The minority, even when accepting the culture of the majority, is never wholly accepted. There is always a distance.

📖

Summer 1964

Looking down from the ninth-floor kitchen window of the projects. Debris flying, cars being overturned, flames and the sounds of sirens. Dad should be home from work. Past midnight, Dad arrives to tell of being caught on Bedford Avenue, bricks and molotov cocktails, lying down on the floorboard of the Corvair till a policeman knocks on the windshield to tell him to get the hell out of there. Riots in Bedford-Stuyvesant and later in Harlem. Mami announces that she will not raise another child in New York. Stela is two. Mami rules, though Dad is ruler.

Dad's cousin (or something) lives in California. November 1964: sad and happy goodbyes to Don Victor, la Comai, Gollo, Papo, and others. Mami, Dad, Stela, Papi, and all possessions in the Corvair, heading across country, to Los Angeles, California.

Events of the trip: a near collision, a first exposure to room service and color television, a waitress charging for water, pronounced *water*, not *wahta*. Scenes of a land that is broad and empty, profound contrast to the crowded cluster that is New York.

California. They Park in Compton

It was a cultural vacuum, California. The first Christmas still marks it. Dad's still unemployed, Mom's income barely covers the rent and food; there's a small tree in the living room with toys others wouldn't buy: a doll with only one winking eye, a toy piano without legs, things for Stela. Mom and Dad and Papi forego Christmas. He walks the streets that day—it's sunny and eighty degrees—staring at palm trees. The tropics belonged to Mom and Dad.

Papi was born during a New York blizzard, had passed out from the heat during his one visit to Puerto Rico. Christmas was supposed to be snow and wind, the comforting weight of an overcoat, vapor from nostrils, the smell of steam and the sound of complaining clanks on radiator pipes. Christmas was supposed to be a giant tree in Rockefeller Center, the Central Park folks ice skating below, Gimbel's and Macy's aglow with Christmas tree lights, mechanical elves and reindeer and Santa, giant train sets in the windows. At home, steam and the smells of the big cooking: *pasteles*. Dad making the *carne gisao*, Mami the *masa*, Papi spreading *achiote* on the paper that would be folded into rectangular bundles tied with twine, the bundles boiled. *Turron* for dessert, nougat from Spain. There would be the visit to the *abuela* Doña Teresa or to Tia Fela or to Carlina in Long Island. But this year there were just the immediate four, a forgotten meal, and oatmeal for dessert, and summer in Christmas.

The blacks live in a world separate from him, confined to Watts for the most part, not knowing of portoricans, he figured, not seeing portoricans as somehow the same as they, even when the portorican is white. And he isn't Mexican, what with Mom and Dad's jabs at Mexicans' funny ways with Spanish. And the white kids speak a different language, listen to a music that sounds foreign to his ears—the Beach Boys and Jan and Dean: surfin' safaris and deuce coupes and sloops John D, meaningless.

He tries to be white, kind of, taking the lead of the cultural hybrid in one of the two friends he made in school, Buzz Unruh: hair in the pompadour of the low rider, not the peaked pomp of the white working-class low rider, more the pomp of the Chicano, the Vato, the Pachuco; and Buzz wears Chicano work shirts, Pendletons for status, buttoned all the way not just at the top; Levis instead of starched khakis; modified fenceclimbers, without the high Cuban heels—a white working-class/Chicano mix. Papi, Victor, follows suit. And the dialect of Brooklyn starts to slip with his attempts at social survival during the peer-importance years of adolescence, even though the peers are two. Yet in his room he listens to the Jazz radio station and plays Tito Rodriguez and Pacheco on his portable record player, the suitcase-like machine with detachable box-like speakers; and he reads *Portnoy's Complaint* and *The Godfather*, stories recalling the mixes of New York, a place he is glad to be away from and a place he misses.

His first school in California is Compton Senior High School. The halls don't look much different from Hamilton. The difference is that Compton seems exclusively African American, none of the poor Irish, the Italians, the Puerto Ricans of Hamilton, not even California's Mexicans. He is alone. But he doesn't remain at Compton High long.

Mom and Dad move the family to another part of town in order to have him be in a better school district. This is different. Single-story buildings linked by concrete trails and clusters of lockers, a large grassy field where PE classes are conducted, a large parking lot where students—*students*—park their cars and motorcycles and Mopeds. And walking about are boys and girls in baggy short pants and T-shirts, a sea of blond hair and pink faces and blue eyes, assemblies on bleachers facing a basketball court, pep rallies with meaningless rhymes, women in short skirts bouncing about, leading the hyperactive rally, a man in plaid pants among the cheerleaders, himself a cheerleader.

At one assembly, a lone black face speaks to the sea of blond and blue about the time for a "nigro" student-body president, and there is silence and a respectful applause. Blond-and-blue are nicer than the Italian greasers were when we ventured outside the block, but the feeling in the air is somehow no different. No nigro student-body president that year.

He doesn't see the clusters of Mexicans at assemblies. But he does see them around the campus: groups of women in short, tight skirts and black hair teased high, thick black lines encircling large black eyes; the men with toothpicks or matchsticks in the corners of their mouths, thick, shiny black hair combed straight back, dark men dressed in plaid work shirts, white undershirts exposed, khakis with waists worn high, bandannas tied around one leg, shiny pointed shoes. They cluster. And he can feel the bristling when black eyes and blue eyes make contact for too long. And he feels that bristling when he makes eye contact with anyone, blue or black. No "Wazzup?" No "¿Y que?" Just loud silences.

First day at Manuel Dominguez Senior High School, a meeting with a counselor. First order of business: a bar of soap and a razor. The first order of business is humiliation. *Que portorro* doesn't have a moustache? His is respectable, neatly trimmed always, never did wear a *chibo*, the little strip of hair from the bottom lip to the chin: never did let the moustache turn into a *chinchow*, the Charlie-Chan like droop below the lipline. He wore his moustache like his father had, like his uncle Diego, like the respectable men of the block, like Zorro. But this is not TV California; it's his new world, and he'll comply. With the now swollen, clean-shaven heavy top lip comes the second order of business, the dress code: shorts must have a pocket, so too must T-shirts, no bare feet—rules for wearing underwear as outerwear, as far as he is concerned. He wears his fenceclimbers, pegged pants, white shirt with tabbed collar, a tie, a jacket, his hair combed back. One dresses for school, not because of a code, just because it is school. He is swimming in foreignness. Third order of business: evaluate transcripts.

He knew there would be no college. Hamilton's consolation prize had been architectural drafting. He had the skills, maybe even the talent. Back at Hamilton, he had taken everything he could to prepare him for the job: carpentry and foundry, electrical design, algebra and trig to qualify for strength-of-materials, strength of materials. He mastered the slide rule (which he supplemented with the abacus that John Lee had given him and taught him to use years back). Back in his Bed-Stuy bedroom he had written to Dietz and to Crane and to American Standard, written of his intention to be an architectural draftsman, asked for brochures and drawing templates, and got them. Mom and Dad had given him a fine compass, dividers, a protractor, high-quality triangles, a desk and a T-square, drawing pens, mechanical pencils. There was the promise of a trade on graduation, and the promise that after seven years as an apprentice he could take the AIA test and become an architect.

Dominguez says architectural drafting requires college. But there would be no college. He had resigned himself. The tests had told him so. Dominguez says only so many of all those shop courses can count toward graduation. Strength-of-materials could be a physics course, but to get credit for physics and for the trigonometry there would have to be geometry and a general science prerequisite. Never mind the "A"; there are rules. Physics and trig can't be learned without geometry, can't be understood without the basics. But he had learned and he did understand. No matter. Six months later he's told he won't graduate on schedule. Seems like he hadn't gotten California history his freshman year. It wasn't offered in Brooklyn. So why is he here?

Lockstep and college prep, except that not everyone goes to college. A drafting teacher gives him a special project: design an extension to the school library. He gets building codes, pulls out his templates, recalls his lessons learned at Hamilton, draws a complete set: floor plans, elevations, specs, the works. Gets an "A"—for mechanical drawing, says the report card, not for architectural drawing. No credit, really. Years later, attempting to convert a GED into a diploma (and being denied), he sees the school library's extension. It's remarkably like the one he had designed. No credit and no cash either.

Lockstep, all prearranged, everything on automatic. The geometry teacher recites lectures while staring at the ceiling, never making eye contact. The English teacher requires two-page stories, literally stories, but no reading. History is dates and dead white guys. And PE assumes everyone knows about flag football and decathlons. The block had been basketball, stick ball, and king-queen, a kind of handball. The PE teacher shouts, "Go home and get a haircut! And don't come back till you do!" Papi never goes back.

It was said to be the oldest apartment house in the city of Seattle: from nineteenth-century loggers' quarters to whorehouse to tenement. It stood on a hill at the gateway to the south side. Nights would be filled with the sounds of foghorns coming in from the Puget Sound and the sounds of gunfire from within the neighborhood.

There were other sounds as well. There was the whirring of a sewing machine long into the night: the Vietnamese family doing piecework for a company that made baseball caps. There were the clucks of chickens or honks of geese from the Cambodian family, the crack of a rock when fowl were slaughtered for food. The whoops of joy from the Nigerian fellow the day he was served with deportation papers (couldn't have afforded to return to his home otherwise). The screams of anguish from the panhandler a few doors down the day the government worker took her children away. The long talks about Latin American coffee from the retired merchant marine with the game leg. There was the occasional shout through the kitchen window: "If you can't beat 'em, join 'em." Angry talk about American academics from the apartment manager: a man from India who had recently gotten his Ph.D. in history from the prestigious university but couldn't land a job. There were the family sounds: children at play; the clickings of a 1941 Remington typewriter long enough into the night to know of the whirring sewing machine next door; the nightly screeching and scratching of rats crawling within the walls; the crunching on cockroach carcasses the day the exterminator came by. These were the sounds that came from and came to the one-bedroom apartment of Victor and Carol and their children. And there was the friendly chatter when all gathered by the mailboxes on the eighth of each month, anticipating the mailman and food stamps, discussing different versions of what that great meal would be that night, enjoying a few days' balm after long sorenesses.

Summer mornings, Carol would walk down to the free-bus zone to get to her job in telemarketing, bothering people in their homes for minimum wage. Victor would go with his daughter to the food bank on Empire Way—mainstreet in the heart of the ghetto, the location of the Welfare office, the empire's way—then to the food bank at the Freemont District, then the food bank at the local Catholic Church. Some bags would contain frozen juices or frozen burritos or frozen turnovers, but the apartment had no working freezer and no working oven. Miles for meals. Carol would return, and Victor would walk the five miles to the University to teach his basic-writing class. Pride at teaching; humiliation at food-bank lines, free government cheese and butter lines, welfare lines. He had known greater affluence as a sergeant in the Army. Dr. V, the college professor, can still make that claim, the difference between then and now, matters of degree rather than kind. But he had made a choice, had opted out of the army.

The morality of war, the morality of military occupation, the morality of forced separation from family, all had become unignorable. Memories of Dad speaking about the Americans who would be in charge of the virtually all Puerto Rican American forces in Puerto Rico, of the resentment Dad heard about from the Panamanians when he had served as an American soldier in Panama; Dad's discharge papers reading "WPR," White Puerto Rican; Dad's dissertations on the large American corporations' profiting by being located in Puerto Rico but not passing on the profits to the majority of Puerto Ricans on the Island—all such memories had come flooding back as he thought of his experiences in the Army, especially in Korea, the similarities unignorable. And there were the officers the sergeant from *el bloque* had served under, particularly those whose sole qualification for leadership seemed to be their college degrees, those who seemed no brighter than he, no more competent. And there was Walter Myles, a peer, from the block, even if in Palo Alto; Walter, of color—and a college graduate. It was time to move on, away from the Army.

I wanted to try my hand at college, go beyond the GED. But college scared me. I had been told long ago that college wasn't my lot.

He drives by the University District of Seattle during his last days in the military and sees the college kids, long hair and sandals, baggy short pants on the men, long, flowing dresses on the women, some men in suits, some women in high heels, all carrying backpacks over one shoulder. There is both purpose and contentment in the air. Storefronts carry names like Dr. Feelgood and Magus Bookstore, reflecting the good feelings and magic he senses. A block away is the University, red tiles and green grass, rolling hills and tall pines, apple and cherry blossoms, the trees shading modern monoliths of gray concrete and gothic, church-like buildings of red brick. And he says to himself, "Maybe in the next life."

He must be content with escaping a life at menial labor, at being able to bank on the skills in personnel management he had acquired in the Army. But there are only two takers. The large department-store chain would hire him as a management trainee—a shoe salesman on commission, no set income, but a trainee could qualify for GI Bill benefits as well as the commissions. Not good enough, not getting paid beyond the GI Bill; and a sales career wasn't good enough either, the thought of his mother's years as a saleslady, years lost, still in memory. A finance corporation offers him a job: management trainee. The title: Assistant Manager. The job: bill collector, with low wage, but as a trainee, qualified to supplement with the GI Bill. The combined pay would be good, but he would surely lose his job in time, would be unable to be righteously indignant like the bill collectors he has too often had to face too often are, unable to bother people like Mom and Dad, knowing that being unable to meet bills isn't usually a moral shortcoming but most often an economic condition.

The GI Bill had come up again, however, setting the "gettinover" wheels in motion. The nearby community college charges ninety dollars a quarter tuition, would accept him on the strength of his GED scores. That would mean nearly four hundred dollars a month from the GI Bill, with only thirty dollars a month for schooling ("forgetting" to account for books and supplies). What a get-over! There would be immediate profit in simply going to school. And if he failed, there would be nothing lost. And if he succeeded, an Associate degree in something. He'd be better equipped to brave the job market again.

So he walks onto the community college campus in the summer of 1976. It's not the campus of the University of Washington. It's more like Dominguez High School in California. But it is a college. Chemistry: a clumsiness at the lab, but relative grace at mathematical equations and memorization. French is listening to audiotapes and filling out workbooks. History is enjoyable stories, local lore from a retired newsman, easy memorization for the grade.

Then there is English. There are the stories, the taste he had always had for reading, now peppered with talk of philosophy and psychology and tensions and textures. Writing is 200 words on anything, preceded by a sentence outline. He'd write about Korea and why *The Rolling Stone* could write about conspiracies of silence, or he'd write about the problems in trying to get a son to understand that he is Puerto Rican when the only Puerto Ricans he knows are his grandparents; he'd write about whatever seemed to be on his mind at the time. The night before a paper would be due, he'd gather pen and pad, and stare. Clean the dishes. Stare. Watch an "I Love Lucy" rerun. Stare. Then sometime in the night the words would come. He'd write; scratch something out; draw arrows shifting paragraphs around; add a phrase or two. Then he'd pull out the erasable bond, making changes even as he typed, frantic to be done before school. Then he'd use the completed essay to type out an outline, feeling a little guilty about having cheated in not having produced the outline first.

The guilt showed one day when Mrs. Ray, the Indian woman in traditional dress with a Ph.D. in English from Oxford, part-time instructor at the community college, said there was a problem with his writing. She must have been able to tell somehow that he was discovering what to write while writing, no prior thesis statement, no outline, just a vague notion that would materialize, magically, while writing. In her stark, small office she hands him a sheet with three familiar sayings mimeoed on it; instructs him to write on one, right there, right then. He writes on "a bird in the hand is worth two in the bush." No memory of what he had written, probably forgotten during the writing. Thirty minutes or so later, she takes the four or five pages he had written; she reads; she smiles; then she explains that she had suspected plagiarism in his previous writings. She apologizes, saying she found his writing "too serious," too abstract, not typical of her students. He is not insulted; he is flattered. He knew he could read; now he knew he could write well enough for college.

English 102, Mr. Lukens devotes a portion of the quarter to Afro-American literature. Victor reads Ishmael Reed, "I'm a Cowboy in the Boat of Ra." It begins,

I am a cowboy in the boat of Ra,
sidewinders in the saloons of fools
bit my forehead like O
the untrustworthiness of Egyptologists
Who do not know their trips. Who was that
dog faced man? they asked, the day I rode
from town.

School marms with halitosis cannot see
the Nefertitti fake chipped on the run by slick
germans, the hawk behind Sonny Rollins' head or
the ritual beard of his axe; a longhorn winding
its bells thru the Field of Reeds.

There was more, but by this point he was already entranced and excited. Poetry has meaning, more than the drama of Mark Antony's speech years back.

Mr. Lukens says that here is an instance of poetry more for effect (or maybe *affect*) than for meaning, citing a line from Archibald MacLeish: "A poem should not mean/But be." But there *was* meaning in this poem. Victor writes about it. In the second stanza, the chipped Nefertitti, a reference to a false black history, with images from "The Maltese Falcon" and war movies. The "School marms" Reed mentions are like the schoolmasters at Hamilton, unknowing and seeming not to know of being unknowing. Sonny Rollins' axe and the Field of Reeds: a saxophone, a reed instrument, the African American's links to Egypt, a history whitewashed by "Egyptologists/Who do not know their trips." He understood the allusions, appreciated the wordplay. The poem had the politics of Bracy, the language of the block, TV of the fifties, together in the medium Mr. D had introduced to Victor, Papi, but now more powerful. This was fun; this was politics. This was Victor's history, his life with language play.

Years later, Victor is on a special two-man panel at a conference of the Modern Language Association. He shares the podium with Ishmael Reed. Victor gives a talk on "Teaching as Social Action," receives applause, turns to see Ishmael Reed looking him in the eye, applauding loudly. He tries to convey how instrumental this "colleague" had been in his life.

He'll be an English major. Mr. Lukens is his advisor, sets up the community college curriculum in such a way as to have all but the major's requirements for a BA from the University of Washington out of the way. The University of Washington is the only choice: it's relatively nearby, tuition for Vietnam veterans is $176 a quarter. "Maybe in this life."

His AA degree in his back pocket, his heart beating audibly with exhilaration and fear, he walks up the campus of the University of Washington, more excited than at Disneyland when he was sixteen. He's proud: a regular transfer student, no special minority waivers. The summer of 1977.

But the community is not college in the same way the University is. The community college is torn between vocational training and preparing the unprepared for traditional university work. And it seems unable to resolve the conflict (see Cohen and Brawer). His high community-college GPA is no measure of what he is prepared to undertake at the University. He fails at French 103, unable to carry the French conversations, unable to do the reading, unable to do the writing, dropping the course before the failure becomes a matter of record. He starts again. French 101, only to find he is still not really competitive with the white kids who had had high school French. But he cannot fail, and he does not fail, thanks to hour after hour with French tapes after his son's in bed.

English 301, the literature survey, is fun. Chaucer is a ghetto boy, poking fun at folks, the rhyming reminding him of when he did the dozens on the block; Chaucer telling bawdy jokes: "And at the wyndow out she putte hir hole . . . 'A berd, a berd!,' quod hende Nicholas." So this is literature. Chaucer surely ain't white. At least he doesn't sound white, "the first to write poetry in the vernacular," he's told. Spenser is exciting; images of knights and damsels distressing, magic and dragons, the *Lord of the Rings* that he had read in Korea paling in the comparison. Donne is a kick: trying to get laid when he's Jack Donne, with a rap the boys from the block could never imagine; building church floors with words on a page when he's Dr. John Donne. Every reading is an adventure, never a nod, no matter how late into the night the reading. For his first paper, Victor, the 3.8 at Tacoma Community College, gets 36 out of a possible 100—"for your imagination," written alongside the grade.

I was both devastated and determined, my not belonging was verified but I was not ready to be shut down, not so quickly. So to the library to look up what the Professor himself had published: *Proceedings of the Spenser Society*. I had no idea what the Professor was going on about in his paper, but I could see the pattern: an introduction that said something about what others had said, what he was going to be writing about, in what order, and what all this would prove; details about what he said he was going to be writing about, complete with quotes, mainly from the poetry, not much from other writers on Spenser; and a "therefore." It wasn't the five-paragraph paper Mr. Lukens had insisted on, not just three points, not just repetition of the opening in the close, but the pattern was essentially the same. The next paper: 62 out of 100 and a "Much better." Course grade: B. Charity.

I never vindicated myself with that professor. I did try, tried to show that I didn't need academic charity. Economic charity was hard enough. I took my first graduate course from him. This time I got an "All well and good, but what's the point?" alongside a "B" for a paper. I had worked on that paper all summer long.

I have had to face that same professor, now a Director of Freshman Writing, at conferences. And with every contact, feelings of insecurity well up from within, the feeling that I'm seen as the minority (a literal term in academics for those of us of color), the feeling of being perceived as having gotten through *because* I am a minority, an insecurity I face often. But though I never got over the stigma with that professor (whether real or imagined), I did get some idea on how to write for the University.

Professorial Discourse Analysis became a standard practice: go to the library; see what the course's professor had published; try to discern a pattern to her writing; try to mimic the pattern. Some would begin with anecdotes. Some would have no personal pronouns. Some would cite others' research. Some would cite different literary works to make assertions about one literary work. Whatever they did, I would do too. And it worked, for the most part, so that I could continue the joy of time travel and mind travel with those, and within those, who wrote about things I had discovered I liked to think about: Shakespeare and work versus pleasure, religion and the day-to-day world, racism, black Othello and the Jewish Merchant of Venice; Dickens and the impossibility of really getting into the middle class (which I read as "race," getting into the white world, at the time), pokes at white folks (though the Podsnaps were more likely jabs at the middle class); Milton and social responsibility versus religious mandates; Yeats and being assimilated and yet other (critically conscious with a cultural literacy, I'd say now); others and other themes. And soon I was writing like I had written in the community college: some secondary reading beforehand, but composing the night before a paper was due, a combination of fear that nothing will come and faith that something would eventually develop, then revising to fit the pattern discovered in the Professorial Discourse Analysis, getting "A's" and "B's," and getting comments like "I never saw that before."

There were failures, of course. One professor said my writing was too formulaic. One professor said it was too novel. Another wrote only one word for the one paper required of the course: "nonsense." But while I was on the campus I could escape and not. I could think about the things that troubled me or intrigued me, but through others' eyes in other times and other places. I couldn't get enough, despite the pain and the insecurity.

School becomes his obsession. There is the education. But the obsession is as much, if not more, in getting a degree, not with a job in mind, just the degree, just because he thinks he can, despite all that has said he could not. His marriage withers away, not with rancor, just melting into a dew. The daily routine has him taking the kid to a daycare/school at 6:00 A.M., then himself to school, from school to work as a groundskeeper for a large apartment complex; later, a maintenance man, then a garbage man, then a plumber, sometimes coupled with other jobs: shipping clerk for the library, test proctor. From work to pick up the kid from school, prepare dinner, maybe watch a TV show with the kid, tuck him into bed, read. There are some girlfriends along the way, and he studies them too: the English major who won constant approval from the same professor who had given him the 36 for being imaginative; the art major who had traveled to France (French practice); the fisheries major whose father was an executive vice president for IBM (practice at being middle class). Victor was going to learn—quite consciously—what it means to be white, middle class. He didn't see the exploitation; not then; he was obsessed. There were things going on in his classes that he did not understand and that the others did. He didn't know what the things were that he didn't understand, but he knew that even those who didn't do as well as he did, somehow did not act as foreign as he felt. He was the only colored kid in every one of those classes. And he hadn't the time nor the racial affiliation to join the Black Student Union or Mecha. He was on his own, an individual pulling on his bootstraps, looking out for number one. He's not proud of the sensibility, but isolation—and, likely, exploitation of others—are the stuff of racelessness.

There were two male friends, Mickey, a friend to this day, and Luis el Loco. Luis was a *puertoriceño*, from Puerto Rico, who had found his way to Washington by having been imprisoned in the federal penitentiary at MacNeal Island, attending school on a prison-release program. Together, they would enjoy talking in Spanglish, listening to *salsa*. But Luis was a Modern Languages major, Spanish literature. Nothing there to exploit. It's a short-lived friendship. Mickey was the other older student in Victor's French 101 course, white, middle class, yet somehow other, one who had left the country during Vietnam, a disc jockey in Amsterdam. The friendship begins with simply being the two older men in the class, longer away from adolescence than the rest; the friendship grows with conversations about politics, perceptions about America from abroad, literature. But Victor would not be honest with his friend about feeling foreign until years later, a literary bravado. Mickey was well read in the literary figures Victor was coming to know. Mickey would be a testing ground for how Victor was reading, another contact to be exploited. Eventually, Mickey and his wife would introduce Victor to their friend, a co-worker at the post office. This is Carol. She comes from a life of affluence, and from a life of poverty, a traveler within the class system, not a journey anyone would volunteer for, but one which provides a unique education, a path not unlike Paulo Freire's. From her, there is the physical and the things he would know of the middle class, discussed explicitly, and there is their mutual isolation. There is love and friendship, still his closest friend, still his lover.

But before Carol, there is simply the outsider obsessed. He manages the B.A. He cannot stop, even as the GI Bill reaches its end. He will continue to gather credentials until he is kicked out. Takes the GRE, does not do well, but gets into the graduate program with the help of references from within the faculty—and with the help of minority status in a program decidedly low in numbers of minorities. "Minority," or something like that, is typed on the GRE test results in his file, to be seen while scanning the file for the references. His pride is hurt, but he remembers All Saints, begins to believe in the biases of standardized tests: back in the eighth grade, a failure top student; now a near-failure, despite a 3.67 at the competitive Big University of State. Not all his grades, he knew, were matters of charity. He had earned his GPA, for the most part. Nevertheless, he is shaken.

More insecure than ever, there are no more overnight papers. Papers are written over days, weeks, paragraphs literally cut and laid out on the floor to be pasted. One comment appears in paper after paper: "Logic?" He thinks, "Yes." He does not understand. Carol cannot explain the problem. Neither can Mickey. He does not even consider asking the professors. To ask would be an admission of ignorance, "stupid spic" still resounding within. This is his problem.

Then by chance (exactly how is now forgotten), he hears a tape of a conference paper delivered by the applied linguist Robert Kaplan. Kaplan describes contrastive rhetoric. Kaplan describes a research study conducted in New York City among Puerto Ricans who are bilingual and Puerto Ricans who are monolingual in English, and he says that the discourse patterns, the rhetorical patterns which include the logic, of monolingual Puerto Ricans are like those of Puerto Rican bilinguals and different from Whites, more Greek than the Latin-like prose of American written English. Discourse analysis takes on a new intensity. At this point, what this means is that he will have to go beyond patterns in his writing, become more analytical of the connections between ideas. The implications of Kaplan's talk, for him at least, will take on historical and political significance as he learns more of rhetoric.

 # Dust Tracks on a Road

Zora Neale Hurston _____

Zora Neale Hurston's (1881–1960) piece is an excerpt from her autobiography, *Dust Tracks on a Road*, published in 1942. She was a folklorist/anthropologist (studied with Franz Boas) and novelist (*Their Eyes were watching God*), part of the Harlem Renaissance, and a friend of Langston Hughes. She died poor and alone of a stroke and was buried in an unmarked grave. Hurston was "rediscovered" by scholars and popular readers alike in the last couple of decades.

I used to take a seat on top of the gate-post and watch the world go by. One way to Orlando ran past my house, so the carriages and cars would pass before me. The movement made me glad to see it. Often the white travelers would hail me, but more often I hailed them, and asked, "Don't you want me to go a piece of the way with you?"

They always did. I know now that I must have caused a great deal of amusement among them, but my self-assurance must have carried the point, for I was always invited to come along. I'd ride up the road for perhaps a half-mile, then walk back. I did not do this with the permission of my parents, nor with their foreknowledge. When they found out about it later, I usually got a whipping. My grandmother worried about my forward ways a great deal. She had known slavery and to her my brazenness was unthinkable.

"Git down offa dat gate-post! You li'l sow, you! Git down! Setting up dere looking dem white folks right in de face! They's gowine to lynch you, yet. And don't stand in dat doorway gazing out at 'em neither. Youse too brazen to live long."

Nevertheless, I kept right on gazing at them, and "going a piece of the way" whenever I could make it. The village seemed dull to me most of the time. If the village was singing a chorus, I must have missed the tune.

Perhaps a year before the old man died, I came to know two other white people for myself. They were women.

PAGES 52–58 from DUST TRACKS ON A ROAD by ZORA NEALE HURSTON. Copyright 1942 by Zora Neale Hurston. Copyright renewed 1970 by John C. Hurston. Reprinted by permission of HarperCollins Publishers, Inc.

It came about this way. The whites who came down from the North were often brought by their friends to visit the village school. A Negro school was something strange to them, and while they were always sympathetic and kind, curiosity must have been present, also. They came and went, came and went. Always, the room was hurriedly put in order, and we were threatened with a prompt and bloody death if we cut one caper while the visitors were present. We always sang a spiritual, led by Mr. Calhoun himself. Mrs. Calhoun always stood in the back, with a palmetto switch in her hand as a squelcher. We were all little angels for the duration, because we'd better be. She would cut her eyes and give us a glare that meant trouble, then turn her face towards the visitors and beam as much as to say it was a great privilege and pleasure to teach lovely children like us. They couldn't see that palmetto hickory in her hand behind all those benches, but we knew where our angelic behavior was coming from.

Usually, the visitors gave warning a day ahead and we would be cautioned to put on shoes, comb our heads, and see to ears and fingernails. There was a close inspection of every one of us before we marched in that morning. Knotty heads, dirty ears and fingernails got hauled out of line, strapped and sent home to lick the calf over again.

This particular afternoon, the two young ladies just popped in. Mr. Calhoun was flustered, but he put on the best show he could. He dismissed the class that he was teaching up at the front of the room, then called the fifth grade in reading. That was my class.

So we took our readers and went up front. We stood up in the usual line, and opened to the lesson. It was the story of Pluto and Persephone. It was new and hard to the class in general, and Mr. Calhoun was very uncomfortable as the readers stumbled along, spelling out words with their lips, and in mumbling undertones before they exposed them experimentally to the teacher's ears.

Then it came to me. I was fifth or sixth down the line. The story was not new to me, because I had read my reader through from lid to lid, the first week that Papa had bought it for me.

That is how it was that my eyes were not in the book, working out the paragraph which I knew would be mine by counting the children ahead of me. I was observing our visitors, who held a book between them, following the lesson. They had shiny hair, mostly brownish. One had a looping gold chain around her neck. The other one was dressed all over in black and white with a pretty finger ring on her left hand. But the thing that held my eyes were their fingers. They were long and thin, and very white, except up near the tips. There they were baby pink. I had never seen such hands. It was a fascinating discovery for me. I wondered how they felt. I would have given those hands more attention, but the child before me was almost through. My turn next, so I got on my mark, bringing my eyes back to the book and made sure of my place. Some of the stories I had reread several times, and this Greco-Roman myth was one of my favorites. I was exalted by it, and that is the way I read my paragraph.

"Yes, Jupiter had seen her (Persephone). He had seen the maiden picking flowers in the field. He had seen the chariot of the dark monarch pause by the maiden's side. He had seen him when he seized Persephone. He had seen the black horses leap down Mount Aetna's fiery throat. Persephone was now in Pluto's dark realm and he had made her his wife."

The two women looked at each other and then back to me. Mr. Calhoun broke out with a proud smile beneath his bristly moustache, and instead of the next child taking up where I had ended, he nodded to me to go on. So I read the story to the end, where flying Mercury, the messenger of the Gods, brought Persephone back to the sunlit earth and restored her to the arms of Dame Ceres, her mother, that the world might have springtime and summer flowers, autumn and harvest. But because she had bitten the pomegranate while in Pluto's kingdom, she must return to him for three months of each year, and be his queen. Then the world had winter, until she returned to earth.

The class was dismissed and the visitors smiled us away and went into a low-voiced conversation with Mr. Calhoun for a few minutes. They glanced my way once or twice and I began to worry. Not only was I barefooted, but my feet and legs were dusty. My hair was more uncombed than usual, and my nails were not shiny clean. Oh, I'm going to catch it now. Those ladies saw me, too. Mr. Calhoun is promising to 'tend to me. So I thought.

Then Mr. Calhoun called me. I went up thinking how awful it was to get a whipping before company. Furthermore, I heard a snicker run over the room. Hennie Clark and Stell Brazzle did it out loud, so I would be sure to hear them. The smart-aleck was going to get it. I slipped one hand behind me and switched my dress tail at them, indicating scorn.

"Come here, Zora Neale," Mr. Calhoun cooed as I reached the desk. He put his hand on my shoulder and gave me little pats. The ladies smiled and held out those flower-looking fingers towards me. I seized the opportunity for a good look.

"Shake hands with the ladies, Zora Neale," Mr. Calhoun prompted and they took my hand one after the other and smiled. They asked me if I loved school, and I lied that I did. There was *some* truth in it, because I liked geography and reading, and I liked to play at recess time. Whoever it was invented writing and arithmetic got no thanks from me. Neither did I like the arrangement where the teacher could sit up there with a palmetto stem and lick me whenever he saw fit. I hated things I couldn't do anything about. But I knew better than to bring that up right there, so I said yes, I *loved* school.

"I can tell you do," Brown Taffeta gleamed. She patted my head, and was lucky enough not to get sandspurs in her hand. Children who roll and tumble in the grass in Florida, are apt to get sandspurs in their hair. They shook hands with me again and I went back to my seat.

When school let out at three o'clock, Mr. Calhoun told me to wait. When everybody had gone, he told me I was to go to the Park House, that was the hotel in Maitland, the next afternoon to call upon Mrs. Johnstone and Miss Hurd. I must tell Mama to see that I was clean and brushed from head to feet, and I must wear shoes and stockings. The ladies liked me, he said, and I must be on my best behavior.

The next day I was let out of school an hour early, and went home to be stood up in a tub of suds and be scrubbed and have my ears dug into. My sandy hair sported a red ribbon to match my red and white checked gingham dress, starched until it could stand alone. Mama saw to it that my shoes were on the right feet, since I was careless about left and right. Last thing, I was given a handkerchief to carry, warned again about my behavior, and sent off, with my big brother John to go as far as the hotel gate with me.

First thing, the ladies gave me strange things, like stuffed dates and preserved ginger, and encouraged me to eat all that I wanted. Then they showed me their Japanese dolls and just talked. I was then handed a copy of *Scribner's Magazine*, and asked to read a place that was pointed out to me. After a paragraph or two, I was told with smiles, that that would do.

I was led out on the grounds and they took my picture under a palm tree. They handed me what was to me then a heavy cylinder done up in fancy paper, tied with a ribbon, and they told me goodbye, asking me not to open it until I got home.

My brother was waiting for me down by the lake, and we hurried home, eager to see what was in the thing. It was too heavy to be candy or anything like that. John insisted on toting it for me.

My mother made John give it back to me and let me open it. Perhaps, I shall never experience such joy again. The nearest thing to that moment was the telegram accepting my first book. One hundred goldy-new pennies rolled out of the cylinder. Their gleam lit up the world. It was not avarice that moved me. It was the beauty of the thing. I stood on the mountain. Mama let me play with my pennies for a while, then put them away for me to keep.

That was only the beginning. The next day I received an Episcopal hymn-book bound in white leather with a golden cross stamped into the front cover, a copy of The Swiss Family Robinson, and a book of fairy tales.

I set about to commit the song words to memory. There was no music written there, just the words. But there was to my consciousness music in between them just the same. "When I survey the Wondrous Cross" seemed the most beautiful to me, so I committed that to memory first of all. Some of them seemed dull and without life, and I pretended they were not there. If white people like trashy singing like that, there must be something funny about them that I had not noticed before. I stuck to the pretty ones where the words marched to a throb I could feel.

A month or so after the two young ladies returned to Minnesota, they sent me a huge box packed with clothes and books. The red coat with a wide circular collar and the red tam pleased me more than any of the other things. My chums pretended not to like anything that I had, but even then I knew that they were jealous. Old Smarty had gotten by them again. The clothes were not new, but they were very good. I shone like the morning sun.

But the books gave me more pleasure than the clothes. I had never been too keen on dressing up. It called for hard scrubbings with Octagon soap suds getting in my eyes, and none too gentle fingers scrubbing my neck and gouging in my ears.

In that box were Gulliver's Travels, Grimm's Fairy Tales, Dick Whittington, Greek and Roman Myths, and best of all, Norse Tales. Why did the Norse tales strike so deeply into my soul? I do not know, but they did. I seemed to remember seeing Thor swing his mighty short-handled hammer as he sped across the sky in rumbling thunder, lightning flashing from the tread of his steeds and the wheels of his chariot. The great and good Odin, who went down to the well of knowledge to drink, and was told that the price of a drink from that fountain was an eye. Odin drank deeply, then plucked out one eye without a murmur and handed it to the grizzly keeper, and walked away. That held majesty for me.

Of the Greeks, Hercules moved me most. I followed him eagerly on his tasks. The story of the choice of Hercules as a boy when he met Pleasure and Duty, and put his hand in that of Duty and followed her steep way to the blue hills of fame and glory, which she pointed out at the end, moved me profoundly. I resolved to be like him. The tricks and turns of the other Gods and Goddesses left me cold. There were other thin books about this and that sweet and gentle little girl who gave up her heart to Christ and good works. Almost always they died from it, preaching as they passed. I was utterly indifferent to their deaths. In the first place I could not conceive of death, and in the next place they never had any funerals that amounted to a hill of beans, so I didn't care how soon they rolled up their big, soulful, blue eyes and kicked the bucket. They had no meat on their bones.

But I also met Hans Andersen and Robert Louis Stevenson. They seemed to know what I wanted to hear and said it in a way that tingled me. Just a little below these friends was Rudyard Kipling in his Jungle Books. I loved his talking snakes as much as I did the hero.

I came to start reading the Bible through my mother. She gave me a licking one afternoon for repeating something I had overheard a neighbor telling her. She locked me in her room after the whipping, and the Bible was the only thing in there for me to read. I happened to open to the place where David was doing some mighty smiting, and I got interested. David went here and he went there, and no matter where he went, he smote 'em hip and thigh. Then he sung songs to his harp awhile, and went out and smote some more. Not one time did David stop and preach about sins and things. All David wanted to know from God was who to kill and when. He took care of the other details himself. Never a quiet moment. I liked him a lot. So I read a great deal more in the Bible, hunting for some more active people like David. Except for the beautiful language of Luke and Paul, the New Testament still plays a poor second to the Old Testament for me. The Jews had a God who laid about Him when they needed Him. I could see no use waiting till Judgment Day to see a man who was just crying for a good killing, to be told to go and roast. My idea was to give him a good killing first, and then if he got roasted later on, so much the better.

In searching for more Davids, I came upon Leviticus. There were exciting things in there to a child eager to know the facts of life. I told Carrie Roberts about it, and we spent long afternoons reading what Moses told the Hebrews not to do in Leviticus. In that way I found out a number of things the old folks would not have told me. Not knowing what we were actually reading, we got a lot of praise from our elders for our devotion to the Bible.

Having finished that and scanned the Doctor Book, which my mother thought she had hidden securely from my eyes, I read all the things which children write on privy-house walls. Therefore, I lost my taste for pornographic literature. I think that the people who love it got cheated in the matter of privy houses when they were children.

In a way this early reading gave me great anguish through all my childhood and adolescence. My soul was with the gods and my body in the village. People just would not act like gods. Stew beef, fried fatback and morning grits were no ambrosia from Valhalla. Raking back yards and carrying out chamber-pots, were not the tasks of Thor. I wanted to be away from drabness and to stretch my limbs in some mighty struggle. I was only happy in the woods, and when the ecstatic Florida springtime came strolling from the sea, trance-glorifying the world with its aura. Then I hid out in the tall wild oats that waved like a glinty veil. I nibbled sweet oat stalks and listened to the wind soughing and sighing through the crowns of the lofty pines. I made particular friendship with one huge tree and always played about its roots. I named it "the loving pine," and my chums came to know it by that name. . . .

The Achievement of Desire

Richard Rodriguez

Richard Rodriguez is a well known editor and author who has appeared frequently as a commentator on the MacNeil/Lehrer News Hour. He recently published *Days of Obligation: An Argument with My Mexican Father.* In *Hunger of Memory*, which was published in 1982 and is the source of the following excerpt, Rodriguez explains the conflicts he experienced as a nonnative speaker of English who desperately sought to enter mainstream culture, even if this meant sacrificing his identity as the son of Mexican immigrants.

The boy who first entered a classroom barely able to speak English, twenty years later concluded his studies in the stately quiet of the reading room in the British Museum. Thus with one sentence I can summarize my academic career. It will be harder to summarize what sort of life connects the boy to the man.

With every award, each graduation from one level of education to the next, people I'd meet would congratulate me. Their refrain always the same: 'Your parents must be very proud.' Sometimes then they'd ask me how I managed it—my 'success.' (How?)After a while, I had several quick answers to give in reply. I'd admit, for one thing, that I went to an excellent grammar school. (My earliest teachers, the nuns, made my success their ambition.) And my brother and both my sisters were very good students. (They often brought home the shiny school trophies I came to want.) And my mother and father always encouraged me. (At every graduation they were behind the stunning flash of the camera when I turned to look at the crowd.)

As important as these factors were, however, they account inadequately for my academic advance. Nor do they suggest what an odd success I managed. For although I was a very good student, I was also a very bad student. I was a 'scholarship boy', a certain kind of scholarship boy. Always successful, I was always unconfident. Exhilarated by my progress. Sad. I became the prized student—anxious and eager to learn. Too eager, too anxious—an imitative and unoriginal pupil. My brother and two sisters enjoyed the advantages I did, and they grew to be as successful as I, but none of them ever seemed so anxious about their schooling. A second-grade student, I was the one who came home and corrected the 'simple' grammatical mistakes of our parents. ("Two negatives make a positive.") Proudly I announced—to my family's startled silence—that a teacher had said I was losing all trace of a Spanish accent. I was oddly annoyed when I was unable to get parental help with a homework assignment. The night my father tried to help me with an arithmetic exercise, he kept reading the instructions, each time more deliberately, until I pried the textbook out of his hands, saying, 'I'll try to figure it out some more by myself.'

When I reached the third grade, I outgrew such behavior. I became more tactful, careful to keep separate the two very different worlds of my day. But then, with ever-increasing inten-

From Hunger of Memory by Richard Rodriguez. Reprinted by permission of DAVID R. GODINE, PUBLISHERS, INC. Copyright © 1982 by Richard Rodriguez.

sity, I devoted myself to my studies. I became bookish, puzzling to all my family. Ambition set me apart. When my brother saw me struggling home with stacks of library books, he would laugh, shouting: 'Hey, Four Eyes!' My father opened a closet one day and was startled to find me inside, reading a novel. My mother would find me reading when I was supposed to be asleep or helping around the house or playing outside. In a voice angry or worried or just curious, she'd ask: 'What do you see in your books?' It became the family's joke. When I was called and wouldn't reply, someone would say I must be hiding under my bed with a book.

(How did I manage my success?)

What I am about to say to you has taken me more than twenty years to admit: *A primary reason for my success in the classroom was that I couldn't forget that schooling was changing me and separating me from the life I enjoyed before becoming a student.* That simple realization! For years I never spoke to anyone about it. Never mentioned a thing to my family or my teachers or classmates. From a very early age, I understood enough, just enough about my classroom experiences to keep what I knew repressed, hidden beneath layers of embarrassment. Not until my last months as a graduate student, nearly thirty years old, was it possible for me to think much about the reasons for my academic success. Only then. At the end of my schooling, I needed to determine how far I had moved from my past. The adult finally confronted, and now must publicly say, what the child shuddered from knowing and could never admit to himself or to those many faces that smiled at his every success. ('Your parents must be very proud. . . .')

📖

At the end, in the British Museum (too distracted to finish my dissertation) for weeks I read, speed-read, books by modern educational theorists, only to find infrequent and slight mention of students like me. (Much more is written about the more typical case, the lower-class student who barely is helped by his schooling.) Then one day, leafing through Richard Hoggart's *The Uses of Literacy*, I found, in his description of the scholarship boy, myself. For the first time I realized that there were other students like me, and so I was able to frame the meaning of my academic success, its consequent price—the loss.

Hoggart's description is distinguished, at least initially, by deep understanding. What he grasps very well is that the scholarship boy must move between environments, his home and the classroom, which are at cultural extremes, opposed. With his family, the boy has the intense pleasure of intimacy, the family's consolation in feeling public alienation. Lavish emotions texture home life. *Then*, at school, the instruction bids him to trust lonely reason primarily. Immediate needs set the pace of his parent's lives. From his mother and father the boy learns to trust spontaneity and nonrational ways of knowing. *Then*, at school, there is mental calm. Teachers emphasize the value of a reflectiveness that opens a space between thinking and immediate action.

Years of schooling must pass before the boy will be able to sketch the cultural differences in his day as abstractly as this. But he senses those differences early. Perhaps as early as the night he brings home an assignment from school and finds the house too noisy for study.

He has to be more and more alone, if he is going to 'get on'. He will have, probably unconsciously, to oppose the ethos of the hearth, the intense gregariousness *of the working-class family group. Since everything centres upon the living-room, there is unlikely to be a room of his own; the bedrooms are cold and inhospitable, and to warm them or the front room, if there is one, would not only be expensive, but would require an imaginative leap—out of the tradition—which most families are not capable of making. There is a corner of the living-room table. On the other side Mother is ironing, the wireless is on, someone is singing a snatch of song or Father says intermittently whatever comes into his head. The boy has to cut himself off mentally, so as to do his homework, as well as he can.*

The next day, the lesson is as apparent at school. There are even rows of desks. Discussion is ordered. The boy must rehearse his thoughts and raise his hand before speaking out in a loud voice to an audience of classmates. And there is time enough, and silence, to think about ideas (big ideas) never considered at home by his parents.

Not for the working-class child alone is adjustment to the classroom difficult. Good schooling requires that any student alter early childhood habits. But the working-class child is usually least prepared for the change. And, unlike many middle-class children, he goes home and sees in his parents a way of life not only different but starkly opposed to that of the classroom. (He enters the house and hears his parents talking in ways his teachers discourage.)

Without extraordinary determination and the great assistance of others—at home and at school—there is little chance for success. Typically most working-class children are barely changed by the classroom. The exception succeeds. The relative few become scholarship students. Of these, Richard Hoggart estimates, most manage a fairly graceful transition. Somehow they learn to live in the two very different worlds of their day. There are some others, however, those Hoggart pejoratively terms 'scholarship boys,' for whom success comes with special anxiety. Scholarship boy: good student, troubled son. The child is 'moderately endowed,' intellectually mediocre, Hoggart supposes—though it may be more pertinent to note the special qualities of temperament in the child. High-strung child. Brooding. Sensitive. Haunted by the knowledge that one *chooses* to become a student. (Education is not an inevitable or natural step in growing up.) Here is a child who cannot forget that his academic success distances him from a life he loved, even from his own memory of himself.

Initially, he wavers, balances allegiance. ('The boy is himself [until he reaches, say, the upper forms] very much of *both* the worlds of home and school. He is enormously obedient to the dictates of the world of school, but emotionally still strongly wants to continue as part of the family circle.') Gradually, necessarily, the balance is lost. The boy needs to spend more and more time studying, each night enclosing himself in the silence permitted and required by intense concentration. He takes his first step toward academic success, away from his family.

From the very first days, through the years following, it will be with his parents—the figures of lost authority, the persons toward whom he feels deepest love—that the change will be most powerfully measured. A separation will unravel between them. Advancing in his studies, the boy notices that his mother and father have not changed as much as he. Rather when he sees them, they often remind him of the person he once was and the life he earlier shared with them. He realizes what some Romantics also know when they praise the working class for the capacity for human closeness, qualities of passion and spontaneity, that the rest of us experience in like measure only in the earliest part of our youth. For the Romantic, this doesn't make working-class life childish. Working-class life challenges precisely because it is an *adult* way of life.

The scholarship boy reaches a different conclusion. He cannot afford to admire his parents. (How could he and still pursue such a contrary life?) He permits himself embarrassment at their lack of education. And to evade nostalgia for the life he has lost, he concentrates on the benefits education will bestow upon him. He becomes especially ambitious. Without the support of old certainties and consolations, almost mechanically, he assumes the procedures and doctrines of the classroom. The kind of allegiance the young student might have given his mother and father only days earlier, he transfers to the teacher, the new figure of authority. '[The scholarship boy] tends to make a father-figure of his form-master,' Hoggart observes.

But Hoggart's calm prose only makes me recall the urgency with which I came to idolize my grammar school teachers. I began by imitating their accents, using their diction, trusting their every direction. The very first facts they dispensed, I grasped with awe. Any book they told me to read, I read—then waited for them to tell me which books I enjoyed. Their every casual opinion I came to adopt and to trumpet when I returned home. I stayed after school 'to help'—to get my teacher's undivided attention. It was the nun's encouragement that mattered most to me. (She understood exactly what—my parents never seemed to appraise so well—all my achievements entailed.) Memory gently caressed each word of praise bestowed in the classroom so that compliments teachers paid me years ago come quickly to mind even today.

The enthusiasm I felt in second-grade classes I flaunted before both my parents. The docile, obedient student came home a shrill and precocious son who insisted on correcting and teaching his parents with the remark: 'My teacher told us. . . .'

I intended to hurt my mother and father. I was still angry at them for having encouraged me toward classroom English. But gradually this anger was exhausted, replaced by guilt as school grew more and more attractive to me. I grew increasingly successful, a talkative student. My hand was raised in the classroom; I yearned to answer any question. At home, life was less noisy than it had been. (I spoke to classmates and teachers more often each day than to family members.) Quiet at home, I sat with my papers for hours each night. I never forgot that schooling had irretrievably changed my family's life. That knowledge, however, did not weaken ambition. Instead, it strengthened resolve. Those times I remembered the loss of my past with regret, I quickly reminded myself of all the things my teachers could give me. (They could make me an educated man.) I tightened my grip on pencil and books. I evaded nostalgia. Tried hard to forget. But one does not forget by trying to forget. One only remembers. I remembered too well that education had changed my family's life. I would not have become a scholarship boy had I not so often remembered.

Once she was sure that her children knew English, my mother would tell us, 'You should keep up your Spanish.' Voices playfully groaned in response. '¡*Pochos!*' my mother would tease. I listened silently.

After a while, I grew more calm at home. I developed tact. A fourth-grade student, I was no longer the show-off in front of my parents. I became a conventionally dutiful son, politely affectionate, cheerful enough, even—for reasons beyond choosing—my father's favorite. And much about my family life was easy then, comfortable, happy in the rhythm of our living together: hearing my father getting ready for work; eating the breakfast my mother had made me; looking up from a novel to hear my brother or one of my sisters playing with friends in the backyard; in winter, coming upon the house all lighted up after dark.

But withheld from my mother and father was any mention of what most mattered to me: the extraordinary experience of first-learning. Late afternoon: In the midst of preparing dinner, my mother would come up behind me while I was trying to read. Her head just over mine, her breath warmly scented with food. 'What are you reading?' Or, 'Tell me all about your new courses.' I would barely respond, "Just the usual things, nothing special." (A half smile, then silence. Her head moving back in the silence. Silence! Instead of the flood of intimate sounds that had once flowed smoothly between us, there was this silence.) After dinner, I would rush to a bedroom with papers and books. As often as possible, I resisted parental pleas to 'save lights' by coming to the kitchen to work. I kept so much, so often, to myself. Sad. Enthusiastic. Troubled by the excitement of coming upon new ideas. Eager. Fascinated by the promising texture of a brand-new book. I hoarded the pleasures of learning. Alone for hours. Enthralled. Nervous. I rarely looked away from my book—or back on my memories. Nights when relatives visited and the front rooms were warmed by Spanish sounds, I slipped quietly out of the house.

It mattered that education was changing me. It never ceased to matter. My brother and sisters would giggle at our mother's mispronounced words. They'd correct her gently. My mother laughed girlishly one night, trying not to pronounce *sheep* as *ship*. From a distance I listened sullenly. From that distance, pretending not to notice on another occasion, I saw my father looking at the title pages of my library books. That was the scene on my mind when I walked home with a fourth-grade companion and heard him say that his parents read to him every night. (A strange-sounding book—*Winnie the Pooh*.) Immediately, I wanted to know, 'What is it like?' My companion, however, thought I wanted to know about the plot of the book. Another day, my mother surprised me by asking for a 'nice' book to read. 'Something not too hard you think I might like.' Carefully I chose one, Willa Cather's *My Antonia*. But when, several weeks later, I happened to see it next to her bed unread except for the first few pages, I was furious and suddenly wanted to cry. I grabbed up the book and took it back to my room and placed it in its place, alphabetically on my shelf.

'Your parents must be very proud of you.' People began to say that to me about the time I was in sixth grade. To answer affirmatively, I'd smile. Shyly I'd smile, never betraying my sense of the irony: I was not proud of my mother and father. I was embarrassed by their lack of education. It was not that I ever thought they were stupid, though stupidly I took for granted their enormous native intelligence. Simply, what mattered to me was that they were not like my teachers.

But, 'Why didn't you tell us about the award?' my mother demanded, her frown weakened by pride. At the grammar school ceremony several weeks after, her eyes were brighter than the trophy I'd won. Pushing back the hair from my forehead, she whispered that I had 'shown' the *gringos*. A few minutes later, I heard my father speak to my teacher and felt ashamed of his labored, accented words. Then guilty for the shame. I felt such contrary feelings. (There is no simple roadmap through the heart of the scholarship boy.) My teacher was so soft-spoken and her words were edged sharp and clean. I admired her until it seemed to me that she spoke too carefully. Sensing that she was condescending to them, I became nervous. Resentful. Protective. I tried to move my parents away. 'You both must be very proud of Richard,' the nun said. They responded quickly. (They were proud.) 'We are proud of all our children.' Then this afterthought: 'They sure didn't get their brains from us.' They all laughed. I smiled.

Tightening the irony into a knot was the knowledge that my parents were always behind me. They made success possible. They evened the path. They sent their children to parochial schools because the nuns 'teach better.' They paid a tuition they couldn't afford. They spoke English to us.

For their children my parents wanted chances they never had—an easier way. It saddened my mother to learn that some relatives forced their children to start working right after high school. To *her* children she would say, 'Get all the education you can.' In schooling she recognized the key to job advancement. And with the remark she remembered her past.

As a girl new to America my mother had been awarded a high school diploma by teachers too careless or busy to notice that she hardly spoke English. On her own, she determined to learn how to type. That skill got her jobs typing envelopes in letter shops, and it encouraged in her an optimism about the possibility of advancement. (Each morning when her sisters put on uniforms, she chose a bright-colored dress.) The years of young womanhood passed, and her typing speed increased. She also became an excellent speller of words she mispronounced. 'And I've never been to college,' she'd say, smiling, when her children asked her to spell words they were too lazy to look up in a dictionary.

Typing, however, was dead-end work. Finally frustrating. When her youngest child started high school, my mother got a full-time office job once again. (Her paycheck combined with my father's to make us—in fact—what we had already become in our imagination of ourselves—middle class.) She worked then for the (California) state government in numbered civil service positions secured by examinations. The old ambition of her youth was rekindled. During the lunch hour, she consulted bulletin boards for announcements of openings. One day she saw mention of something called an 'anti-poverty agency.' A typing job. A glamorous job, part of the governor's staff. 'A knowledge of Spanish required.' Without hesitation she applied and became nervous only when the job was suddenly hers.

'Everyone comes to work all dressed up,' she reported at night. And didn't need to say more than that her co-workers wouldn't let her answer the phones. She was only a typist, after all, albeit a very fast typist. And an excellent speller. One morning there was a letter to be sent to a Washington cabinet officer. On the dictating tape, a voice referred to urban guerrillas. My mother typed (the wrong word, correctly): 'gorillas.' The mistake horrified the anti-poverty bureaucrats who shortly after arranged to have her returned to her previous position. She would go no further. So she willed her ambition to her children. 'Get all the education you can; with an education you can do anything.' (With a good education *she* could have done anything.)

When I was in high school, I admitted to my mother that I planned to become a teacher someday. That seemed to please her. But I never tried to explain that it was not the occupation of teaching I yearned for as much as it was something more elusive: I wanted to *be* like my teachers, to possess their knowledge, to assume their authority, their confidence, even to assume a teacher's persona.

In contrast to my mother, my father never verbally encouraged his children's academic success. Nor did he often praise us. My mother had to remind him to 'say something' to one of his children who scored some academic success. But whereas my mother saw in education the opportunity for job advancement, my father recognized that education provided an even more startling possibility: It could enable a person to escape from a life of mere labor.

In Mexico, orphaned when he was eight, my father left school to work as an 'apprentice' for an uncle. Twelve years later, he left Mexico in frustration and arrived in America. He had great expectations then of becoming an engineer. ('Work for my hands and my head.') He knew a Catholic priest who promised to get him money enough to study full time for a high school diploma. But the promises came to nothing. Instead there was a dark succession of warehouse, cannery, and factory jobs. After work he went to night school along with my mother. A year, two passed. Nothing much changed, except that fatigue worked its way into the bone; then everything changed. He didn't talk anymore of becoming an engineer. He stayed outside on the steps of the school while my mother went inside to learn typing and shorthand.

By the time I was born, my father worked at 'clean' jobs. For a time he was a janitor at a fancy department store. ('Easy work; the machines do it all.') Later he became a dental technician. ('Simple.') But by then he was pessimistic about the ultimate meaning of work and the possibility of ever escaping its claims. In some of my earliest memories of him, my father already seems aged by fatigue. (He has never really grown old like my mother.) From boyhood to manhood, I have remembered him in a single image: seated, asleep on the sofa, his head thrown back in a hideous corpselike grin, the evening newspaper spread out before him. 'But look at all you've accomplished,' his best friend said to him once. My father said nothing. Only smiled.

It was my father who laughed when I claimed to be tired by reading and writing. It was he who teased me for having soft hands. (He seemed to sense that some great achievement of leisure was implied by my papers and books.) It was my father who became angry while watching on television some woman at the Miss America contest tell the announcer that she was going to college. ('Majoring in fine arts.') 'College!' he snarled. He despised the trivialization of higher education, the inflated grades and cheapened diplomas, the half education that so often passed as mass education in my generation.

It was my father again who wondered why I didn't display my awards on the wall of my bedroom. He said he liked to go to doctors' offices and see their certificates and degrees on the wall. ('Nice.') My citations from school got left in closets at home. The gleaming figure astride one of my trophies was broken, wingless, after hitting the ground. My medals were placed in a jar of loose change. And when I lost my high school diploma, my father found it as it was about to be thrown out with the trash. Without telling me, he put it away with his own things for safekeeping.

These memories slammed together at the instant of hearing that refrain familiar to all scholarship students: 'Your parents must be very proud . . . .' Yes, my parents were proud. I knew it. But my parents regarded my progress with more than mere pride. They endured my early precocious behavior—but with what private anger and humiliation? As their children got older and would come home to challenge ideas both of them held, they argued before submitting to the force of logic or superior factual evidence with the disclaimer, 'It's what we were taught in our time to believe.' These discussions ended abruptly, though my mother remembered them on other occasions when she complained that our 'big ideas' were going to our heads. More acute was her complaint that the family wasn't close anymore, like some others she knew. Why weren't we close, 'more in the Mexican style'? Everyone is so private, she added. And she mimicked the yes and no answers she got in reply to her questions. Why didn't we talk more? (My father never asked.) I never said.

I was the first in my family who asked to leave home when it came time to go to college. I had been admitted to Stanford, one hundred miles away. My departure would only make physically apparent the separation that had occurred long before. But it was going too far. In the months preceding my leaving, I heard the question my mother never asked except indirectly. In the hot kitchen, tired at the end of her workday, she demanded to know, 'Why aren't the colleges here in Sacramento good enough for you? They are for your brother and sister.' In the middle of a car ride, not turning to face me, she wondered, 'Why do you need to go so far away?' Late at night, ironing, she said with disgust, 'Why do you have to put us through this big expense? You know your scholarship will never cover it all.' But when September came there was a rush to get everything ready. In a bedroom that last night I packed the big brown valise, and my mother sat nearby sewing initials onto the clothes I would take. And she said no more about my leaving.

Months later, two weeks of Christmas vacation: The first hours home were the hardest. ('What's new?') My parents and I sat in the kitchen for a conversation. (But, lacking the same words to develop our sentences and to shape our interests, what was there to say? What could I tell them of the term paper I had just finished on the 'universality of Shakespeare's appeal'?) I mentioned only small, obvious things: my dormitory life; weekend trips I had taken; random events. They responded with news of their own. (One was almost grateful for a family crisis about which there was much to discuss.) We tried to make our conversation seem like more than an interview.

📖

The scholarship boy pleases most when he is young—the working-class child struggling for academic success. To his teachers, he offers great satisfaction; his success is their proudest achievement. Many other persons offer to help him. A business man learns the boy's story and promises to underwrite part the cost of his college education. A woman leaves him her entire library of several hundred books when she moves. His progress is featured in a newspaper article. Many people seem happy for him. They marvel. 'How did you manage so fast?' From all sides, there is lavish praise and encouragement.

In his grammar school classroom, however, the boy already makes students around him uneasy. They scorn his desire to succeed. They scorn him for constantly wanting the teacher's attention and praise. 'Kiss Ass,' they call him when his hand swings up in response to every question he hears. Later, when he makes it to college, no one will mock him aloud. But he detects annoyance on the faces of some students and even some teachers who watch him. It puzzles him often. In college, then in graduate school, he behaves much as he always has. If anything is different about him it is that he dares to anticipate the successful conclusion of his studies. At last he feels that he belongs in the classroom, and this is exactly the source of the dissatisfaction he causes. To many persons around him, he appears too much the academic. There may be some things about him that recall his beginnings—his shabby clothes; his persistent poverty; or his dark skin (in those cases when it symbolizes his parents' disadvantaged condition)—but they only make clear how far he has moved from his past. He has used education to remake himself.

It bothers his fellow academics to face this. They will not say why exactly. (They sneer.) But their expectations become obvious when they are disappointed. They expect—they want—a student less changed by his schooling. If the scholarship boy, from a past so distant from the classroom, could remain in some basic way unchanged, he would be able to prove that it is possible for anyone to become educated without basically changing from the person one was.

Here is no fabulous hero, no idealized scholar-worker. The scholarship boy does not straddle, cannot reconcile, the two great opposing cultures of his life. His success is unromantic and plain. He sits in the classroom and offers those sitting beside him no calming reassurance about their own lives. He sits in the seminar room—a man with brown skin, the son of working-class Mexican immigrant parents. (Addressing the professor at the head of the table, his voice catches with nervousness.) There is no trace of his parents' accent in his speech. Instead he approximates the accents of teachers and classmates. Coming from *him* those sounds seem suddenly odd. Odd too is the effect produced when *he* uses academic jargon—bubbles at the tip of his tongue: 'Topos . . . negative capability . . . vegetation imagery in Shakespearean comedy.' He lifts an opinion from Coleridge, takes something else from Frye or Empson or Leavis. He even repeats exactly his professor's earlier comment. All his ideas are clearly borrowed. He seems to have no thought of his own. He chatters while his listeners smile—their look one of disdain.

When he is older and thus when so little of the person he was survives, the scholarship boy makes only too apparent his profound lack of *self*-confidence. This is the conventional assessment that even Richard Hoggart repeats:

> [The scholarship boy] tends to over-stress the importance of examinations, of the piling-up of knowledge and of received opinions. He discovers a technique of apparent learning, of the acquiring of facts rather than of the handling and use of facts. He learns how to receive a purely literate education, one using only a small part of the personality and challenging only a limited area of his being. He begins to see life as a ladder, as a permanent examination with some praise and some further exhortation at each stage. He becomes an expert imbiber and doler-out; his competence will vary, but will rarely be accompanied by genuine enthusiasms. He rarely feels the reality of knowledge, of other men's thoughts and imaginings, on his own pulses . . . He has something of the blinkered pony about him. . .

But this is criticism more accurate than fair. The scholarship boy is a very bad student. He is the great mimic; a collector of thoughts, not a thinker; the very last person in class who ever feels obliged to have an opinion of his own. In large part, however, the reason he is such a bad student is because he realizes more often and more acutely than most other students—than Hoggart himself—that education requires radical self-reformation. As a very young boy, regarding his parents, as he struggles with an early homework assignment, he knows this too well. That is why he lacks self-assurance. He does not forget that the classroom is responsible for remaking him. He relies on his teacher, depends on all that he hears in the classroom and reads in his books. He becomes in every obvious way the worst student, a dummy mouthing the opinions of others. But he would not be so bad—nor would he become so successful, a *scholarship* boy—if he did not accurately perceive that the best synonym for primary 'education' is 'imitation.'

A Room of One's Own

Virginia Woolf

Virginia Woolf was born in 1882 into an upper class intellectual British family. While she is probably best known for innovative novels, novels that in many ways typify the "modern," (including *To the Lighthouse* and *Mrs. Dalloway*), she has recently been "discovered" by scholars interested in women writers and in feminist theory. In *A Room of One's Own*, she makes a compelling argument about how women—viewed in the early 20th century as "weaker vessels"—had been denied the economic, educational, and social advantages that would allow them to "create," specifically to write.

But, you may say, we asked you to speak about women and fiction—what has that got to do with a room of one's own? I will try to explain. When you asked me to speak about women and fiction I sat down on the banks of a river and began to wonder what the words meant. They might mean simply a few remarks about Fanny Burney; a few more about Jane Austen; a tribute to the Brontës and a sketch of Haworth Parsonage under snow; some witticisms if possible about Miss Mitford; a respectful allusion to George Eliot; a reference to Mrs. Gaskell and one would have done. But at second sight the words seemed not so simple. The title women and fiction might mean, and you may have meant it to mean, women and what they are like; or it might mean women and the fiction that they write; or it might mean women and the fiction that is written about them; or it might mean that somehow all three are inextricably mixed together and you want me to consider them in that light. But when I began to consider the subject in this last way, which seemed the most interesting, I soon saw that it had one fatal drawback. I should never be able to come to a conclusion. I should never be able to fulfil what is, I understand, the first duty of a lecturer—to hand you after an hour's discourse a nugget of pure truth to wrap up between the pages of your notebooks and keep on the mantelpiece forever. All I could do was to offer you an opinion upon one minor point—a woman must have money and a room of her own if she is to write fiction; and that, as you will see, leaves the great problem of the true nature of woman and the true nature of fiction unsolved. I have shirked the duty of coming to a conclusion upon these two questions—women and fiction remain, so far as I am concerned, unsolved problems. But in order to make some amends I am going to do what I can to show you how I arrived at this opinion about the room and the money. I am going to develop in your presence as fully and freely as I can the train of thought which led me to think this. Perhaps if I lay bare the ideas, the prejudices, that lie behind this statement you will find that they have some bearing upon women and some upon fiction. At any rate, when a subject is highly controversial—and any question about sex is that—one cannot hope to tell the truth. One can only show how one came to hold whatever opinion one does hold. One can only give one's audience the chance of drawing their own conclusions as they observe the limitations,

Excerpts from A ROOM OF ONE'S OWN by Virginia Woolf, copyright 1929 by Harcourt Brace & Company and renewed 1957 by Leonard Woolf, reprinted by permission of the publisher.

the prejudices, the idiosyncrasies of the speaker. Fiction here is likely to contain more truth than fact. Therefore I propose, making use of all the liberties and licences of a novelist, to tell you the story of the two days that preceded my coming here—how, bowed down by the weight of the subject which you have laid upon my shoulders, I pondered it, and made it work in and out of my daily life. I need not say that what I am about to describe has no existence; Oxbridge is an invention; so is Fernham; "I" is only a convenient term for somebody who has no real being. Lies will flow from my lips, but there may perhaps be some truth mixed up with them; it is for you to seek out this truth and to decide whether any part of it is worth keeping. If not, you will of course throw the whole of it into the wastepaper basket and forget all about it.

Here then was I (call me Mary Beton, Mary Seton, Mary Carmichael or by any name you please—it is not a matter of any importance) sitting on the banks of a river a week or two ago in fine October weather, lost in thought. That collar I have spoken of, women and fiction, the need of coming to some conclusion on a subject that raises all sorts of prejudices and passions, bowed my head to the ground. To the right and left bushes of some sort, golden and crimson, glowed with the colour, even it seemed burnt with the heat, of fire. On the further bank the willows wept in perpetual lamentation, their hair about their shoulders. The river reflected whatever it chose of sky and bridge and burning tree, and when the undergraduate had oared his boat through the reflections they closed again, completely, as if he had never been. There one might have sat the clock round lost in thought. Thought—to call it by a prouder name than it deserved—had let its line down into the stream. It swayed, minute after minute, hither and thither among the reflections and the weeds, letting the water lift it and sink it, until—you know the little tug—the sudden conglomeration of an idea at the end of one's line: and then the cautious hauling of it in, and the careful laying of it out? Alas, laid on the grass how small, how insignificant this thought of mine looked; the sort of fish that a good fisherman puts back into the water so that it may grow fatter and be one day worth cooking and eating. I will not trouble you with that thought now, though if you look carefully you may find it for yourselves in the course of what I am going to say.

But however small it was, it had, nevertheless, the mysterious property of its kind—put back into the mind, it became at once very exciting, and important; and as it darted and sank, and flashed hither and thither, set up such a wash and tumult of ideas that it was impossible to sit still. It was thus that I found myself walking with extreme rapidity across a grass plot. Instantly a man's figure rose to intercept me. Nor did I at first understand that the gesticulations of a curious-looking object, in a cut-away coat and evening shirt, were aimed at me. His face expressed horror and indignation. Instinct rather than reason came to my help; he was a Beadle; I was a woman. This was the turf; there was the path. Only the Fellows and Scholars are allowed here; the gravel is the place for me. Such thoughts were the work of a moment. As I regained the path the arms of the Beadle sank, his face assumed its usual repose, and though turf is better walking than gravel, no very great harm was done. The only charge I could bring against the Fellows and Scholars of whatever the college might happen to be was that in protection of their turf, which has been rolled for 300 years in succession, they had sent my little fish into hiding.

What idea it had been that had sent me so audaciously trespassing I could not now remember. The spirit of peace descended like a cloud from heaven, for if the spirit of peace dwells anywhere, it is in the courts and quadrangles of Oxbridge on a fine October morning. Strolling through those colleges past those ancient halls the roughness of the present seemed smoothed away; the body seemed contained in a miraculous glass cabinet through which no sound could penetrate, and the mind, freed from any contact with facts (unless one trespassed on the turf again), was at liberty to settle down upon whatever meditation was in harmony with the moment. As chance would have it, some stray memory of some old essay about revisiting Oxbridge in the long vacation brought Charles Lamb to mind— Saint Charles, said Thackeray, putting a letter of Lamb's to his forehead. Indeed, among all the dead (I give you my thoughts as they came to me), Lamb is one of the most congenial; one to whom one would have liked to say, Tell me then how you wrote your essays? For his essays are superior even to Max Beerbohm's, I thought, with all their perfection, because of that wild flash of imagination, that lightning crack of genius in the middle of them which leaves them flawed and imperfect, but starred with poetry. Lamb then came to Oxbridge perhaps a hundred years ago. Certainly he wrote an essay—the name escapes me—about the manuscript of one of Milton's poems which he saw here. It was *Lycidas* perhaps, and Lamb wrote how it shocked him to think it possible that any word in *Lycidas* could have been different from what it is. To think of Milton changing the words in that poem seemed to him a sort of sacrilege. This led me to remember what I could of *Lycidas* and to amuse myself with guessing which word it could have been that Milton had altered, and why. It then occurred to me that the very manuscript itself which Lamb had looked at was only a few hundred yards away, so that one could follow Lamb's footsteps across the quadrangle to that famous library where the treasure is kept. Moreover, I recollected, as I put this plan into execution, it is in this famous library that the manuscript of Thackeray's *Esmond* is also preserved. The critics often say that *Esmond* is Thackeray's most perfect novel. But the affectation of the style, with its imitation of the eighteenth century, hampers one, so far as I remember; unless indeed the eighteenth-century style was natural to Thackeray—a fact that one might prove by looking at the manuscript and seeing whether the alterations were for the benefit of the style or of the sense. But then one would have to decide what is style and what is meaning, a question which—but here I was actually at the door which leads into the library itself. I must have opened it, for instantly there issued, like a guardian angel barring the way with a flutter of black gown instead of white wings, a deprecating, silvery, kindly gentleman, who regretted in a low voice as he waved me back that ladies are only admitted to the library if accompanied by a Fellow of the College or furnished with a letter of introduction.

That a famous library has been cursed by a woman is a matter of complete indifference to a famous library. Venerable and calm, with all its treasures safe locked within its breast, it sleeps complacently and will, so far as I am concerned, so sleep for ever. Never will I wake those echoes, never will I ask for that hospitality again, I vowed as I descended the steps in anger.

📖

The scene, if I may ask you to follow me, was now changed. The leaves were still falling, but in London now, not Oxbridge; and I must ask you to imagine a room, like many thousands, with a window looking across people's hats and vans and motor-cars to other windows, and on the table inside the room a blank sheet of paper on which was written in large letters WOMEN AND FICTION, but no more. The inevitable sequel to lunching and dining at Oxbridge seemed, unfortunately, to be a visit to the British Museum. One must strain off what was personal and accidental in all these impressions and so reach the pure fluid, the essential oil of truth. For that visit to Oxbridge and the luncheon and the dinner had started a swarm of questions. Why did men drink wine and women water? Why was one sex so prosperous and the other so poor? What effect has poverty on fiction? What conditions are necessary for the creation of works of art?—a thousand questions at once suggested themselves. But one needed answers, not questions; and an answer was only to be had by consulting the learned and the unprejudiced, who have removed themselves above the strife of tongue and the confusion of body and issued the result of their reasoning and research in books which are to be found in the British Museum. If truth is not to be found on the shelves of the British Museum, where, I asked myself, picking up a notebook and a pencil, is truth?

Thus provided, thus confident and enquiring, I set out in the pursuit of truth. The day, though not actually wet, was dismal, and the streets in the neighborhood of the Museum were full of open coal-holes, down which sacks were showering; four-wheeled cabs were drawing up and depositing on the pavement corded boxes containing, presumably, the entire wardrobe of some Swiss or Italian family seeking fortune or refuge or some other desirable commodity which is to be found in the boarding-houses of Bloomsbury in the winter. The usual hoarse-voiced men paraded the streets with plants on barrows. Some shouted; others sang. London was like a workshop. London was like a machine. We were all being shot backwards and forwards on this plain foundation to make some pattern. The British Museum was another department of the factory. The swing-doors swung open; and there one stood under the vast dome, as if one were a thought in the huge bald forehead which is so splendidly encircled by a band of famous names. One went to the counter; one took a slip of paper; one opened a volume of the catalogue, and. . . . the five dots here indicate five separate minutes of stupefaction, wonder and bewilderment. Have you any notion how many books are written about women in the course of one year? Have you any notion how many are written by men? Are you aware that you are, perhaps, the most discussed animal in the universe? Here had I come with a notebook and a pencil proposing to spend a morning reading, supposing that at the end of the morning I should have transferred the truth to my notebook. But I should need to be a herd of elephants, I thought, and a wilderness of spiders, desperately referring to the animals that are reputed longest lived and most multitudinously eyed, to cope with all this. I should need claws of steel and beak of brass even to penetrate the husk. How shall I ever find the grains of truth embedded in all this mass of paper, I asked myself, and in despair began running my eye up and down the long list of titles. Even the names of the books gave me food for thought. Sex and its nature might well attract doctors and biologists; but what was surprising and difficult of explanation was the fact that sex—woman, that is to say—also attracts agreeable essayists, light-fingered novelists, young men who have taken the M.A. degree; men who have taken no degree; men who have no apparent qualification save that they are not women. Some of these books were, on the face of it, frivolous and facetious; but many, on the other hand, were serious and prophetic, moral and hortatory. Merely to read the titles suggested innumerable schoolmasters, innumerable clergymen mounting their platforms and pulpits and holding forth with a loquacity which far exceeded the hour usually allotted to such discourse on this one subject. It was a most strange phenomenon; and apparently—here I consulted the letter M—one confined to male sex. Women do not write books about men—a fact that I could not help welcoming with relief, for if I had first to read all that men have written about women, then all that women have written about men, the aloe that flowers once in a hundred years would flower twice before I could set pen to paper. So, making a perfectly arbitrary choice of a dozen volumes or so, I sent my slips of paper to lie in the wire tray, and waited in my stall, among the other seekers for the essential oil of truth.

What could be the reason, then, of this curious disparity, I wondered, drawing cart-wheels on the slips of paper provided by the British taxpayer for other purposes. Why are women, judging from this catalogue, so much more interesting to men than men are to women? A very curious fact it seemed, and my mind wandered to picture the lives of men who spend their time in writing books about women; whether they were old or young, married or unmarried, red-nosed or hump-backed-anyhow,it was flattering, vaguely, to feel oneself the object of such attention, provided that it was not entirely bestowed by the crip-pled and the infirm—so I pondered until all such frivolous thoughts were ended by an avalanche of books sliding down on to the desk in front of me. Now the trouble began. The student who has been trained in research at Oxbridge has no doubt some method of shep-herding his question past all distractions till it runs into its answer as a sheep runs into its pen. The student by my side, for instance, who was copying assiduously from a scientific manual was, I felt sure, extracting pure nuggets of the essential ore every ten minutes or so. His little grunts of satisfaction indicated so much. But if, unfortunately, one has had no train-ing in a university, the question far from being shepherded to its pen flies like a frightened flock hither and thither, helter-skelter, pursued by a whole pack of hounds. Professors, schoolmasters, sociologists, clergymen, novelists, essayists, journalists, men who had no qualification save that they were not women, chased my simple and single question—Why are women poor?—until it became fifty questions; until the fifty questions leapt frantically into mid-stream and were carried away. Every page in my notebook was scribbled over with notes. To show the state of mind I was in, I will read you a few of them, explaining that the page was headed quite simply, WOMEN AND POVERTY, in block letters; but what followed was something like this:

Condition in Middle Ages of,
Habits in the Fiji Islands of,
Worshipped as goddesses by,
Weaker in moral sense than,
Idealism of,
Greater conscientiousness of,
South Sea Islanders, age of puberty among,
Attractiveness of,
Offered as sacrifice to,
Small size of brain of,
Profounder sub-consciousness of,
Less hair on the body of,
Mental, moral and physical inferiority of,
Love of children of,

Greater length of life of,
Weaker muscles of,
Strength of affections of,
Vanity of,
Higher education of,
Shakespeare's opinion of,
Lord Birkenhead's opinion of,
Dean Inge's opinion of,
La Bruyère's opinion of,
Dr. Johnson's opinion of,
Mr. Oscar Browning's opinion of,. . .

Here I drew breath and added, indeed, in the margin, Why does Samuel Butler say, "Wise men never say what they think of women"? Wise men never say anything else apparently. But, I continued, leaning back in my chair and looking at the vast dome in which I was a single but by now somewhat harassed thought, what is so unfortunate is that wise men never think the same thing about women. Here is Pope:

Most women have no character at all.

And here is La Bruyère:

Les femmes sont extrêmes; elles sont meilleures ou pires que les hommes—

a direct contradiction by keen observers who were contemporary. Are they capable of education or incapable? Napoleon thought them incapable. Dr. Johnson thought the opposite.[1] Have they souls or have they not souls? Some savages say they have none. Others, on the contrary, maintain that women are half divine and worship them on that account.[2] Some sages hold that they are shallower in the brain; others that they are deeper in the consciousness. Goethe honoured them; Mussolini despises them. Wherever one looked men thought about women and thought differently. It was impossible to make head or tail of it all, I decided, glancing with envy at the reader next door who was making the neatest abstracts, headed often with an A or a B or a C, while my own notebook rioted with the wildest scribble of contradictory jottings. It was distressing, it was bewildering, it was humiliating. Truth had run through my fingers. Every drop had escaped.

I could not possibly go home, I reflected, and add as a serious contribution to the study of women and fiction that women have less hair on their bodies than men, or that the age of puberty among the South Sea Islanders is nine—or is it ninety?—even the handwriting had become in its distraction indecipherable. It was disgraceful to have nothing more weighty or respectable to show after a whole morning's work. And if I could not grasp the truth about W. (as for brevity's sake I had come to call her) in the past, why bother about W. in the future? It seemed pure waste of time to consult all those gentlemen who specialize in woman and her effect on whatever it may be—politics, children, wages, morality—numerous and learned as they are. One might as well leave their books unopened.

🕮

It was certainly an odd monster that one made up by reading the historians first and the poets afterwards—a worm winged like an eagle; the spirit of life and beauty in a kitchen chopping up suet. But these monsters, however amusing to the imagination, have no existence in fact. What one must do to bring her to life was to think poetically and prosaically at one and the same moment, thus keeping in touch with fact—that she is Mrs. Martin, aged thirty-six, dressed in blue, wearing a black hat and brown shoes; but not losing sight of fiction either—that she is a vessel in which all sorts of spirits and forces are coursing and flashing perpetually. The moment; however, that one tries this method with the Elizabethan woman, one branch of illumination fails; one is held up by the scarcity of facts. One knows nothing detailed, nothing perfectly true and substantial about her. History scarcely mentions her. And I turned to Professor Trevelyan again to see what history meant to him. I found by looking at his chapter headings that it meant—

"The Manor Court and the Methods of Open-field Agriculture . . . The Cistercians and Sheep-farming . . . The Crusades . . . The University . . . The House of Commons . . . The Hundred Years' War . . . The Wars of the Roses . . . The Renaissance Scholars . . . The Dissolution of the Monasteries . . . Agrarian and Religious Strife . . . The Origin of English Sea-power . . . The Armada . . . " and so on. Occasionally an individual woman is mentioned, an Elizabeth, or a Mary; a queen or a great lady. But by no possible means could middle-class women with nothing but brains and character at their command have taken part in any one of the great movements which, brought together, constitute the historian's view of the past. Nor shall we find her in any collection of anecdotes. Aubrey hardly mentions her. She never writes her own life and scarcely keeps a diary; there are only a handful of her letters in existence. She left no plays or poems by which we can judge her. What one wants, I thought—and why does not some brilliant student at Newnham or Girton supply it?—is a mass of information; at what age did she marry; how many children had she as a rule; what was her house like; had she a room to herself; did she do the cooking; would she be likely to have a servant? All these facts lie somewhere, presumably, in parish registers and account books; the life of the average Elizabethan woman must be scattered about somewhere, could one collect it and make a book of it. It would be ambitious beyond my daring, I thought, looking about the shelves for books that were not there, to suggest to the students of those famous colleges that they should re-write history, though I own that it often seems a little queer as it is, unreal, lop-sided; but why should they not add a supplement to history? calling it, of course, by some inconspicuous name so that women might figure there without impropriety? For one often catches a glimpse of them in the lives of the great, whisking away into the background, concealing, I sometimes think, a wink, a laugh, perhaps a tear. And, after all, we have lives enough of Jane Austen; it scarcely seems necessary to consider again the influence of the tragedies of Joanna Baillie upon the poetry of Edgar Allan Poe; as for myself, I should not mind if the homes and haunts of Mary Russell Mitford were closed to the public for a century at least. But what I find deplorable, I continued, looking about the bookshelves again, is that nothing is known about women before the eighteenth century. I have no model in my mind to turn about this way and that. Here am I asking why women did not write poetry in the Elizabethan age, and I am not sure how they were educated; whether they were taught to write; whether they had sitting-rooms to themselves; how many women had children before they were twenty-one; what, in short, they did from eight in the morning till eight at night. They had no money evidently; according to Professor Trevelyan they were married whether they liked it or not before they were out of the nursery, at fifteen or sixteen very likely. It would have been extremely odd, even upon this showing, had one of them suddenly written the plays of Shakespeare, I concluded, and I thought of that old gentleman, who is dead now, but was a bishop, I think, who declared that it was impossible for any woman, past, present, or to come, to have the genius of Shakespeare. He wrote to the papers about it. He also told a lady who applied to him for information that cats do not as a matter of fact go to heaven, though they have, he added, souls of a sort. How much thinking those old gentlemen used to save one! How the borders of ignorance shrank back at their approach! Cats do not go to heaven. Women cannot write the plays of Shakespeare.

Be that as it may, I could not help thinking, as I looked at the works of Shakespeare on the shelf, that the bishop was right at least in this; it would have been impossible, completely and entirely, for any woman to have written the plays of Shakespeare in the age of Shakespeare. Let me imagine, since facts are so hard to come by, what would have happened had Shakespeare had a wonderfully gifted sister, called Judith, let us say. Shakespeare himself went, very probably—his mother was an heiress—to the grammar school, where he may have learnt Latin—Ovid, Virgil and Horace—and the elements of grammar and logic. He was, it is well known, a wild boy who poached rabbits, perhaps shot a deer, and had, rather sooner than he should have done, to marry a woman in the neighbourhood, who bore him a child rather quicker than was right. That escapade sent him to seek his fortune in London. He had, it seemed, a taste for the theatre; he began by holding horses at the stage door. Very soon he got work in the theatre, became a successful actor, and lived at the hub of the universe, meeting everybody, knowing everybody, practising his art on the boards, exercising his wits in the streets, and even getting access to the palace of the queen. Meanwhile his extraordinarily gifted sister, let us suppose, remained at home. She was as adventurous, as imaginative, as agog to see the world as he was. But she was not sent to school. She had no chance of learning grammar and logic, let alone of reading Horace and Virgil. She picked up a book now and then, one of her brother's perhaps, and read a few pages. But then her parents came in and told her to mend the stockings or mind the stew and not moon about with books and papers. They would have spoken sharply but kindly, for they were substantial people who knew the conditions of life for a woman and loved their daughter—indeed, more likely than not she was the apple of her father's eye. Perhaps she scribbled some pages up in an apple loft on the sly, but was careful to hide them or set fire to them. Soon, however, before she was out of her teens, she was to be betrothed to the son of a neighbouring wool-stapler. She cried out that marriage was hateful to her, and for that she was severely beaten by her father. Then he ceased to scold her. He begged her instead not to hurt him, not to shame him in this matter of her marriage. He would give her a chain of beads or a fine petticoat, he said; and there were tears in his eyes. How could she disobey him? How could she break his heart? The force of her own gift alone drove her to it. She made up a small parcel of her belongings, let herself down by a rope one summer's night and took the road to London. She was not seventeen. The birds that sang in the hedge were not more musical than she was. She had the quickest fancy, a gift like her brother's, for the tune of words. Like him, she had a taste for the theatre. She stood at the stage door; she wanted to act, she said. Men laughed in her face. The manager— a fat, loose-lipped man—guffawed. He bellowed something about poodles dancing and women acting—no woman, he said, could possibly be an actress. He hinted—you can imagine what. She could get no training in her craft. Could she even seek her dinner in a tavern or roam the streets at midnight? Yet her genius was for fiction and lusted to feed abundantly upon the lives of men and women and the study of their ways. At last—for she was very young, oddly like Shakespeare the poet in her face, with the same grey eyes and rounded brows—at last Nick Greene the actor-manager took pity on her; she found herself with child by that gentleman and so—who shall measure the heat and violence of the poet's heart when caught and tangled in a woman's body?—killed herself one winter's night and lies buried at some cross-roads where the omnibuses now stop outside the Elephant and Castle.

That, more or less, is how the story would run, I think, if a woman in Shakespeare's day had had Shakespeare's genius. But for my part, I agree with the deceased bishop, if such he was—it is unthinkable that any woman in Shakespeare's day should have had Shakespeare's genius. For genius like Shakespeare's is not born among labouring, uneducated, servile people. It was not born in England among the Saxons and the Britons. It is not born today among the working classes. How, then, could it have been born among women whose work began, according to Professor Trevelyan, almost before they were out of the nursery, who were forced to it by their parents and held to it by all the power of law and custom? Yet genius of a sort must have existed among women as it must have existed among the working classes. Now and again an Emily Brontë or a Robert Burns blazes out and proves its presence. But certainly it never got itself on to paper. When, however, one reads of a witch being ducked, of a woman possessed by devils, of a wise woman selling herbs, or even of a very remarkable man who had a mother, then I think we are on the track of a lost novelist, a suppressed poet, of some mute and inglorious Jane Austen, some Emily Brontë who dashed her brains out on the moor or mopped and mowed about the highways crazed with the torture that her gift had put her to. Indeed, I would venture to guess that Anon, who wrote so many poems without signing them, was often a woman. It was a woman Edward Fitzgerald, I think, suggested who made the ballads and the folk-songs, crooning them to her children, beguiling her spinning with them, or the length of the winter's night.

This may be true or it may be false—who can say?—but what is true in it, so it seemed to me, reviewing the story of Shakespeare's sister as I had made it, is that any woman born with a great gift in the sixteenth century would certainly have gone crazed, shot herself, or ended her days in some lonely cottage outside the village, half witch, half wizard, feared and mocked at. For it needs little skill in psychology to be sure that a highly gifted girl who had tried to use her gift for poetry would have been so thwarted and hindered by other people, so tortured and pulled asunder by her own contrary instincts, that she must have lost her health and sanity to a certainty. No girl could have walked to London and stood at a stage door and forced her way into the presence of actor-managers without doing herself a violence and suffering an anguish which may have been irrational—for chastity may be a fetish invented by certain societies for unknown reasons—but were nonetheless inevitable. Chastity had then, it has even now, a religious importance in a woman's life, and has so wrapped itself round with nerves and instincts that to cut it free and bring it to the light of day demands courage of the rarest. To have lived a free life in London in the sixteenth century would have meant for a woman who was poet and playwright a nervous stress and dilemma which might well have killed her. Had she survived, whatever she had written would have been twisted and deformed, issuing from a strained and morbid imagination. And undoubtedly, I thought, looking at the shelf where there are no plays by women, her work would have gone unsigned.

Endnotes

1. " 'Men know that women are an overmatch for them, and therefore they choose the weakest or the most ignorant. If they did not think so, they never could be afraid of women knowing as much as themselves.'. . . In justice to the sex, I think it but candid to acknowledge that, in a subsequent conversation, he told me that he was serious in what he said."—**BOSWELL**, *The Journal of a Tour to the Hebrides*.
2. "The ancient Germans believed that there was something holy in women, and accordingly consulted them as oracles."—**FRAZER**, *Golden Bough*.

From Silence to Words: Writing as Struggle

Min-zhan Lu

Min-Zhan Lu is a professor at Drake University, who has used autobiographical writing as a tool for exploring problems of language and language use in the context of both the multicultural classroom and society. She has contributed a great deal to educators' understanding of basic writing, challenging deficit models of basic, or underprepared, writers with more culturally-sensitive approaches to teaching writing. This article appeared in *College English*, a journal for college English faculty, Vol. 49, no. 4, April 1987.

Imagine that you enter a parlor. You come late. When you arrive others have long preceded you, and they are engaged in a heated discussion. . . . You listen for a while, until you decide that you have caught the tenor of the argument: then you put in your oar. Someone answers; you answer him; another comes to your defense; another aligns himself against you, to either the embarrassment or gratification of your opponent, depending upon the quality of your ally's assistance. However, the discussion is interminable. The hour grows late, you must depart. And you do depart, with the discussion still vigorously in progress.

> —Kenneth Burke, *The Philosophy of Literary Form*

Men are not built in silence, but in word, in work, in action-reflection.

> —Paulo Freire, *Pedagogy of the Oppressed*

My mother withdrew into silence two months before she died. A few nights before she fell silent, she told me she regretted the way she had raised me and my sisters. I knew she was referring to the way we had been brought up in the midst of two conflicting worlds—

From Silence to Words: Writing as Struggle by Min-zhan Lu, College English, April, 1987. Copyright 1987 by the National Council of Teachers of English. Reprinted with permission.

the world of home, dominated by the ideology of the Western humanistic tradition, and the world of a society dominated by Mao Tse-tung's Marxism. My mother had devoted her life to our education, an education she knew had made us suffer political persecution during the Cultural Revolution. I wanted to find a way to convince her that, in spite of the persecution, I had benefited from the education she had worked so hard to give me. But I was silent. My understanding of my education was so dominated by memories of confusion and frustration that I was unable to reflect on what I could have gained from it.

This paper is my attempt to fill up that silence with words, words I didn't have then, words that I have since come to by reflecting on my earlier experience as a student in China and on my recent experience as a composition teacher in the United States. For in spite of the frustration and confusion I experienced growing up caught between two conflicting worlds, the conflict ultimately helped me to grow as a reader and writer. Constantly having to switch back and forth between the discourse of home and that of school made me sensitive and self-conscious about the struggle I experienced every time I tried to read, write, or think in either discourse. Eventually, it led me to search for constructive uses for such struggle.

From early childhood, I had identified the differences between home and the outside world by the different languages I used in each. My parents had wanted my sisters and me to get the best education they could conceive of—Cambridge. They had hired a live-in tutor, a Scot, to make us bilingual. I learned to speak English with my parents, my tutor, and my sisters. I was allowed to speak Shanghai dialect only with the servants. When I was four (the year after the Communist Revolution of 1949), my parents sent me to a local private school where I learned to speak, read, and write in a new language—Standard Chinese, the official written language of New China.

In those days I moved from home to school, from English to Standard Chinese to Shanghai dialect, with no apparent friction. I spoke each language with those who spoke the language. All seemed quite "natural"—servants spoke only Shanghai dialect because they were servants; teachers spoke Standard Chinese because they were teachers; languages had different words because they were different languages. I thought of English as my family language, comparable to the many strange dialects I didn't speak but had often heard some of my classmates speak with their families. While I was happy to have a special family language, until second grade I didn't feel that my family language was any different than some of my classmates' family dialects.

My second grade homeroom teacher was a young graduate from a missionary school. When she found out I spoke English, she began to practice her English on me. One day she used English when asking me to run an errand for her. As I turned to close the door behind me, I noticed the puzzled faces of my classmates. I had the same sensation I had often experienced when some stranger in a crowd would turn on hearing me speak English. I was more intensely pleased on this occasion; however, because suddenly I felt that my family language had been singled out from the family languages of my classmates. Since we were not allowed to speak any dialect other than Standard Chinese in the classroom, having my teacher speak English to me in class made English an official language of the classroom. I began to take pride in my ability to speak it.

This incident confirmed in my mind what my parents had always told me about the importance of English to one's life. Time and again they had told me of how my paternal grandfather, who was well versed in classic Chinese, kept losing good-paying jobs because he couldn't speak English. My grandmother reminisced constantly about how she had slaved and saved to send my father to a first-rate missionary school. And we were made to understand that it was my father's fluent English that had opened the door to his success. Even though my family had always stressed the importance of English for my future, I used to complain bitterly about the extra English lessons we had to take after school. It was only after my homeroom teacher had "sanctified" English that I began to connect English with my education. I became a much more eager student in my tutorials.

What I learned from my tutorials seemed to enhance and reinforce what I was learning in my classroom. In those days each word had one meaning. One day I would be making a sentence at school: "The national flag of China is red." The next day I would recite at home, "My love is like a red, red rose." There seemed to be an agreement between the Chinese "red" and the English "red," and both corresponded to the patch of color printed next to the word. "Love" was my love for my mother at home and my love for my "motherland" at school; both "loves" meant how I felt about my mother. Having two loads of homework forced me to develop a quick memory for words and a sensitivity to form and style. What I learned in one language carried over to the other. I made sentences such as, "I saw a red, red rose among the green leaves," with both the English lyric and the classic Chinese lyric—red flower among green leaves—running through my mind, and I was praised by both teacher and tutor for being a good student.

Although my elementary schooling took place during the fifties. I was almost oblivious to the great political and social changes happening around me. Years later, I read in my history and political philosophy textbooks that the fifties were a time when "China was making a transition from a semi-feudal, semi-capitalist, and semi-colonial country into a socialist country," a period in which "the Proletarians were breaking into the educational territory dominated by Bourgeois Intellectuals." While people all over the country were being officially classified into Proletarians, Petty-bourgeois, National-bourgeois, Poor-peasants, and Intellectuals, and were trying to adjust to their new social identities, my parents were allowed to continue the upper middle-class life they had established before the 1949 Revolution because of my father's affiliation with British firms. I had always felt that my family was different from the families of my classmates, but I didn't perceive society's view of my family until the summer vacation before I entered high school.

First, my aunt was caught by her colleagues talking to her husband over the phone in English. Because of it, she was criticized and almost labeled a Rightist. (This was the year of the Anti-Rightist movement, a movement in which the Intellectuals became the target of the "socialist class-struggle.") I had heard others telling my mother that she was foolish to teach us English when Russian had replaced English as the "official" foreign language. I had also learned at school that the American and British Imperialists were the arch-enemies of New China. Yet I had made no connection between the arch-enemies and the English our family spoke. What happened to my aunt forced the connection on me. I began to see my parents' choice of a family language as an anti-Revolutionary act and was alarmed that I had participated in such an act. From then on, I took care not to use English outside home and to conceal my knowledge of English from my new classmates.

Certain words began to play important roles in my new life at the junior high. On the first day of school, we were handed forms to fill out with our parents' class, job, and income. Being one of the few people not employed by the government, my father had never been officially classified. Since he was a medical doctor, he told me to put him down as an Intellectual. My homeroom teacher called me into the office a couple of days afterwards and told me that my father couldn't be an Intellectual if his income far exceeded that of a Capitalist. He also told me that since my father worked for Foreign Imperialists, my father should be classified as an Imperialist Lackey. The teacher looked nonplussed when I told him that my father couldn't be an Imperialist Lackey because he was a medical doctor. But I could tell from the way he took notes on my form that my father's job had put me in an unfavorable position in his eyes.

The Standard Chinese term "class" was not a new word for me. Since first grade, I had been taught sentences such as, "The Working class are the masters of New China." I had always known that it was good to be a worker, but until then, I had never felt threatened for not being one. That fall, "class" began to take on a new meaning for me. I noticed a group of Working-class students and teachers at school. I was made to understand that because of my class background, I was excluded from that group.

Another word that became important was "consciousness." One of the slogans posted in the school building read, "Turn our students into future Proletarians with socialist consciousness and education!" For several weeks we studied this slogan in our political philosophy course, a subject I had never had in elementary school. I still remember the definition of "socialist consciousness" that we were repeatedly tested on through the years: "Socialist consciousness is a person's political soul. It is the consciousness of the Proletarians represented by Marxist Mao Tse-tung thought. It takes expression in one's action, language, and lifestyle. It is the task of every Chinese student to grow up into a Proletarian with a socialist consciousness so that he can serve the people and the motherland." To make the abstract concept accessible to us, our teacher pointed out that the immediate task for students from Working-class families was to strengthen their socialist consciousnesses. For those of us who were from other class backgrounds, the task was to turn ourselves into Workers with socialist consciousnesses. The teacher never explained exactly how we were supposed to "turn" into Workers. Instead, we were given samples of the ritualistic annual plans we had to write at the beginning of each term. In these plans, we performed "self-criticism" on our consciousnesses and made vows to turn ourselves into Workers with socialist consciousnesses. The teacher's division between those who did and those who didn't have a socialist consciousness led me to reify the notion of "consciousness" into a thing one possesses. I equated this intangible "thing" with a concrete way of dressing, speaking, and writing. For instance, I never doubted that my political philosophy teacher had a socialist consciousness because she was from a steelworker's family (she announced this the first day of class) and was a Party member who wore grey cadre suits and talked like a philosophy textbook. I noticed other things about her. She had beautiful eyes and spoke Standard Chinese with such a pure accent that I thought she should be a film star. But I was embarrassed that I had noticed things that ought not to have been associated with her. I blamed my observation on my Bourgeois consciousness.

At the same time, the way reading and writing were taught through memorization and imitation also encouraged me to reduce concepts and ideas to simple definitions. In literature and political philosophy classes, we were taught a large number of quotations from Marx, Lenin, and Mao Tse-tung. Each concept that appeared in these quotations came with a definition. We were required to memorize the definitions of the words along with the quotations. Every time I memorized a definition, I felt I had learned a word: "The national red flag symbolizes the blood shed by Revolutionary ancestors for our socialist cause"; "New China rises like a red sun over the eastern horizon." As I memorized these sentences, I reduced their metaphors to dictionary meanings: "red" meant "Revolution" and "red sun" meant "New China" in the "language" of the Working class. I learned mechanically but eagerly. I soon became quite fluent in this new language.

As school began to define me as a political subject, my parents tried to build up my resistance to the "communist poisoning" by exposing me to the "great books"—novels by Charles Dickens, Nathaniel Hawthorne, Emily Brontë, Jane Austen, and writers from around the turn of the century. My parents implied that these writers represented how I, their child, should read and write. My parents replaced the word "Bourgeois" with the word "cultured." They reminded me that I was in school only to learn math and science. I needed to pass the other courses to stay in school, but I was not to let the "Red doctrines" corrupt my mind. Gone were the days when I could innocently write, "I saw the red, red rose among the green leaves." collapsing, as I did, English and Chinese cultural traditions. "Red" came to mean Revolution at school, "the Commies" at home, and adultery in *The Scarlet Letter*. Since I took these symbols and metaphors as meanings natural to people of the same class, I abandoned my earlier definitions of English and Standard Chinese as the language of home and the language of school. I now defined English as the language of the Bourgeois and Standard Chinese as the language of the Working class. I thought of the language of the Working class as someone else's language and the language of the Bourgeois as my language. But I also believed that, although the language of the Bourgeois was my real language, I could and would adopt the language of the Working class when I was at school. I began to put on and take off my Working class language in the same way I put on and took off my school clothes to avoid being criticized for wearing Bourgeois clothes.

📖

Despite my parents' and teachers' attempts to keep home and school discrete, the internal conflict between the two discourses continued whenever I read or wrote. Although I tried to suppress the voice of one discourse in the name of the other, having to speak aloud in the voice I had just silenced each time I crossed the boundary kept both voices active in my mind. Every "I think . . ." from the voice of home or school brought forth a "However . . ." or a "But . . ." from the voice of the opponents. To identify with the voice of home or school, I had to negotiate through the conflicting voices of both by restating, taking back, qualifying my thoughts.

📖

Not long ago, my daughter told me that it bothered her to hear her friend "talk wrong." Having come to the United States from China with little English, my daughter has become sensitive to the way English, as spoken by her teachers, operates. As a result, she has amazed her teachers with her success in picking up the language and in adapting to life at school. Her concern to speak the English taught in the classroom "correctly" makes her uncomfortable when she hears people using "ain't" or double negatives, which her teacher considers "improper." I see in her the me that had eagerly learned and used the discourse of the Working class at school. Yet while I was torn between the two conflicting worlds of school and home, she moves with seeming ease from the conversations she hears over the dinner table to her teacher's words in the classroom. My husband and I are proud of the good work she does at school. We are glad she is spared the kinds of conflict between home and school I experienced at her age. Yet as we watch her becoming more and more fluent in the language of the classroom, we wonder if, by enabling her to "survive" school, her very fluency will silence her when the scene of her reading and writing expands beyond that of the composition classroom.

For when I listen to my daughter, to students, and to some composition teachers talking about the teaching and learning of writing, I am often alarmed by the degree to which the metaphor of a survival tool dominates their understanding of language as it once dominated my own. I am especially concerned with the way some composition classes focus on turning the classroom into a monological scene for the students' reading and writing. Most of our students live in a world similar to my daughter's, somewhere between the purified world of the classroom and the complex world of my adolescence. When composition classes encourage these students to ignore those voices that seem irrelevant to the purified world of the classroom, most students are often able to do so without much struggle. Some of them are so adept at doing it that the whole process has for them become automatic.

However, beyond the classroom and beyond the limited range of these students' immediate lives lies a much more complex and dynamic social and historical scene. To help these students become actors in such a scene, perhaps we need to call their attention to voices that may seem irrelevant to the discourse we teach rather than encourage them to shut them out. For example, we might intentionally complicate the classroom scene by bringing into it discourses that stand at varying distances from the one we teach. We might encourage students to explore ways of practicing the conventions of the discourse they are learning by negotiating through these conflicting voices. We could also encourage them to see themselves as responsible for forming or transforming as well as preserving the discourse they are learning.

As I think about what we might do to complicate the external and internal scenes of our students' writing, I hear my parents and teachers saying: "Not now. Keep them from the wrangle of the marketplace until they have acquired the discourse and are skilled at using it." And I answer: "Don't teach them to 'survive' the whirlpool of crosscurrents by avoiding it. Use the classroom to moderate the currents. Moderate the currents, but teach them from the beginning to struggle." When I think of the ways in which the teaching of reading and writing as classroom activities can frustrate the development of students, I am almost grateful for the overwhelming complexity of the circumstances in which I grew up. For it was this complexity that kept me from losing sight of the effort and choice involved in reading or writing with and through a discourse.

References

Burke, Kenneth. *The Philosophy of Literary Form: Studies in Symbolic Action*. 2nd ed. Baton Rouge: Louisiana State UP, 1967.
—. *A Rhetoric of Motives*. Berkeley: U of California P, 1969.
Freire, Paulo. *Pedagogy of the Oppressed*. Trans. M. B. Ramos. New York: Continuum, 1970.
Williams, Raymond. *Marxism and Literature*. New York: Oxford UP, 1977.

Due West of What?

Charlayne Hunter-Gault

Charlayne Hunter-Gault, the first Black woman to attend the University of Georgia, is an award-winning journalist and correspondent for the MacNeil/Lehrer News Hour. In both "Due West of What?" and "Wayne State," she writes about her experiences of segregation in school and the ways that her education prepared her to face the challenges she describes. These selections are from her book In My Place, *1992.*

The first of many places that I would call "my place" was a tiny village tucked away in a remote little corner of South Carolina: Due West. There may have been bigger, better known, and happier places on February 27, 1942, but you couldn't have told my mother anything about them. Not even a difficult labor at home, which lasted four days, with the doctor popping in from time to time with encouraging words but little else, could diminish my mother's happiness.

When I was old enough to appreciate just what a remote little town Due West, South Carolina, was, and what a mostly country girl my mother was, I really became curious about how she came up with what then and for many years to come was a very unusual name. She explained that I was supposed to have been Charles. During the four years she had unsuccessfully tried to get pregnant, she had dreamed of having a boy. She would name him Charles, after my father, whom she adored. It would have been the third Charles in the Hunter family, and she had planned for me to have all the names of the two previous ones—Charles Shepherd Henry. If I had been a boy, I would have been called Henry, as was my first brother eight years later, because my grandfather was known to his friends and close associates as "Shep" and my father was called Charles, sometimes Chace, by his family.

For as long as I can remember, I loved my name. Mother chose Alberta as my middle name, in honor of my father's mother. My mother, her mother, my brothers, and my closest, oldest friends sometimes called me "Char," and I liked that, too, but it was a long time before I heard anything that sounded remotely like Charlayne. After a while, I heard the name Charlene—the way most people pronounced mine. And though I was always quick to correct them, most people still had trouble getting it right. I didn't like that part. But I did like the idea that people had to think about my name, and sometimes exert some effort to get it right. It was a long time before I ever asked my mother, who also had an unusual name—Althea—how she came up with Charlayne.

The conversation went something like this:

"Mother [I always called her Mother, because everyone else I knew called their mothers Mama or Ma and I wanted to be different], how did a little country girl like you, off in this isolated little town of Due West, come up with a name as different as Charlayne? Had you ever heard anything like it before?"

From IN MY PLACE by Charlayne Hunter-Gault. Copyright © 1992 by Charlayne Hunter-Gault. Reprinted by permission of Farrar, Straus & Giroux, Inc.

"Well," she said in her usual nonchalant and soft-spoken way, "I just made it up."

I persisted. "But how could you just come up with a name like that?"

"Well," she began again, nonplussed by my insistence, "I wanted it to be as close to Charles as possible and yet make it feminine."

And that, to me, always meant strong-and-feminine—which could cut two ways. In fact, whenever my mother would get annoyed with me in later years, like most mothers who have an unerring instinct for getting under their daughter's skin, she would say, "You're just like your father."

In those circumstances I didn't mind her saying that, because my father was quite a man. But when speaking in anger, my mother usually had that "nobody can tell you anything" tone of voice. And it hurt, because all I wanted was for her to think of me the way I thought of her—as smart, but also soft, beautiful, and feminine. At that point in my life I wanted more than anything else to be like my mother; I even worried whether I would be smart enough to come up with a wonderfully original name for my own daughter.

I didn't grow up in Due West. And yet ask any Southerner where he is from and he will tell you every place he has ever been from. I am no exception. I always say, "Well, I grew up in Georgia, but I'm from South Carolina. That always leads to the question of where in South Carolina, and I can always count on anyone I tell to ask me, "Due West of what?" And that is one of the things that have given me a strong sense of place. My place.

As far as I can tell, no one knows for sure just how Due West got its name. Since most people always ask, "Due West of what?" it is easy to assume that it was Due West of something. It is actually a town tucked away in a small spot in the northwestern part of the state, west of Abbeville and Greenwood. There is local history that traces it back to the days when it was the land of the Cherokees, who first used the term Due West in 1768. According to Donald Calhoun, in *The Golden Quill*, the town of Hones Path got its name from the corruption of a junction point in what is now Abbeville County, which the Cherokees had named Hee-na-heena, meaning "many paths."

According to Calhoun's history, sometime before the Revolutionary War, an Indian trader named Charles DeWitt set up a post near there that he called DeWitt's Corner. It was located on the Little River, the dividing line between the present Abbeville and Anderson Counties. Then came the Revolutionary War.

As Calhoun wrote:

The Cherokee Indians rushed with savage ferocity upon the exposed inhabitants of the frontier, and on the day rendered memorable by the Declaration of Independence, DeWitt's Corner was destroyed. [But, the story goes] a little army of militia was gathered together on a field near Hogskin Creek, and advancing into the Indian territory, they so decimated the Cherokees that they were forced to sue for peace, and concluded a treaty by which they acknowledged themselves vanquished. As if by a sort of poetic justice, this treaty was signed at DeWitt's Corner.

The trading post was never reestablished, but "some five or six miles southeast" the town of Due West sprang up. There is speculation that the name was a corruption of Dewitt's Corner, or possibly Duett's Corner, or Duesse's Corner.

Due West could easily have qualified as just another of South Carolina's one-horse towns, like Ninety-Six, Honea Path, Traveler's Rest, Prosperity, Society Hill, Promised Land, Moncks Corner. But Due West had a distinction that the others didn't: it was a college town. Erskine College was founded for white male students, in 1839, by members of the Associate Reformed Presbyterian Church.

As Calhoun recounted:

As for the inhabitants of this post, that story goes back to far earlier events in Scotland. In particular, a woman by the name of Jennie Gedes (there is a large clan of Gettys in the A.R.P. Church) made herself famous, or infamous, by throwing a footstool at the head of a bishop who attempted to say mass in the presence of the good Scotch Presbyterian brethren. It was here that the revolution began that culminated in the dissolution of the Presbyterian Church of Scotland, marked by the secession of a group led by Ebenezer Erskine, who quickly became known as the Seceders. The sons and the daughters of these early valiant seceders appear to have settled at this crossroad which came to bear the name of Due West Corner. And in the course of time Due West became the holy city of the A.R.P.'s, the Mecca toward which all the brethren of Psalm-singing faith turn in reverent awe.[1]

The church defined Due West, earning it its other, informal name, the Holy City. Its inhabitants were so religious that they referred to Sunday only as the Sabbath. According to legend, as recapitulated by Calhoun, they went so far as to decapitate a rooster who crowed on the Holy Day. "It is even rumored," according to Calhoun, "that when Billy Sunday came to Due West to perform his gyrations before the people of the town, he was referred to not by his usual name but as William Sabbath."

My mother recalls: "You weren't supposed to do anything on Sunday but go to church—no reading the paper even. They had a train called *The Dinky* that ran each day to the next town, where it had to back up all the way back, as there was no place to turn it around. But it didn't run on Sunday."

Except for the college, there was little else to Due West. In fact, all there was of "town" resembled what a Hollywood set designer would have created to look like a small town—a mile and a half long and a mile wide. Main Street consisted of one drugstore, a few grocery stores, a lumber-and-paint store, a furniture store, a shoe-repair shop, an oil mill, an ice plant, a dry cleaner, a garage, four filling stations, a printing office, a barbershop, one restaurant, one hotel, three private boardinghouses, and a doctor's office, which at one time was a miniature hospital. Even if you drove slowly, it would have been easy to drive right through Due West without realizing a town was there.

Being born in a town called Due West would have been enough to give me a distinct sense of place. But I was born in 1942, and being Black in those days meant not only that Due West was the place where I was born but that people of color—Negroes or colored people in those days—had their place. The area where we lived was situated around the Mr. Lebanon A.ME. Church. It was called Rabbit Stew. Here again, no one is quite sure why. But WPA researcher Ben Carlton, canvassing for the WPA in 1938, came up with two explanations, both equally plausible. He wrote that the name "derived from the fact that soon after 'freedom' several negro families moved to the outskirts of Due West in what was then pines. Rabbits were cheap. One of the elderly Negroes, from whom I got some of my information concerning [Mt. Lebanon] said his uncle's 'fondness for rabbits' caused the name." But that's where a lot of the Black folks lived, in an assortment of mostly ramshackle, unpainted houses of various sizes, on craggy, unpaved streets. In 1938, there were some 105 white families and 50 Negro families in Due West. Like my grandmother, most of the Black folks worked for the white people of Due West—either for the college as maids, janitors, and the like, or in the homes of people who worked for or were in some way associated with the college.

My mother's people were from Georgia. But sometime after my grandfather, Rochell Brown, died, my grandmother, Frances Wilson Layson Brown, was asked by the Todds, a white family for whom she had worked in Covington, Georgia, to come to Due West to take care of their mother, who had suffered a stroke and was confined to a wheelchair. Unlike some white folks she had worked for, the Todds were good employers, and I never heard any complaints about them. When Black folks stayed in their place, they got along just fine with the white folks of Due West.

Not long after my grandmother moved to Due West, old lady Todd died and my grandmother married a part-time bricklayer named Ollie Jones. Few people could understand why, although one longtime resident of Due West speculated it was because "opposites attract"; another ventured that it might have been their shared love of baseball. They had a garden, where they grew a lot of the food they ate, and also a modest cotton field, which was a source of additional income for them. It was her third marriage—her last and her worst. But before it got bad, my mother moved to Due West to live with her. My mother had been living with my father, who had just begun his career as an army officer at Camp Livingston, Louisiana. She was in the early stages of her long-awaited pregnancy and having a rough time of it. I'm not sure whether it was a need to be nurtured by her mother, whom she was extremely close to, or a desire not to be a burden on her newly commissioned young husband, but she made the decision to go to Due West and remain there until I was born. She remembered that on December 7, 1941, she sat pregnant and heavy-hearted, listening to the stunning and foreboding news, on the old radio, that the Japanese had attacked Pearl Harbor, declaring war on the United States.

There was no hospital in Due West—only an infirmary associated with the college. Ollie Jones's sister, Jenny Vauss, whom I called Aunt Jenny, worked as a nurse there, and also as nurse/midwife to Dr. W. L. "Buck" Pressly, one of the two physicians in town, highly respected by both Blacks and whites. (Interestingly enough for the times, the other was a woman.) It was a comfort to my mother that we lived next door to Aunt Jenny. Anybody seriously ill either suffered through it, died, or went twenty miles to the town of Anderson. My mother once had what the doctor diagnosed as appendicitis, and he sent her to Anderson to have her appendix removed. When the pain persisted long after the tiny intestinal organ had been cut out and placed in a jar of formaldehyde on the mantelpiece in the bedroom, my mother told the doctor that he must have taken out the wrong thing. She told me he said, "I took out what I went after." And that was that. Years later, my mother told me that she believed the reason the doctor ordered the operation was that he knew she had just gotten an army check of close to $700 from my father. I asked her how he would have known and she told me that everybody in Due West knew everybody else's business, especially if it came through Western Union. It was wartime and money was scarce.

My mother recalled: "We had ration books and I had purchased a little Ford car, so I'd collect the neighbors' books in case I ran into scarce items like fatback, butter, cheese, etc., when I shopped in Abbeville or Anderson . . . Sometimes we'd go to Honea Path and other small towns where Jenny and Wallace [her husband] had family or friends. Erskine College, founded by Dr. Pressly's family, was being used as an army base, and since my mother's sister-in-law was a nurse at the infirmary, I never had to worry about gas stamps. The soldiers would give them to her."

There was a CCC camp for Negroes on the outskirts of Rabbit Stew. My mother says she can remember some Black folks saying, "Thank God for Hitler," not because they were unpatriotic or liked Hitler, but because the war brought desperately needed work to the poor folks of Due West.

My mother supplemented her income—and, I suspect, filled some of her lonely hours—by teaching school. She did not have a college degree, but she had graduated from Hyde Park, one of the most prestigious high schools in Chicago back then. My mother remembers that Nat "King" Cole, who was just starting out, used to play for their high-school dances. I think she overcame some of her innate shyness and enjoyed going around with some of the most popular young people in Chicago at the time.

My grandmother had sent her to Chicago to live with my grandfather's sister. When I asked her why, she said that her parents were deeply committed to her getting a good education and didn't feel she could get it in the colored school in Covington. There was an additional factor: her parents were concerned that some of the white men in Covington had their eyes on my mother, who was quite beautiful, and although their shy young daughter stayed mostly at home, they had sent her away to protect her from advances that they could have done little about.

At Hyde Park, my mother learned typing and shorthand, and got a good grounding in all the basics. She loved writing reports, and once pulled out one of her favorites—on the Standard Oil Company—when I was preparing one of my first long papers in school.

I would suspect that the high-school education she received "up North" was far superior to anything in either Black or white high schools in the South, and maybe even the equivalent of some Southern colleges. It certainly helped nurture the love *for* learning—especially reading—she inherited from my grandmother and grandfather. For as long as I can remember, my mother devoured books, often reading one a day. And she spoke well—with a Southern drawl, to be sure—and always with perfect grammar. She loved to work crossword puzzles, too, and had a gift for understanding the meaning of words. We always had a highly visible dictionary in the house.

Calhoun describes the "colored school" in Due West four years before I was born. He wrote:

It exists, and that is about all. The facilities consist of a large frame building, probably used in the pre-Civil War days, which contains rooms which are bereft of blackboard facilities to speak of and blessed by only the roughest of seating arrangements. The windows are mostly conspicuous by their absence, and the roof undoubtedly leaks. As to the type of instruction afforded, I do not have any specific information, but if it is influenced by the environment, it is poor indeed.

In 1940–41, the WPA built a new school named after George Washington Carver, improving upon the physical features of the old "colored school," but not on the facilities. The school where my mother taught first through third grade was, as she put it, "in the country"—several miles outside town—and was comparable to, if not worse than, Calhoun's "colored" school in Due West. When I asked her about how she got the job without a college degree, she said, "The white folks didn't care what the Black folks got, so all they cared about was that I was willing to do it. It was the preacher at the church we went to that told me about the job."

Five years later, halfway across the state in the town of Summerton, the Reverend J. A. Delaine and a group of Black parents, including Harry Briggs, a Black mechanic, petitioned their local, all-white school board for help—not even in bringing the poor Black schools up to par with the white schools but just to get a bus so that the Black children, like the white children, would have a somewhat easier time going the often long distances they had to travel to their little country schools. The school board turned them down, and they went to court, asking then not just for a bus but for school buildings, services, and education equal to whites. It was to be the first in a long series of steps that would lead to the United States Supreme Court's decision that not only outlawed such segregated and unequal school systems but provided still another road leading me to my place in American society.

The preacher who told my mother about the teaching position was the Reverend B. J. Glover. Like the Reverend Delaine, he, too, was a social activist, "using his pulpit as a platform for social reform. He promoted a variety of causes never particularly popular among Southern whites."[2]

Black folks were not allowed to vote in those days, and the Reverend Glover, who had been sent away from his home in nearby Promised Land (pronounced locally as Promiseland) and had returned to Due West after training in theology up North, at Wilberforce University in Ohio, had that on his public agenda, too. In the late thirties the Reverend Glover attempted to register at the Abbeville County Courthouse (Abbeville was the county in which Due West was situated). As recounted in Elizabeth Rauh Bethel's *Promiseland*:

> The clerk routinely administered required by the 1895 state constitution; and Glover, literate in three languages, easily read and interpreted the passages from the constitution as they were presented to him. The clerk had no guidelines for such a situation and quickly conferred with other officials, leaving Glover on a bench in the courthouse corridor. The clerk returned and dismissed Glover with a simple and final decision: "I just can't register you." There was no additional explanation. Glover left the courthouse quietly but filled with deep emotion. The following Sunday, he rose to his pulpit in Due West and "talked about black people registering to vote and the unfairness" of his Abbeville courthouse experience.

Such episodes drew the attention of whites, including the Ku Klux Klan. And one day, between Due West and Greenwood, they confronted the Reverend Glover. As he later told the story: "A group of white men stopped me at that time and asked me my name. I told them, but I didn't say 'yes, sir' and 'no, sir.' It was five to begin with." It was said that Glover's cool dignified responses further enraged the angry group of white men, for he failed to follow the proper Southern pattern of Negro deference.

Glover continues:

> They took me from there in a car, blindfolded, out in the country . . . They did every kind of thing you can imagine. I was stripped completely. I wore nylon shorts, and I can still hear them talking about my nylon shorts. They beat me and made me say "yes, sir," and made me do all kinds of personal things. They were sexually cruel, talking about my sex organs and things like that. They made me do things. They would do it and talk to me. "What you doing, nigger? Why don't you leave things like they are?" The KKK said they had to make an example of me. I was an uppity, smart nigger from the North. I had come back with Northern ideas. They came up with the idea of beating me, and they did . . . for five or six hours. I fought until I couldn't fight anymore. Then they left me for dead in the woods.

But the Reverend Glover survived. His assailants, all known in nearby Promised Land, were never brought to justice.

It was the seeds of such experiences, as shared from the pulpit of my mother's church, that were sown in her consciousness as I lay developing in her womb. It would be a generation before they made a difference, a generation after the morning of February 27, 1942. In a bedroom of the small unpainted frame house that was within eyeshot of the church, my mother lay suffering perhaps the greatest pain she had ever known. Labor started on Wednesday, and by Friday there was still no sign that I was ready to enter the world. Dr. Pressly, who had been stopping by daily, and who probably didn't want to work on the weekend, told my mother she was going to have the baby that day, come hell or high water. She vaguely remembers that he gave her something, and for the next several hours he worked and worked, trying to maneuver my head out, alternately inserting a pair of metal clamps, then his hands. Despite her own pain, my mother remembers screaming for the doctor to "stop mashing the baby's head. You're going to mash it to death."

When I finally did emerge, she said the sides of my head were bruised from the imprint of the clamps, and the space on my forehead between my eyes was red from the apparent pressure of a thumb. My head also was so ill-formed that for days my mother and Aunt Jenny took turns massaging it, trying to get it back to its original round shape. But I cried spontaneously—all nine pounds of me. And, despite the fact that I was not the boy my mother had been anticipating, she felt herself the luckiest woman in the world. I asked her later if she was frightened. "No," she answered. "Momma was there."

There were no telephones. A telegram to the army base in California where my father was then stationed told him the news. For four and a half months, my young mother struggled with her new baby. She told me, "You didn't like to sleep at night, and I would often rock you half the night. Mr. Ollie said I used to start off singing church songs, and by the time I finished I'd be singing the blues."

After four and a half months, during a trip to my father's people in Florida, Mother got word that my father wanted us to join him. She wasted no time and left straight from Florida by train for the long trip across country. It took something like four or five days. She said it wasn't too bad, because we had a sleeper. A white woman with a baby was company for a while, but during one conversation the woman "confided" to my fair-skinned mother that she was really upset that the previous night a "nigger" had boarded the train and slept in the bunk above her. After my mother told her that she didn't see anything wrong with that, the conversations came to a halt. My mother spent the rest of the trip taking care of me and silently enjoying the scenery.

My father had been preparing for our arrival by gathering autographs of famous Hollywood people who had performed on the post after I was born. Two of the most well-known radio personalities of the day, Jack Benny and Eddie "Rochester" Anderson, were among them. Years later, I would look at those autographs in the little pink-satin autograph book my mother had carefully tucked them into and feel really great—not so much because I had the autographs of these stars, but because it was clear to me that my father had made sure that they all spelled my name right.

The next few months in Riverside, California, were to be the closest I would come to having my father and mother together and us living as a family. At first, we stayed with a nice Black lady who was a Christian Scientist. Then my parents found a small apartment, but before they could move in, my father got orders to report overseas, to North Africa, the scene of the most intense fighting between the Axis forces under Field Marshal Rommel and the Allies, led by General Montgomery. It would be months into 1943 before the Allied forces could claim victory. Meanwhile, rather than go all the way back to Due West, my mother decided to go partway and settle temporarily in Cleveland, where her half brother lived—Robert Layson, my grandmother's son by her first marriage. He and his wife lived in a house behind an apartment building and were happy to have my mother and me, but my mother recalls that for her it was wrong from the start.

Mother said: "I knew the moment I got there I couldn't live there. Cleveland was so dirty. So much concrete and no grass. Just grease all over the place. And I always kept you so clean. As soon as we got there, the pretty little white things I had on you got dirty and you got dirt all over you. It was the first time you had ever been dirty. I got in touch with Momma and she came up and we rerouted our belongings back to Due West."

Once there, the two women grew even closer. I think they had ceased to be mother and daughter and had become each other's best friend. And they both needed a best friend. My grandmother's husband was an alcoholic and was becoming increasingly abusive. So my mother rented a small house on the highway that ran through town and she and my grandmother moved.

My mother lived for the days when "Old Man Wharton," a friend who walked to town to collect the mail, would come back down the road and, spotting her from a distance, would begin shouting, "I got it! I got it! I got it!" all the way down the road, so that she and the whole neighborhood would know that a letter had arrived from my father. But, she said sadly, there weren't many. By now my father, in the North African theater of operations, was one of the few Black chaplains serving overseas at the time, fighting both the war and the racists who regarded the all-Black fighting forces with suspicion and often treated them with contempt and disdain.

He was always pretty closed-mouth about the bad experiences, not even telling my mother until after he had returned home that he had been wounded and was awarded the Purple Heart as a direct result of enemy action somewhere near Bari, Italy. But he did tell us the story of his experience walking through an Italian town. He said that the local people kept running up behind the Black soldiers and lifting up their jackets. My father spoke fluent Italian, among several other languages, and when he asked them why they were doing this, one of the Italians told him it was because the white American soldiers had told them to stay away from the Black soldiers because they had tails. When he told us that story, my father was more bemused than bitter, almost as if he pitied them for their ignorance and fear. The pictures he brought home, bearing such warm inscriptions as "To My Dear Chaplain Hunter," and often signed "Affettuosamente," illustrated what little effect the story had on the Italians—especially the Italian women at whom the warnings were certainly directed. Still, it was surely a demanding and trying time for men like my father, who were expected to act as liaisons between the men and the white leaders. Even though the chaplains themselves were leaders, they had to defer to the white commanding officers. There were no Black commanding officers.

Meanwhile, my mother began preparing for the time when my father would be coming home. She corresponded with Mrs. Mary Daniel Martin, a wealthy Black lady, and eventually decided to buy a house from her in Covington, Georgia. She told me, "I felt we would enjoy life more, as I had lived there so long, and I wanted to be away from Due West when Charles came home." And so we left my first place before I really came to know it, but not before it had become a part of me.

Endnotes

1. Donald W. Calhoun. "Due West—An Objective Sketch," *The Golden Quill*, May 1938, pp. 4–6.
2. Elizabeth Rauh Bethel. *Promiseland* (Philadelphia: Temple University Press. 1961). pp 215–17.

● Wayne State

Charlayne Hunter-Gault

"5050 Cass Avenue," I said to the cabdriver after I arrived in Detroit. It was supposed to be the dormitory, which I had tried to imagine during the long ride from Atlanta to Detroit. Uppermost in my mind were the images of the campuses in the Atlanta University complex, with their stately old neoclassical buildings and their long brick walkways lined with dogwood and magnolia trees. When the cabdriver stopped and announced that we had arrived at 5050 Cass, I was not ready for what I saw before me—a massive twelve-story building, larger than anything I had ever seen in Atlanta, let alone on a college campus, but not nearly as large as the disappointment welling up in me at the sight. This couldn't be the campus, I thought to myself. But I was soon to discover that this dormitory housed not only both men and women students (a unique concept in 1959) but also the main college cafeteria, faculty offices, and many of the other major offices of Wayne State University. I couldn't believe it. I was instantly engaged in beating back the wave of homesickness that was about to engulf me. It was a preoccupation that absorbed me throughout my tour of the place: the three floors for students—one for undergraduate men, one for undergraduate women, and one that was really coed, for the graduate students. On the tenth floor, I was directed to a compact two-room suite in the corner at the far end of the hall. My roommates had already arrived: two white girls from small towns in Michigan, Alpina and Dowagiac. Since this was

From IN MY PLACE by Charlayne Hunter-Gault. Copyright © 1992 by Charlayne Hunter-Gault. Reprinted by permission of Farrar, Straus & Giroux, Inc.

"up North," I had thought about having two white roommates, but not a lot. They seemed curious but not hostile. It looked like a good beginning.

The freshmen were required to come in early for orientation, which would take place away from the campus, somewhere outside Detroit, on an outing called Frosh Weekend. That's where I met Kathi Fearn, a tall, slim, somewhat reserved Black girl from Washington, D.C., and the only other Black freshman there. In many ways, it was Ursa Major all over again. At Frosh Weekend, square dances and square mixers and square conversation. I remember thinking that I was glad I had grown up deprived, because there was absolutely nothing I liked about camping out.

At first glance, Wayne resembled a slightly larger version of Georgia State—a bare-bones kind of place that offered a no-frills education. Many, if not most, of the students had already been out in the workaday world or had served in the military. They did not come from college families or families that could afford to send them to college, so many of them were still working. As a result, they had a very different attitude and approach toward school. They were dead serious about making it and making every minute count, because in all probability they were paying for it themselves. In addition, most of the students who attended Wayne lived in Detroit. This was their city college, so there was no real need to provide housing. The few students who signed up to live in the few rooms that were available tended to be the younger, recent high-school graduates, who wanted to have a college experience but could afford only the price of a ticket in their own back yard.

Even though the undergraduate women were all on the same floor, it was some time before we got past our preoccupation with getting settled into college and began socializing with one another. The configuration of the floor added to the delay. It was basically a kind of horseshoe, where you emerged from the elevator into a corridor that branched off to the left and to the right. The corridors ran for several yards in opposite directions before breaking at a sharp right angle and extending another several yards. For the non-social or the antisocial, it was possible to live on one side of the dorm and almost never come in contact with anyone from the other side, except possibly during the elevator ride to the lobby. I had seen some other Black girls in the elevator, but the only one I ever saw on my side of the horseshoe was Kathi Fearn. She lived alone, although she was supposed to have a roommate, another Black girl who had shown up at the door, taken one look at the room, and announced that she was going back to Cleveland. She had never been heard from since.

As it turned out, I was the only Black person in an integrated situation. Furthermore, once I started to get to know some of the other Black girls and be invited to their rooms, it dawned on us that the "dorm" was really quite segregated. Except for Kathi and me, the right side of the corridor was all white, and without exception, the left side was all Black. When we tried to figure out how the authorities could have planned this layout so effectively, the Detroit girls realized that it was their high schools that gave them away. Even though Detroit was "up North," most of them had come from predominantly, if not entirely, Black high schools, in predominantly Black neighborhoods. In Kathi's case, she had gone to Eastern High School, in Washington, D.C., and although she was on the white side, as it were, had it not been for the sister who had gone back to Cleveland, she would have been segregated as well. The only exception was me, and we figured out that the authorities thought anybody coming from so far away had to be white and never noticed that I, too, had come from a Black school, albeit one that was segregated by law.

We were more amused than angry over the discovery, in part because the Black side of the floor was always jumping. We used to get together and fix each other's hair, and listen to music, talk about guys, make plans for dinner (the cafeteria was open only during the day to accommodate the day students; there were no meals for the live-ins; we were on our own at night), and sometimes study, although most of that was done in the library or elsewhere.

Except for my roommates and me, there was hardly any communication between the Blacks and the whites on the floor. We lived in *two separate worlds.*

It was at Wayne, in the *"separate but equal" dorm,* that I first learned that Jews were considered different from white people. Unlike in the South, where you were Black or you were white, both Black and white Northerners made those distinctions, and so did Jews. One of the few Jewish girls on the floor was a girl named Rochelle Katz, who was almost as dark as I was and whose hair was thicker and kinkier. She always used to ask us how we "fixed" our hair and did we think it would work on hers, until one day we heated up a straightening comb and waited until she had come out of the shower. "Rochelle," we called, "we've got something for you," and after she had wrapped a towel around herself we led her off to one of our rooms, sat her down, and fried her hair until it was straight. She loved it.

There were also some cultural differences between me and my Northern sisters. They found it amusing that I said "Yes, ma'am" and "No, ma'am," to all adults, and they found it downright fall-on-the-floor hilarious when, waiting for the elevator, I would ask, "Did anyone mash the button?" I also remember coming in from the scene of an accident nearby and asking if anybody had seen the wreck outside. All of a sudden, Doris Jeffries, one of the Black students from Detroit, burst out laughing. It was fully five minutes before she could stop long enough to tell me what she was laughing at.

If I had loved the freedom of changing classes in high school, I was ecstatic about the schedule of college classes. I continued the pattern of perfect attendance that I had established as far back as elementary school. I hated to miss a class—even one I didn't particularly like.

Much to my dismay, Wayne wouldn't allow any student to major until junior year, and no journalism classes were offered to freshmen. Instead, the university had the good sense to require a core curriculum of basic liberal-arts courses. There was also a foreign language requirement. Everybody I knew from Turner who had taken a foreign language other than Latin in high school had taken French. I wanted to be different, so I decided to take German instead. I had no real problems with any of my courses freshman year, except German. In class, I did extremely well. I studied and had a good German accent, and my hand was one of the few that were always up as I volunteered to answer a question, translate a passage from German to English, or vice versa. But I absolutely froze on tests.

One day, Herr Professor asked to see me in his office. "Fräulein Hunter," he began, "you unnerstond ze Churman language ferry well. Your classroom participation is excellent. But what is heppening to you on ze tests? Iz not so goot, correct?"

I couldn't explain what was "heppening" to me on the test, but I knew as well as he that the tests were not an accurate reflection of the German I knew. I studied and I *spracht,* and did all the things I was supposed to do; yet I froze on the test.

Herr Doktor Poster then suggested that maybe for a while I should take ze tests in his office. Just to see if it made a difference. I was stunned. Here I had expected absolutely no slack from this rigidly correct Prussian. He was going out of his way to help me. Of all the white professors, I had expected the least sympathy from him, and yet here he was making an offer that I never heard before. I accepted it, but alas, in the end, I was just not a good test-taker. I could converse *auf Deutsch* with Herr Doktor Poster about what I had done wrong and how I needed to correct it (umlaut here, accent there, verb at the end), but for some reason I couldn't function once the clock was on in a test situation. I nevertheless managed to pass first-year German with a C average and move on to the next level. German, with its guttural and umlaut sounds, was about as alien to the slow, drawling, sweet sound of the South as anything I had ever known. And while I can't say that I really liked it, what was appealing to me was that nobody would expect me, of all people, to speak German or know anything about Mozart or Rainer Maria Rilke or Friedrich von Schiller. And then there was my father, who had introduced me to Hegel. One day, I might be able to tell him more about Hegelian dialectic than he himself knew.

For all its lack of campus and charm, in time Wayne offered still another world for me. Not just the world of college, but the world of the urban North and of bohemian intellectualism. I fell in love with ideas and art, discourse and debate. And in time I even started to pay less attention to the "fine" clothes I had brought from the best stores in Atlanta and adopted a style that was more in keeping with the cost-consciousness displayed by most of the students on campus.

In fact, starting in the second semester of my freshman year, since most of the students I knew worked, I, too, got a job. It was a terrific position in the McGregor Memorial Community Conference Center, the newest and most modern structure on campus. Designed by the up-and-coming Japanese architect Minoru Yamasaki, it was a stunning ultra-modern structure, standing in stark contrast to the urban pedestrian style that surrounded it. It had many wonderful features—especially its lovely, serene rock garden. I worked behind a counter, near the front of the gallery, selling pens and pencils and other small items. Sometimes I worked the coat check. It was while I was doing this job that I learned this song:

Don't cry, lady,
I'll buy your goddamn violets.
Don't cry, lady, I'll buy your pencils, too.
Don't cry, lady,
Take off those old dark glasses.
 Hello, Mother, I knew it was you.

Surrounded by art and art students, I loved McGregor's creative energy, and its atmosphere, which was somehow more open than any other place on campus. With the money I made, I bought all my clothes and other necessities for the remainder of the school year.

My roommate Lila loved my clothes and often asked to borrow items to wear. As an only girl, I never had to share, and this was a new experience for me. I wasn't sure I liked it, but I acquiesced in the face of Lila's earnest admiration. Leather was still in vogue, and I had a beige leather coat that I liked a lot, especially because, unlike most of the leather coats I had seen, this one had two huge pockets in the front. I usually wore it only to parties or to Mass, or when I wanted to feel dressed up. One evening, as I was preparing to go out with a group of friends, I reached into my closet for my leather coat and it was gone. I looked everywhere in the room for it. I couldn't imagine what had happened to it. Later, when my other roommate came in, she told me that Lila had taken it home for the weekend. I was livid. When she returned, we had a discussion about it, and that ended the clothes borrowing. The exchange, however, was not really rancorous.

Lila was like an up-North, small-town Southern girl, obliging her parents by attending college but lacking any real interest in it. She had no idea what she was going to major in, and I think she really wanted to be a nurse. She was especially naïve when it came to men. I sometimes had to run interference for her after she had blithely walked into some situation that was on the verge of being out of control. I remember once when she had started seeing a guy she had met at a dance. She knew nothing about him, and even on their first date he drank too much. She really didn't want to continue seeing him, but she didn't know how to tell him. Often, when he was in his cups, he would call. She would get so worked up over just going to the phone that we would all be miserable. So one day, when he called, I picked up the phone and, as she shook her head and gestured that she didn't want to talk to him, I said, "She's not here, and don't call her anymore!" Lila was so grateful, she hugged me.

By mid-year, I, too, was getting a lot of calls from male students, and so were some of the other girls who lived in the dorm. I think it was because we lived on campus and were easy to reach. But it really used to bug the switchboard operator. One night, she complained over the intercom. "I don't know what you're going to do," she said. "You've got two people here in the lobby." It was really none of her business. The guys were well behaved and polite, but they were Black, and we decided that what was really bothering her was just having to deal with Black guys. So my friend Kathi Fearn and I decided to teach her a lesson. We invited several guys to come to the dorm and ask for us, and we left to go to dinner before they arrived. We laughed throughout dinner thinking about her probable reaction to all those Blacks.

That was the dinner, however, where there was also a big laugh on me. We had gone to a soul-food restaurant that everybody had been talking about. There was one nice Black restaurant in Atlanta, Pascal Brothers, but going out to eat was not something Black folks in the South did. So I was still adjusting to the fact that eating out was routine; it still felt pretty special to me. My mouth was watering as the waiter recited the menu, and I was the first to order.

"I'll have a pork chop," I said, and with a display of growing worldly sophistication, I added, "Rare, please."

The waiter, a tall Black man with the air of an efficient Pullman porter (which he may have been at one time), shot me a look. "Did you say rare?" he asked.

Dismissing his tone as probably being due to the infrequency of requests for rare meat in a place whose pride lay in its capacity to cook a piece of meat to its most extreme state of doneness and still maintain the taste, I repeated my order, this time with emphasis.

"Yes," I said, somewhat arrogantly. "Rare!" "Okay," he said, somewhat indulgently. "One rare pork chop coming up."

Actually, since everybody was following my lead and feigning sophistication, it was a long time before I got the joke on myself. Fortunately, before the next time and before I contracted trichinosis, I learned better.

Because of my work at McGregor, I started getting interested in art. Whenever I had the time, I wandered over to the Detroit Institute of Art, which was within easy walking distance. If there were museums in Atlanta, they were for white people and we wouldn't have been allowed inside. So this was an awakening for me, and it was like the smell of morning coffee. I would spend hours there, usually by myself, getting acquainted with Rodin, whose *Thinker* sat, elbow positioned on knee, at the entrance, the Diego Rivera murals, ancient Egyptian artifacts, the armor of the Middle Ages. But in time the artist who interested me most was the Flemish painter Hieronymus Bosch. I was initially drawn to the unusual figures in his work—strange, monstrous creatures, weird and diabolical human figures—and I spent hours in front of the huge canvases, drifting into a world that stimulated my imagination and appreciation of the fantasy and wonder that had lived someplace inside me since the days of my Covington childhood, when I would crawl inside a comic book and disappear into the world of Wonder Woman or Nyoka, Jungle Girl. I remember once renaming myself and sharing it only with Horace and Tommy, my constant doll companions. They were to call me Charlayne Alberta Ruth Nyoka, Queen of the Jungle and All Places. I told them that they could call me Nyoka for short. Bosch took me back to the fantasies I had known, but also propelled me forward, opening regions in my mind that I would revisit at a critical time, a few months down the road, in another place, on a cold day.

As on the dorm floor upstairs, there was a racial division on campus. It could best be observed in the dining hall during lunch. That's when you would see mostly all-white tables and mostly all-Black tables. And while the all-Black tables were clustered together and collegial, there were also divisions among them—primarily along Greek lines. The Black fraternity groupings—Alpha Phi Alpha, Omega Psi Phi, and Kappa Alpha Psi—ate at separate tables, as did the Black sororities: Delta Sigma Theta, Alpha Kappa Alpha, Sigma Gamma Rho.

Almost all the Black socializing was done around Greek activities. Freshmen could not join Greek organizations, but because Greek life was central to Black campus life, most freshmen attended "Rush Week" events where the Greek groups introduced themselves and their programs. Throughout my freshman year, I observed the women in all the sororities, and there was no question in my mind that I would eventually pledge one. The issue for me was which one. I was already familiar with Greeks from the Atlanta college community. Frats and sororities were a stable part of life on all Southern college campuses. They conferred a sense of belonging, but also established a social pecking order, although the prestige of any single group could vary from one campus to another. At Clark, where Carolyn was now a sophomore, she had pledged Delta. But I was keeping an open mind. At Wayne, the Black Greek organizations played an even more important role. On a campus with only 2,500 Blacks out of a student body of 25,000, they were a virtual necessity. It was within those organizations that Black students found respect and reinforced identity.

And it was within these groups that some small note was taken of an event on February 1, 1960. Four Black students from North Carolina A & T College sat down at a lunch counter in Greensboro, North Carolina, and refused to move until they were served. The event made headlines all over America. The sit-in movement had begun. By the time I got home on spring break, it had reached Atlanta. And a dramatic change, which was more like a final coming of age than a transformation, had taken place in my best friends. Carolyn and Wylma (now with a y) had stepped up to fulfill the historic mission of the talented tenth, joining with some 4,000 other students in the Atlanta University Center—the largest and most impressive group of Negro students in the country. In the simplest terms, they were the Student Movement. But in time they acquired the more impressive title of the Committee on Appeal for Human Rights. As Carolyn explained at the time, "Our plan is to end segregation once and for all over Atlanta. We're never going to shop at Rich's again until we can eat in the Magnolia Room. And that goes for everything in Atlanta that right now is closed to us." Their tactic was civil disobedience. Their philosophy was nonviolence. In fact, they required that everyone participating in a demonstration take an oath, swearing to be nonviolent.

Carolyn explained: "We had studied what happened at A & T [North Carolina], and we decided to build on that. And yet we wanted to have a movement that was an outgrowth of the historical legacy of Negro Atlanta. So we approached the problem very scientifically. We studied it, went downtown, and actually counted the numbers of seats at lunch counters. We came up with solutions, and we mapped out strategies. We were really organized. We got our hard facts from *A Second Look* [a study by a group of ACCA members, including Whitney M. Young, dean of the Atlanta University School of Social Work, and Carl Holman, which examined patterns of segregation in Atlanta], and confirmed them with the Southern Regional Council, and then we went to the students who were in the various English Department clubs and societies and asked them to draft a document reflecting the problems outlined in these reports. Then Julian Bond and I took the best parts and synthesized them into one document. That became the Committee on Appeal for Human Rights."

Carolyn also told me why and how the Atlanta students got a reputation for being the best-organized Student Movement in the country. Now, instead of who had the best sports team, there was a lot of rivalry among Black colleges as to who had the best-organized movement. "In our group," she said, "we had students who had been in the military, like Lonnie King, who became one of the major leaders, and Morris Dillard, a graduate student at Atlanta University. They brought to bear their military experience on the organization. They mapped out march routes and organized advance teams equipped with walkie-talkies, to report back to the church we were using—Rush Memorial Baptist—and to keep track of where everybody was and what everybody was doing. It was in guys like Lonnie that you could see the underlying bitterness from the contradiction that they saw of being on the front lines serving their country, and then coming home and not being able to get served at all.

"The veterans also taught us tactics for survival during nonviolent demonstrations. They taught us things like how to crouch and cover our heads with our hands in the event of being clubbed by the police; also how to fall down and pull our knees up to our stomachs in a fetal position, so that the brunt of the blows would be on the meat of our bodies, like the back and behind. One of the things we decided was that we wouldn't have any high-school student demonstrators, because we didn't think they could take the pressure and the harassment that we anticipated from the white waitresses, the white customers, and the white police."

The group's first official act as a committee was the drafting of a document outlining their grievances and their demands. Written primarily by Carolyn (Clark), Julian Bond and Morris Dillard (Morehouse), Roslyn Pope, Hershel Sullivan (Spelman), it was published in all the Atlanta newspapers except the one Black paper, the *Atlanta Daily World*, whose editor, C. A. Scott, was a conservative Republican who was opposed to direct action and wanted no part of any threats to the white establishments that advertised in his newspaper.

When I got home from Wayne on spring break, Carolyn showed me the document and told me what had happened in the wake of its publication. I thought I knew my friends, but I was now seeing a side of them that had never before been tested, and I listened in awe. Their manifesto was called "An Appeal for Human Rights," and it read as follows:

We, the students of the six affiliated institutions forming the Atlanta University Center—Clark, Morehouse, Morris Brown, and Spelman Colleges, Atlanta

University, and the Interdenominational Theological Center—have joined our hearts, minds, and bodies in the cause of gaining those rights which are inherently ours as members of the human race and as citizens of these United States.

We pledge our unqualified support to those students in this nation who have recently been engaged in the significant movement to secure long awaited rights and privileges. This protest, like the bus boycott in Montgomery, has shocked many people throughout the world. Why? Because they had not quite realized the unanimity of spirit and purpose which motivated the thinking and action of the great majority of the Negro people. The students who instigate and participate in these sit-down protests are dissatisfied, not only with the existing conditions, but with the snail-like speed at which they are being ameliorated. Every normal human being wants to walk the earth with dignity and abhors any and all proscriptions placed upon him because of race or color. In essence, this is the meaning of the sit-down protests that are sweeping this nation today.

We do not intend to wait placidly for those rights which are already legally and morally ours to be meted out to us one at a time. Today's youth will not sit by submissively, while being denied all of the rights, privileges, and joys of life. We want to state clearly and unequivocally that we cannot tolerate, in a nation professing democracy and among people professing Christianity, the discriminatory conditions under which the Negro is living today in Atlanta, Georgia—supposedly one of the most progressive cities in the South.

We hold that:

1. The practice of racial segregation is not in keeping with the ideals of Democracy and Christianity.
2. Racial segregation is robbing not only the segregated but the segregator of his human dignity. Furthermore, the propagation of racial prejudice is unfair to the generations of yet unborn.
3. In times of war, the Negro has fought and died for his country; yet he still has not been accorded first-class citizenship.
4. In spite of the fact that the Negro pays his share of taxes, he does not enjoy participation in city, county, and state government at the level where laws are enacted.
5. The social, economic, and political progress of Georgia is retarded by segregation and prejudices.
6. America is fast losing the respect of other nations by the poor example which she sets in the area of race relations.

It is unfortunate that the Negro is being forced to fight, in any way, for what is due him and is freely accorded to other Americans. It is unfortunate that even today some people should hold to the erroneous idea of racial superiority, despite the fact that the world is fast moving toward an integrated humanity.

The time has come for the people of Atlanta and Georgia to take a good look at what is really happening in this country, and to stop believing those who tell us that everything is fine and equal, and that the Negro is happy and satisfied.

It is to be regretted that there are those who still refuse to recognize the overriding supremacy of the Federal Law.

Our churches, which are ordained by God and claim to be the houses of all people, foster segregation of the races to the point of making Sunday the most segregated day of the week.

We, the students of the Atlanta University Center, are driven by past and present events to assert our feelings to the citizens of Atlanta and to the world.

We, therefore, call upon the people in authority—State, County, and City officials; all leaders in civic life—ministers, teachers, and businessmen; and all people of good will to assert themselves and abolish these injustices. We must say in all candor that we plan to use every legal and nonviolent means at our disposal to secure full citizenship rights as members of this great Democracy of ours.

On the day the document was published, March 9, 1960, Carolyn told me, she put on her best Sunday clothes, including high heels, and, along with Wylma and many of the 4,000 students of the Atlanta University Center colleges, marched through the streets of Atlanta, saying, in effect, "Our time has come."

A week later, fanning out to places of public accommodation and facilities supported by tax dollars, the students held their first sit-in. Their goal was to draw attention to their demands and to get arrested in order to make cases that would challenge the Jim Crow laws that sent us to the separate "colored" water fountains, that sent us to the separate "colored" toilets, or that kept us from eating at all. Eventually, it would include places like the Fox Theater, a movie house designed like a medieval castle. There were over one hundred stone steps winding against the outer wall leading up to the tower. That's where they made the Black folks sit. Many a time I remember going with my mother to the Fox, and while I don't remember any of the movies I saw there, I have not forgotten, and shall never forget, the stairs.

One of the main stores that we targeted was Rich's, the multi-story, moderate-to-upscale department store where most of Black Atlanta shopped.

In those days, Blacks may not always have liked the treatment they got, but they had no options. In addition to all my other memories now about the subtle and not so subtle indignities Blacks suffered at Rich's, I remember once suggesting to my mother that she go to Rich's and get her hair done in the beauty salon. It was long and straight, and about all she could do with it was put it in a ponytail or a bun. I wasn't suggesting that she try to pass, I was merely telling her that she could go there and, as fair as she was, I was sure no questions would ever be asked.

My mother's reaction was typical of an attitude all over the Black community at that time. "Oh no," she said, without bitterness, "I'm not going down there and take the chance they'd find out I was a Negro and let them burn up my hair."

But something had now changed in Atlanta. And something had changed in us. *We had been protected and privileged within the confines of our segregated communities. But now that we stu-*

dents had removed the protective covering, we could see in a new light both our past and our future. We could see that past—the slavery, the segregation, the deprivation and denial—for what it was: a system designed to keep us in our place and convince us, somehow, that it was our fault, as well as our destiny. Now, without either ambivalence or shame, we saw ourselves as the heirs to a legacy of struggle, but struggle that was, as Martin Luther King was teaching, ennobling; struggle that was enabling us to take control of our destiny. And, as a result, we did not see ourselves or the other young people demonstrating in one way or another throughout the South as heroes to be praised, celebrated, or fretted over. We were simply doing what we were born and raised to do.

While not everybody in the adult Black community was on board, the Atlanta Student Movement had spoken in terms that became the watchwords for all of us: "Ain't gonna let nobody turn me roun'."

Ideas for Discussion, Writing and Research

1. Virginia Woolf, Victor Villanueva, and Mike Rose provide accounts of how gender, class, and race can influence educational experiences and the development of literacy. How and why do their views differ? What is your own position about what factors shape literate practice and/or educational opportunity?

2. Using the pieces written by Charlayne Hunter-Gault, Zora Neale Hurston, Richard Rodriguez, and other sources—oral or written—explore and discuss the extent to which education can change people's views of themselves and the world.

3. How do personal narratives about education in this chapter illustrate and support Mike Rose's view that students will "float to the level" that teachers set? What is your own position about the role that teachers play in learning?

4. Richard Rodriguez suggests that education and the development of a public voice inevitably lead people to give up their cultural identity. How might Victor Villanueva and Min-Zhan Lu respond to such an argument? Is it inevitable that people need to shed their identity in order to be educated?

5. With classmates, interview people in school and the community about their experiences with reading, writing, and schooling when they were growing up. How do their experiences extend or perhaps challenge what the authors in this chapter say about education in the United States?

6. How do Min-Zhan Lu's observations about conflict and struggle relate to the personal narratives written by Richard Rodriguez and Charlayne Hunter-Gault?

7. Research the issue of tracking (placing students in classes according to test scores or future ambitions) that Mike Rose discusses in order to reach your own conclusions about this issue. (See related reading sections in Chapters Two and Five, as well.) Based on this research and your own experiences in school, can you think of circumstances when tracking might benefit students? What are some possible arguments against tracking? What is your position?

8. Victor Villanueva discusses the importance of knowing how to use and interpret language in different communities, pointing out that "the skillful speaker" is one who knows how to "code-switch." Relate his comments to those made in any other three selections in this chapter.

9. Charlayne Hunter-Gault brings into focus the relationship between education and democracy, questioning the extent to which people in the United States have had equal access to quality education. Using this chapter and information from other sources, discuss the extent to which educational opportunities in the United States have changed during the past three decades.

CHAPTER 2

Stepping Inside America's Schools and Classrooms

🍎 The Classroom World

Robert B. Everhart

Like many of the authors in this chapter, Robert B. Everhart is a professor and researcher who studies life in school. The following selection is excerpted from his book-length study of a junior high school, Reading, Writing, and Resistance: Adolescence and Labor in a Junior High School, 1983. Everhart explains in the book's preface that "this is a story of everyday life in a junior high school—a story I wrote from two years of fieldwork in one such school. The study focuses on 'everyday' life of junior high schools, and is a chronicle of the daily routine of students and, to a much lesser degree, teachers."

'Then if this is true,' I said, 'our belief about these matters must be this, that the nature of education is not really as some say it is; as you know, they say that there is not understanding in the soul, but they put it in as if they were putting sight into blind eyes.' (Plato, *The Republic*, Book vii).

The typical day begins with the yellow buses rolling up to the breeze-way in front of the school at about 8.10 A.M. By 8.25—only five minutes before the first class—some students have already filed into their first-period class and are sitting on the desks or standing around in groups talking to each other. Others stand around in the hall outside the classroom, talking to friends who are going to other classes. At 8.30, the shrill electronic pitch of the bell pierces throughout the school, and at that instant those still left in the halls and outside corridors scurry into their first-period class; those in the rooms proceed to their assigned seats. The halls are empty and quiet as doors to the classrooms are shut. It is time for the schoolday to begin 'officially.'

The first-period class starts as students listen to the notices for the day. Following these announcements, the class settles down and students begin the work which the teacher has planned for that period. The bell rings at the end of the fifty-five minute period and students flood into the halls to go to their second-period class. The second period proceeds much as the first with some variations occurring depending on the class, be it shop, PE, art or the typical 'academic' courses such as English, math, social studies or science. In the middle of the day, students go to the cafeteria for one of three thirty-minute lunch periods during which time they eat lunch and talk to each other. More classes follow lunch until 3.00 P.M. when the students who had arrived on the buses pile back on to them for the return trip home while others take to the streets and roads and walk home. Various students remain for athletic practices, club meetings, detention, and other activities of a required or optional nature.

To the casual observer, the student day seems fairly typical and not unlike those schooldays they may have experienced five, ten, maybe thirty years ago. But beneath this rather pal-

Excerpts from "The Classroom World" from READING, WRITING, AND RESISTANCE: ADOLESCENCE AND LABOR IN JUNIOR HIGH SCHOOL by Robert Everhart. Published by Routledge. Reprinted by permission.

lid veneer is a distinctive way of life that students lead: this life reflects their confrontation and interpretation of a given environment and the meaning they draw from it. First, we will examine the environment of the classroom more closely; later in this chapter we'll examine the *meaning* of classroom life for the students at Harold Spencer who lived it.

Time in Class[1]

Waiting and Getting Ready

'Hey Bob, get your math done for today?' Don, a seventh-grade student, poked me on the shoulder as he came into the math room, grabbed his math folder from the large file hanging from the wall, and walked toward his assigned seat.

'Yeah, got it all done,' I replied.

'I'll bet,' he said in disbelief as he sat down.

Just then the bell rang, signaling the beginning of the school day. Mr Glenn (one of the math teachers) went to his office to get a copy of the daily bulletin and then walked to the middle of the large room where students were sitting around tables and at study carrels located along the wall. 'OK, listen up for the announcements.' He paused a moment, waiting for the class to stop talking and then proceeded to read the daily notices: 'The *Spencer* [the weekly school newspaper] arrives first period today. Room representatives should go to room 100 to pick them up. Cost is five cents with a student body card, ten cents without a card. After the announcements, Chris, you and Midget take a count of those who want the paper and collect the money.' He continued: 'OK, there will be a Thespian meeting on Wednesday after school in room 500. Officers will be elected and all new members are encouraged to attend. There will be a Camera Club meeting after school in Mr Jackson's room on Wednesday. Any ninth-grade students who wish to apply for a position on the photography staff at North High next year should turn their applications in to Mr Jackson by the time of the meeting.'

Mr Glenn then looked around and asked if there were any questions. A student shouted from the side of the room, 'The paper, don't forget to collect for the paper.'

'Yeah, that's right. Chris, you and Midget count hands. Raise your hands so they can see and don't take all morning doing this.' Chris and Midget counted the number of hands for the school paper, then left the room to pick them up in the journalism class.

Glenn turned to the class and said, 'OK, you people know what you're supposed to be doing, let's get humming on those math problems. For those of you who have tests to take, get into that test room.' The students slowly opened their math notebooks and began moving around the room to take tests, to get problem books; some raised their hand for help. There was the usual line at the pencil sharpener to fine tune the pencils.

Some of the math classes at Harold Spencer were 'individualized' and the class that I usually attended with Chris, Don, and other seventh-grade boys was one of these classes. At the beginning of the year, students in this class took a placement test, used to designate at what level of math difficulty they should be placed. Once the students were placed, they then used their math notebook in which was outlined the types of problems they had to do at each level. The answers to problems were found in the various 'teacher's editions' of textbooks located on a table at the side of the room. The students could periodically check their answers in these books and, once they had mastered the problems, they were then eligible to take a test over the whole unit. If they passed the test, they then went on to the next level; if they did not pass it they were given a 'prescription' by Mr Glenn or Mr Charles (the other teacher in the room) that outlined the type of work on which they needed additional review.

About ten minutes after they had left, Chris and Midget returned to distribute the papers. 'Papers here, get them while they're hot. "No-no Song" voted number one song at Spencer,' Midget chanted as he walked into the room. Chris started singing in a low voice: 'A lady that I know came from Columbia, she smiled because I did not understand. Then she held out some . . .' Mr Glenn seemed mildly irritated by this interruption. 'All right, let's knock this routine off; get the papers passed out and then get back to work.' As Chris and Midget distributed the papers, Don and Steve began reading them, commenting on the top ten songs at Spencer as listed in the paper.

'God, "Angie Baby" is number two, what a lousy song.'

'There aren't even any Pink Floyd songs on here.'

'Everyone get those papers put away or you'll find out you won't have any,' said Mr Charles, looking at Don and Steve and then the rest of the class, most of whom were also looking at the papers. With that admonition, everyone put the papers away.

Soon a number of students had their hands in the air either wanting help or desiring to be certified to take a test. Carl, a friend of Chris's, was sitting at the table next to me complaining that he had his hand up off and on for twenty minutes in order to get permission to take a test and still he was waiting. Bobby, sitting at the same table and talking to Tony about skiing, replied, 'That's nothing, I've been waiting almost the whole period just to see if I passed the test which I took yesterday.' Finally, Mr Charles walked over to Carl, checked the work that he had done, and told him he could take the post-test—but then noted that the test room was full so he would have to wait until someone left it. Carl then went over to sit with Bobby and entered into the conversation about skiing. Finally, Carl shot into the test room and had been there for about ten minutes when Glenn announced that there were five minutes left in the class and that everyone should put their materials away.

The individualized mathematics class was not representative of all classes, yet it still illustrates that much of the time spent in the classroom situation was time spent waiting—waiting to do something, waiting to begin something, waiting to go on to a new activity. I say individualized math classes were not representative because there was somewhat less waiting there. Waiting was even more pronounced in most of the other classes at Spencer as the class moved along in unison rather than in smaller segments, an activity that happened to some greater degree in the individualized math class.

Waiting abounded and was so pervasive in most classes that it is impossible to enumerate all of its manifestations. Waiting for students to give up books needed by other students, waiting to use filmstrips, reading machines, or other instructional devices, waiting for grades to be recorded or waiting to have papers distributed—all were events that affected large segments of the class at any one time. Individual students had to sit through exercise reviews, oral reading sessions, and class discussions, all of which may have been irrelevent to them at any one point in time. The fact that waiting itself was pervasive is clear, but takes on even more meaning when looked at in the context of the entire school day.

We can safely assume that the announcements, attendance taking, the passing out of school papers and registration forms, head counts on a variety of topics on which the school needed information (like the number of students whose parents worked for the federal government, number planning on coming to open houses) consumed anywhere from five to ten minutes of the first period of every day. Announcements and attendance taking in each of the other five class periods also took at least five minutes from the beginning of each class. It is also safe to eliminate at least the last five minutes of each class for papers to be collected, books to be returned, desks to be lined up, and for other classroom maintenance activities. Thus, at least ten minutes was taken from each class for these procedural activities—time during which students essentially waited around for the class to begin or end. Add to this the five minutes passing time between each class and the thirty minutes for lunch, and the sum of 115 minutes each day were *formally* set aside for the student to move, eat, get ready to do something, or wait for a class to end. If we round this off to 120 minutes, two hours out of a six-and-a-half hour day, or almost one-third of the student's time in school, was formally used for activities necessitated by the fact that certain activities such as passing, attendance taking, and announcements were required, yet this figure of one-third of the time does not even include the time spent *between* the first and last five minutes in any class during which the student was required to adjust to the pace of instruction. Now let us turn to see what students did during instructional activities.

The Pacing of Instruction

Instructional events for a given student are determined by a number of considerations. One is the time available within any one class period and the pacing of events within the limits of time. In this respect, the constraints on the teacher are set and unyielding—the period begins at a certain time and ends fifty-five minutes later, and within these limits whatever instruction the teacher has planned will and must occur. This simple observation carries considerable weight when used to describe and interpret the students' environment in the school.

Instruction at Spencer was organized so that things 'came out' in such a fashion that the majority of students ended up with the same product at essentially the same time. In Marcy's English class, for example, the group had been writing a business letter in order to learn the proper format, style, and content of such a letter. First, Marcy asked the class to turn to the chapter on business letters in their grammer books and read that section. After five minutes Marcy asked the class, 'How many have not yet finished?' Initially, about one-third of the class raised their hands. Roy, sitting in the rear near where I was sitting, nudged John. John then spoke up, 'I'm not finished.'

'I ain't finished either,' Roy added, smiling. Needless to say, they both had finished; I had seen them close their books a few minutes earlier and then proceed to trade a *Mad* magazine back and forth.

'Well, I'll give you a few more minutes, but hurry up,' said Marcy. Those not finished continued reading while the rest of the class began engaging in different activities: looking out the window, doodling, and pulling pictures from their wallets and looking at them. Roy then pulled a copy of *Cycle* magazine from beneath his desk and began leafing through it. After a few minutes Marcy went to the blackboard and began outlining the structure of the business letter.

'Ok, first thing we do is to place the return address—where, class?'

'On the paper,' said one boy slouched in his chair and tapping his pencil.

'All right, comedian, that's obvious. Where else?'

'On the front side of the paper.'

'Come on class, get serious! Where do you place the return address? Larry?' Marcy obviously was in no mood for students' wisecracks although she was usually tolerant of this constant undertone of comments.

'I don't know . . . on the top?'

'OK, good, now where on the top?' Larry thought for a moment and then Marcy said impatiently, 'Larry come on, you just read it in the book.'

Steve volunteered, 'He can't read.' Someone let out a 'Duh' from the back of the room. A few people snickered, Marcy stared at Steve for an instant, then turned to Larry and asked him to turn to page 236 in his grammar book and look at the example on the page to see where the return address was. Larry looked at it and finally answered, 'In the upper right-hand corner.'

'Right.' She then proceeded through a description and explanation of the form of the business letter. After a discussion lasting between ten and fifteen minutes, she then asked the students to begin thinking about writing their own business letter, an assignment due at the end of the following week (this was Tuesday). First they were to write an initial paragraph for a business letter to anyone they chose and concerning any subject. After about ten minutes of writing, Marcy asked, 'How many are not finished with their paragraph?' About six students raised their hands. 'OK, I'll give you a few minutes to finish up. The rest of you, I want to read your paragraphs to each other because I want you to read them to the class tomorrow and they'd better be clear; if they aren't clear to you now they won't be clear to the class tomorrow.'

One of the students at the back of the room seemed somewhat surprised at this. 'Hey, you didn't say anything about having to read these in front of the class.'

'Yeah, I don't want to read mine in front of the class,' added Phil.

Marcy put her hands on her hips and stated emphatically, 'Now come on, class, you'll all want to do a good job and this will give you a chance to practice and improve your paragraphs before they're submitted for grades. And you all want to get "A's", I'm sure.' There was a chorus of laughs from most of the class and Marcy smiled.

"I don't care,' I heard one girl say under her breath.

'Yeah, I don't care either, just so I get this stupid thing done.'

After saying that, Don turned to Art and said, 'Hey, Art, what you writing your letter on?'

'I am writing the Elephant Rubber Company, telling them that their rubbers were too small.'

'Wow,' Ron replied.

'Don't think I'll write that letter though, Marcy will have a bird.'

'For sure,' Art replied.

The students continued talking to each other, which finally prompted Marcy to get up from her desk and say, 'Class, get busy or some of you will be in after school.'

This incident, typical of classes at Spencer, illustrates how instruction was paced in most of the classes and demonstrates the different uses of time for both teachers and students. For the teacher, instruction was paced in such a manner that the different rates of student progress were 'leveled,' resulting in large blocks of students moving along to approximately the same spot at the same time. However, this pacing provided a different situation both for the individual student and groups of students. The uniform orchestration of instruction provided, for the students, gaps, sometimes small and sometimes large, in the attention they had to pay to the formal requirements of the classroom. When these gaps were present, students filled them readily with their own activities. Thus Don and Steve talked about motor cycles, Karen and Terry talked about going to the store after school, and Larry doodled on his peechie.

Management of Time

This incident in Marcy's class points to the perennial problem in the classroom where students serve basically as respondents bounded in time and space by the limitations of legitimate behavior happening within the physical boundaries of the classroom. The problem at Spencer revolved around the teacher having to organize between thirty and thirty-five students within these limits. Since it was physically impossible to fill the allotted time for all these students, the best the teacher could do was to manage activities within a restrictive time frame and, as in the case just explained, to stretch out tasks so that time was filled with relevant activities, all accomplished at about the same pace, and involving something close to a majority of the students at any one time.

This 'staging' procedure had other ramifications in terms of the management of time. Usually, teachers taught multiple sections of the same class. Ideally, the teacher attempted to keep these sections at approximately the same place so as to avoid confusion on his part in ordering films, preparing handouts, grading papers, and preparing lesson plans. But disjuncture was often unavoidable when assemblies, school-wide testing, early dismissals, and field trips cut into one period's time but not the other. While some might question the legitimacy of such time management, innumerable situations made it seemingly unavoidable. This was most pronounced in Creadley's science class wherein he had students involved in laboratory work between 40 and 50 per cent of the time. Preparing labs meant setting up experiments the night before, and having to prepare two different sets of labs the same day with equipment restrictions, space limitations, and the like was difficult. So if, for reasons of schedule changes, the two seventh-grade science sections got out of 'synch' as he used to say, Creadley often let the students do whatever they wanted (which involved anything from playing chess to doing assignments for other classes to the usual talking about sports and after-school activities) until the other class had caught up. Realistically, there was probably little choice in his holding the class up as he too was a victim of time and its limitations.

The management of time also created a situation wherein students who did not relate to a certain pace of classroom instruction and desired to deviate were compelled to adjust to the normal procedure. In reading class, for example, Don and the other students were reading a book called *The Peddler War*, a book that they read out loud in class and individually. Don was mumbling to himself about what a 'chicken shit' way of reading a book this was—'just like a bunch of candy assed fourth graders,'—so he raised his hand.

'Can we take these books home to read them?'

Mrs McBride said, 'No, hand them in at the end of the period, we have to use them for another class tomorrow.' Hearing that, Don then simply closed his book and, propping his chin on his hand, stared out the window for about five minutes. Finally, McBride said, 'Don, get to work, you can't read staring out of the window.'

Don raised his hand and asked, 'Can I go to my locker, we're not doing anything in here anyhow?'

'No, you'll have to wait until the period ends. Tomorrow, we're going to work right up to the bell instead of having five minutes left over like we do almost everyday.'

Time and its uses were an important regularity of classroom life. In virtually every class and throughout the school year, variations of waiting and getting ready, the manner by which instruction was paced, and the management of time defined a large part of the daily instructional happenings.

Classroom Demands

The fact that the students at Harold Spencer spent such a significant portion of their time governed by the contingencies of time has parallels with what was required while they attended school. The constant reality of waiting, moving with the group, and fitting in with the stream of instructional events as they were arranged by the teacher meant that the student's involvement in 'learning' had to fit into that stream as he was caught by the flow. That the stream bypassed the students or was not flowing for significant portions of their existence in the school speaks to the instructional demands placed on them.

Not all classes were alike, of course, but the social studies taught by Richards and Mr Bruce illustrates some typical requirements placed on students. One day in the Fall I walked into the class with Chris, John, and Don. We took our assigned seats and were talking before the bell rang. As usual, Chris and I were trading Polish jokes. The bell rang and Mr Bruce directed everyone's attention to the side blackboard on which was written the cycle of events for the unit that they were beginning:

Monday:　work in large room on summary charts and watch film.

Tuesday:　work in small groups reading from text and working on worksheets.

Wednesday:　work in large groups correcting worksheets and on maps.

Thursday:　work in large room on essay assignments and watch film.

Friday:　small groups, reading and worksheets.

Monday:　large groups, review of unit.

Tuesday:　test on unit.

Bruce said, 'OK, now that you have that [the schedule] you can decide on which days you want to stay home.' He smiled as he looked around the room for responses.

'Far out,' Roger said, 'how about everyday?'

Bruce replied, 'Roger, your mind is home everyday anyhow.'

'What mind?' Carl chimed in a low voice that Bruce could not hear at the front of the room. 'His mind is like a sponge that's been squeezed dry.'

Roger looked over at Carl, smiled drolly, and produced an obscene gesture. Ann, sitting in the seat between them, giggled.

Richards then passed out the worksheets for the summary charts (papers the students kept on salient data such as climate, population, products produced, major landforms and other such 'encyclopedic' information as it pertained to countries being studied). The week began with Richards listing on the overhead projector the information that should be included on the summary sheet. As the period progressed, most of the students in the class dutifully filled in the information as Richards outlined it.

The next day (Tuesday), Richards passed out a worksheet that was to be used in class to answer some questions on the assignment. 'Remember, on these worksheets you should print rather than write. Since many of you people never had writing in grade school, you're going to have to communicate so I can read it. That means PRINT. Next, the answers on the worksheet must be the same as those given in the text—none of your own thought about what you think the answer should be. Just write the answer as it appears in the book. Next, number 12 asks you to underline the correct answer, and this means to underline it, not circle it. Finally, number 13–25, the directions state to circle the correct word and this means the whole word, not just the number in front of the word. Any questions? Get going.'

The students slowly opened their books and began to work at the required material. I was sitting near John, who was soon busily talking to Steve sitting next to him about the intramural touch football game after school tomorrow night. They did this while simultaneously working on the assignment and keeping vaguely aware of Richard's and Bruce's location in the room.

'Which team are you on?' Steve asked. John responded that he was on 'Fillmore's Fighters,' each team being named after its captain.

'God, you guys really got killed last week,' said Steve.'Hey, what kind of farming do they practice in Switzerland?'

'What do ya mean, "What kind of farming?" How the hell do I know?'

'Well, it's question number seven.'

John ignored the question and went on to recount the horrors of their loss to 'Victor's Victors' last week, and added that they were not at full strength then but they would kill Steve's team. A few minutes later he said rather nonchalantly, 'Oh, here it is.'

'Here's what?'

'The kind of farming they practice in Switzerland; it's called vertical farming.'

They both began copying the answer in but Steve hesitated and looked over at John.

'V-E-R-T-I-C-L-E, is that how you spell vertical?'

'Na ya dummy, it's "al" not "le." Hey, is Runger playing for your team?' And on they went like that for the remainder of the period, talking while paying minimal attention to the work required.

The next day they watched a film on Switzerland and corrected the worksheets that they had completed the previous day. Friday was spent as the previous Wednesday except that Steve and John talked about the game the night before in which 'Fillmore's Fighters' had won by one touch-down in the last minute.

The following Monday was devoted to review for the unit test on Switzerland to be given the following day. Richards was his usual ultra-organized and precise self in providing directions for the review. He asked students to take a piece of paper on which they would write answers to various review questions he would pose. Bruce turned the overhead projector on and wrote in large block letters on the overlay, 'Review for unit tests.'

John immediately shot his hand in the air. 'Are we supposed to center the title like that, like you have it on the overhead?'

Bruce responded, 'Well, this is for your own use so it's really not crucial at this time.'

Another hand went up toward the back of the room. 'Well, I put my title on the right-hand side and not in the center and besides it's lower than yours. Is that all right?'

John and Steve both snickered as Bruce responded. 'Come on, people, this is for your own use so it's not all that important where you put it now. All right, the first thing we are going to review is the mountain climate region. Now, one of the things that characterizes a mountain climate is that there is a variety in the climate.' Bruce underlined the word 'variety' but in such a manner that the line looked like it had a period at the end. John then raised his hand and asked, 'Should we put a period after variety?' Bruce turned around to look at the overhead, extended the line to the 'y' and then explained that there was no period there. This made little difference as half the class was smiling to themselves over Bruce's penchant for detail.

Characteristic of the demand placed on students was what seemed to be a 'quota' placed on acquired knowledge. The dominant form of instruction was the acquisition of information dispensed by the teacher, a form that resulted in the teacher being unable to provide all students with enough to keep them busy on instructional tasks for the entire period. It also made the teacher tend toward minimizing variety, effectively placing a ceiling upon what was required of the typical student.

Students and Classroom Life

Thus far I have discussed some regularities of classroom life that clarify the role of students in the school. We now begin to see that organizational forces within Harold Spencer create, in part, an environment that defines students' lives in particular ways. First, students are massed in the learning process in such a manner that relatively little differentiation occurs among them. Given this approach, academic involvement does not require much of the students' energy—so little in fact that students often are at a loss for something to do. Finally, because of the standardization of treatment, standardized outcomes (answers) tend to be what is expected.

If this is the organizational life that students experience, then we would expect them to form some relatively consistent set of beliefs about those experiences. In turn we would expect these beliefs to influence subsequent actions. Since classroom life is pregnant with attempts by teachers to create these academic products—these constellations of right answers—we need to understand how students come to interpret this process.

Work

As a result of structured interviews with students I was able to construct a composite map of what students said they did in school. When I asked this question of them a typical response was 'we work.'

I became intrigued with the notion of work for two reasons. First, in my two years within the school I was somewhat puzzled by the relative infrequency with which it was discussed by students among themselves. Quite simply, the subject of schoolwork rarely was entertained during student chatter, and I wondered why. Second, when it was mentioned, I noticed what appeared to be subtle distinctions between activities assigned to the notion of 'work' and those that were discussed as 'non-work.' As I explored more fully how students saw work in the school, I began to understand their perspectives within the ongoing regularities of the classroom environment.

Toward the end of the seventh grade, I asked Don and Steve, Chris, Bill, and John and a number of other students what type of activities constituted work. From what they told me, the list reflected in Table 1 was generated.

The students, by their categorization, were telling me that work was something that characteristically came from teachers. Of course, not all things that teachers did in class constituted work, but then most of what came to be seen as work emanated from the teacher. This distinction became clear after I talked to three girls, Sharon, Susan and Anna, about work in school. I asked them what activities constituted work.

'Assignments.'

'You know, sentences, stupid stuff.'

'Yeah, I forgot to do mine today too,' Sharon replied.

I asked them if work was the same in all classes or if it differed from class to class. 'Like how about social studies, what kind of work do you do in social studies?'

'Write down different stuff about a story. . . watching a film.'

'Is watching a film work?' I asked.

TABLE 1   Work and Non-Work Activities

Work	Writing.
	Having to write on paper.
	Read so many pages in so much time.
	Do assignments.
	Things teachers make you do.
	Films if there is a quiz or notes to take.
	Piling it on.
	Doing questions at the end of the chapter.
	Graded assignments.
	Doing the same thing over and over.
	Memorizing.
	Something you have to do alone.
	Do exercises.
Non-work	Experiments.
	Listening.
	Extra credit.
	Art.
	Science.
	Going at your own speed.
	Things where you can get away with doing other things.
	Things assigned I never do.
	Watching films.
Easy work---------------	Just reading stuff you already know.
	Assignments with lots of time.
Chorus.	

'It's boring, it's not work.'

'Where does work come from?' I asked.

'Teachers,' replied Anna.

I continued in a somewhat different vein. 'But what if you write a story yourself; for example I noticed you were writing a story about your horse the other day in Creadley's class. Was that work?'

'Oh no,' Anna replied emphatically. 'That was extra credit. I was doing that for English class. You get extra credit on your grade for doing that.'

Thus for these girls (and for most of the students to whom I talked) 'work' or 'doing work' did not depend so much on the type of activity being done as much as on whether or not the person in authority required it be done. Anna made this clear by emphasizing that writing things down about a story was considered work because it was *required* in Richards's class, but writing a story in English class was not envisioned as work because Anna herself had *initiated* the writing of the story. Without the imperative of the teacher standing over her telling her she had to do it, she saw what was essentially the same activity in a different light.

The notion of requirements—having to do something stated by the teacher—helps to distinguish analytically between what were considered 'work' and 'non-work' activities. In this respect, a film could be perceived as 'work' or 'non-work,' depending upon whether the students needed to pay attention in order to fulfill the expectations of the teacher. Thus, a film might be considered work if students had to watch it to pass a test, but be considered non-work if they could ignore it.

Another criterion, already alluded to, that made work distasteful and which tended to be a definer of work was that it was something you did alone. The preponderance of activities listed under work were those where the students had to sit at their seats, pay attention to the lesson that the teacher had arranged for them, and do what was required by themselves. On the other hand, most of the activities classified as 'non-work' were those in which some semblance of social interaction could go on while the activity was being performed. Science and art were the two classes where students could usually do what was required of them and discuss personal subjects at the same time, and these two classes appeared most frequently on the 'non-work' list; no other specific classes appeared with any regularity on the 'work' list.

The perception of work as a required activity coming from someone in a position of authority and an activity the product of which had an exchange-value (usually by the submission of a paper indicating the satisfactory completion of the work) made sense in the world of the student at Harold Spencer. Work itself was something done not so much because of its intrinsic interest or value, but rather as it was commensurate with the student role that demanded students selling labor power (or the physical and mental capabilities of a person used through labor) in exchange for some symbolic reward. Such a role helps explain the location in Table 1 of such activities as 'doing exercises,' 'memorizing,' 'doing the same thing over and over again,' 'doing questions at the end of the chapter' and similar activities listed under the rubric of work. These activities all were congruent with the position of the student as a recipient of knowledge—as one who not so much created knowledge as consumed it. Classrooms were dominated by the teacher. These mandatory activities were subsequently evaluated by the teacher and a grade assigned to them. Such activities were not 'individualized' but were required of the entire class to be done at approximately the same time. Work then developed a negative connotation because work, rather than something emanating from within students themselves, was something that controlled them.

Students' views of my role further illustrate their over-all perspective on work. To them, I was not working most of the time I was in the school. 'You get paid for this?' was a comment. I replied that I did, and their response was to ask who was crazy enough to pay someone to sit around in a school all day with junior high students. But what made my role one of non-work was the students' perceptions of my liberties to come and go as I pleased and to decide for myself what needed attention. Since I was in the school almost every day of the first year, my infrequent absences were noticeable and many wondered how I could work and still 'skip' from the location of my work—the school. The fact that I could choose which classes to attend, which lunch to go to, which students to hang around—all were conditions simply not connected with work. To the students, work meant having to do something, being regulated, the presence of tight parameters and the like. They had come to see work as the absence of control over the conditions of their own labor.

Teachers and Teaching

Parallel with students' perspective on work were the visions they carried with them on teachers and what teachers did. I should note here that, like the subject of work, characteristics of teachers were not frequently discussed either. As students filed from classes, they immediately began or continued their conversations relating to their personal interests with few comments on either how interesting or how boring the class had been. Minimal discussion does not mean that students did not construct certain perspectives on teachers and the teaching process, for they obviously did. Yet these perspectives must be placed in context, for other activities were far more important and occupied a much more pre-eminent space in the student's cognitive framework than did any discussion of work or the teachers who parceled out the work.

Table 2 is an arrangement of the comments made regarding teachers throughout the year, gathered mostly by my being with the students when the subject was raised but also during formal interviews which I held with a number of students near the end of the seventh grade. Generally, students believed that teachers could be divided into two groups, those labeled 'teachers with negative attributes' and 'teachers with positive attributes.' It is interesting to note the distinction that the students made between the two groups.

Two conditions characterized teachers with negative attributes. The first centered around *physical or personal characteristics* and included such characterizations as 'bastards,' 'screwy,' 'weirdo,' 'fairies,' 'hard to get along with teachers,' 'fish,' 'those that think they're funny,' 'crabs,' or 'snappers.' There was not uniform agreement on what every one of these terms meant as distinguished from the other, but it was obvious that certain ones were reserved for specific people. The term 'bastard,' for example, was usually reserved for teachers who carried on in ways that were seen as unfair or demeaning. Don and Steve, for example, thought Richards was a bastard because 'he's always yelling, standing up there getting red in the face, making a fool out of himself.' 'Treating us like kids,' was another of Richards's attributes.

Terms like 'screwy,' 'weirdo,' 'fairies,' 'fish,' 'pick and flick' related to personal habits such as voice inflections, mannerisms of walking and other movements, and dress. Discussions frequently occurred over whether Mr Bruce really was 'queer' simply because he had a high

TABLE 2 Kinds of Teachers

Teachers with negative attributes	Strict.
	Those with favorites.
	Those that hate the whole class.
	Bastards.
	Screwy.
	Fairies.
	Femmies.
	Busters.
	Mean.
	Those who don't communicate.
	Worse teachers.
	Narcs.
	Hard to get along with teachers.
	Fish.
	Pick n'flicks.
	Those that think they're funny.
	Those that do the same thing over and over.
	Slave drivers.
	Crabs.
	Snappers.
Teachers with positive attributes	Nice---------- They respect us. They trust us. They listen to us.
	Those that let you chew gum.
	Neat teachers.
	Cool teachers.

voice, dressed fairly well, and bounced a little while he walked. A few students even debated the same issue about Mr Charles simply because he called people 'honey' or 'sweetheart,' and because often he put his arm on a student's shoulder while helping him with a math problem.

Personal appearance, too, often served as a basis for students' discriminations among teachers. Mrs Ansel was considered 'weird' because she wore what students considered to be mismatched clothing. Students usually picked on Mr Von Hoffman because of his short hair-cut, a butch cut from the 1950s. Mr Franks was considered 'screwy' because he wore old ties and was reputed to pick the wax out of his ears and flick it across the room while talking, an act that I never personally observed although Steve and others swore a hunk of wax once landed on their science book. Mr Hackett, who often had bloodshot eyes, was suspected of being a heavy drinker; the students never placed much credence in the fact that he wore contact lenses and held down a part-time job in the evenings, a combination that, I imagined, would give anyone bloodshot eyes.

The *specific actions* of teachers in the classroom was a second criterion used to assign negative attributes to teachers. Such attributes as 'strictness,' 'those with favorites,' 'those that hate the whole class,' 'those that think they're funny,' 'those that do the same things over and over,' and 'slave drivers' were included. These conditions often overlapped and many were assigned to the same teacher as an over-all negative indictment.

Negative attributes connected with specific actions usually were connected with the notion of 'teachers who don't communicate.' Chris described this during a discussion about Von Hoffman. 'I don't think he communicates with kids. Like he's giving a spelling test and the word is supposed to be "entered," like "He entered the door quickly." He pronounced it "innard" so I said out loud, "You mean entered." He just says, "Look buddy, you have a detention slip." He's one of the most self-conscious persons I have ever met, he's always worried about another person looking at him . . . you see him talking to himself a lot and doing things like pointing and hitting his fist and maybe frowning and hitting the table and you think "What's going through that guy's mind?"'

The characterization of 'hard to get along with teachers' was another category that included a variety of descriptors and that reflected the over-all flexibility of the teacher in the school. I once asked Chris and John what a hard-to-get-along-with teacher was.

'They're the ones who have been at Harold Spencer since the first year . . . they've seen year after year of kids come through here and I think it just gives them the impression when a new group of students comes in that "Oh man, here comes another group of those brats," and they think that they have to push their thumb on someone completely and if they let half their thumb off the class is going to go wild.' To many students, these teachers were inflexible and students had to meet them on their terms, which meant 'doing the same thing over and over.' Barry and John, both good students, commented that their English teacher was hard to get along with because they did the same thing in class over and over again: 'prepositional phrases, prepositional phrases, just do it over everyday, do assignments three and four times, and it gets so boring, you just sit there. Everyday I hate to go to that class because I know we are going to do the same things again.'

Hard-to-get-along-with teachers, in other words, were like bad bosses—they extracted the most from the students and viewed work as an exchange process that operated on the basis of the controllers of production having authority over the means of production.

To understand characteristics about teachers that students did not like is also to understand the characteristics of the teachers they viewed positively. I found surprisingly little disagreement among the students when they specified what it was about a teacher that made them, in their terms, 'nice,' 'neat,' or 'cool.' John said that most of the kids thought Mr Creadley was the best teacher in the school. 'He just says, "Okay, we have some work to do, let's do it and keep the talking down." He gives you work and he expects you to have it done. It's not that it's that hard, he just gives you a little incentive.'

Chris added, 'He's the only teacher I know who gives you an opportunity to go ahead and do other things. Like with Mr Franks, he just wants you to answer the questions and then you sit around waiting for everyone else to finish but Mr Creadley encourages you to do things other than just answer the questions.'

While John and Chris mentioned some ways in which Creadley ran his class, it was Creadley's style and personality rather than what they learned in class that appealed most to them. Most of the other students liked him because he treated the students 'fairly,' was not 'uptight,' did not 'yell a lot,' and so on. When most students talked about 'cool' or 'neat' teachers, these seemed to be the attributes to which they were referring.

Also common were comments such as 'they respect us,' or 'they listen to us.' In their more reflective moments, many of the students could tell what they saw in teachers they valued positively, and usually this had little to do with how or what they taught, but rather how they interacted with the students as people. One boy who spent considerable time in the office for minor discipline problems told me he thought the vice-principal, Mr Pall, was really quite fair and that 'at least he usually listens to you.' He could not speak as highly of his other teachers for, as he saw them, 'they don't look at you as an individual, they look at you as a group like they want you to be. In fact a lotta times the only time a teacher remembers your name is if you're always getting into trouble or if you're especially good, but if you're just sort of average they don't notice you.'

Most teachers fell between what students perceived to be completely positive and negative attributes when they did talk about teachers, but I never felt that this signified a real resentment against most of the teachers.

What teachers did in the school appeared, at least on the surface, in conflict with what the students thought was best or desirable, as shown in Table 3, wherein I have presented the students' belief about what the teachers did. This list dramatizes that students saw themselves as passive and the adults as the active member of the relationship. In the area of what I have called 'interaction with students' students portrayed a picture of themselves as being less than or below adults. Students saw many adults in terms of authority hierarchies where the adults interacted with students on the basis of the authority vested in their office. Thus, when teachers interacted with students, the students perceived they were underestimated and treated 'like third-graders' through a simplification of work and assignments. Students also thought they were talked down to and that little allowance was made for their input as individuals.

The tendency of the teachers to give out work and the students to do it is clear in Table 3. Teachers 'pile it [work] on' and then turn around and 'write,' 'sit at their desk,' 'correct papers,' and 'grade us.' If there were problems with the class, teachers 'scream,' 'watch people,' and 'be strict.' From the student point of view, there was little else involved in what teachers did in the classroom other than that represented in this simple 'factory model' of learning; that is, the teachers pouring in the facts and the students pouring them back in the form of papers and tests. Students had little, if any, conception of teachers planning lessons, debating alternatives of what to teach, agonizing over grading, the treatment of a student, wondering if their teaching had an effect, or anything like that. The student picture of teachers provided little room for emotion, with the exception of that associated with student violation of school standards. The teacher's world, in the student's eyes, was straightforward and linear, hardly complex at all.

Such viewpoints on teachers—their characteristics and what they do, confirms the presence of a separate student culture—one poised at odds with the adult culture in the school.[2] First, students saw their academic activities consisting mostly of 'work' and it was the teacher who so defined their task, thereby providing students with little formal control over their own labor. Second, upon examining student-held beliefs about teachers, we see that teachers were viewed negatively owing to the extent to which they maintained tight control over student activities in the classroom; teachers who were viewed more positively were those who provided some greater degree of self-determination, although this did not necessarily mean that these teachers might be less demanding. Finally, students' beliefs about what teachers 'did' was remarkably congruous to their own conception of what they, as students, did. Accordingly, the student-generated belief system held that the teacher's job consisted mostly of handing out work and enforcing the standards by which work was done. Most social interaction with students by teachers existed from a position of authority, making even sharper the divisions between the adult and student way of understanding the junior high school.

TABLE 3 Things Teachers Do

Interaction with students	Simplify things like third-graders. Don't treat us as individuals. Don't listen to us. Not congratulate you. Embarrass us. Take for granted you know what to do. Try to build a reputation with students. Sit around and expect you to learn by yourself.	
Duties	Run projector. Sit. Talk------------------------------- Pile it on. Read papers. Correct papers. Sit at desk. Give work. Tap pencils. Grade us. Write. Read stories. Give detention.	to us. to each other.
Discipline	Catch people smoking. Scream. Argue. Eye you. Stare at the girls. Cuss. Give hacks. Throw people out.	Study people's jaws. Watch people. Tell us to stop talking. Be strict. Send us to the office. Nag. Give sentences.
Actions	Be self-conscious. Act like commandos. Try to be cool-------------------	Dumb jokes to us. Dirty jokes to each other. Don't take things seriously.

Endnotes

1. For additional perspectives on time in classrooms, see for example Philip Jackson's *Life in Classrooms* (New York: Holt, Rinehart, & Winston, 1968), Jules Henry's *Culture Against Man* (New York: Random House, 1963), and Philip Cusick's *Inside High School* (New York: Holt, Rinehart, & Winston, 1972).

2. Waller described this most aptly when he said 'a second and more universal conflict between students and teachers arises from the fact that teachers are adults and students are not, so the teachers are the bearers of the culture of the society of adults and try to impose that culture upon students, whereas students represent the indigenous culture of the group of children. 'Willard Waller, *The Sociology of Teaching* (New York: John Wiley, 1965), p. 104.

What High School Is

Theodore R. Sizer

Theodore R. Sizer is chair of the Education Department at Brown University and formerly Dean of the Graduate School of Education at Harvard. "What High School Is" is a chapter from his book *Horace's Compromise: The Dilemma of the American High School*, a book-length study of American high schools published in 1984 as part of a five-year inquiry into secondary education called A Study of High Schools and co-sponsored by the National Association of Secondary School Principals and the Commission on Educational Issues of the National Association of Independent Schools. Sizer explains in the introduction to this book that some of the teachers and students he describes are "composites, a blending of people and places." Mark, the student described in this selection, is such a composite. While Mark—the individual—does not exist, Sizer explains that all the classes he describes are "real" classes, but their juxtaposition is invented.

Mark, sixteen and a genial eleventh-grader, rides a bus to Franklin High School, arriving at 7:25. It is an Assembly Day, so the schedule is adapted to allow for a meeting of the entire school. He hangs out with his friends, first outside school and then inside, by his locker. He carries a pile of textbooks and notebooks; in all, it weighs eight and a half pounds.

From 7:30 to 8:19, with nineteen other students, he is in Room 304 for English class. The Shakespeare play being read this year by the eleventh grade is *Romeo and Juliet*. The teacher, Ms. Viola, has various students in turn take parts and read out loud. Periodically, she interrupts the (usually halting) recitations to ask whether the thread of the conversation in the play is clear. Mark is entertained by the stumbling readings of some of his classmates. He hopes he will not be asked to be Romeo, particularly if his current steady, Sally, is Juliet. There is a good deal of giggling in class, and much attention paid to who may be called on next. Ms. Viola reminds the class of a test on this part of the play to be given next week.

The bell rings at 8:19. Mark goes to the boys' room, where he sees a classmate who he thinks is a wimp but who constantly tries to be a buddy. Mark avoids the leech by rushing off. On the way, he notices two boys engaged in some sort of transaction, probably over marijuana. He pays them no attention. 8:24. Typing class. The rows of desks that embrace big office machines are almost filled before the bell. Mark is uncomfortable here: typing class is girl country. The teacher constantly threatens what to Mark is a humiliatingly female future: "Your employer won't like these erasures." The minutes during the period are spent copying a letter from a handbook onto business stationery. Mark struggles to keep from looking at his work; the teacher wants him to watch only the material from which he is copying. Mark is frustrated, uncomfortable, and scared that he will not complete his letter by the class's end, which would be embarrassing.

Theodore Sizer, Horace's Compromise: The Dilemma of the American School. Copyright © 1984 by Houghton Mifflin Company. Reprinted with permission.

Nine tenths of the students present at school that day are assembled in the auditorium by the 9:18 bell. The dilatory tenth still stumble in, running down aisles. Annoyed class deans try to get the mob settled. The curtains part; the program is a concert by a student rock group. Their electronic gear flashes under the lights, and the five boys and one girl in the group work hard at being casual. Their movements on stage are studiously at three-quarter time, and they chat with one another as though the tumultuous screaming of their schoolmates were totally inaudible. The girl balances on a stool; the boys crank up the music. It is very soft rock, the sanitized lyrics surely cleared with the assistant principal. The girl sings, holding the mike close to her mouth, but can scarcely be heard. Her light voice is tentative, and the lyrics indecipherable. The guitars, amplified, are tuneful, however, and the drums are played with energy.

The students around Mark—all juniors, since they are seated by class—alternately slouch in their upholstered, hinged seats, talking to one another, or sit forward, leaning on the chair backs in front of them, watching the band. A boy near Mark shouts noisily at the microphone-fondling singer, "Bite it . . . ohhh," and the area around Mark explodes in vulgar male laughter, but quickly subsides. A teacher walks down the aisle. Songs continue, to great applause. Assembly is over at 9:46, two minutes early.

9:53 and biology class. Mark was at a different high school last year and did not take this course there as a tenth-grader. He is in it now, and all but one of his classmates are a year younger than he. He sits on the side, not taking part in the chatter that goes on after the bell. At 9:57, the public address system goes on, with the announcements of the day. After a few words from the principal ("Here's today's cheers and jeers. . ." with a cheer for the winning basketball team and a jeer for the spectators who made a ruckus at the gymnasium), the task is taken over by officers of ASB (Associated Student Bodies). There is an appeal for "bat bunnies." Carnations are for sale by the Girls' League. Miss Indian American is coming. Students are auctioning off their services (background catcalls are heard) to earn money for the prom. Nominees are needed for the ballot for school bachelor and school bachelorette. The announcements end with a "thought for the day. When you throw a little mud, you lose a little ground."

At 10:04 the biology class finally turns to science. The teacher, Mr. Robbins, has placed one of several labeled laboratory specimens—some are pinned in frames, others swim in formaldehyde—on each of the classroom's eight laboratory tables. The three or so students whose chairs circle each of these benches are to study the specimen and make notes about it or drawings of it. After a few minutes each group of three will move to another table. The teacher points out that these specimens are of organisms already studied in previous classes. He says that the period-long test set for the following day will involve observing some of these specimens—then to be without labels—and writing an identifying paragraph on each. Mr. Robbins points out that some of the printed labels ascribe the specimens names different from those given in the textbook. He explains that biologists often give several names to the same organism.

The class now falls to peering, writing, and quiet talking. Mr. Robbins comes over to Mark, and in whispered words asks him to carry a requisition form for science department materials to the business office. Mark, because of his "older" status, is usually chosen by Robbins for this kind of errand. Robbins gives Mark the form and a green hall pass to show to any teacher who might challenge him, on his way to the office, for being out of a classroom. The errand takes Mark four minutes. Meanwhile Mark's group is hard at work but gets to only three of the specimens before the bell rings at 10:42. As the students surge out, Robbins shouts a reminder about a "double" laboratory period on Thursday.

Between classes one of the seniors asks Mark whether he plans to be a candidate for schoolwide office next year. Mark says no. He starts to explain. The 10:47 bell rings, meaning that he is late for French class.

There are fifteen students in Monsieur Bates's language class. He hands out tests taken the day before: *"C'est bien fait, Etienne . . . c'est mieux, Marie . . . Tch, tch, Robert . . ."* Mark notes his C+ and peeks at the A—in front of Susanna, next to him. The class has been assigned seats by M. Bates; Mark resents sitting next to prissy, brainy Susanna. Bates starts by asking a student to read a question and give the correct answer. *"James question un."* James haltingly reads the question and gives an answer that Bates, now speaking English, says is incomplete. In due course: *"Mark, question cinq."* Mark does his bit, and the sequence goes on, the eight quiz questions and answers filling about twenty minutes of time.

"Turn to page forty-nine. *Maintenant, lisez après moi. . ."* and Bates reads a sentence and has the class echo it. Mark is embarrassed by this and mumbles with a barely audible sound. Others, like Susanna, keep the decibel count up, so Mark can hide. This I-say-you-repeat drill is interrupted once by the public address system, with an announcement about a meeting for the cheerleaders. Bates finishes the class, almost precisely at the bell, with a homework assignment. The students are to review these sentences for a brief quiz the following day. Mark takes note of the assignment, because he knows that tomorrow will be a day of busy-work in French class. Much though he dislikes oral drills, they are better than the workbook stuff that Bates hands out. Write, write, write, for Bates to throw away, Mark thinks.

11:36. Down to the cafeteria, talking noisily, hanging out, munching. Getting to Room 104 by 12:17: U.S. history. The teacher is sitting cross-legged on his desk when Mark comes in, heatedly arguing with three students over the fracas that had followed the previous night's basketball game. The teacher, Mr. Suslovic, while agreeing that the spectators from their school certainly were provoked, argues that they should neither have been so obviously obscene in yelling at the opposing cheerleaders nor have allowed Coke cans to be rolled out on the floor. The three students keep saying that "it isn't fair." Apparently they and some others had been assigned "Saturday mornings" (detentions) by the principal for the ruckus.

At 12:34, the argument appears to subside. The uninvolved students, including Mark, are in their seats, chatting amiably. Mr. Suslovic climbs off his desk and starts talking: "We've almost finished this unit, chapters nine and ten. . ." The students stop chattering among themselves and turn toward Suslovic. Several slouch down in their chairs. Some open notebooks. Most have the five-pound textbook on their desks.

Suslovic lectures on the cattle drives, from north Texas to railroads west of St. Louis. He breaks up this narrative with questions ("Why were the railroad lines laid largely east to west?"), directed at nobody in particular and eventually answered by Suslovic himself. Some students take notes. Mark doesn't. A student walks in the open door, hands Mr. Suslovic a list, and starts whispering with him. Suslovic turns from the class and hears out this messenger. He then asks, "Does anyone know where Maggie Sharp is?" Some one answers, "Sick at home"; someone else says, "I thought I saw her at lunch." Genial consternation. Finally Suslovic tells the messenger, "Sorry, we can't help you," and returns to the class: "Now, where were we?" He goes on for some minutes. The bell rings. Suslovic forgets to give the homework assignment.

1:11 and Algebra II. There is a commotion in the hallway: someone's locker is rumored to have been opened by the assistant principal and a narcotics agent. In the five-minute passing time, Mark hears the story three times and three ways. A locker had been broken into by another student. It was Mr. Gregory and a narc. It was the cops, and they did it without Gregory's knowing. Mrs. Ames, the mathematics teacher, has not heard anything about it. Several of the nineteen students try to tell her and start arguing among themselves. "O.K., that's enough." She hands out the day's problem, one sheet to each student. Mark sees with dismay that it is a single, complicated "word" problem about some train that, while traveling at 84 mph, due west, passes a car that was going due east at 55 mph. Mark struggles: Is it $d = rt$ or $t = rd$? The class becomes quiet, writing, while Mrs. Ames writes some additional, short problems on the blackboard. "Time's up." A sigh; most students still writing. A muffled "Shit." Mrs. Ames frowns. "Come on, now." She collects papers, but it takes four minutes for her to corral them all.

"Copy down the problems from the board." A minute passes. "William, try number one." William suggests an approach. Mrs. Ames corrects and cajoles, and William finally gets it right. Mark watches two kids to his right passing notes; he tries to read them, but the handwriting is illegible from his distance. He hopes he is not called on, and he isn't. Only three students are asked to puzzle out an answer. The bell rings at 2:00. Mrs. Ames shouts a homework assignment over the resulting hubbub.

Mark leaves his books in his locker. He remembers that he has homework, but figures that he can do it during English class the next day. He knows that there will be an in-class presentation of one of the *Romeo and Juliet* scenes and that he will not be in it. The teacher will not notice his homework writing, or won't do anything about it if she does.

Mark passes various friends heading toward the gym, members of the basketball teams. Like most students, Mark isn't an active school athlete. However, he is associated with the yearbook staff. Although he is not taking "Yearbook" for credit as an English course, he is contributing photographs. Mark takes twenty minutes checking into the yearbook staff's headquarters (the classroom of its faculty adviser) and getting some assignments of pictures from his boss, the senior who is the photography editor. Mark knows that if he pleases his boss and the faculty adviser, he'll take that editor's post for the next year. He'll get English credit for his work then.

After gossiping a bit with the yearbook staff, Mark will leave school by 2:35 and go home. His grocery market bagger's job is from 4:45 to 8:00, the rush hour for the store. He'll have a snack at 4:30, and his mother will save him some supper to eat at 8:30. She will ask whether he has any homework, and he'll tell her no. Tomorrow, and virtually every other tomorrow, will be the same for Mark, save for the lack of the assembly: each period then will be five minutes longer.

Most Americans have an uncomplicated vision of what secondary education should be. Their conception of high school is remarkably uniform across the country, a striking fact, given the size and diversity of the United States and the politically decentralized character of the schools. This uniformity is of several generations' standing. It has, however, two appearances, each quite different from the other, one of words and the other of practice, a world of political rhetoric and Mark's world.

A California high school's general goals, set out in 1979, could serve equally well most of America's high schools, public and private. This school had as its ends:

🍎 Fundamental scholastic achievement . . . to acquire knowledge and share in the traditionally accepted academic fundamentals . . . to develop the ability to make decisions, to solve problems, to reason independently, and to accept responsibility for self-evaluation and continuing self-improvement.

🍎 Career and economic competence . . .

🍎 Citizenship and civil responsibility . . .

🍎 Competence in human and social relations . . .

🍎 Moral and ethical values . . .

🍎 Self-realization and mental and physical health . . .

🍎 Aesthetic awareness . . .

🍎 Cultural diversity . . . [1]

In addition to its optimistic rhetoric, what distinguishes this list is its comprehensiveness. The high school is to touch most aspects of an adolescent's existence—mind, body, morals, values, career. No one of these areas is given especial prominence. School people arrogate to themselves an obligation to all.

An example of the wide acceptability of these goals is found in the courts. Forced to present a detailed definition of "thorough and efficient education," elementary as well as secondary, a West Virginia judge sampled the best of conventional wisdom and concluded that

> there are eight general elements of a thorough and efficient system of education: (a) Literacy, (b) The ability to add, subtract, multiply, and divide numbers, (c) Knowledge of government to the extent the child will be equipped as a citizen to make informed choices among persons and issues that affect his own governance, (d) Self-knowledge and knowledge of his or her total environment to allow the child to intelligently choose life work—to know his or her options, (e) Work-training and advanced academic training as the child may intelligently choose, (f) Recreational pursuits, (g) Interests in all creative arts such as music, theater, literature, and the visual arts, and (h) Social ethics, both behavioral and abstract, to facilitate compatibility with others in this society.[2]

That these eight—now powerfully part of the debate over the purpose and practice of education in West Virginia—are reminiscent of the influential list, "The Seven Cardinal Principles of Secondary Education," promulgated in 1918 by the National Education Association, is no surprise.[3] The rhetoric of high school purpose has been uniform and consistent for decades. Americans agree on the goals for their high schools.

That agreement is convenient, but it masks the fact that virtually all the words in these goal statements beg definition. Some schools have labored long to identify specific criteria beyond them; the result has been lists of daunting pseudospecificity and numbing earnestness. However, most leave the words undefined and let the momentum of traditional practice speak for itself. That is why analyzing how Mark spends his time is important: from watching him one uncovers the important purposes of education, the ones that shape practice. Mark's day is similar to that of other high school students across the country, as similar as the rhetoric of one goal statement to others'. Of course, there are variations, but the extent of consistency in the shape of school routine for a large and diverse adolescent population is extraordinary, indicating more graphically than any rhetoric the measure of agreement in America about what one does in high school, and, by implication, what it is for.

The basic organizing structures in schools are familiar. Above all, students are grouped by age (that is, freshman, sophomore, junior, senior), and all are expected to take precisely the same time—around 720 school days over four years, to be precise—to meet the requirements for a diploma. When one is out of his grade level, he can feel odd, as Mark did in his biology class. The goals are the same for all, and the means to achieve them are also similar.

Young males and females are treated remarkably alike; the schools' goals are the same for each gender. In execution, there are differences, as those pressing sex discrimination suits have made educators intensely aware. The students in metalworking classes are mostly male; those in home economics, mostly female. But it is revealing how much less sex discrimination there is in high schools than in other American institutions. For many young women, the most liberated hours of their week are in school.

School is to be like a job: you start in the morning and end in the afternoon, five days a week. You don't get much of a lunch hour, so you go home early, unless you are an athlete or are involved in some special school or extracurricular activity. School is conceived of as the children's workplace, and it takes young people off parents' hands and out of the labor market during prime-time work hours. Not surprisingly, many students see going to school as little more than a dogged necessity. They perceive the day-to-day routine, a Minnesota study reports, as one of "boredom and lethargy." One of the students summarizes: School is "boring, restless, tiresome, puts ya to sleep, tedious, monotonous, pain in the neck."[4]

The school schedule is a series of units of time: the clock is king. The base time block is about fifty minutes in length. Some schools, on what they call modular scheduling, split that fifty-minute block into two or even three pieces. Most schools have double periods for laboratory work, especially in the sciences, or four-hour units for the small numbers of students involved in intensive vocational or other work-study programs. The flow of all school activity arises from or is blocked by these time units. "How much time do I have with my kids" is the teacher's key question.

Because there are many claims for those fifty-minute blocks, there is little time set aside for rest between them, usually no more than three to ten minutes, depending on how big the school is and, consequently, how far students and teachers have to walk from class to class. As a result, there is a frenetic quality to the school day, a sense of sustained restlessness. For the adolescents, there are frequent changes of room and fellow students, each change giving tempting opportunities for distraction, which are stoutly resisted by teachers. Some schools play soft music during these "passing times," to quiet the multitude, one principal told me.

Many teachers have a chance for a coffee break. Few students do. In some city schools where security is a problem, students must be in class for seven consecutive periods, interrupted by a heavily monitored twenty-minute lunch period for small groups, starting as early as 10:30 A.M. and running to after 1:00 P.M. A high premium is placed on punctuality and on "being where you're supposed to be." Obviously, a low premium is placed on reflection and repose. The student rushes from class to class to collect knowledge. Savoring it, it is implied, is not to be done much in school, nor is such meditation really much admired. The picture that these familiar patterns yield is that of an academic supermarket. The purpose of going to school is to pick things up, in an organized and predictable way, the faster the better.

What is supposed to be picked up is remarkably consistent among all sorts of high schools. Most schools specifically mandate three out of every five courses a student selects. Nearly all of these mandates fall into five areas—English, social studies, mathematics, science, and physical education. On the average, English is required to be taken each year, social studies and physical education three out of the four high school years, and mathematics and science one or two years. Trends indicate that in the mid-eighties there is likely to be an increase in the time allocated to these last two subjects. Most students take classes in these four major academic areas beyond the minimum requirements, sometimes in such special areas as journalism and "yearbook," offshoots of English departments.[5]

Press most adults about what high school is for, and you hear these subjects listed. *High school? That's where you learn English and math and that sort of thing.* Ask students, and you get the same answer. High school is to "teach" these "subjects."

What is often absent is any definition of these subjects or any rationale for them. They are just there, labels. Under those labels lie a multitude of things. A great deal of material is supposed to be "covered"; most of these courses are surveys, great sweeps of the stuff of their parent disciplines.

While there is often a sequence *within* subjects—algebra before trigonometry, "first-year" French before "second-year" French—there is rarely a coherent relationship or sequence *across* subjects. Even the most logically related matters—reading ability as a precondition for the reading of history books, and certain mathematical concepts or skills before the study of some of physics—are only loosely coordinated, if at all. There is little demand for a synthesis of it all; English, mathematics, and the rest are discrete items, to be picked up individually. The incentive for picking them up is largely through tests and, with success at these, in credits earned.

Coverage within subjects is the key priority. If some imaginative teacher makes a proposal to force the marriage of, say, mathematics and physics or to require some culminating challenges to students to use several subjects in the solution of a complex problem, and if this proposal will take "time" away from other things, opposition is usually phrased in terms of what may be thus forgone. If we do that, we'll have to give up colonial history. We won't be able to get to programming. We'll not be able to read *Death of a Salesman*. There isn't time. The protesters usually win out.

The subjects come at a student like Mark in random order, a kaleidoscope of worlds: algebraic formulae to poetry to French verbs to Ping-Pong to the War of the Spanish Succession, all before lunch. Pupils are to pick up these things. Tests measure whether the picking up has been successful.

The lack of connection between stated goals, such as those of the California high school cited earlier, and the goals inherent in school practice is obvious and, curiously, tolerated. Most striking is the gap between statements about "self-realization and mental and physical growth" or "moral and ethical values"—common rhetoric in school documents—a practice. Most physical education programs have neither the time nor the focus really to ensure fitness. Mental health is rarely defined. Neither are ethical values, save at the negative extremes, such as opposition to assault or dishonesty. Nothing in the regimen of a day like Mark's signals direct or implicit teaching in this area. The "schoolboy code" (not ratting on a fellow student) protects the marijuana pusher, and a leechlike associate is shrugged off without concern. The issue of the locker search was pushed aside, as not appropriate for class time.

Most students, like Mark, go to class in groups of twenty to twenty-seven students. The expected attendance in stone schools, particularly those in low-income areas, is usually higher, often thirty-five students per class, but high absentee rates push the actual numbers down. About twenty-five per class is an average figure for expected attendance, and the actual numbers are somewhat lower. There are remarkably few students who go to class in groups much larger or smaller than twenty-five.[6]

A student such as Mark sees five or six teachers per day; their differing styles and expectations are part of his kaleidoscope. High school staffs are highly specialized: guidance counselors rarely teach mathematics, mathematics teachers rarely teach English, principals rarely do any classroom instruction. Mark, then, is known a little bit by a number of people, each of whom sees him in one specialized situation. No one may know him as a "whole person"—unless he becomes a special problem or has special needs.

Save in extracurricular or coaching situations, such as in athletics, drama, or shop classes, there is little opportunity for sustained conversation between student and teacher. The mode is a one-sentence or two-sentence exchange: *Mark, when was Grover Cleveland president? Let's see, was 1890 . . . or something . . . wasn't he the one . . . he was elected twice, wasn't he? . . . Yes . . . Gloria, can you get the dates right?* Dialogue is strikingly absent, and as a result the opportunity of teachers to challenge students' ideas in a systematic and logical way is limited. Given the rushed, full quality of the school day, it can seldom happen. One must infer that careful probing of students' thinking is not a high priority. How one gains (to quote the California school's statement of goals again) "the ability to make decisions, to solve problems, to reason independently, and to accept responsibility for self-evaluation and continuing self-improvement" without being challenged is difficult to imagine. One certainly doesn't learn these things merely from lectures and textbooks.

Most schools are nice places. Mark and his friends enjoy being in theirs. The adults who work in schools generally like adolescents. The academic pressures are limited, and the accommodations to students are substantial. For example, if many members of an English class have jobs after school, the English teacher's expectations for them are adjusted, downward. In a word, school is sensitively accommodating, as long as students are punctual, where they are supposed to be, and minimally dutiful about picking things up from the clutch of courses in which they enroll.

This characterization is not pretty, but it is accurate, and it serves to describe the vast majority of American secondary schools. "Taking subjects" in a systematized, conveyer-belt way is what one does in high school. That this process is, in substantial respects, not related to the rhetorical purposes of education is tolerated by most people, perhaps because they do not really either believe in those ill-defined goals or, in their heart of hearts, believe that schools can or should even try to achieve them. The students are happy taking subjects. The parents are happy, because that's what they did in high school. The rituals, the most important of which is graduation, remain intact. The adolescents are supervised, safely and constructively most of the time, during the morning and afternoon hours, and they are off the labor market. That is what high school is all about.

Endnotes

1. Shasta High School, Redding, California. An eloquent and analogous statement, "The Essentials of Education," one stressing explicitly the "interdependence of skills and content" that is implicit in the Shasta High School statement, was issued in 1980 by a coalition of education associations. Organizations for the Essentials of Education (Urbana, Illinois).

2. Judge Arthur M. Recht, in his order resulting from *Pauley v. Kelly*, 1979, as reprinted in *Education Week*, May 26, 1982, p. 10. See also, in *Education Week*, January 16, 1983, pp. 21, 24, Jonathan P. Sher, "The Struggle to Fulfill at Judicial Mandate: How Not to 'Reconstruct' Education in W. Va."

3. Bureau of Education, Department of the Interior, "Cardinal Principles of Secondary Education: A Report of the Commission on the Reorganization of Secondary Education, appointed by the National Education Association," *Bulletin*, no. 35 (Washington: U.S. Government Printing Office, 1918).

4. Diane Hedin, Paula Simon, and Michael Robin, *Minnesota Youth Poll: Youth's Views on School and School Discipline*, Minnesota Report 184 (1983), Agricultural Experiment Station, University of Minnesota, p. 13.

5. I am indebted to Harold F. Sizer and Lyde E. Sizer for a survey of the diploma requirements of fifty representative secondary school, completed for A Study of High Schools.

6. Education Research Service, Inc. *Class Size: A Summary of Research* (Arlington, Virginia, 1978); and *Class Size Research: A Critique of Recent Meta-Analyses* (Arlington, Virginia, 1980).

The Shopping Mall High School

Arthur G. Powell, Eleanor Farrar, and David K. Cohen _____

The following selection is a chapter from the book *The Shopping Mall High School: Winners and Losers in the Educational Marketplace* by Arthur G. Powell, Eleanor Farrar, and David K. Cohen. In the introduction to their book, they state that "the argument of *The Shopping Mall High School* was develop jointly by the authors during three years spent visiting fifteen schools and analyzing field notes made on interviews and classroom observations." This book, published in 1985, is the Second Report from A Study of High Schools, co-sponsored by the National Association of Secondary School Principals and the Commission on Educational Issues of the National Association of Independence Schools.

If Americans want to understand their high schools at work, they should imagine them as shopping malls. Secondary education is another consumption experience in an abundant society. Shopping malls attract a broad range of customers with different tastes and purposes. Some shop at Sears, others at Woolworth's or Bloomingdale's. In high schools a broad range of students also shop. They too can select from an astonishing variety of products and services conveniently assembled in one place with ample parking. Furthermore, in malls and schools many different kinds of transactions are possible. Both institutions bring hopeful purveyors and potential purchasers together. The former hope to maximize sales but can take nothing for granted. Shoppers have wide discretion not only about what to buy but also about whether to buy.

Some shoppers know just what they want and efficiently make their purchases. Others come simply to browse. Still others do neither; they just hang out. The mall and the school are places to meet friends, pass the time, get out of the rain, or watch the promenade. Shopping

Excerpts from THE SHOPPING MALL HIGH SCHOOL. Copyright © 1985 by Arthur G. Powell, Eleanor Farrar and David K. Cohen. Reprinted by permission of Houghton Mifflin Co. All rights reserved.

malls or their high school equivalents can be entertaining places to onlookers with no intention of buying anything. Yet not everyone goes to the mall. Unenticed by its shops or its scene, some pass the time elsewhere.

Many contemporary high schools even look like shopping malls. Blessed by a favorable climate, one is a complex of attached single-story buildings whose classrooms open to the outdoors rather than to locker-lined corridors. Between periods students go outside to find their next destination, entering and leaving classrooms as if they were adjacent stores. Another school appears massive and mysterious from the outside, but its architecture looks inward: everything radiates from a lively covered promenade. This mall, in a less forgiving climate, is appropriately enclosed.[1]

It is not surprising, then, that teachers often regard themselves as salespeople. Their business is to attract customers and persuade them to buy. Marketing skills are important; teachers become educational pitchmen. Recognizing that necessity, one teacher lamented, "It would be nice to believe we had a culture that so endorsed the products we have to sell that we don't have to do that." But lacking cultural endorsement, many strive to "build up a constituency" of buyers. They recruit through the reputations they establish and speak of how teaching is "perceived as an art of capturing audiences and entertaining them." Sometimes marketing is directly encouraged by the school, as in the case of one that gives an entire day to a series of faculty commercials for what they hope to teach the forthcoming year. The supply of particular subjects flows directly from student demand. An angry math teacher remembered the elimination of a carefully planned program in technical mathematics for vocational students simply because not enough signed up for it. It is easy to see who really makes decisions about what schools teach: "The kids do."

Not only do teachers compete with one another for the business of students, they also are acutely aware of external competition. Students who always browse but never buy and students who avoid the mall whenever possible are a lost market. A common complaint is that high schools have lost some of their competitive edge for students' time and attention. "School has ceased to be the focus of their lives," teachers often say of students. They have other things to do. Part-time employment, in particular, enables students to work in malls and purchase the goods sold there. Scheduling afternoon classes is often difficult. "A lot of our kids," an administrator explained, "really have no reason to work other than that they just want a car, or they want something special." They insist on attending school only half a day. "They look at you and demand that you approve their half-day schedule." Such students often regard high school, not paid employment, as their real part-time job. "When I have nights off, I study," said one boy who worked twenty hours a week.

Shopkeepers in malls try to coax voluntary attendance through collective efforts that combine convenience and entertainment. Despite competition among themselves, their common goal is to attract people to the mall. Celebrity appearances, live concerts, and food service are only a few of their common strategies. A passive browser may one day become a willing buyer, but no one can even browse if he or she is not drawn to the mall in the first place. So, too, the shopping mall high school is committed to luring and holding the largest possible crowd. Today's casual browser is tomorrow's educational consumer. Compulsory attendance laws, which generally reach only to age sixteen and can be easily subverted through chronic or selective absenteeism, do not guarantee a captive, much less an attentive, audience. Like shopping malls, high schools of necessity offer more than a collection of stores.

One girl gratefully contrasted her school with a local parochial school where "there's nothing to do . . . except go to classes all day long." Browsers like her are drawn to school for social reasons. "I like to come to school because my friends are here," another admitted, "but otherwise than that I don't have any reason," Since "everyone else is in school . . . there's no one to be with" if you stay away. Because their peers are present, teenagers sometimes view high school as "one big party" or a "fun place" where "there is not always reading and writing." Alienated from the educational offerings of his institution, a boy nonetheless emphasized that "school is where it's at. When you put a lot of people in one place, something's bound to happen every day, Right? You can count on having a joint." An exasperated counselor agreed there were "kids who come only to play in our sandbox. They bring a bucket and a shovel and play hour after hour and do nothing. They skip class, . . . go to the bathroom, and stay there."

But complaints about the "big babysitting service" provided by high schools are infrequent. Most educators are resigned to a long-term marketing strategy that helps explain the sandbox approach. School professionals grudgingly tolerate such uses of high schools for the same reasons that mall shopkeepers spend money on live entertainment: no good purpose is served if potential customers stay away. "The kid who just stays in school for seat time," one principal said, "will eventually convert it to learning time; so . . . our philosophy here is to first get students to come . . . Ultimately, what we hope is that while they're in school some of the things that the school has to offer will begin to interest them and involve them, so that they will not only be in school for seat time but will be really learning."

Most educators are proud of the mall-like features of high schools. "The nice thing about [our] school," a teacher explained, "is that students can do their own thing. They can be involved in music, fine arts, athletics, sitting out on the south lawn—and nobody puts them down for it." Here three crucial institutional features are nicely summarized. Schools offer a wide *variety* of consumer opportunities, from curricular opportunities like fine arts to extracurricular opportunities like sports and noncurricular opportunities like hanging out. Schools place *choice* clearly in the hands of the consumer. Students can do their own thing. In general, the customer is always right. Finally, the institution is largely *neutral* about the choices students make. Adults are unlikely to put them down for their decisions.

But why are these features "really something that helps this school be what it is"? Why is the mall a triumph? Part of the answer, the teacher said, was that the features helped "overcome a lot of the problems that high schools today are going through." The mall is a solution, but what were the problems? The teacher concluded that "there are all different kinds of kids" in the school. Everything follows from that. Variety of opportunities, choice among them, and neutrality about choices are all accommodations made by the school to an inclusive and diversified student body. They are intimately related adaptations, successful ones in the teacher's judgment, essential ones in any case. A deeper look at these central features is necessary for understanding the logic of the shopping mall high school and for judging its results.

The Vertical Curriculum

Shopping malls sell not only different products—color televisions and blue jeans, for instance—but also different kinds of TV sets and jeans, with different features and price tags. There is almost as much variety within product categories as there are products. Malls themselves differ from each other not by product categories alone but by the styles and prices of what is sold. There are "upscale" malls for more affluent tastes. In a similar way, high school goods with apparently generic labels—introductory algebra, American history, junior English—are available in different versions within the same school. Each version has distinct features designed to appeal to a particular set of consumer tastes, formed by previous education, ability, motivation, family background, peer pressure, and the blandishments of the purveyors. There are upscale high schools, too.

Not all courses are available in different versions, but most of those that generate large enrollments and require some cognitive dexterity are offered in a vertical curriculum complementing the horizontal. This greatly enhances variety. The vertical curriculum is usually described by "levels"; the word "track" is not fashionable in the 1980s. The names and numbers of levels within a subject vary according to local traditions. Some schools speak of honors, college-preparatory, general, and basic levels. Others use words such as accelerated and regular, and still others employ a letter designation or Arabic or Roman numerals.

Whatever system of product labeling is used, the main purpose is to disclose in advance to prospective consumers the degree of difficulty in courses with similar titles. This is a more subtle undertaking than differentiating between kinds of products—between, say, Child and Family and Advanced Physics—and catalogs therefore often expend considerable effort in making the differences clear. At times the advertising campaign is remarkably candid. Students in one school were told they should elect one level of sophomore English if they were "willing and able to read two or three books a term and to write about experience or books once a week." Another level was appropriate "if you read and write only when you have to," while a third made sense for those who had trouble with reading and writing. At this level, "most of the reading and writing assignments can be completed during class time."

An important function of such candor is to minimize consumer complaints by clarifying in advance the expectations and responsibilities. When courses at various levels have the same name, the descriptions make clear that what is offered and what is expected vary enormously from one course to another. In general, the vertical curriculum is not an instrument to achieve similar ends by different means. Levels usually embody different notions of proficiency and of what a subject is, rather than the notion of different roads to a common destination. One level of junior English often resembles another no more than Child and Family resembles Advanced Physics.[2]

Variety within the vertical curriculum is further enhanced because even courses at the same level are frequently taught by different teachers with considerable freedom to shape their classes as they choose. Students everywhere understand that the experience of a course depends as much (if not more) on who the teacher is as it does on the catalog description. Consumerism allows students in some schools to select teachers as well as courses. Even at the Advanced Placement level, where a common national examination supposedly enforces a common standard, students and their parents understand that dramatic differences exist among teachers and therefore among courses.

In an AP science course, for example, students knew that two teachers brought contrasting philosophies and personalities to the same subject. One version emphasized theory and was designed for prospective scientists; the instructor, like Dr. McBride, was brusque and sarcastic. The other version was more relaxed, proceeded at a slower pace, and had a more hands-on approach and a more nurturing instructor; it was not designed for the budding scientist despite its AP status. Each teacher had defenders and detractors. But in the opinion of students and parents, variety should properly extend this far. "You can't blame them for looking," one satisfied parent commented on the consumerism of his children. An experienced administrator remarked, "There's more feeling now that I don't need to have *you* as a teacher. I can get somebody else."

Junior English as a label masks an extraordinary range of intentions, materials, and methods. Consider three classes; all met the junior English graduation requirement. Applied Communication met the junior English requirement in one school at the level of least difficulty. The class gathered in an attractive theater where attendance ranged from thirty to forty on any given day. Mr. Lynch stood on stage, lecturing and asking questions about comic books as a literary form. Armed with a theatrical flair and considerable knowledge of the history of comics, he held the attention of most students throughout the period.

He began by reviewing the link between comics and the broader themes of the course. "Remember, the function of this is to see how the plot relates to literature. Does anyone know what 'plot' is?" After several seconds of silence, he continued, "A plot is the action of a story—the action that takes place. That's very important." He described two other literary concepts that could be found in comics: "character—people in it" and "setting—time and place, when it takes place and where it takes place." Gradually he increased the complexity of his talk. He reviewed the "three purposes of comics," emphasizing in particular that comics reflected the times in which they were written.

Midway through the period Mr. Lynch changed his approach. He projected on a screen the earliest depictions of Superman. "Superman is one of the most important characters . . . I'd like you to remember Siegel and Shuster." When he asked about Superman's abilities, there was far more response than before. "Faster than a speeding bullet," one student called out. Another asked, "Do we still have to take notes?" "No," Mr. Lynch replied, "this is for your own education . . . This is going to take me about fifteen minutes. Just sit back and enjoy."

The class became pure entertainment. As various Superman strips were projected, Lynch spoke the dialogue with dramatic skill, altering voices according to character. From time to time students shouted out their reactions: "Check out his hair already!" When a response took the form of a question—"Are these the same people writing the comics?"—he swiftly followed it up: "No, let's take some time to talk about this." To reinforce his point, he told the story of how Siegel and Shuster gave up their rights to Superman for one hundred dollars.

Two days later Batman and Robin were the subjects of his scrutiny. Again Mr. Lynch made interesting historical asides about the characters—for instance, he mentioned the controversy over whether their relationship was homosexual—and connected these facts to the idea of plot. Batman could not carry a gun because he could not be placed in a position to kill off central characters, like Joker. Villains needed to live to continue the story line. In this class Mr. Lynch also announced the main writing project for the term. Each student (or pair: two could work together) would create an eight-page comic book. Two pages had to be ads; one had to contain letters to the editor. They would be given seven full classroom periods to execute the project, and he emphasized their obligation to use this time well. "You need to take responsibility," he said. Writing the comic strip was really like writing a short story.

Mr. Lynch knew that the goods available in his class were a far cry from what most people, including himself, imagined junior English to be. Variety in the vertical curriculum allowed for a primary focus on entertainment. Because the content was something that students might relate to, he hoped they would attend, be orderly, and perhaps learn something about plot, character, and setting. Everybody knew the course was a dumping ground for the unproficient and uncommitted. He expected few to buy, and only hoped enough would remain to browse. There were no illusions about product quality in Applied Communication.

Contrast that course with a middle-level or "regular" version of junior English. Unlike Applied Communication, this class was designed as college preparation, and most of the students planned to attend four-year colleges. Mrs. Austin greeted the seventeen students with jokes and puns as they trooped boisterously into her room. She promptly announced that there were two activities on the day's agenda. They would read favorite passages from *The Catcher in the Rye* to each other—selecting the passages had been the homework assignment—and they would play a quiz game.

After everyone's book had been opened to the correct place, a girl read haltingly for a minute. "What does he mean by that last couple of lines?" the teacher probed at the end. The student countered, "Can't I tell you why I like it?" "Oh yes," Mrs. Austin said, "tell us why you like the last part." "The reason is because he finally admits that he likes everybody," "That's right. Who else has a favorite passage?" No one volunteered, so Mrs. Austin read for four minutes in a style nicely expressive of Holden Caulfield's adolescent sarcasm. Everyone listened with evident amusement and many laughed from time to time.

Mrs. Austin liked her own passage because it was humorous and reminded her of contrived, silly movies. The best part was "where he's talking about the lady that cries in the movie but won't take her son to the bathroom. What kind of thing do you think he's trying to get at in real life?" After a long silence she continued, "Psychiatrists are saying now—I've heard it someplace—that people who spend an inordinate amount of time watching soap operas, for example, and living the lives of characters, are often themselves not very humane to other people. They lead a false kind of life, so they can't really feel sympathetic or empathetic with real people. There might be a grain of truth in that, who knows?" Then she asked for more volunteers.

None of the three other students who read aloud remembered to tell why he or she liked the passage chosen, and none was asked to do so. At the beginning of each reading, everyone's visual attention was fixed on the speaker, but during the readings attention noticeably waned. One student surreptitiously opened a package of Fritos and munched away; another nonchalantly combed her hair. Some stared out of the window and a few initiated whispered conversations. Basic order was never lost, though. There were no reprimands or calls for silence. Mrs. Austin later said that she hadn't had a discipline problem in years.

Then the quiz game began. The class split into two teams, with the boys at one side of the room and the girls on the other. The point was for the girls to answer written questions posed by the boys, and vice versa. The questions had been prepared ahead of time as part of a homework assignment. A correct answer earned a team one point; talking among team members gave two points to the team's opponents. The game served as a relaxed review for an upcoming test.

Virtually all of the questions called for the recall of minute plot details. What was the name of the elevator operator? What title did Holden hold on the fencing team? What was the name of Holden's mistress? As the game progressed the noise level grew. Team members talked to one another—more points were accumulated this way than through correct answers—and friendly banter shot back and forth. One boy yelled, "I can't remember, but give me a point anyway." Everyone laughed at that, including the teacher. When another boy protested that the girls would win "'cause these guys never even read the book," everyone laughed again. When a girl paused a moment before answering, a boy called out, "Hey! Come on!" "Shut up, I'm trying," she yelled back. "Now, now," interrupted Mrs. Austin, suddenly the domestic peacemaker, "no fighting until you get married." A roar of knowing laughter rocked the room.

After class she emphasized the importance of choosing books "that I know they're going to like." Extensive experience with the regular level, at which she much preferred to teach, was that "the pie-in-the-sky *Scarlet Letter* and that type of thing" would just not work. She had assigned it anyway because it was a classic and this was a college-prep class. The students didn't like it but at least they were good sports; "I didn't like it either," she said. *Catcher* was far more congenial to both sides. "We get into the fact that even though it was written thirty or forty years ago, that it is still universal, that it has a lot of truths for today's living." That was her goal. "I tell my students that in reading they learn a lot about themselves. And about others. Even though it's fiction."

This class was a more familiar version of junior English. Students read an acknowledged high school classic, were assigned homework, and discussed the book. Unlike the Applied Communication class, where everyone understood that something other than English was being offered, Mrs. Austin's class had an unmistakable product. But the goods were bogus. Illusions abounded in this middle-level college-prep course. Mrs. Austin did not push her students or herself. She settled for poor reading or no reading; no examination of why passages were chosen; brief answers to trivial questions; and an environment nearly as relaxed and entertaining as that of the other class. Yet she clearly "covered" reputable material. The class was about junior English without taking it seriously. Here was another kind of product available and consumed in the shopping mall high school.

Contrast that product with another level of junior English. Ms. Fish sat in a circle with twenty-one advanced students. The work under scrutiny was Ibsen's play *A Doll's House,* and, as in the other class, students had generated a list of questions. Ms. Fish had duplicated the questions and handed out copies. Her plan was to break the class into small groups to consider some of the questions, and later reconvene to make summary reports. But protests ensued. "We want to hear *everyone's* reaction," one student said. A unanimous student vote confirmed this preference and the lesson plan was discarded.

The first question was whether it was fair to force particular values, such as religious ones, on a child too young to know whether he or she in fact preferred them. Immediately the discussion became animated; six students volunteered responses from personal experience within five minutes. Suddenly Ms. Fish cut the discussion off, skipped over several questions, and finally settled on one farther down. Was it right for Nora to have left her family? After class she explained that her intention at this point in the period was to move the discussion into the play rather than staying with personal experiences. The students were charming talkers, and the danger of neglecting the play was always present.

"No," replied a girl whom Ms. Fish called on, "it was another childish thing to do." From this point on, student comments, which had previously been directed to Ms. Fish, were directed mainly to each other. They began to argue about a highly charged issue: under what circumstances can a parent responsibly abandon a family in order to grow into a more independent person? Some vehemently disagreed with the first speaker. In the family, Nora "never had a chance to be independent." Her withdrawal was not selfish; she merely realized her inadequacies and was attempting to deal with them. Besides, another pointed out, she rarely saw her children even when she was in the family. Such thinking, the first girl rejoined, smacked of the "me-first" mentality of today's generation. Nora was saying that her needs were greater than the responsibilities she had accumulated. "It's childish to say that she's not an ideal mother so let's scrap the whole relationship."

Ms. Fish participated in the debate in two ways. She tried to ensure that a maximum number of students spoke: "Give John a chance and then Blair, who has been extraordinarily patient." And she intervened when necessary, as she later put it, "to get them into the experience of the play and away from intellectualizing." Intellectualizing, like talking only about personal experiences, was a way to evade the play. She explained that there were students who liked to talk but would only talk about the play as a disembodied historical artifact; they would mention, for example, that it had shocked its own generation. When one boy spoke this way, Ms. Fish pressed for a personal reaction to the play itself. "What do you think of this? Do you think Nora ought to have left the family?" "It's heavy." "But what do you personally think?" "She had to leave. Torvald wouldn't have changed. She couldn't have changed had she stayed there." Ms. Fish confronted the initial speaker the same way. "What if she can't change? . . . I'm trying to get you to answer a question you don't want to answer." The girl replied, "I don't disagree with her leaving. I just disagree with her doing it that way." At the end of the hour, a boy said, "Torvald has treated her as something to have around the house—a garnishment." Cheers and laughter followed. "A vocabulary word!" someone shouted in delight.

Afterward Ms. Fish said she was relieved at the openness with which a tough issue had been discussed. She planned to assign Alice Walker's *Meridian* next. This book, about a black woman growing up in the South, was filled with complex racial and sexual issues. Now she thought the students had sufficient sensitivity to begin the task.

The product Ms. Fish offered was more than coverage. By ceaseless questioning, she attempted to engage students in the material. She wouldn't let them alone. Her class was more exhausting than relaxing. Variety within the vertical curriculum thus takes many forms. Students, teachers, and materials can differ profoundly in their conception of junior English. What linked these otherwise different classes was the consumerism they embodied. Each teacher was intent on—and successful at—satisfying the demands of very different consumer tastes. They were all proud of their popularity and pleased by a system that allowed them to teach in a manner that was as comfortable to them as it was congenial to their students.

The Extracurriculum

No high school phrase is more misleading than "extracurricular activities." There is nothing extra about the extracurriculum, whether schools are rich or poor, public or private, large or small. Most teachers and students regard the extracurriculum as constructively educational. It supplements the rest of the curriculum and lures many students and teachers even when academic credit is not given. It is as integral to high schools as food service and celebrity appearances are integral to shopping malls.

Sports are the most visible part of the extracurriculum. Whatever external uses they may have in stimulating community support or providing public entertainment, their internal educational function is widely acknowledged. Curiously, they have supplied the most powerful pedagogical metaphor in recent educational discussion—"coaching"—to reformers with intellectual rather than athletic objectives. And they are defended on educational grounds that extol their usefulness in vocational preparation and in teaching cooperation and personal self-esteem.

One boy assumed as a matter of course that high school should provide vocational education in sports as well as in other fields. "My athletics have really suffered," he lamented, although he found nothing wrong with his school's academic program. There were "a lot of things that I haven't learned that these coaches should have taught me." They "haven't really prepared me for college ball." His sympathetic coaches agreed that the school had not invested sufficiently in equipment, facilities, and qualified instructors. The education of many youngsters had therefore been shortchanged. They thought the problem was not that sports were unimportant in their school, but rather that they were viewed less as a route to college scholarships or eventual jobs and more as a route to developing self-esteem. Achieving the latter goal required little more than the fielding of teams.

The extracurriculum, whether it is sports or some other activity, usually gets better reviews. Andy, for example, freely admitted he was overextended in extracurricular activities. "Really, I'm amazed I make it. But that's one of the reasons I enjoy school that much, because I have something to come to other than the note-taking. Like I say, it's a whole learning experience if you can use that to your advantage."

As a student council member, a position that carried course credit, Andy could try to implement some of his ideas. The council's theme for the year was "Dare!" To Andy this meant "daring for people to attend sports events, and to just become involved." He didn't want teenagers to be able to say at the end of high school, "Hey, the school didn't do anything for me. It just made me sit in the classroom and take notes." He wanted instead "to make school a place where you're not restricted to book-learning, but life-learning." He would only be satisfied when more students came to high school with the attitude that "you're going to experience so many things that you're going to come out ahead either way it goes, even if you don't take classes or something you need for college." They had to understand that education was more than academics.

Besides the Dare program Andy spent time on a council effort to prepare eighth-graders for entry into high school, founded a youth and government club, and gave presentations to student groups on topics ranging from birth control to values clarification. He did gymnastics, cross-country, and track, and he numbered Advanced Dance and Public Speaking among his favorite courses. He knew his way around the extracurriculum sufficiently well to know that for him, as a black, gaining access to traditionally white enclaves like the student newspaper was too complicated to be worth the trouble. He was proud that various teachers had told him he had a serious future in politics.

Andy's savvy in using the extracurriculum did not carry over to the horizontal or vertical curricula. He regarded these as peripheral to his high school education. Although he fully expected to go on to college, he was taking introductory algebra as a senior. If he failed the course, he reasoned, he would simply repeat it in college. He had had an unpleasant conflict with his junior English teacher and claimed that he had been prevented from taking biology until the end of high school because years earlier the school had misread his reading scores. To no avail he had attempted to take an advanced-level course. This astute young man, who had used one part of the school to his constructive advantage, was at sea in negotiating access to the academic curriculum: "Me on my own, I can't do it." His energies remained in the extracurriculum, where he felt in charge.

Brad also loved high school. "I think I look forward more to school than anything else. It puts order in my life, which I need." High school was his world, and increasingly he found that the best part was the extracurriculum. As a freshman he had dreamed of becoming a veterinarian, but quickly learned that neither math nor chemistry was his strong suit. What he was good at was politics and public speaking. "I just love to speak in front of people," he said excitedly. "It gets me all pumped up inside. It's a great feeling."

Admittedly behind in several academic subjects, he had made deliberate decisions about where to allocate his considerable energy. Student council was his biggest arena; he had ambitions for a major elective office the next year. "The purpose of the student council is to teach you how to be a leader." He was also active in school plays, and a member of the soccer team. He saw all these things in part as vocational education: "I am looking for a career in political science or politics. I'm not going to look in math." But he saw in them a liberal education as well: "I have to be a human being, and I have to be a compassionate human being. If I spend all my time wrapped up in books, maybe I won't take time enough for what goes on around our world. That's what I'm starting to learn from [high school]. That's what I really truly appreciate." Like Andy, Brad appreciated his school's willingness to give him room to find his way. "Of course," he admitted, high school "can't accommodate everybody. It can't look after everybody in the way they want to be looked after," But his school came pretty close to saying "if you want to do this, we are here. We'll back you up." Brad believed "people have chances here."

High schools are proud of their Andys and Brads, solid citizens despite their distance from the academic curriculum. They are institutional success stories. The goods they have purchased are decency and direction, and for the schools that is more than enough. Schools often permit such youngsters to gain substantial graduation credit for their various activities. Student council, the newspaper, the yearbook, the magazine, the debate club, are all usually credit offerings. One school allows students to take up to 36 percent of their credits during grades ten through twelve in Marching and Concert Band. Several others *require* students participating in these activities to take connected courses for credit.

But the penetration of the extracurriculum into the credit curriculum sometimes meets the preferences of those who, unlike Brad and Andy, simply want the easiest path to graduation. One such student, Beth, reduced the number of truly extracurricular activities she engaged in and incorporated them when possible into her regular credit program. By the time she was a senior, her main after-school activity was "to go home and be bored. Because there's nothing to do here and it's more comfortable to sit around at home or talk on the phone." Brad believed that high school gave students chances; Beth wanted only the chance to graduate, and was sure the school would accommodate her wish.

Performance Expectations

Shopping mall high schools are especially neutral about performance expectations for students. Mrs. Jefferson, for example, would not demand minimum mastery of Child and Family as a condition for passing the course: "I feel it's very unfair if a child comes and really puts forth an effort and is doing his very best and is there every day trying, and yet you defeat him with an F." Failure and defeat were inextricably linked. Despite her genuine commitment to the value of what she taught, the psychological ideal of feeling successful took precedence in her class over learning a crucial life skill. "I am going to do, what I can to enhance his self-image and to make him think that the world is good." (Perhaps she was remembering the student who was sure it was not.) "I'm not going to give him F's just because he's not capable of doing what the average student in the room is doing."

Her feelings were shared by most teachers regardless of subject, level, or geographical region. In the shopping mall high school, failure comes from not attending or not behaving. Performance is remarkably irrelevant. Poor performance in fact is sometimes accompanied by acceptable and even honors grades. A teacher of advanced math thought the only way to fail was "not come . . . The kids really have to fail themselves." Those who could not handle the work were simply put in a lower level. Once there, they were graded "almost solely on attitude. If a student comes and has tried his hardest, he will get a B." Dr. McBride said it took far more work for his advanced students to fail than to pass. They had to try to fail, "do it actively." He considered C a "pejorative" mark in the high-level classes, and would give everyone who did decent work an A or a B. Both were officially regarded as honors grades. Another physics teacher explained, "I'm an easy grader. It's hard to get kids into physics in the first place, and I don't want to destroy their GPAs, so I think that a youngster in that class should have no trouble getting a B." High grades were part of his advertising campaign to lure customers. A social studies teacher said that "a kid who's given his best shot" could never do worse than a C, although students who never showed up could fail. After all, agreed a Spanish teacher, "you have to look at kids now from all angles. You can't just look at their performance in Spanish." A girl in her Advanced Placement class was "really not very good at all" in the language. "But she tries very, very hard, and she always attends, and it makes you feel very sorry for her. So she'll get a B or a B minus."

Well aware that passing her course was a diploma requirement, an American history teacher reasoned that "you can't penalize the kids just because we don't have a place to put them." She coped by careful test design. Even though she usually included a little essay question, she made sure "that the kids can pass just by answering the objective portion—pass with a C usually." She did this because many of her students could not write a paragraph. For similar reasons she excluded questions requiring critical thinking in her regular (that is, college-preparatory) classes: "Two thirds of your kids are not able to do that work." Instead, she used questions that "depend primarily on recognition and recall." When asked how her students would ever learn critical thinking, she answered confidently, "The average student never learns it." Bright students learned it intuitively. Others learned it at home. She was "not sure the schools provide it" to anybody.

Students know they will pass in return for orderly attendance because teachers tell them so. There are no covert arrangements here. One group recalled how their history teacher had said the first day of class, "You give me thirty-five minutes [per day in class] and show me you're working and you'll pass the course." Another group remembered that the first words spoken by their eminent English teacher were, "You can just sit there and you'll pass with a D minus." They explained matter-of-factly that "she focuses just on the few who care . . . She doesn't care about the other kids in the class." This seemed to make perfect sense to the students. "I get a lot out of it if I'm prepared," one concluded.

Of course not all teachers accommodate student diversity in this way. "I tell them point-blankly," one dissenter reported, "'You will pass my final in order to pass my course.' I think I'm one of the few who does it." She thought their reaction confirmed the rarity of her action. "You would think I told them to rape their mother at high noon in the town square." Such behavior seemed rigid and insensitive to many colleagues as well. An administrator explained that "teachers today are more humanistic in their approach with kids . . . A lot of them don't have an ironclad set of standards on achievement. It used to be that if you got sixty percent on a test you were all right, but if you got fifty-nine you were finished." But now they realized that "more and more kids have personal problems, more and more kids have twenty things to deal with as well as school, and they'll take that into account."

Even when students volunteer neither order nor attendance, schools go to enormous lengths to make passing possible. "Most teachers give them a way out," one confided, "or else the system gives them a way out . . . They can go to summer school, they can make up their work, they can take a correspondence course. Miraculously they pass and weasel out." Teachers often don't enforce policies that make failure automatic after a certain number of absences. "I talk to the kid. I tell him, 'If you find the course so distasteful, drop it and take something else.'" At least one school offered a Pass/No Credit course where failure was theoretically impossible.

The shopping mall high school is thus profoundly neutral about mastery. No one opposes it, but few require or expect it. Of course many schools mandate a minimum competency test of some sort as a graduation hurdle. But these test basic skills that have traditionally been the purview of elementary education, are usually first made available to students near the beginning of their high school careers, and are rarely connected to the regular curriculum. Further, there are ways to adjust the competency tests so that everyone may pass. One special-needs teacher pointed out that if a student could not pass the reading test, she could decide what would be appropriate competency for that student: "If I said this student will spell 'cat' by June, and he did, then that student will pass his competency." The regular competency examination was somewhere "between a fifth- and a seventh-grade level. The general public isn't aware of that, and so they assume they're doing twelfth-grade work, and they're not."

Separating passing from even minimal notions of mastery has the effect of making the high school diploma little more than an emblem of good behavior. Despite considerable criticism of this situation by reformers outside the schools and by some professionals in the schools, most schoolpeople do not regard it as scandalous at all. They do not regard the high school experience as exclusively about mastery of the formal curriculum. The centrality of variety, choice, and neutrality in the mall is not seen by insiders as a cop-out, a conspiracy to expect the least. They regard these features, instead, as enabling high schools to meet as many adolescent needs as possible.

Perhaps the need that best explains the commitment to passing is the need to avoid failure. "Failure" in this sense is rarely defined diagnostically, that is, as evidence of some important deficiency whose remediation is at the heart of educational purpose. Failing is never seen in such positive terms. "I believe," one teacher said passionately, "if a kid has done all he can and you fail him, I think you've done him an injustice. He'll feel like he's a nobody. So if he tries, he'll pass my class. A lot of people say kids need to know there are failures in lifetimes, but they're not going to have to spend their lifetime going to school."

Failure is anathema because success—*feeling* success—is so deeply cherished as both a goal and a means to other goals. Many teachers seem preoccupied by the psychological costs of failure and the therapeutic benefits of success. That was what one teacher was talking about when she said, "If you don't get it done, you don't fail. You don't get credit, but you don't experience failure." "The most important thing to me is to make them feel they are human beings, that they are worthwhile," another teacher emphasized. Still another's primary goals were to "build confidence, to build trust . . . I try to affirm them as people." A math teacher prescribed "a daily dose of self-respect." And a social studies teacher explained why he didn't stress thinking skills: "I just encourage them to make the most of their ability to have pride in themselves." In all these instances, the need for students to feel success is disconnected from the idea of students mastering something taught. A wide gap separates the two notions. "Let's face it," a teacher said by way of partial explanation. "A kid could get through their life without having my course." Many teachers believe more in the value of self-esteem than in the value of what they teach. Mastery and success are like ships that pass in the night.

Therapeutic ideology is not the only reason why passing is mainly contingent on orderly attendance, but it is the most noble one. Some teachers also believe, for example, that attendance is more important than course content because it is a marketable skill. Students need to learn "to be on time at their job." Furthermore, these arrangements make life easier for teachers. The bargain is, after all, an attractive one for everyone. Alternatives might cause unwanted conflict. And teachers do not have to work as hard or be as competent if students can do well without learning much.

For teenagers to feel success, pass, and graduate, they must attend. Even in schools where truancy is not a significant dilemma, expensive computers and sophisticated monitoring systems keep track of where everyone is—sometimes before computers are seriously deployed for instructional purposes. "Holding" teenagers is a preoccupation. "They don't want to let anyone leave," a teacher remarked. "They want to bend over backwards to keep them."

The importance of holding students is most deeply felt where transiency is high and family income low. One thoughtful principal contrasted the safety and security of his building to "the street" where "gangs, organizations, prostitution, pimping, drug sales, house-breaking, and robbery" were routine occurrences. Families were simply "no longer there." His primary objective was for adolescents to "survive" better at the end of high school than at the beginning. Mastery in courses was a "secondary goal." After all, as one of his teachers put it, "if they come to class all the time, they must be learning something." Learning was never absent from this principal's mind. But it was a hope, not an expectation and certainly not a demand. High school in his community was a place of last resort, a haven in a heartless world.

Far away another principal agreed: "We're trying to keep kids inside who weren't all that turned on by being in school, so we come up with more programs." Only fifteen years earlier, he recalled, things were different. Then kids were belligerent and challenged authority. Getting rid of some was a survival tactic. Now "the war is over." Order prevailed, for at least a while. He said the current idea was to keep students in school, with the diploma within easy reach, because everyone understood that there was no better place for them to be. High school had become, as the century progressed, not a special place for those who cared about learning and the opportunities that it opened, but the *only* place for teenagers. "The thing I resent most," he complained, "is that society is saying it's our job." Parents would throw up their hands and say, "I can't do anything with the kid. It's your job. Don't call us. Don't bother us."

It was true, he admitted, that in a time of declining enrollments more students meant more dollars for his school. There was "pressure on teachers to maintain their numbers." A cynical colleague concluded, "They aren't trying to keep kids in school because it's good for them, They're trying to keep the kids in school because it keeps their enrollments up. If they don't have enough kids in those seats, it means they lose jobs." But such cynicism disguises the basic reality that the schools that do *not* face loss of population have the same commitment to holding teenagers as the schools that do.

If schools are now judged by their holding power, any attendance problem suggests institutional failure. "It's interesting how it works against you," the principal reflected. "You take a marginal student and do everything you can to encourage him to stay in school and don't drop out of school. 'We'll build you a program, we'll hand-pick your teachers.' So he reluctantly comes on board. And then he's showing up over here as an absenteeism, increasing your percentage of your absentee kids . . . The more you work trying to keep that marginal kid in, the more statistics can make you look somewhat embarrassed." For the marginal student, he speculated, "you could have taken a different tack and say, 'We agree with you.' " You don't have to come. But that approach ran counter to the prevailing wisdom. Suspending students for truancy, the school's attendance officer pointed out, was downright illogical. It would only bring about what the school was trying to avoid. "If you knew you only had to cut a few classes to be thrown out, and you didn't want to be there anyway, that would be the way to do it . . . The kids don't have to go if they don't want to, and there's no way for the school to enforce their attendance. Yet the school clearly feels they ought to be present."[5]

That is the puzzling dilemma. School and community alike assume that all teenagers should be in high school. High school attendance and graduation are nearly a social entitlement. They are things people take for granted. Perhaps the most valued product offered by high school, the diploma itself, is purchasable for the least effort. "We're successful," one teacher explained, "in that most of them stay in school. They get some minimum degree of skill development. They get a high school diploma. They seem generally happy. They have a lot of freedom moving around the building." These do not seem ambitious indices of success. Another teacher put the matter bluntly. "The problem is, we're trying to retain kids . . . We don't know what to do with these kids . . . Our society doesn't know what to do. The operant goal is to get people to graduate, and they can graduate if they are barely literate."

The neutrality criticized by this teacher captures the successes and problems of the shopping mall high school. In this consumer-oriented institution, students and teachers alike say with considerable truth that everything is there, everybody is there, and there is something for everyone. But it is there only if you want it and will go get it. You can get as much or as little as you choose. If you choose to buy little, the problem is yours, not the mall's. The mall is neutral about the kinds of purchases you make and about how informed a consumer you are. The mall wants your regular presence and your good behavior, and for that alone it will sell you a diploma. From one point of view it is a very good buy. Students, parents, and teachers seem generally satisfied with the deal.

These arrangements, after all, reflect two fundamental realities. First, Americans want high school to be genuinely accessible to virtually everyone, and on a basis such that everyone who wants to can complete it. Second, Americans have profoundly different notions of what a proper high school education should be. There is no consensus at all, no moral equivalent of the early grades' "three Rs." In these circumstances the shopping mall is more than an apt metaphor; it provides high schools with a workable model. In their imitation of the shopping mall, high schools accommodate these two realities with a minimum of friction. But to what extent is this successful accommodation also an abdication of responsibility toward those students and families, who, for whatever reasons, do not make the wise choice that distinguishes between accommodating students and educating them?

Endnotes

1. The movie *Fast Times at Ridgemont High* also makes the comparison of high schools to shopping malls. Its opening titles comes up over scenes of a mall, not a school, and the mall continues throughout as the main setting where students live out their adolescence. See Pauline Kael's review in *The New Yorker*, November 1, 1982, p. 146.
2. In rare instances a semester's work in a foreign language may be offered over two semesters for those who learn languages slowly. The level of mastery aimed for in the spread-out version is the same as that in the one-semester course. A longer time is provided to reach the same end. But levels rarely have this intention.

 # Mad

Jerome Stern _____

Jerome Stern teaches English at Florida State University. "Mad" appeared in the journal *Writing on the Edge*. "What They Learn in School" aired March 17, 1989 on National Public Radio's "All Things Considered" and was later reprinted in *Harper's Magazine*.

So I don't know, I don't know what the teacher wants from us, I mean the teacher gives us these notes on John Milton and then he asks us if we have any questions and we can't have any questions because we don't know what to ask and so we are quiet and then he gets mad at us, and then he asks us if we heard of Jean Paul Sartre and Reinhold Niebuhr who we never heard of and are not on the syllabus, and then he gets mad at us for not having heard of people no one ever told us about, and then he says what about *Crime and Punishment* and *War and Peace?* Which it turns out are books that nobody even ever mentioned in our lives, and then he gets mad at us.

And then he gives us things to read which are very sad and confusing and then he gets mad at us because we don't like things that are sad and confusing.

Then he says life doesn't have happy endings and we say why does it have to be that way, and that's why we want to read things that have happy endings and then he gets mad at us.

And we tell him we would do what we are supposed to, but he won't tell us what we are supposed to do.

"Mad" by Jerome Stern. Reprinted by permission of the author.

Think he says, think, why don't you think. And then, when we tell him what we think is that we don't understand what he is saying, and what will be on the exam, and will we be responsible for everything in the syllabus, or just what we cover in class, then he gets mad at us, and says all we care about is grades and money.

And then he gets sarcastic and asks us when World War II was, and then he gets unhappy because we don't know, and never heard of Mussolini or Mao or Molotov cocktails, and we don't know why we should have heard of those things so there doesn't seem to be any reason to know those things and then he gets mad at us and says all we care about is ourselves and we don't even know who we are, and that is not the way it was at some time before, but what that time was is not clear.

We do not know that time because it was a time maybe before we were born, and he seems mad at us because we were not born when he was, and did not do the things he said he did, and that it is all our fault.

He does not like what we like and is mad at us for liking the things we do like instead of other things which no one ever told us about, and so he is almost always mad, but we hope he likes us and gives us good grades anyway.

🍎 What They Learn in School

Jerome Stern _____

📖

In the schools now, they want them to know all about marijuana, crack, heroin, and amphetamines,

Because then they won't be interested in marijuana, crack, heroin, and amphetamines,

But they don't want to tell them anything about sex because if the schools tell them about sex, then they will be interested in sex,

But if the schools don't tell them anything about sex,

Then they will have high morals and no one will get pregnant, and everything will be all right,

And they do want them to know a lot about computers so they will outcompete the Japanese,

But they don't want them to know anything about real science because then they will lose their faith and become secular humanists,

And they do want them to know all about this great land of ours so they will be patriotic,

But they don't want them to learn about the tragedy and pain in its real history because then they will be critical about this great land of ours and we will be passively taken over by a foreign power,

And they want them to learn how to think for themselves so they can get good jobs and be successful,

But they don't want them to have books that confront them with real ideas because that will confuse their values,

"What They Learn in School" by Jerome Stern. Reprinted by permission of the author.

And they'd like them to be good parents,

But they can't teach them about families because that takes them back to how you get to be a family,

And they want to warn them about how not to get AIDS

But that would mean telling them how not to get AIDS,

And they'd like them to know the Constitution,

But they don't like some of those amendments except when they are invoked by the people they agree with,

And they'd like them to vote,

But they don't want them to discuss current events because it might be controversial and upset them and make them want to take drugs, which they already have told them all about,

And they want to teach them the importance of morality.

But they also want them to learn that Winning is not everything—it is the Only Thing,

And they want them to be well-read,

But they don't want them to read Chaucer or Shakespeare or Aristophanes or Mark Twain or Ernest Hemingway or John Steinbeck, because that will corrupt them,

And they don't want them to know anything about art because that will make them weird,

But they do want them to know about music so they can march in the band,

And they mainly want to teach them not to question, not to challenge, not to imagine, but to be obedient and behave well so that they can hold them forever as children to their bosoms as the second millennium lurches toward its panicky close.

Life on the Mississippi: East St. Louis, Illinois

Jonathan Kozol

Jonathan Kozol has written a number of acclaimed books on education, the poor, and the homeless in the United States. The following selection is from the first chapter of his book Savage Inequalities: Children in America's Schools, published in 1991. At the beginning of this book, Kozol explains that "the events in this book take place for the most part between 1988 and 1990, although a few events somewhat precede this period." In the following excerpt from the book's preface, Kozol explains his goals:

It occurred to me that we had not been listening much to children in these recent years of "summit conferences" on education, of severe reports and ominous pre-scriptions. The voices of children, frankly, had been missing from the whole discus-

From SAVAGE INEQUALITIES by Jonathan Kozol. Copyright © 1991 by Jonathan Kozol. Reprinted by permission of Crown Publishers, Inc.

sion. *This seems especially unfortunate because the children often are more inter-esting and perceptive than the grown-ups are about the day-to-day realities of life in school. For this reason, I decided early in my journey, to attempt to listen very carefully to children and, whenever possible, to let their voices and their judgments and their longings find a place within this book—and maybe, too, within the nation's dialogue about their destinies.(5–6)*

📖

"East of anywhere," writes a reporter for the *St. Louis Post-Dispatch*, "often evokes the other side of the tracks. But, for a first-time visitor suddenly deposited on its eerily empty streets, East St. Louis might suggest another world." The city, which is 98 percent black, has no obstetric services, no regular trash collection, and few jobs. Nearly a third of its families live on less than $7,500 a year; 75 percent of its population lives on welfare of some form. The U.S. Department of Housing and Urban Development describes it as "the most distressed small city in America."

Only three of the 13 buildings on Missouri Avenue, one of the city's major thoroughfares, are occupied. A 13-story office building, tallest in the city, has been boarded up. Outside, on the sidewalk, a pile of garbage fills a ten-foot crater.

The city, which by night and day is clouded by the fumes that pour from vents and smokestacks at the Pfizer and Monsanto chemical plants, has one of the highest rates of child asthma in America.

It is, according to a teacher at the University of Southern Illinois, "a repository for a nonwhite population that is now regarded as expendable." The *Post-Dispatch* describes it as "America's Soweto."

Fiscal shortages have forced the layoff of 1,170 of the city's 1,400 employees in the past 12 years. The city, which is often unable to buy heating fuel or toilet paper for the city hall, recently announced that it might have to cashier all but 10 percent of the remaining work force of 230. In 1989 the mayor announced that he might need to sell the city hall and all six fire stations to raise needed cash. Last year the plan had to be scrapped after the city lost its city hall in a court judgment to a creditor. East St. Louis is mortgaged into the next century but has the highest property-tax rate in the state.

Since October 1987, when the city's garbage pickups ceased, the backyards of residents have been employed as dump sites. In the spring of 1988 a policeman tells a visitor that 40 plastic bags of trash are waiting for removal from the backyard of his mother's house. Public health officials are concerned the garbage will attract a plague of flies and rodents in the summer. The policeman speaks of "rats as big as puppies" in his mother's yard. They are known to the residents, he says, as "bull rats." Many people have no cars or funds to cart the trash and simply burn it in their yards. The odor of smoke from burning garbage, says the *Post-Dispatch*, "has become one of the scents of spring" in East St. Louis.

Railroad tracks still used to transport hazardous chemicals run through the city. "Always present," says the *Post-Dispatch*, "is the threat of chemical spills . . . . The wail of sirens warning residents to evacuate after a spill is common." The most recent spill, the paper says, "was at the

Monsanto Company plant . . . . Nearly 300 gallons of phosphorous trichloride spilled when a railroad tank was overfilled. About 450 residents were taken to St. Mary's Hospital . . . . The frequency of the emergencies has caused Monsanto to have a 'standing account' at St. Mary's."

In March of 1989, a task force appointed by Governor James Thompson noted that the city was in debt by more than $40 million, and proposed emergency state loans to pay for garbage collection and to keep police and fire departments in continued operation. The governor, however, blamed the mayor and his administrators, almost all of whom were black, and refused to grant the loans unless the mayor resigned. Thompson's response, said a Republican state legislator, "made my heart feel good . . . . It's unfortunate, but the essence of the problem in East St. Louis is the people" who are running things.

Residents of Illinois do not need to breathe the garbage smoke and chemicals of East St. Louis. With the interstate highways, says a supervisor of the Illinois Power Company, "you can ride around the place and just keep going . . . ."

East St. Louis lies in the heart of the American Bottoms—the floodplain on the east side of the Mississippi River opposite St. Louis. To the east of the city lie the Illinois Bluffs, which surround the floodplain in a semicircle. Towns on the Bluffs are predominantly white and do not welcome visitors from East St. Louis.

"The two tiers—Bluffs and Bottoms—" writes James Nowlan, a professor of public policy at Knox College, "have long represented . . . different worlds." Their physical separation, he believes, "helps rationalize the psychological and cultural distance that those on the Bluffs have clearly tried to maintain." People on the Bluffs, says Nowlan, "overwhelmingly want this separation to continue."

Towns on the Bluffs, according to Nowlan, do not pay taxes to address flood problems in the Bottoms, "even though these problems are generated in large part by the water that drains from the Bluffs." East St. Louis lacks the funds to cope with flooding problems on its own, or to reconstruct its sewer system, which, according to local experts, is "irreparable." The problem is all the worse because the chemical plants in East St. Louis and adjacent towns have for decades been releasing toxins into the sewer system.

The pattern of concentrating black communities in easily flooded lowland areas is not unusual in the United States. Farther down the river, for example, in the Delta town of Tunica, Mississippi, people in the black community of Sugar Ditch live in shacks by open sewers that are commonly believed to be responsible for the high incidence of liver tumors and abscesses found in children there: Metaphors of caste like these are everywhere in the United States. Sadly, although dirt and water flow downhill, money, and services do not.

The dangers of exposure to raw sewage, which backs up repeatedly into the homes of residents in East St. Louis, were first noticed, in the spring of 1989, at a public housing project, Villa Griffin. Raw sewage, says the *Post-Dispatch*, over-flowed into a playground just behind the housing project, which is home to 187 children, "forming an oozing lake of . . . tainted water." Two schoolgirls, we are told, "experienced hair loss since raw sewage flowed into their homes."

While local physicians are not certain whether loss of hair is caused by the raw sewage, they have issued warnings that exposure to raw sewage can provoke a cholera or hepatitis outbreak. A St. Louis health official voices her dismay that children live with waste in their backyards. "The development of working sewage systems made cities livable a hundred years ago," she notes. "Sewage systems separate us from the Third World."

"It's a terrible way to live," says a mother at the Villa Griffin homes, as she bails raw sewage from her sink. Health officials warn again of cholera—and, this time, of typhoid also.

The sewage, which is flowing from collapsed pipes and dysfunctional pumping stations, has also flooded basements all over the city. The city's vacuum truck, which uses water and suction to unclog the city's sewers, cannot be used because it needs $5,000 in repairs. Even when it works, it sometimes can't be used because there isn't money to hire drivers. A single engineer now does the work that 14 others did before they were laid off. By April the pool of overflow behind the Villa Griffin project has expanded into a lagoon of sewage. Two million gallons of raw sewage lie outside the children's homes.

In May, another health emergency develops. Soil samples tested at residential sites in East St. Louis turn up disturbing quantities of arsenic, mercury and lead—as well as steroids dumped in previous years by stockyards in the area. Lead levels found in the soil around one family's home, according to lead-poison experts, measure "an astronomical 10,000 parts per million." Five of the children in the building have been poisoned. Although children rarely die of poisoning by lead, health experts note, its effects tend to be subtle and insidious. By the time the poisoning becomes apparent in a child's sleep disorders, stomach pains and hyperactive behavior, says a health official, "it is too late to undo the permanent brain damage." The poison, she says, "is chipping away at the learning potential of kids whose potential has already been chipped away by their environment."

The budget of the city's department of lead-poison control, however, has been slashed, and one person now does the work once done by six.

Lead poisoning in most cities comes from lead-based paint in housing, which has been illegal in most states for decades but which poisons children still because most cities, Boston and New York among them, rarely penalize offending landlords. In East St. Louis, however, there is a second source of lead. Health inspectors think it is another residue of manufacturing—including smelting—in the factories and mills whose plants surround the city. "Some of the factories are gone," a parent organizer says, "but they have left their poison in the soil where our children play." In one apartment complex where particularly high quantities of lead have been detected in the soil, 32 children with high levels in their blood have been identified.

"I anticipate finding the whole city contaminated," says a health examiner.

📖

The problems of the streets in urban areas, as teachers often note, frequently spill over into public schools. In the public schools of East St. Louis this is literally the case.

"Martin Luther King Junior High School," notes the *Post-Dispatch* in a story published in the early spring of 1989, "was evacuated Friday afternoon after sewage flowed into the kitchen . . . . The kitchen was closed and students were sent home." On Monday, the paper continues, "East St. Louis Senior High School was awash in sewage for the second time this year." The school had to be shut because of "fumes and backed-up toilets." Sewage flowed into the basement, through the floor, then up into the kitchen and the students' bathrooms. The backup, we read, "occurred in the food preparation areas."

School is resumed the following morning at the high school, but a few days later the overflow recurs. This time the entire system is affected, since the meals distributed to every student in the city are prepared in the two schools that have been flooded. School is called off for all 16,500 students in the district. The sewage backup, caused by the failure of two pumping stations, forces officials at the high school to shut down the furnaces.

At Martin Luther King, the parking lot and gym are also flooded. "It's a disaster," says a legislator. "The streets are underwater; gaseous fumes are being emitted from the pipes under the schools," she says, "making people ill."

In the same week, the schools announce the layoff of 280 teachers, 166 cooks and cafeteria workers, 25 teacher aides, 16 custodians and 18 painters, electricians, engineers and plumbers. The president of the teachers' union says the cuts, which will bring the size of kindergarten and primary classes up to 30 students, and the size of fourth to twelfth grade classes up to 35, will have "an unimaginable impact" on the students. "If you have a high school teacher with five classes each day and between 150 and 175 students . . . . it's going to have a devastating effect." The school system, it is also noted, has been using more than 70 "permanent substitute teachers," who are paid only $10,000 yearly, as a way of saving money.

Governor Thompson, however, tells the press that he will not pour money into East St. Louis to solve long-term problems. East St. Louis residents, he says, must help themselves. "There is money in the community," the governor insists. "It's just not being spent for what it should be spent for."

The governor, while acknowledging that East St. Louis faces economic problems, nonetheless refers dismissively to those who live in East St. Louis. "What in the community," he asks, "is being done right?" He takes the opportunity of a visit to the area to announce a fiscal grant for sewer improvement to a relatively wealthy town nearby.

In East St. Louis, meanwhile, teachers are running out of chalk and paper, and their paychecks are arriving two weeks late. The city warns its teachers to expect a cut of half their pay until the fiscal crisis has been eased.

The threatened teacher layoffs are mandated by the Illinois Board of Education, which, because of the city's fiscal crisis, has been given supervisory control of the school budget. Two weeks later the state superintendent partially relents. In a tone very different from that of the governor, he notes that East St. Louis does not have the means to solve its education problems on its own. "There is no natural way," he says, that "East St. Louis can bring itself out of this situation." Several cuts will be required in any case—one quarter of the system's teachers, 75 teacher aides, and several dozen others will be given notice—but, the state board notes, sports and music programs will not be affected.

East St. Louis, says the chairman of the state board, "is simply the worst possible place I can imagine to have a child brought up . . . . The community is in desperate circumstances." Sports and music, he observes, are, for many children here, "the only avenues of success." Sadly enough, no matter how it ratifies the stereotype, this is the truth; and there is a poignant aspect to the fact that, even with class size soaring and one quarter of the system's teachers being given their dismissal, the state board of education demonstrates its genuine but skewed compassion by attempting to leave sports and music untouched by the overall austerity.

Even sports facilities, however, are degrading by comparison with those found and expected at most high schools in America. The football field at East St. Louis High is missing almost everything—including goalposts. There are a couple of metal pipes—no crossbar, just the pipes. Bob Shannon, the football coach, who has to use his personal funds to purchase footballs and has had to cut and rake the football field himself, has dreams of having goalposts someday. He'd also like to let his students have new uniforms. The ones they wear are nine years old and held together somehow by a patchwork of repairs. Keeping them clean is a problem, too. The school cannot afford a washing machine. The uniforms are carted to a corner laundromat with fifteen dollars' worth of quarters.

Other football teams that come to play, according to the coach, are shocked to see the field and locker rooms. They want to play without a halftime break and get away. The coach reports that he's been missing paychecks, but he's trying nonetheless to raise some money to help out a member of the team whose mother has just died of cancer.

"The days of the tight money have arrived," he says. "It don't look like Moses will be coming to this school."

He tells me he has been in East St. Louis 19 years and has been the football coach for 14 years. "I was born," he says, "in Natchez, Mississippi. I stood on the courthouse steps of Natchez with Charles Evers. I was a teen-age boy when Michael Schwerner and the other boys were murdered. I've been in the struggle all along. In Mississippi, it was the fight for legal rights. This time, it's a struggle for survival.

"In certain ways," he says, "it's harder now because in those days it was a clear enemy you had to face, a man in a hood and not a statistician. No one could persuade you that you were to blame. Now the choices seem like they are left to you and, if you make the wrong choice, you are made to understand you are to blame. . . .

"Night-time in this city, hot and smoky in the summer, there are dealers standin' out on every street. Of the kids I see here, maybe 55 percent will graduate from school. Of that number, maybe one in four will go to college. How many will stay? That is a bigger question.

"The basic essentials are simply missing here. When we go to wealthier schools I look at the faces of my boys. They don't say a lot. They have their faces to the windows, lookin' out. I can't tell what they are thinking. I am hopin' they are saying, 'This is something I will give my kids someday.'"

Tall and trim, his black hair graying slightly, he is 45 years old.

"No, my wife and I don't live here. We live in a town called Ferguson, Missouri. I was born in poverty and raised in poverty. I feel that I owe it to myself to live where they pick up the garbage."

In the visitors' locker room, he shows me lockers with no locks. The weight room stinks of sweat and water-rot. "See, this ceiling is in danger of collapsing. See, this room don't have no heat in winter. But we got to come here anyway. We wear our coats while working out. I tell the boys, 'We got to get it done. Our fans don't know that we do not have heat.'"

He tells me he arrives at school at 7:45 A.M. and leaves at 6:00 P.M.—except in football season, when he leaves at 8:00 P.M. "This is my life. It isn't all I dreamed of and I tell myself sometimes that I might have accomplished more. But growing up in poverty rules out some avenues. You do the best you can."

In the wing of the school that holds vocational classes, a damp, unpleasant odor fills the halls. The school has a machine shop, which cannot be used for lack of staff, and a woodworking shop. The only shop that's occupied this morning is the auto-body class. A man with long blond hair and wearing a white sweat suit swings a paddle to get children in their chairs. "What we need the most is new equipment," he reports. "I have equipment for alignment, for example, but we don't have money to install it. We also need a better form of egress. We bring the cars in through two other classes." Computerized equipment used in most repair shops, he reports, is far beyond the high school's budget. It looks like a very old gas station in an isolated rural town.

Stopping in the doorway of a room with seven stoves and three refrigerators, I am told by a white teacher that this is a class called "Introductory Home Ec." The 15 children in the room, however, are not occupied with work. They are scattered at some antiquated tables, chatting with each other. The teacher explains that students do no work on Friday, which, she says, is "clean-up day." I ask her whether she regards this class as preparation for employment. "Not this class," she says. "The ones who move on to Advanced Home Ec. are given job instruction." When I ask her what jobs they are trained for, she says: "Fast food places— Burger King, McDonald's."

The science labs at East St. Louis High are 30 to 50 years outdated. John McMillan, a soft-spoken man, teaches physics at the school. He shows me his lab. The six lab stations in the room have empty holes where pipes were once attached. "It would be great if we had water," says McMillan.

Wiping his hand over his throat, he tells me that he cannot wear a tie or jacket in the lab. "I want you to notice the temperature," he says. "The heating system's never worked correctly. Days when it's zero outside it will be 100 Fahrenheit within this room. I will be here 25 years starting September—in the same room, teaching physics. I have no storage space. Those balance scales are trash. There are a few small windows you can open. We are on the side that gets the sun."

Stepping outside the lab, he tells me that he lives in East St. Louis, one block from the school. Balding and damp-looking in his open collar, he is a bachelor 58 years old.

The biology lab, which I visit next, has no laboratory tables. Students work at regular desks. "I need dissecting kits," the teacher says. "The few we have are incomplete." Chemical supplies, she tells me, in a city poisoned by two chemical plants, are scarce. "I need more microscopes," she adds.

The chemistry lab is the only one that's properly equipped. There are eight lab tables with gas jets and water. But the chemistry teacher says he rarely brings his students to the lab. "I have 30 children in a class and cannot supervise them safely. Chemical lab work is unsafe with more than 20 children to a teacher. If I had some lab assistants, we could make use of the lab. As it is, we have to study mainly from a text."

Even texts are scarce, however. "We were short of books for four months last semester. When we got replacement copies, they were different from the texts that we already had. So that presented a new problem. . . .

"Despite these failings, I have had two students graduate from MIT."

"In how many years?" I ask.

He tells me, "Twenty-three."

Leaving the chemistry labs, I pass a double-sized classroom in which roughly 60 kids are sitting fairly still but doing nothing. "This is supervised study hall," a teacher tells me in the corridor. But when we step inside, he finds there is no teacher. "The teacher must be out today," he says.

Irl Solomon's history classes, which I visit next, have been described by journalists who cover East St. Louis as the highlight of the school. Solomon, a man of 54 whose reddish hair is turning white, has taught in urban schools for almost 30 years. A graduate of Brandeis University in 1961, he entered law school but was drawn away by a concern with civil rights. "After one semester, I decided that the law was not for me. I said, 'Go and find the toughest place there is to teach. See if you like it.' I'm still here. . . .

"This is not by any means the worst school in the city," he reports, as we are sitting in his classroom on the first floor of the school. "But our problems are severe. I don't even know where to begin. I have no materials with the exception of a single textbook given to each child. If I bring in anything else—books or tapes or magazines—I pay for it myself. The high school has no VCRs. They are such a crucial tool. So many good things run on public television. I can't make use of anything I see unless I can unhook my VCR and bring it into school. The AV equipment in the building is so old that we are pressured not to use it."

Teachers like Mr. Solomon, working in low-income districts such as East St. Louis, often tell me that they feel cut off from educational developments in modern public schools. "Well, it's amazing," Solomon says. "I have done without so much so long that, if I were assigned to a suburban school, I'm not sure I'd recognize what they are doing. We are utterly cut off."

Of 33 children who begin the history classes in the standard track, he says, more than a quarter have dropped out by spring semester. "Maybe 24 are left by June. Mind you, this is in the junior year. We're speaking of the children who survived. Ninth and tenth grades are the more horrendous years for leaving school.

"I have four girls right now in my senior home room who are pregnant or have just had babies. When I ask them why this happens, I am told, 'Well, there's no reason not to have a baby. There's not much for me in public school.' The truth is, that's a pretty honest answer. A diploma from a ghetto high school doesn't count for much in the United States today. So, if this is really the last education that a person's going to get, she's probably perceptive in that statement. Ah, there's so much bitterness—unfairness—there, you know. Most of these pregnant girls are not the ones who have much self-esteem . . . .

"Very little education in the school would be considered academic in the suburbs. Maybe 10 to 15 percent of students are in truly academic programs. Of the 55 percent who graduate, 20 percent may go to four-year colleges: something like 10 percent of any entering class. Another 10 to 20 percent may get some other kind of higher education. An equal number join the military . . . .

"I get $38,000 after nearly 30 years of teaching. If I went across the river to one of the suburbs of St. Louis, I'd be earning $47,000, maybe more. If I taught in the Chicago suburbs, at a wealthy high school like New Trier, for example, I'd be getting close to $60,000. Money's not an issue for me, since I wouldn't want to leave; but, for new, incoming teachers, this much differential is a great deterrent. When you consider that many teachers are afraid to come here in the first place, or, if they are not afraid, are nonetheless offended by the setting or intimidated by the challenge of the job, there should be a premium and not a punishment for teaching here.

"Sometimes I get worried that I'm starting to burn out. Still, I hate to miss a day. The department frequently can't find a substitute to come here, and my kids don't like me to be absent."

Solomon's advanced class, which soon comes into the room, includes some lively students with strong views.

"I don't go to physics class, because my lab has no equipment," says one student. "The typewriters in my typing class don't work. The women's toilets . . ." She makes a sour face. "I'll be honest," she says. "I just don't use the toilets. If I do, I come back into class and I feel dirty."

"I wanted to study Latin," says another student. "But we don't have Latin in this school."

"We lost our only Latin teacher," Solomon says.

A girl in a white jersey with the message DO THE RIGHT THING on the front raises her hand. "You visit other schools," she says. "Do you think the children in this school are getting what we'd get in a nice section of St. Louis?"

I note that we are in a different state and city.

"Are we citizens of East St. Louis or America?" she asks.

A tall girl named Samantha interrupts. "I have a comment that I want to make." She then relates the following incident: "Fairview Heights is a mainly white community. A friend of mine and I went up there once to buy some books. We walked into the store. Everybody lookin' at us, you know, and somebody says, 'What do you want?' And lookin' at each other like, 'What are these black girls doin' here in Fairview Heights?' I just said, 'I want to buy a book!' It's like they're scared we're goin' to rob them. Take away a privilege that's theirs by rights. Well, that goes for school as well.

"My mother wanted me to go to school there and she tried to have me transferred. It didn't work. The reason, she was told, is that we're in a different 'jurisdiction.' If you don't live up there in the hills, or further back, you can't attend their schools. That, at least, is what they told my mother."

"Is that a matter of race?" I ask. "Or money?"

"Well," she says, choosing her words with care, "the two things, race and money, go so close together—what's the difference? I live here, they live there, and they don't want me in their school."

A boy named Luther speaks about the chemical pollution. "It's like this," he says. "On one side of us you have two chemical corporations. One is Pfizer—that's out there. They make paint and pigments. The other is Monsanto. On the other side are companies incinerating toxic waste. So the trash is comin' at us this direction. The chemicals is comin' from the other. We right in the middle."

Despite these feelings, many of the children voice a curiously resilient faith in racial integration. "If the government would put a huge amount of money into East St. Louis, so that this could be a modern, well-equipped and top-rate school," I ask, "with everything that you could ever want for education, would you say that racial segregation was no longer of importance?"

Without exception, the children answer, "No."

"Going to a school with all the races," Luther says, "is more important than a modern school."

"They still believe in that dream," their teacher says. "They have no reason to do so. That is what I find so wonderful and . . . ah, so moving. . . . These kids are the only reason I get up each day."

I ask the students, "What would happen if the government decided that the students in a nearby town like Fairview Heights and the students here in East St. Louis had to go to school together next September?"

Samantha: "The buses going to Fairview Heights would all be full. The buses coming to East St. Louis would be empty."

"What if East St. Louis had the very best computer classes in the state—and if there were no computer classes in the school of Fairview Heights?"

"The buses coming here," she says, "would still be empty."

When I ask her why, she answers in these quiet words: "I don't know why."

Sam Morgan, principal of East St. Louis High, was born and raised in East St. Louis. He tells me he didn't go to East St. Louis High, however. "This was the white high school in those days," he says.

His office was ruined in a recent fire, so he meets me in a tiny room with space for three chairs and a desk. Impeccably dressed in a monogrammed shirt with gold links in his cuffs, a purple tie and matching purple handkerchief in his suit pocket, he is tall, distinguished-looking and concerned that I will write a critical report on East St. Louis High. When I ask, however, what he'd do if he were granted adequate funds, he comes up with a severe assessment of the status quo.

"First, we're losing thousands of dollars in our heating bills because of faulty windows and because the heating system cannot be controlled. So I'd renovate the building and install a whole new heating system and replace the windows. We've had fire damage but I see that as a low priority. I need computers—that's a low priority as well. I'd settle for a renovation of the typing rooms and new typewriters. The highest priorities are to subdivide the school and add a modern wing, then bring the science laboratories up to date. Enlarge the library. Buy more books. The books I've got, a lot of them are secondhand. I got them from the Catholic high school when it closed. Most of all, we need a building renovation. This is what I'd do to start with, if I had an extra $20 million."

After he's enumerated all the changes he would like to make, he laughs and looks down at his hands. "This, of course, is pie in the sky. You asked me what I need so I have told you. If I'm dreaming, why not dream the big dreams for our children?"

His concerns are down-to-earth. He's not pretentious and does not appropriate the cloudy jargon that some educators use to fill a vacuum of specifics—no talk of "restructuring," of "teacher competency" or any of the other buzzwords of the decade. His focus is on the bare necessities: typewriters, windows, books, a renovated building.

While we are speaking in his temporary office, a telephone call from the police informs him that his house has just been robbed—or that the theft alarm, at least, has just gone off. He interrupts the interview to try to reach his wife. His poise and his serene self-discipline do not desert him. I gain the impression this has happened before. He's a likable man and he smiles a lot, but there is tremendous tension in his body and his fingers grip the edges of his desk as if he's trying very hard to hold his world together.

Before I leave the school, I take a final stroll along the halls. In a number of classrooms, groups of children seem to be involved in doing nothing. Sometimes there's a teacher present, doing something at his desk. Sometimes there's no adult in the room. I pass the cooking class again, in which there is no cooking and no teaching taking place. The "supervised" study hall is still unsupervised.

In one of the unattended classrooms on the second floor, seven students stand around a piano. When I stick my head into the room, they smile and invite me to come in. They are rehearsing for a concert: two young women, five young men. Another young man is seated at the piano. One of the students, a heavyset young woman, steps out just before the others. When she sings, her pure soprano voice transforms the room. "Sometimes I feel like a motherless child," she begins. The pianist gazes up at her with an attentive look of admiration.

The loveliness and the aesthetic isolation of the singer in the squalor of the school and city bring to my mind the words of Dr. Lillian Parks, the superintendent of the East St. Louis schools. "Gifted children," says Dr. Parks, "are everywhere in East St. Louis, but their gifts are lost to poverty and turmoil and the damage done by knowing they are written off by their society. Many of these children have no sense of something they belong to. They have no feeling of belonging to America. Gangs provide the boys, perhaps, with something to belong to . . . .

"There is a terrible beauty in some of these girls—terrible, I mean, because it is ephemeral, foredoomed. The language that our children speak may not be standard English but there still is wisdom here. Our children have become wise by necessity."

Clark Junior High School is regarded as the top school in the city. I visit, in part, at the request of school officials, who would like me to see education in the city at its very best. Even here, however, there is a disturbing sense that one has entered a backwater of America.

"We spend the entire eighth grade year preparing for the state exams," a teacher tells me in a top-ranked English class. The teacher seems devoted to the children, but three students sitting near me sleep through the entire period. The teacher rouses one of them, a girl in the seat next to me, but the student promptly lays her head back on her crossed arms and is soon asleep again. Four of the 14 ceiling lights are broken. The corridor outside the room is filled with voices. Outside the window, where I see no schoolyard, is an empty lot.

In a mathematics class of 30 children packed into a space that might be adequate for 15 kids, there is one white student. The first white student I have seen in East St. Louis, she is polishing her nails with bright red polish. A tiny black girl next to her is writing with a one-inch pencil stub.

In a seventh grade social studies class, the only book that bears some relevance to black concerns—its title is *The American Negro*—bears a publication date of 1967. The teacher invites me to ask the class some questions. Uncertain where to start, I ask the students what they've learned about the civil rights campaigns of recent decades.

A 14-year-old girl with short black curly hair says this: "Every year in February we are told to read the same old speech of Martin Luther King. We read it every year. 'I have a dream . . . . ' It does begin to seem—what is the word?" She hesitates and then she finds the word: "perfunctory."

I ask her what she means.

"We have a school in East St. Louis named for Dr. King," she says. "The school is full of sewer water and the doors are locked with chains. Every student in that school is black. It's like a terrible joke on history."

It startles me to heard her words, but I am startled even more to think how seldom any press reporter has observed the irony of naming segregated schools for Martin Luther King. Children reach the heart of these hypocrisies much quicker than the grown-ups and the experts do.

"I would like to comment on that," says another 14-year-old student, named Shalika. "I have had to deal with this all of my life. I started school in Fairview Heights. My mother pushes me and she had wanted me to get a chance at better education. Only one other student in my class was black. I was in the fifth grade, and at that age you don't understand the ugliness in people's hearts. They wouldn't play with me. I couldn't understand it. During recess I would stand there by myself beside the fence. Then one day I got a note: 'Go back to Africa.'

"To tell the truth, it left a sadness in my heart. Now you hear them sayin' on TV, 'What's the matter with these colored people? Don't they care about their children's education?' But my mother did the best for me she knew. It was not my mother's fault that I was not accepted by those people."

"It does not take long," says Christopher, a light-skinned boy with a faint mustache and a somewhat heated and perspiring look, "for little kids to learn they are not wanted."

Shalika is small and looks quite young for junior high. In each ear she wears a small enameled pin of Mickey Mouse. "To some degree I do believe," she says, "that this is caused by press reports. You see a lot about the crimes committed here in East St. Louis when you turn on the TV. Do they show the crimes committed by the government that *puts* black people here? Why are all the dirty businesses like chemicals and waste disposal here? This is a big country. Couldn't they find another place to put their poison?"

"Shalika," the teacher tells me afterward, "will go to college."

"Why is it this way?" asks Shalika in a softer voice again. But she doesn't ask the question as if she is waiting for an answer.

"Is it 'separate but equal,' then?" I ask. "Have we gone back a hundred years?"

"It is separate. That's for sure," the teacher says. She is a short and stocky middle-aged black woman. "Would you want to tell the children it is equal?"

Christopher approaches me at the end of class. The room is too hot. His skin looks warm and his black hair is damp. "Write this down. You asked a question about Martin Luther King. I'm going to say something. All that stuff about 'the dream' means nothing to the kids I know in East St. Louis. So far as they're concerned, he died in vain. He was famous and he lived and gave his speeches and he died and now he's gone. But we're still here. Don't tell students in this school about 'the dream.' Go and look into a toilet here if you would like to know what life is like for students in this city."

Before I leave, I do as Christopher asked and enter a boy's bathroom. Four of the six toilets do not work. The toilets stalls, which are eaten away by red and brown corrosion, have no doors. The toilets have no seats. One has a rotted wooden stump. There are no paper towels and no soap. Near the door there is a loop of wire with an empty toilet-paper roll.

"This," says Sister Julia, "is the best school that we have in East St. Louis."

Possible Lives

Mike Rose _____

Mike Rose is on the faculty of the UCLA Graduate School of Education and Information Studies and UCLA Writing Programs. The following selection contains excerpts from his book *Possible Lives: The Promise of Public Education in America*, 1995. As Rose explains in the introduction, excerpted below, he spent nearly four years visiting classrooms across the country to research this book.

Introduction

During a time when so many are condemning public schools—and public institutions in general—I have been traveling across the country, visiting classrooms in which the promise of public education is being powerfully realized. These are classrooms judged to be good and decent places by those closest to them—parents, principals, teachers, students—

Excerpts from POSSIBLE LIVES: The Promise of Public Education in America. Copyright © 1995 by Mike Rose. Reprinted by permission of Houghton Mifflin Company. All rights reserved.

classrooms in big cities and small towns, preschool through twelfth grade, places that embody the hope for a free and educated society that has, at its best, driven this extraordinary American experiment from the beginning.

We seem to be rapidly losing that hope. Our national discussion about public schools is despairing and dismissive, and it is shutting down our civic imagination. I visited schools for three and a half years, and what struck me early on—and began to define my journey—was how rarely the kind of intellectual and social richness I was finding was reflected in the public sphere.

We have instead a strange mix of apocalyptic vignettes—violent classrooms, incompetent teachers, students who think Latin is spoken in Latin America—and devastating statistics: declines in SAT scores and embarrassing cross-national comparisons. We hear—daily, it seems—that our students don't measure up, either to their predecessors in the United States or to their peers in other countries, and that, as a result, our position in the global economy is in danger. We are told, by politicians, by pundits, that our cultural values, indeed our very way of life is threatened. We are offered, by both entertainment and news media, depictions of schools as mediocre places, where students are vacuous and teachers are not so bright; or as violent and chaotic places, places where order has fled and civility has been lost. It's hard to imagine anything good in all this.

Though researchers have for some time challenged the simplicity of these representations—reports from the Rand Corporation and the Sandia National Laboratories, for example, dispute the much-broad-casted declines in student achievement—their challenges rarely enter our public discourse in any significant way. We seem beguiled by a rhetoric of decline, this ready store of commonplaces about how awful our schools have become. "America's schools are the least successful in the Western world," declare the authors of a book on the global economy. "Face it, the public schools have failed," a bureau chief for a national news magazine tells me, offhandedly. "The kids in the Los Angeles Unified School District are garbage," a talk-radio host exclaims.

There are many dangers in the use of such language. It blinds us to the complex lives lived out in the classroom. It pre-empts careful analysis of one of the nation's most significant democratic projects. And it engenders a mood of cynicism and retrenchment, preparing the public mind for extreme responses: increased layers of testing and control, denial of new resources—even the assertion that money doesn't affect a school's performance—and the curative effects of free market forces via vouchers and privatization. What has been seen historically as a grand republican venture is beginning to be characterized as a failed social experiment, noble in intention but moribund now, perhaps headed toward extinction. So, increasing numbers of people who can afford to don't even consider public schools as an option for their children, and increasingly we speak, all of us, about the schools as being in decline. This is what is happening to our public discussion of education, to our collective vision of the schools.

But if you would travel with me to those classrooms in Baltimore or Kentucky or Chicago or LA, sit and watch those teachers work, listen in as students reason through a problem, walk around the neighborhoods to see what the schools provide—then the importance of public education and the limits of our portraits of it would become clear. To be sure, the visitor traveling through our nation's schools would find burned-out teachers, lost students, boredom, violence, inertia. But if our understanding of schooling and the conception we have of what's possible emerge primarily from these findings, then what we can imagine for public education will be terribly narrow and impoverished.

If, for example, we try to organize schools and create curriculum based on an assumption of failure and decay, then we make school life a punitive experience. If we think about education largely in relation to our economic competitiveness, then we lose sight of the fact that school has to be about more than economy. If we determine success primarily in terms of test scores, then we ignore the social, moral, and aesthetic dimensions of teaching and learning— and, as well, we'll miss those considerable intellectual achievements which aren't easily quantifiable. If we judge one school according to the success of another, we could well diminish the particular ways the first school serves its community. In fact, a despairing vision will keep us from fully understanding the *tragedies* in our schools, will reduce their complexity, their human intricacy. We will miss the courage that sometimes accompanies failure, the new directions that can emerge from burn-out, the desire that pulses in even the most depressed schools and communities.

Why are we thinking about our schools in such limited and limiting ways? To begin with, the way we perceive problems in schools is profoundly affected by our concerns about broad social conditions that exist well beyond the schoolhouse door. Since the mid-nineteenth century, that period when we began the standardization of the "common" elementary school and the development of the high school, most major periods of national concern about education— and the reform movements that have emerged from them—have coincided with periods of social and economic disruption, and in some ways have been responses to them. As historians David Tyack and Larry Cuban put it, "Americans have translated their cultural anxieties and hopes into dramatic demands for educational reform." The last fifteen years have seen conflict and uncertainty about economic competitiveness, changing demographics and national identity, and our position in the world order. These anxieties shape our perception of the schools— our schools have placed "our very future as a Nation and a people" at risk, states the most prominent of 1980s' reform documents—and manifest themselves in the sweeping but one-dimensional remedies we pose as a corrective, the remedies of siege and devastation.

There are other reasons for our limited perception; some are longstanding, others more immediate, all are interrelated. Though the teacher has been a respected figure in some communities, as a nation we have had little regard for teaching. It has been low-pay, low-status work, devalued as "women's work," judged to have limited intellectual content. In addition, we have little appreciation for the richness and mystery of "everyday cognition," for the small, commonplace intellectual challenges and achievements of the school day. It is also true that through most of this century our society has been in the grip of narrow conceptions of intellectual development and academic achievement; we operate with inadequate, even damaging notions of what it means to be "excellent." For all the hope we place in what school will do for our children—and we have always placed great hope in the benefits of education—we have a tendency to diminish the day-to-day practice of schooling. This has been especially true for our intellectual elite. Few discussions of schooling in policy papers, in legislation, in the endless flow of books by nonteachers telling us how to make it right, few of these discussions take us in close to teaching and learning. They tend to work at a high level of generality and opinion, thereby relying more easily on one-dimensional portrayals of the classroom. Class and race bias play into all this, keeping us from seeing the good in poor schools and orienting us toward stereotype and sweeping condemnation—and this distortion will get worse as public schools increasingly become the domain of the working classes, immigrants, and minorities. Contributing as well to our disillusion with the schools is a general loss of faith in public institutions and an idealization of the private sphere and the free market. Finally, these tendencies have been skillfully manipulated during the last decade by legislators, policy analysts, and entrepreneurs who want to restrict funding to public education, subject it to market forces, and, ultimately, privatize it.

I have written this book to help us think in a different way.

In doing so, I am not trying to ignore the obvious misery in our schools nor the limitations of too many of those who teach in and manage them. Nor have I disregarded the complaints of those whose schools are failing them; they have a strong voice in this book. This is not a call to abandon the critical perspective a citizenry should have when it surveys its institutions. What I am suggesting is that we lack a public critical language adequate to the task. We need a different kind of critique, one that does not minimize the inadequacies of curriculum and instruction, the rigidity of school structure, or the "savage inequalities" of funding, but that simultaneously opens discursive space for inspired teaching, for courage, for achievement against odds, for successful struggle, for the insight and connection that occur continually in public school classrooms around the country. Without a multiplicity of such moments, criticism becomes one-dimensional, misses too much, is harsh, brittle, the humanity drained from it.

Public education demands a capacious critique, one that encourages both dissent and invention, fury and hope. Public education is bountiful, crowded, messy, contradictory, exuberant, tragic, frustrating, and remarkable. We need an expanded vocabulary, adequate to both the daily joy and daily sorrow of our public schools. And we are in desperate need of rich, detailed images of possibility. In the stories that follow, I try to provide some of those images.

📖

The LA Basin

Continue north from Monterey Park about six winding miles to the foothills of the San Gabriel mountains, and you'll enter Pasadena, located along the northeast rim of the LA Basin. It is linked to downtown Los Angeles by the first freeway built in California, the Arroyo Seco Parkway, a six-mile route built by the WPA and opened in 1940. Though Pasadena is now a middle-class community, it has a history of privilege. Founded in 1874 on the site of an old *rancho* by settlers from Indiana ("The California Colony of Indiana"), Pasadena would quickly develop from what John Muir called "an aristocratic little colony" of orange and lemon orchards, exotic gardens, and learned societies into a booming resort for people of means looking to ease the chill of Boston or Chicago. It hosted the Rose Parade (the first in 1890) and, from 1916, when football replaced chariot racing in the festivities, the Rose Bowl. The city was one of the wealthiest in California until its tourism was devastated by the Great Depression. It was saved—as were a number of other Southern California cities—by World War II, for a local polytechnic institute had developed into Cal Tech, a hub for the region's aerospace and electronics industries. To this day, a large number of residents have undergraduate and graduate degrees and hold managerial and professional positions. Until recently, the power base of the city was exclusively White. Though Mexican and Chinese immigrants were present from the first days of the settlement—employed primarily as field hands—and African Americans migrated in to fill jobs as hotel domestics and chauffeurs (developing eventually a small but active middle class), all non-Whites were strictly segregated in housing, schools, and medical facilities. Such patterns of segregation—restrictive covenants, separate schools—could be found in most Southern California suburbs.

In the last two decades, the demographic mix of Pasadena's citizenry has changed considerably. As the population increased (from 113,000 in 1970 to 132,000 in 1990), the White majority became a minority. The number of African Americans decreased slightly, as well. The Asian population expanded, and the Latino population has increased significantly (from 21,772 in 1980 to 35,912 in 1990), reflecting trends evident throughout Southern California. But the ethnic shifts in the Southland have been marked not only in Latino and Asia numbers. There is a growing Armenian population in Pasadena, migrating in from their point of entry in East Hollywood and Glendale. The 250,000 Armenians in Los Angeles County form the largest concentration outside their homeland.

Pasadena High School graduated its first class in 1890, moved and rebuilt two times to accommodate the city's boom cycles, and opened the doors of its newest campus in 1960. The large, well-equipped facility (it has two swimming pools) served a White middle- and upper-middle-class constituency until 1970, when the courts judged Pasadena to be in violation of school desegregation laws, and busing was mandated. The demographic changes, combined with busing and massive White flight to private schools, have yielded a current ethnic composition of 38 percent Hispanic, 32 percent African American, 25 percent Caucasian (many of whom are Armenian), and about 5 percent Asian. But these percentages do not tell the full story of Pasadena High School. Within the demographer's broad categories, there are forty-two nationalities represented on campus and thirty-eight languages spoken. And since the early 1970s, there has been a shift in class: PHS has the largest number of low-income students in the Pasadena school district, many of whom live in foster homes and/or public housing projects. A lot of these young people see little meaning in school, are regularly truant, are getting in trouble with the law, and show all the signs of dropping out.

These problems have absorbed Principal Judy Codding. How, she wondered, could she develop services and programs that would "give our students hope that school can do something for them." One thing she did was establish two academies—one in Graphic Arts and one in Visual Arts and Design—small programs within the school that each enroll 100 to 150 students and attempt an integration of vocational and academic coursework. Such career-academic programs, which have been gaining national attention, can be little more than deceptive tracks away from college and toward low-level employment. But if they are carried out with integrity, they can provide an engaging curriculum, a feeling of specialness, and an expansion of opportunity. Ruby, a junior in the Graphic Arts Academy, saw it like this: the program will enable her to do two things she really wants to do—she wants to go to college, but she has to get a job to support herself. When she graduates, she figures, she'll be able to do both. To ensure that students like Ruby will be able to achieve such goals, Principal Codding has secured mentors and internships from the local printing industry, arranged for students to take courses during their senior year at nearby Pasadena City College, and established agreements so that coursework will be given credit at California State University at Los Angeles.

When I visited it, the Graphic Arts Academy was in its second experimental year. Students entered as sophomores and took some courses in the regular curriculum—a foreign language or physical education or an art elective—but the majority of their courses were taken with academy faculty, teachers chosen because of their skill in the classroom and their interest in creating an interdisciplinary curriculum. There were five: Ellen Abraham and Kirk Odegard taught humanities, Elaine Mirkin taught biology and mathematics, Mary Tsotsis handled chemistry, and Mark Hall was head of the Graphic Arts Lab. They met every week, and conferred on the fly, to develop ways to integrate their curricula: How can you teach humanities or chemistry with an orientation toward graphic arts? What kind of projects can bring the disciplines together in fruitful ways? So, for example, early in their first term, sophomores wrote a haiku or limerick or quatrain in humanities, made their own paper in the Graphic Arts Lab—and tested its weight and thickness and determined its gloss and texture—and made the ink they used to letter their verse in chemistry, testing its reflective density, opacity, and absorbency. At the heart of the academy was one critical question: How is graphic arts a science, an art, and a language?

I was standing by the Heidelberg computerized printing press in the Graphic Arts Lab with Alena Bayramyan, a sophomore who, with her parents, had emigrated from Armenia. "This program is so special," she said. "The teachers don't want you to get a low grade. They really care about you. It's like we're a family." Alena was petite and full of feeling, and she had taken it on herself to walk me around the lab. It was a big room, white brick walls, lots of windows covered with blinds to regulate the light, a gray linoleum floor. Student-made signs with bright safety warnings were everywhere: DON'T RUN, KEEP HANDS AND LOOSE CLOTHING AWAY FROM ALL MACHINES, DO NOT THROW OBJECTS, and, by the door to the teacher's small office, DON'T MESS WITH MR. HALL! Alena had started us off at the entrance, where students were sitting at computers composing and formating text for their projects. Between the terminals were backpacks, bookbags, jackets and sweaters piled in small heaps, folders full of paper, a couple of dictionaries. Next came four "light tables," tables with opaque glass tops illuminated from below. Students were bent over the soft glow, laying out their negatives, using T-squares and angles to get the images just right. Then came a long sink with curled negatives hanging from a string overhead, and then the darkroom—its red warning light on. "I'm just learning all of this," Alena said. "I can't wait to get really proficient at it."

Once past the darkroom, we paused at the electrostatic plate maker, a kind of high-intensity photocopying machine that created a plastic "plate" from the texts the students had made. "You have to be careful," Alena explained, "if you make it too hot, it'll burn." From there we passed the paper cutter, where two Armenian boys looked up long enough to tease Alena. "Don't you know," one said to me, "she's an illegal alien!" Alena rolled her eyes and sighed as if to say "How pathetic" and shot something back in Armenian—and we continued on to the Heidelberg printer.

On this day, the academy students were making business cards. Some had a personal slant, the student's name and phone number inscribed under or around a cartoon with a simple exhortation to call, to use the number, to dial and see what happens. Others were for a family business, an auto shop or wrecking yard or shoe repair. Dimple and Lynita, best friends, were over at the computers formating their cards, giving each other a little friendly grief, moving, occasionally, to the hip-hop tape playing low on a portable recorder, Lynita now and then executing a gliding dance step. Three or four boys were in close over the light tables, their cheeks and foreheads illuminated a gentle gold, touching up scratches on their negatives with a fine brush—no talking here—or concentrating on a precise cut with an Exacto knife, squinting, biting a lip. The Graphic Arts Academy, according to its position paper, stressed "the central importance of learning how to learn, how to reason, and how to investigate complex issues that require collaboration, personal responsibility, and a tolerance for uncertainty." Two girls traded off at the darkroom. Over by the plate maker, Truc Pham was showing Jack Zabounian how to fuse an electrostatic plate without overheating it. And here at the printing press, the instructor, Mark Hall, stood back as Anthony Willis, a gifted cartoonist, was explaining to a sophomore named Davida how to run the machine. Alena, my guide, stepped to the back of the whirring printer, where sheets of business cards were flapping into a tray. "Hey, Davida," Alena asked, slipping a sheet quickly from the pile, "why did this corner come out so light?" "Oh," Davida answered, "that's 'cause the printer is still loading with ink—right, Anthony?" Anthony nodded and showed her how to adjust a knob on the side of the machine. Mr. Hall watched, arms folded across his lab coat. "Hey, Alena, see," Davida said, grabbing a new sheet. "Look at this—it's darker." Alena's eyes brightened. "Oh, OK, I got it!" "Tell me what just became clear to you, Alena," Mr. Hall said. A few feet away, a Lebanese-Armenian boy named Pierre (there are Lebanese, Egyptian, Iranian, Turkish, and Soviet Armenians in Los Angeles) was standing over the electrostatic plate maker, hesitating. "Hey, Mr. Hall," he called out, "I forgot—do I put this transparency face up or face down?" Mr. Hall looked up from the Heidelberg press. "Where's the light coming from, Pierre?" " Oh, yeah," Pierre said quickly, "yeah, yeah, OK, face down." The bell for lunch rang, and Alena and Davida and Anthony and Pierre and Jack Zabounian and Truc Pham kept working. Across the room, Dimple and Lynita walked over to the printer to get hard copies of their texts, and Lynita started picking, slowly, through the piles of clothing for her jacket, keeping an eye on the printer. Mr. Hall leaned over and tapped my shoulder. "I just love it," he said softly, "when the bell rings and nobody moves."

Mark Hall, thirty-one, six-one, a big man with glasses, both irreverent and sentimental, worked in the printing industry until three years ago, when he decided to become a teacher. "I just found that what I enjoyed most about the work I was doing was training new people. You know, we would hustle, push hard to get out advertising inserts—that's what we printed—and it hit me one day: So what if someone didn't get their Kmart ad? Who would care? They'd just miss that week's lining for their cat box. I wanted to work with someone or something that would matter to people, would make a difference in their lives, so I began to think about teaching. What I guess I like most about this program is that it gives kids a reason to come to school—and once they're here and with it, you have a better shot at everything else."

A few hundred feet south of the Graphic Arts Lab, the chemistry teacher Mary Tsotsis was preparing a class of academy sophomores to conduct experiments on polar and nonpolar materials. For a long time, Mary had been interested in developing ways to integrate the teaching of science and art, and the Graphic Arts Academy provided her the opportunity. She would select a procedure or problem in graphic arts and then focus on the chemistry involved, both concepts and techniques.

She began this day by reviewing for the class the defining characteristics of polarity and nonpolarity (the absence or presence of free electrons), and then asked why they, as future graphic artists, need to know "whether polar materials and nonpolar materials can mix." Billy, a sharp kid who could be a teacher's bad day, answered, "Because we'll be using lots of different materials when we make plates." He slid down in his chair, continuing, "We'll hafta know what'll mix, or we'll mess up." Mary nodded. She was formal, serious, dressed meticulously. "Yes," she said in slightly accented English—she was of Greek heritage—"you would mess up."

She asked the students to go to the small laboratory in the back of the room and begin the experiments. Along a wood counter was a row of neatly labeled polar materials (salt, water-based ink, hydrochloric acid, water, and water-based pigment) and a row of nonpolar materials: carbon tetrachloride, ink solvent, oil, and oil-based pigment—in this case, crayon shavings. Some of these would be found in a print shop; others were commonplace, thrown in to complicate the experiment. There was a tray of beakers behind the materials and, alongside the tray, a cabinet and a sink and draining rack filled with clean test tubes. In front of all this were several Formica-covered tables on which Mary's students began laying out large sheets of white paper. The sheets were lined with dark grids. Along the top and down the left side, the students had written the names of the polar materials—NaCl, water-based ink, HCl—and nonpolar materials, CCl_4, ink solvent, and so on. (Some boys wrote these names in the stylized tagger script you'd usually see in graffiti.) As the students began systematically mixing one material with another (a polar with a polar, a nonpolar with a polar), they were to place a drop of each mix in the appropriate square on the grid, thereby illustrating at a glance if a solution had resulted—a nice blot on white—or a bad mix—little clumps of salt or crayon or unblended streaks and stains. A graphic representation of data. Mary would put these sheets on the wall, and later—as the class created further displays of basic concepts and experimental results—they would be stored in a set of bulging portfolios of student work.

Around the room, the students were washing test tubes, holding them up to the windows for the glint of sunlight, checking for a bad rinse; mixing salt and water to prepare one of their polar materials; shaving more crayons, thin slivers of magenta and violet and black, to replenish their store of nonpolar oil-based pigment; cautiously filling droppers with hydrochloric acid or carbon tetrachloride or ink solvent; stirring solutions with glass rods—*tink, tink, tink*—squinting to see the results. There was chatter and school-yard news and crude flirtation and rebuff, lots of questions of Mrs. Tsotsis and of one another, and an occasional line from a song, sung under breath during the washing and stinting. And Mary Tsotsis walked from student to student, asking what they were doing and why and what they were finding out.

I had been with the academy students in other classes and walked around the school yard at lunchtime. Some of them would probably do well in a traditional academic program. Others would have a hard time of it, would get discouraged, and possibly not see the point of it all. And still others—four or five boys—would most likely end up in a continuation school . . . or worse. In the yard they challenged each other, pushing the verbal limits, and in some of their classes they jockeyed continually for the funny line, a desperate impulsivity, not laughing at one another's jokes, but elbowing for the delinquent limelight. A few boys bore so much anger, such a charged resistance to any authority, that the air seemed to pop when a teacher walked by their desks, trying in vain to cool them out.

But here in chemistry and in Mark Hall's Graphic Arts Lab, the work seemed to focus these students' energies and, at times, virtually demanded collaboration rather than street-culture combativeness. So while you certainly heard young people insulting each other, or, on the other hand, saw them congregating in small groups by gender or ethnicity or neighborhood affiliation, you also saw interaction around joint problems or projects, shared needs. Many of the tasks in Mary's or Mark's classes were hard to do alone, and because of the mix of back-grounds' and interests and skill, some students would simply be more adept at the technology, some better artists, some in possession of a sharper eye, some quicker to grasp concepts behind procedures. Working together made sense. "You know," Mark had said to me, "sometimes I think the really big benefit of this program is social. It would be hard to prove—how would I get stats on such a thing—but I see some remarkable things happening with my students." By bringing together young people who would traditionally be in separate academic tracks and by integrating applied vocational and college-oriented curricula, the Graphic Arts Academy was creating an institutional and instructional space that encouraged the formation of a microsociety that valued both hand and brain.

But over the brief history of the academy's existence, the creation of that space had proven to be a challenge of the first order. To begin with, nowhere in their professional education are teachers taught how to work together, jointly solve problems, develop mutual curricula; teaching is defined as a highly individualized pursuit. The isolation is reinforced by the rigid borders our colleges and universities establish between disciplines; for all the current talk in higher education about "interdisciplinarity," chemists rarely interact with physicists, let alone social scientists or humanists. This conceptual insularity is, of course, passed on to those who will eventually move into the schools. Add to the problem society's class-laden distinction between manual work and mental work, demonstrated in school by the fierce gulf between vocational education and college preparation. (John Dewey called this distinction "the most deep-seated antithesis . . . in educational history.") And to all this, add one further complication: the linkages that Principal Judy Codding established with industry, with Pasadena City College, with Cal State LA—connections that will assist academy students as they move beyond high school, but that affect here and now the curriculum Mark and Mary and the others must develop for them. "We make a lot of mistakes," Mark told me. "It's not like we have the time to sit back and think all this through, troubleshoot it. We have to create it and teach it at the same time. You just hope it goes right."

And some things did go right. On a shelf by Mark Hall's office in the Graphic Arts Lab was a neat row of hand-bound books with multicolored cloth covers. The students had been reading Sandra Cisneros's *The House on Mango Street* in their humanities class, and they were asked to write a series of vignettes—following Cisneros's episodic style—about their name, their house, their neighbors, the language(s) they spoke, their first job, and so on. They were to write their own *Mango Street*. Since this structure allowed for a lot of variation, it occurred to the biology teacher that students could incorporate brief chapters on science that would thematically play off the autobiographical vignettes. So if you paged through, for example, Dimple's and Lynita's books, you'd find a chapter called "Tears" (about the death of a grandmother) followed by a brief chapter on the lacrimal glands, and a summary of genetics following a chapter on the family. Dimple's chapter on her name was accompanied by a definition of *dimple*. Lynita's chapter called "Me" was paired with an illustration of the human brain. The whole project took about three weeks, and at the end, the students had to plan, measure, illustrate, cut, lay out, and bind the book in the Graphic Arts Lab. When the teachers first came up with the idea, they were unsure about it. Could the students pull it off? Could it be sufficiently interdisciplinary? But once they introduced the project, it began to take shape, the students further developing it. Mark remembered the last few days, watching the students going from biologist to humanities teacher to graphic artist for help, working with them after school to get the binding right, driving Dimple and Lynita to the bus stop as the sky was turning deep blue.

📖

Polaris, Montana

The two-lane highway extended with an intermittent dip and rise as far as I could see, no cars coming or going, a clear band of asphalt running pasture beyond pasture. On either side of State Highway 278 were grasslands and grazing cattle, creeks and ponds, bales of hay and isolated haystacking machines called "beaverslides", beyond that grew clumps of brush and a little juniper. Then came rolling meadows, then foothills and fir trees, rising in the far distance to snow-covered mountains, crisp and striking. In addition to cattle, there were occasional sheep, deer, magpies with white-tipped wing and tail, coyote, sandhill cranes, and two humpbacked moose making their way into willow.

I was traveling with Claudette Morton, director of the Rural Education Center at Western Montana College in Dillon, the seat of this county called Beaverhead, the largest in Montana, as big as Rhode Island and Connecticut combined, with a population of eighty-four hundred, half of whom lived in Dillon. We were headed northwest to a one-room school near the ghost town of Polaris, in the middle of the Grasshopper Valley, surrounded by the Beaverhead National Forest. There are nearly a hundred single-teacher elementary schools in Montana alone, Claudette told me, and another sixty or so schools with two to four teachers, combining children from more than one grade level in a single classroom. It's the scale, the size of the land, she explained, and the population density. Montana is the fourth largest state in the union, yet has a population of just under 800,000—and a large proportion reside in and around a dozen or so cities. Vast stretches of the state, especially in the eastern plains, are sparsely populated. By one rough estimate, there is in Montana about one kindergarten-through-twelfth-grade student per square mile. So the single-teacher elementary, the current incarnation of the one-room country school that for a good part of our history defined nonurban public education, is still a necessity. Approximately 830 such schools are to be found in half of the states in the union, Maine to California, the largest numbers in Nebraska, Montana, and South Dakota, states with expansive, sparsely populated rural landscape.

The drive to Polaris out of Dillon was just over thirty-five miles and took about forty-five minutes, though the time varied depending on weather—at about 6500 feet Claudette had to slow to fifteen miles per hour as we passed through clouds that surrounded us in thick whiteness. There were always potential delays, even in good weather. One morning Claudette's husband, George, and I encountered a transfer of cattle from one pasture to another, somewhere between seventy-five and a hundred cows and calves lumbering along the highway, mooing, bleating, breaking into a heavy trot as George tried to inch his way through, an occasional cowboy assisting our passage.

The one-room schoolhouse has been characterized many ways in our history: as a symbol of progress, as the forge of rural culture, as, in Hamlin Garland's words, "a barren temple of the arts," as provincial and backward. It was all these things and more—a complex institution. What is clear, though, is that since before the turn of this century, there has been a systematic attempt to close down these little schools, to consolidate them into larger systems. In 1910 there were 200,000 one-teacher schools in the United States; fifty years later that number dropped to 23,695. The consolidation was driven by shifts in population and the disrepair of older buildings, by unfavorable comparison with the large urban (or suburban) school and its multiple facilities and services, and by the desire of policymakers to concentrate control and to achieve uniformity and efficiency in finance and governance. ("The best," asserted an influential big city superintendent, "is the best everywhere.") Recent analyses of rural education have undermined the assumption that big is necessarily more effective—and, in many quarters, as we have seen, the model of the large urban school is under attack. But the drive for consolidation continues (in Montana there were 820 one-teacher schools recorded in a 1958–59 survey; by 1984 there were 99), held at bay only in those areas where citizens can organize and argue that distance, transportation, weather, and community need make it impossible to close their local school. This battle has been going on in rural America for over a hundred years, and is basically a conflict between local control—governance by a small independent school board that has say over location, hiring, curriculum, resources, and policies—and control by more distant governing bodies and agencies that redistribute (and attempt to equalize) resources, certify and hire teachers, establish curriculum and policy, and determine central, strategic (sometimes equally inconvenient) locations for school buildings. Traveling to Polaris, I began to understand the conflict. At one point, we passed two children waiting at roadside, their house in the distance, off a crooked pathway, no other house in sight. A school bus was coming toward them from the north, red lights flashing.

As Claudette and I ascended into the national forest, it began to snow, flurries coming at the windshield in an upward curl, light powder on the highway, light as confectioner's sugar, blowing in rippling waves across the road. Claudette steadied herself—she knew the snowfall would get heavier—and continued talking about the region and about rural schools. It seemed that people were finally beginning to appreciate the potential of small schools, she said, the possibilities of individualized instruction, independent work, children tutoring other children. And the close attention, the intimate connection of school and community. Nobody gets lost. For a long time, it was just assumed that kids from these rural schools got an inadequate education and did poorly as they moved on. Anything so small and so country had to be inferior. While it is true that the transition to larger town high schools can be a problem, some new studies, and reviews of old ones, suggest that, on average, children from rural schools do as well as everybody else. And in some cases, from some schools or regions, they do better. These little schools have gotten, Claudette believed, a bad rap.

We passed two large ranches, cattle dotting broad snow-covered pastures, and came on the unmarked dirt road, white now, that led to Polaris, veering suddenly off Highway 278. It curved for about four miles through grassland and shrubbery, past old fences and sporadic power poles. Polaris, named after the polestar, or North Star, at the tip of the handle of the Little Dipper, was, in the mid-1880s, a silver-mining town, not too far north of the region being homesteaded by some of the families who, today, hold two or three of the largest ranches in the area. Polaris was now the site of a post office, a house owned by an old cowboy named Walt Melcher, and the Polar Bear, once run by Walt and his wife, closed these days—though Walt would open it for the occasional traveler who needed a drink to cut the chill. Polaris School, about a mile south of the town, was established in 1892—four and five generations of some local families have attended it—and the first variation of the present schoolhouse was erected in 1925. A teacherage was built onto the side of the school by one Junior Stallings in 1949—before that, teachers boarded with local families—and a first-year teacher named Andy Bayliss now lived and worked there, finishing up the last month of a one-year contract.

Claudette had hooked me up with Andy because, though he was still finding his way, he was already a knowledgeable and creative teacher who played to the strengths of the one-room school. On Claudette's recommendation, I had read some books and articles—ones sympathetic to rural education—that lamented the unimaginative nature of instruction in some rural classrooms: materials were limited and dated, resources were scarce, teaching practices tended toward recitation and rote learning, without much variability. This was not always the fault of the teachers. Some were isolated, out of contact with other teachers or teacher-education institutions. Publishers produced few materials geared toward rural schools—too diverse and diffused to be a lucrative market. And community norms some-times constrained experimentation. But Andy was inventive and ambitious, eager to extend what children could do. On this day of my stay with him I was going to try to record the flow of his practice, capture a day in the life of this rural schoolteacher and his students.

Even with the delays, Claudette and I got to Polaris early, pulling in through an open gate, rolling to a stop by the wooden walkway that led to the school. She set the brake, and I opened the door, confirming that I would ride back to Dillon with Andy, who would be need-ing supplies and a little company. She handed me a package of materials to give to him and pulled away, leaving no other sound but a meadowlark and the soft rippling of Farlin Creek, running amid sedges and willows along the northern border of the school yard. Just beyond the creek, behind a simple fence, cows, powdered with snow, stood quietly, nosing the ground.

Polaris School faced the road. It was a neat frame building, clapboard siding, gray with white trim, with a raised front porch and a dormer jutting out from a pitched roof. There was a large propane tank on the side and, farther back, an old log barn from the days when stu-dents rode their horses to school. Behind the school was a swing set and slide, a tool shed, also gray and white, and an abbreviated basketball court. A boy, an early arrival, dressed in a slicker and cowboy hat, was shooting baskets, finding his footing on the slippery concrete, propelling the wet ball in a heavy arc through the air.

Andy Bayliss sat at the table closest to the tall windows in the back wall of the schoolhouse, eating a bowl of cereal, listening to Peanuts Wilson on an old rockabilly tape he had found in the discount bin at the Safeway in Dillon, gazing out beyond the silhouette of Tyler shooting baskets to the sharp, white peak of Bald Mountain. In the midst of this vast expanse of meadow and mountain, Andy lived in tight quarters. The teacherage had a separate entrance, leading to a narrow living room, a desk covered with textbooks and school supplies, a couch, a VCR and stacks of videotapes, six pairs of skis. Off to one side was a bedroom only partly closed off from the classroom, the dividing wall running three quarters of the way to the ceil-ing. Straight through the living room was a kitchen—skillets, loose dishes, canned goods— that, through a rear door, led to the restrooms Andy shared with his students. So Andy liked to come into the classroom early, put a cassette into the radio-tape player, and look out at the mountains. Morning light flooded across the counter along the base of the windows: rocks, sprouting geraniums, a microscope and slides, a spider plant sitting on the *New World*

Dictionary. Andy Bayliss was the sixty-first teacher to lead instruction at Polaris School. He bobbed his head in time with the slapping bass, the wailing, stuttering saxophone, enjoying the full light, a lick of his brown hair sticking straight up.

His day was about to begin.

Eight-twenty, and Andy saw James and Russell joining Tyler on the basketball court. The three oldest boys in the school, all good athletes. He clicked off the tape and rinsed his bowl and spoon. The troublesome tuft of hair would not lie down. His slacks were already dusty with chalk. He was a meticulous planner, charting curriculum for each of his fifteen students—they ranged from second grade to eighth—and writing on the blackboard daily schedules and lists of assignments for various groups of children. This was the general plan for today:

8:30	Morning Business
9:00	Math 7, Math 3–4
9:30	Habitat Studies, Montana Studies
10:00	Snack, Recess
10:20	Math 5–6, Montana Studies
11:00	Science
11:30	Silent Reading
12:00	Lunch
12:30	Native American Role Play
1:30	Art
2:30	Track
3:15	*Ciao*

In addition, there were recommended readings, due dates, page numbers in textbooks. The class, as Andy conceived it, wouldn't work without such detail, such clarity of expectation.

To successfully teach children from so many grade levels required the ability to manage a classroom efficiently and resourcefully. It was common for Andy to conduct a lesson for one group of children while the remainder worked separately or in pairs on math problems or reading assignments or on an art or science project begun earlier in the week. Andy was fortunate to have a skillful aide, Michele Reynolds, who could assist those children working independently. Or she could tutor Colt, the one second-grader, or James, the sole eighth-grade student. Or she could seclude herself in the tiny library attached to the classroom to prepare materials for children who needed more time with one lesson or were ready to move ahead on another, beyond the assignment, beyond grade level. There were also multiple possibilities for students helping other students, tapping into their own experience and achievement, pairing one of the older kids with one of the younger to listen to a story or review math homework or edit a piece of writing. And Andy and Michele could split the class, Andy explaining a project for Montana Studies to the fifth- through eight-graders while Michele played a math game with the younger children. Sometimes things got a little hectic—I was reminded of a description of a nineteenth-century country school where "the teacher was mending pens for one class . . . hearing another spell . . . [and] calling a covey of small boys to be quiet"—but, overall, there was a good deal of effective individualized instruction as well as movement in and out of groups, a fluid configuration. It is interesting to note that such practice is currently receiving a good deal of attention in teacher education programs; in the good multi-grade classroom, it exists of necessity.

At 8:30 sharp, Andy led the class in the Pledge of Allegiance, then asked them to choose a song. This was a morning ritual. On this day, a number of the children wanted to hear country singer Alan Jackson, a favorite in this community, so Dustin, a fourth-grader, clattered through the pile of cassettes by the tape player and selected "Chattahoochee":

Way down yonder on the Chattahoochee
It gets hotter than a hootchie-kootchie

Almost everyone knew the words, or at least the driving chorus, so the class, squeezed into a soft couch facing the blackboard or sitting on the floor with backs against it, sang about a wild Friday night all the way across the United States. When the song was over, Andy reached up for a map over the blackboard, pulled it down with a *flap*, and traced the Chattahoochee River, running his finger along the Alabama-Georgia border. "See? That's the river he's singing about. It forms a natural boundary." Then Andy chose a song, a traditional one, from a loose cluster of lyric sheets he had hanging by the piano and asked Melissa to put another cassette in the player. A scratchy piano came on, and a woman's voice announced "The Little Black Bull." Andy stood by the lyrics, hand under the first line, and the class began:

Oooooh, the little black bull
came down the meadow . . .
    a long time ago . . .

The classroom at Polaris School was about twenty-eight by thirty-five feet. If you began at the front of the room, you would have before you the black chalkboard and maps, a rack of books and handouts, and the old piano. Toward the corner there were cupboards and a large heater, run on propane, with a tall silver stovepipe. The intersection of piano and cupboard formed a kind of cubbyhole, and in it was a pile of worn, fluffy pillows where, occasionally, you would find Erica curled up reading a novel. She loved this school, she would tell you if asked. Everyone knows you, and you aren't made to feel stupid, and its safe. She had a friend near Denver, and that girl talked a lot about kids who already had problems with drugs. At thirteen, Erica's age. But it did get lonely out here. So she studied Spanish by audiotape at night and wrote stories and read.

Continuing along the west wall, you entered the library, an eight-by-twelve-foot room with crammed shelves along three walls: children's and adolescent literature, six different encyclopedias, *National Geographic*, reference books on subjects ranging from plants and rocks and grains to Indians, oceans, music, and light. Back out to the classroom, continuing along the wall through a long anarchy of shelves, both metal and wooden, and tables, card and kitchen, on which you would find glue, scissors, files for rock sculpture, tape, athletic trophies, a poinsettia, rulers, yarn, a three-hole punch, piles of books on Montana, displays of books the students had made, and, finally, a computer in a wooden console.

Turning the next corner, against the south wall, beyond which the teacherage lay, there were blue-green plastic tubs stacked on metal shelves, each tub with a student's name affixed, filled with tools and art supplies. Then a small table with cups full of brushes and a cardboard box of crayons, peeled and broken, the microwave (the school's hot lunch program, Andy joked), and the restrooms and rear entrance to the teacherage. At the southeast corner was a noisy wall heater and a large piece of corkboard on a stand, like a movable blackboard, The corkboard became a flimsy partition, farming another cubby of sorts, and sometimes Russell or Tyler or James or Stephen went there to read under an old parlor lamp. Then came the long counter under the full windows that looked out onto Bald Mountain, the counter rich with plants and field guides and sparkling rocks. Then Andy's desk, the light from the last of the windows slanting over half of it, a bright, warm triangle. Turn around in the desk's swivel chair, the one Andy was now retrieving, and you're facing the blackboard at the front of the room.

Before the blackboard was that fat couch into which the children crammed to sing, and throughout the rest of the room were folding chairs and dark Formica tables. Andy's students moved often from couch to table to rug to nook—the floor creaking beneath their step—or to the library, or outdoors, leaving a trail of paper and pencil and crayon behind them. During the first month or so of the term, some parents and board members visited the room, and, as one put it to me, wondered, "What in God's name was going on here?" Andy had found those tables and chairs in the storeroom—they were used for civic functions—and had replaced the old school desks with them, and there was all this activity. The board was not heavy-handed—Andy enjoyed good relations with them—but that was not a comfortable position for a first-year teacher to be in. Over time, Andy was able to explain in detail and with polite assurance his methods and goals to individual parents and to the board. And after a while, the district came to see that something interesting was going on here.

Student work was on bold display. Along the top third of the west wall, from the jamb of the library door nearly to the computer console, extended a hand-drawn map of the region, embellished in greens and blues and browns. Mountain ranges and rivers were marked, as were roadways, forests, Polaris School, the post office, and each of the children's homes. Over the microwave was a large bar chart depicting the results of six hundred coin tosses, a lesson in probability. There were paper constructions and crayon mosaics, dense and bright, over shelves, by the bathrooms, in small free spaces. There were data sheets on science experiments, and illustrated summaries of novels and short stories, and large interpretive maps drawn up during geography and social studies—like the one of Alaska pinned to the corkboard partition. And above the door of the girls' bathroom was Leo's science lesson *cum* personal narrative, printed on a large piece of brown wrapping paper cut into an irregular circle:

> 1) I am the sun. 2) All of the planets orbit around me. 3) I am the only star you can see in the daytime. 4) I am the hottest object in the solar system. 5) I produce energy.

Student writing was everywhere, like Erica's reminiscence of ice fishing with her father, placed amid paper mosaics:

> I went ice fishing with Dad . . . There was a small fire, and my ears were kept warm by a hat pulled tight over my head. Dad, who is always trying to do the

strangest things, put bait in two different places on my pole. I put it in the water
. . . The only clouds I remember were white, pure; they looked like cotton in the
sky. I was so happy, my cheeks rosy, and having Dad there beside me waiting in
silence was such an awesome comfort. It wasn't until Dad pulled out my pole
that I had the most incredible feeling. I was awed at the sight—two different fish on my pole. I felt a gratitude for Dad, a feeling for him that had
never been quite as strong as it was then. . .

And Charlie's story "Mean Miss Gorf," bound into a cloth-covered book, shown to me
within ten minutes of my arrival by an admiring Reba and Melissa. It began:

Once there as a mean teacher at Polaris school. Her name was Miss Gorf. She was
skinny as a rail and mean as a rattlesnake. She had the power to turn a kid into a
shiny red apple. First she would wiggle her right ear, then her left ear, and then
she'd stick out her tongue.

One day Miss Gorf was teaching arithmetic, and the problem was
6,503,526,679 divided by 6. After three minutes she yelled, "Time's up," and we
turned in our answers.

She looked them over and said, "Good job Charlie, James, Crystal, Russell, Tyler,
but I am disappointed in you Erica. Sorry." She wiggled her left ear, then her right
ear, then struck on her tongue, and there was a nice shiny red apple where Erica
once was standing.

And the collaborative poem composed by the class on a long sheet of butcher paper—what
do you do when you don't have an overhead projector, Andy explained—hanging in the
nook by the piano:

My Surroundings

In fall it's colorful, bright,
Foxes hide fast in the red,
dead trees.

Moose covered with frost.
As we climb we look and see
white on the top of the mountains.

Great blocks of rock are
wintery white, rough on my hands.

Eagle fly on wind, black
above me.

Then we see a mountain cat
battling a rat.

Picturesque sunsets.

"What you're doing down there is different," one parent told Andy after a few months had passed, "But I think it's beneficial." "The kids seem interested," said another, "in going to school." The combination of Andy's congeniality, the rationale for his practice and the specificity of his goals, and, pure and simple, the quality of the work the class was producing—it all became persuasive.

Andy was sitting in his swivel chair facing the couch, where seventh-graders Heather, Russell, Erica, and Tyler were working in teams of two, studying patterns and number theory and making their way through story problems like the following:

Loren was studying the meaning of new words. After the first day he had 15 words left to learn. After the second day he had 12 words left to learn. The next day he had 9 words left. At that rate, how many days will it take him to learn all the words?

Heather suggested to Russell that the two of them count down on their collective fingers. They quickly did so, then she ventured, "It'll take a total of six days." Erica and Tyler were solving the problem with a factor tree, arriving at multiples of 5 and 3. The answer, they said in disagreement with Heather and Russell, was five. Any pointed out the different strategies they were using, then asked each team to justify their answers. "It's going in a number pattern." Heather said, leaning over Russell to Erica and Tyler, "and they're losing three words a day." Erica agreed that there was a pattern, but pointed to the factor tree she and Tyler had calculated, arguing that the answer had to lie in the multiples. Andy urged more cross-talk, which led, within the next two minutes or so, to Tyler asking Heather to review her procedure; Erica defending her answer, for "maybe the problem doesn't give us enough information"; and Erica lighting up suddenly and saying, "Oh, it is six!" In a recent rural math contest, students from Polaris won an award for group problem-solving, and this exchange demonstrated why. Andy encouraged students to work together, articulate strategies, consider alternatives, and come to consensus.

Across the room, Michele sat cross-legged on the floor between two teams of third- and fourth-graders playing a math game. The school board wanted students to develop facility with estimating and rapid calculation, necessary in ranch life. Historically, rural boards were responsible for curriculum, and some still exercise control over what gets taught. That was not so at Polaris, but the board did want there to be some "basic skills" work combined with Andy's more reflective, conceptual approach. Andy agreed that such skills were necessary, so he and Michele worked up activities like this.

The students had their multiplication tables in front of them; Leo, Dustin, and Rossy on one side, Melissa, Reba, and Clarissa on the other. Michele had fashioned two oversized cardboard dice, one displaying the numbers 1 through 6, the other 7 through 12. Each team would throw a die and create a division problem that had, as its remainder, the number that came up on the roll. So when Rossy threw a 4, her team hurriedly consulted the multiplication table to figure out that if, say 21 divided by 7 equals 3, then, well, 25 divided by 7 would leave a remainder of 4—the number Rossy threw. *See you add a four to it. Put the four there. We've gotta get a remainder of four. That'll do it. The four'll do it. Oh, oh, I see. Yes. Yessss.* The team that created the most division problems at the end of the period would win, gaining familiarity with the multiplication table and some arithmetic flexibility along the way.

During this period, Sheryl, the itinerant speech therapist, had quietly entered the room and taken second-grader Colt to the library. One way that small independent rural districts like Polaris try to meet the special needs of their students is by joining a cooperative to get services like those Sheryl provided. This co-op included ten schools in two counties, so sometimes Sheryl covered 120 miles in a day, spending anywhere from a half-hour to two hours at each site, depending on need. On this day, she worked with Colt on blends (*gl, pl*) and digraphs (*sh, ch*). Then, when Andy had a moment, she conferred with him on strategies to address them in the more natural language flow of the classroom—she was especially concerned with the "l" sound—and I would see Andy play out her suggestion throughout the day.

At nine-thirty, Michele went into the library to review with the older students their works-in-progress on Montana Studies. One segment of their research required them to plan for a visiting historian or geographer a road tour that would cover at least three hundred miles and include sites important in Native American history, early trapping and mining, home-steading, agriculture, and the like. The assignment involved maps, written text, and an oral report, and Andy asked Michele to check in on Tyler, Russell, Erica, Heather, and James. Were the maps developing? Was the accompanying text more than just a bare-bones sketch?

Meanwhile, Andy convened the younger students at the couch to make sure they understood a new science assignment on habitat and adaptation. Each was to select a grassland animal, a forest animal, and an animal from a habitat of their own choosing and describe how body and behavior were adapted to environment, how various adaptations help the animal to eat, move, regulate temperature, and avoid enemies. "Let's say my forest animal is a squirrel," Andy speculated. "Think of what it eats and how its body has adapted to that." "A squirrel eats nuts," said Clarissa, her arms resting on her knees. "Yeah," added Rossy, thrusting herself out of the cushioned recesses of the couch, "so he'd have to have strong jaw muscles." "Good," said Andy, "Anything else?" "Mr. Bayliss"—Melissa waved her hand—"he'd have *sharp* teeth." "Yes, he would, Melissa. Thank you." Andy wanted the students to "think about animals in a new way, as beings adapted over time to their environments," and that was beginning to happen.

The discussion continued, and later that day Andy picked up the subject again when he tutored Colt.

Colt was a very good student, but, still, the adaptation assignment would be a challenge for a second-grader. Many traditional one-room schools had children follow lessons in text-books for their grade level, but, whenever possible, Andy liked to give the same assignment to a range of kids, encouraging them to engage it as best they could. This was one of the things, he believed, that made the multigrade classroom an exciting place. It could be especially rich for younger children, for it gave them opportunity to stretch beyond grade level. So he clicked on the computer and pulled Colt in beside him.

"What grassland animal did you choose, Colt?" "The antelope," Colt replied. "Great," said Andy, "let's get that in a sentence." "My grassland animal," Colt began, leaning in on his forearm to watch the screen as Andy typed, "is an antelope." "Good," said Andy. "Now how about adaptation? What about the antelope helps it live in its environment?" Colt ran the fingers of his left hand over his short bristly hair, thought a moment, and began: "It kind of has flat teeth and they eat grass." Andy typed and Colt watched. Then, appropriating the recommendations of the speech therapist, Andy had Colt read the text he had generated so far, paying special attention to the *l* sound in *land, animal, antelope,* and *flat*. Colt's pronunciation sounded good, and Andy had him read one more time.

"OK, Colt, what else do they have that helps them live?" "I know that they have leg-bones. . ." Colt checked himself. "I think that their hip," he revised, "is how they walk. . .because, uh, because if they didn't have a hip, they couldn't walk." Andy typed, then had Colt read. This wasn't particularly an example of adaptation—though with elaboration it might be—but Colt was on a roll, and Andy knew he could return to this hip business later in the week. "What about temperature, Colt? Like with the lambs you're raising, how do antelope keep warm or cool?" "Antelope have fur," Colt said, leaning in closer to the screen as his words appeared letter by quick letter. "It makes them warm." "Great!" said Andy, "and protection, avoiding enemies?" Colt let out a mild sigh of exasperation and rubbed his blond stubble again. "Mr. Bayliss . . ." "C'mon Colt, one more line." Colt looked back at the screen. "They put their horns down." Andy typed, Colt watching. "You know, Colt," Andy prodded, "it wouldn't be a complete report, would it, if we didn't say *why* the antelope does that." Colt said, "No, it wouldn't," and added "to protect themselves."

Once the students completed their individual projects—another week or so down the line—Andy would push their thinking by having them create "imaginary animals with weird adaptations and strange habitats." Melissa would write about the porcupine-octopus that lives at the edge of the ocean and protects itself from other animals with its quills; and Colt would draw a fierce baboon-lion, a monkeylike creature with big claws, able to leap about the savanna to both hunt prey and avoid danger.

● Ideas for Discussion, Writing and Research

1. Robert Everhart in "The Classroom World" describes how students at one junior high characterize "'teachers with negative attributes'" and "'teachers with positive attributes.'" With classmates, survey other students, asking them to describe the qualities of the best and worst teachers they remember from high school or junior high. Share your findings in groups and compare them with Everhart's. Do the students you interviewed use the same kinds of criteria to describe teachers? What conclusions can you draw about how students evaluate their teachers after reading Everhart's piece and conducting your own research?

2. In his composite picture of a day-in-the-life of Mark, a high school student, Theodore Sizer compares the American high school to "an academic supermarket." Similarly, in their piece, Arthur Powell, Eleanor Farrar, and David Cohen claim that "if Americans want to understand their high schools at work, they should imagine them as shopping malls." Do you agree with these authors' metaphors for describing secondary education in America? Using information from these authors' pieces and from your own experiences, explain why you agree or disagree. If you disagree, try to offer another extended metaphor for secondary schooling.

3. According to Theodore Sizer in "What High School Is," "young males and females are treated remarkably alike" in most high schools. He claims that "for many young women, the most liberated hours of their week are in school." Do you agree with Sizer's views? With your classmates, create your own "day-in-the-life profile" about a high school student, but make the main character a young woman. Compare your profiles and discuss similarities and differences.

4. Several of the authors in this chapter focus on the kinds of learning that students are expected to demonstrate in school. Drawing from information presented in at least three selections in this chapter, describe the kinds of knowledge that students are expected to acquire and produce in secondary schools. How do your own experiences in junior high or high school compare with these authors' views? Do you think schools expect too much or too little from students?

5. According to Arthur Powell et al., what is the "vertical curriculum" (formerly known as "tracking")? What is its purpose? Did your high school or your classmates's schools have this kind of curriculum? If so, how were the different levels of classes described (for example, "college-preparatory, general, accelerated . . . ")? How were students placed in these different levels of courses—according to personal choice, standardized test scores, a counselor's recommendation . . . ? Based on your own inquiries and on the examples of the "vertical curriculum" described in *The Shopping Mall High School*, what is your position about the use of this kind of curriculum in schools? Is it good or bad for students?

6. In his poem "Mad," Jerome Stern describes how college students feel when their teacher gets mad at them for reasons that they cannot fully understand. Why do you think this teacher gets mad at his students? Relate Stern's picture of frustrated college students to the accounts of secondary school teaching practices offered by Robert Everhart, Theodore

Sizer, and Arthur Powell et al. What conclusions can you draw about the factors that shape students' attitudes toward teachers and learning?

7. According to Jerome Stern in "What They Learn in School," schools and parents want to teach students "not to question, not to challenge, not to imagine, but to be obedient and behave well so that they can hold them forever as children to their bosoms as the second milennium lurches toward its panicky close." How do your experiences in secondary school challenge or corroborate Stern's views about hypocrisy in education?

8. In "Life on the Mississippi," Jonathan Kozol describes the surrounding neighborhood and the teaching and learning conditions at three schools in the largely African-American city of East St. Louis, Illinois: Martin Luther King Junior High, East St. Louis High, and Clark Junior High, "regarded as the top school in the city." How do Kozol's depictions of life at these schools compare with other authors' depictions of classroom life in this chapter? Drawing from related reading selections, discuss how you might account for the differences or similarities you find. (See in particular, selections by Harold Howe II and David Berliner and Bruce Biddle in Chapter Five.)

9. Using Jonathan Kozol's piece and others, explore the issue of equal access to quality education in America. (See related selections in Chapters One and Five.)

10. Mike Rose explains that his purpose in writing *Possible Lives* is to document and celebrate classrooms "in which the promise of public education is being powerfully realized." How do Rose's detailed descriptions of the Graphic Arts Academy in Pasadena, California and of Polaris School in rural Montana relate to his stated goal? How do these positive images of effective classrooms and curricula affect your own developing views about education in America?

11. While Mike Rose acknowledges that "the visitor traveling through our nation's schools would find burned-out teachers, lost students, boredom, violence, inertia," he argues that "if our understanding of schooling and the conception we have of what's possible emerge primarily from these findings, then what we can imagine for public education will be terribly narrow and impoverished." Discuss what you think Rose means by this statement and why you agree or disagree with him.

CHAPTER 3

Defining the Goals of Education and Literacy

153

The Paideia Proposal:
An Educational Manifesto

Mortimer J. Adler

Mortimer J. Adler is Chair of the Board of Editors of Encyclopedia Britannica
and the Chair of the Paideia Group, a group of concerned authors and
educators whose vision for improving public schooling in America is
described in the book *The Paideia Proposal: An Educational Manifesto*,
published in 1982; the following selection is an excerpt from this book. Adler
defines the meaning of "Paideia" on the book's opening page:

PAIDEIA (py-dee-a) from the Greek *pais, paidos*: the upbringing of a child. (Related
to pedagogy and pediatrics.) In an extended *sense*, the equivalent of the Latin
humanitas (from which the "humanities"), signifying the general learning that
should be the possession of all human beings.

We are on the verge of a new era in our national life. The long-needed educational
reform for which this country is at last ready will be a turning point toward that
new era.

Democracy has come into its own for the first time in this century. Not until this century
have we undertaken to give twelve years of schooling to all our children. Not until this century have we conferred the high office of enfranchised citizenship on all our people, regardless of sex, race, or ethnic origin.

The two—universal suffrage and universal schooling—are inextricably bound together.
The one without the other is a perilous delusion. Suffrage without schooling produces
mobocracy, not democracy—not rule of law, not constitutional government by the people as
well as for them.

The great American educator, John Dewey, recognized this early in this century. In
Democracy and Education, written in 1916, he first tied these two words together and let each
shine light upon the other.

A revolutionary message of that book was that a democratic society must provide equal
educational opportunity not only by giving to all its children the same quantity of public education—the same number of years in school—but also by making sure to give to all of them,
all with no exceptions, the same quality of education.

The ideal Dewey set before us is a challenge we have failed to meet. It is a challenge so difficult that it is understandable, perhaps excusable, that we have so far failed. But we cannot
continue to fail without disastrous consequences for all of us. For the proper working of our

Reprinted with the permission of Simon & Schuster from THE PAIDEIA PROPOSAL: AN EDUCATIONAL MANI-
FESTO by Mortimer Adler. Copyright © 1982 by The Institute for Philosophical Research.

political institutions, for the efficiency of our industries and businesses, for the salvation of our economy, for the vitality of our culture, and for the ultimate good of our citizens as individuals, and especially our future citizens—our children—we must succeed.

We are all sufferers from our continued failure to fulfill the educational obligations of a democracy. We are all the victims of a school system that has only gone halfway along the road to realize the promise of democracy.

At the beginning of this century, fewer than 10 percent of those of an age eligible for high school entered such schools. Today, almost 100 percent of our children enter, but not all complete such secondary schooling; many drop out for many reasons, some of them understandable.

It has taken us the better part of eighty years to go halfway toward the goal our society must achieve if it is to be a true democracy. The halfway mark was reached when we finally managed to provide twelve years of basic public schooling for all our children. At that point, we were closer to the goal that Horace Mann set for us more than a century ago when he said: "Education is the gateway to equality."

But the democratic promise of equal educational opportunity, half fulfilled, is worse than a promise broken. It is an ideal betrayed. Equality of educational opportunity is not, in fact, provided if it means no more than taking all the children into the public schools for the same number of hours, days, and years. If once there they are divided into the sheep and the goats, into those destined solely for toil and those destined for economic and political leadership and for a quality of life to which all should have access, then the democratic purpose has been undermined by an inadequate system of public schooling.

It fails because it has achieved only the same quantity of public schooling, not the same quality. This failure is a downright violation of our democratic principles.

We are politically a classless society. Our citizenry as a whole is our ruling class. We should, therefore, be an educationally classless society.

We should have a one-track system of schooling, not a system with two or more tracks, only one of which goes straight ahead while the others shunt the young off onto sidetracks not headed toward the goals our society opens to all. The innermost meaning of social equality is: *substantially the same quality of life for all.* That calls for: *the same quality of schooling for all.*

We may take some satisfaction, perhaps, in the fact that we have won half the battle—the quantitative half. But we deserve the full development of the country's human potential. We should, therefore, be vexed that we have not yet gone further. We should be impatient to get on with it, in and through the schools.

Progress toward the fulfillment of democracy by means of our educational system should and can be accelerated. It need not and must not take another century to achieve uniform quality for all in our public schools.

There are signs on all sides that tell us the people want that move forward now. The time is ripe. Parents, teachers, leaders of government, labor unions, corporations—above all, the young themselves—have uttered passionate complaints about the declining quality of public schooling.

There is no acceptable reason why trying to promote equality should have led to a lessening or loss of quality. Two decades after John Dewey, another great American educator, Robert Maynard Hutchins, as much committed to democracy as Dewey was before him, stated the fundamental principle we must now follow in our effort to achieve a true equality of educational conditions. "The best education for the best," he said, "is the best education for all."

The shape of the best education for the best is not unknown to us. But we have been slow to learn how to provide it. Nor have we always been honest in our commitment to democracy and its promise of equality. A part of our population—and much too large a part—has harbored the opinion that many of the nation's children are not fully educable. Trainable for one or another job, perhaps, but not educable for the duties of self-governing citizenship and for the enjoyment of things of the mind and spirit that are essential to a good human life.

We must end that hypocrisy in our national life. We cannot say out of one side of our mouth that we are for democracy and all its free institutions including, preeminently, political and civil liberty for all; and out of the other side of our mouth, say that only some of the children—fewer than half—are educable for full citizenship and a full human life.

With the exception of a few suffering from irremediable brain damage, every child is educable up to his or her capacity. Educable—not just trainable for jobs! As John Dewey said almost a century ago, vocational training, training for particular jobs, is not the education of free men and women.

True, children are educable in varying degrees, but the variation in degree must be of the same kind and quality of education. If "the best education for the best is the best education for all," the failure to carry out that principle is the failure on the part of society—a failure of parents, of teachers, of administrators—not a failure on the part of the children.

There are no unteachable children. There are only schools and teachers and parents who fail to teach them.

📖

At the very heart of a multitrack system of public schooling lies an abominable discrimination. The system aims at different goals for different groups of children. One goal, higher than the others, is harder to accomplish. The other goals are lower—and perhaps easier, but, ironically, they are all too frequently not attained.

The one-track system of public schooling that *The Paideia Proposal* advocates has the same objectives for all without exception.

These objectives are not now aimed at in any degree by the lower tracks onto which a large number of our underprivileged children are shunted—an educational dead end. It is a dead end because these tracks do not lead to the result that the public schools of a democratic society should seek, first and foremost, for all its children—preparation to go on learning, either at advanced levels of schooling, or in adult life, or both.

Nor, in the present state of our schools, is that main objective aimed at or attained in any satisfactory measure by the higher track along which a minority of favored children move during their years of basic schooling. That track is higher only in the sense that its aims are more difficult to accomplish. But even it is not now directed to the right objectives.

In the early years, before basic schooling branches out in different directions, it failed badly to teach proficiency in the indispensable skills of learning. Even in these years, when it is still a one-track system, it falls far short of delivering the goods.

To achieve the desired quality of democratic education, a one-track system of public schooling for twelve years must aim directly at three main objectives and make every effort to achieve them to a satisfactory degree.

These three objectives are determined by the vocations or callings common to all children when they grow up as citizens, earning their living and putting their free time to good use.

The first of these objectives has already been mentioned. It relates to that aspect of adult life which we call personal growth or self-improvement—mental, moral, and spiritual. Every child should be able to look forward not only to growing up but also to continued growth in all human dimensions throughout life. All should aspire to make as much of their powers as they can. Basic schooling should prepare them to take advantage of every opportunity for personal development that our society offers.

A second main objective has to do with another side of adult life—the individual's role as an enfranchised citizen of this republic. Citizens are the principal and permanent rulers of our society. Those elected to public office for a term of years are instrumental and transient rulers—in the service of the citizenry and responsible to the electorate.

The reason why universal suffrage in a true democracy calls for universal public schooling is that the former without the latter produces an ignorant electorate and amounts to a travesty of democratic institutions and processes. To avoid this danger, public schooling must be universal in more than its quantitative aspect. It must be universal also in its qualitative aspect. Hence, the second objective of basic schooling—an adequate preparation for discharging the duties and responsibilities of citizenship.

This requires not only the cultivation of the appropriate civic virtues, but also a sufficient understanding of the framework of our government and of its fundamental principles.

The third main objective takes account of the adult's need to earn a living in one or another occupation.

The twelve years of basic schooling must prepare them for this task, *not* by training them for one or another particular job in our industrial economy, but by giving them the basic skills that are common to all work in a society such as ours.

Here then are the three common callings to which all our children are destined: to earn a living in an intelligent and responsible fashion, to function as intelligent and responsible citizens, and to make both of these things serve the purpose of leading intelligent and responsible lives—to enjoy as fully as possible all the goods that make a human life as good as it can be.

To achieve these three goals, basic schooling must have for all a quality that can be best defined, *positively*, by saying that it must be general and liberal; and *negatively*, by saying that it must be nonspecialized and non-vocational.

Describing it as nonvocational may appear to be inconsistent with what has been said about its relation to earning a living. However, the schooling proposed is truly vocational in the sense that it aims to prepare children for the three vocations or callings common to all.

It is truly vocational in a further sense. It will prepare the young for earning a living by enabling them to understand the demands and workings of a technologically advanced society, and to become acquainted with its main occupations. It is nonvocational only in the sense that it does not narrowly train them for one or another particular job.

That kind of specialized or particularized job training at the level of basic schooling is in fact the reverse of something practical and effective in a society that is always changing and progressing. Anyone so trained will have to be retrained when he or she comes to his or her job. The techniques and technology will have moved on since the training in school took place.

Why, then, was such false vocationalism ever introduced into our schools? As the school population rapidly increased in the early decades of this century, educators and teachers turned to something that seemed more appropriate to do with that portion of the school population which they incorrectly and unjustly appraised as being uneducable—only trainable. In doing this, they violated the fundamental democratic maxim of equal educational opportunity.

As compared with narrow, specialized training for particular jobs, general schooling is of the greatest practical value. It is good not only because it is calculated to achieve two of the three main objectives at which basic schooling should aim—preparation for citizenship and for personal development and continued growth. It is also good practically because it will provide preparation for earning a living.

Of all the creatures on earth, human beings are the least specialized in anatomical equipment and in instinctive modes of behavior. They are, in consequence, more flexible than other creatures in their ability to adjust to the widest variety of environments and to rapidly changing external circumstances. They are adjustable to every clime and condition on earth and perpetually adjustable to the shock of change.

That is why general, nonspecialized schooling has the quality that most befits human nature. That is why, in terms of practicality and utility, it is better than any other kind of schooling.

But when we recognize that twelve years of general, nonspecialized schooling for all is the best policy—the most practical preparation for work—we should also realize that that is not its sole justification. It is not only the most expedient kind of schooling, but it is also best for the other reasons stated above: because it prepares our children to be good citizens and to lead good human lives.

To give the same quality of schooling to all requires a program of study that is both liberal and general, and that is, in several, crucial, overarching respects, one and the same for every child. All sidetracks, specialized courses, or elective choices must be eliminated. Allowing them will always lead a certain number of students to voluntarily downgrade their own education.

Elective choices are appropriate only in a curriculum that is intended for different avenues of specialization or different forms of preparation for the professions or technical careers. Electives and specialization are entirely proper at the level of advanced schooling—in our colleges, universities, and technical schools. They are wholly inappropriate at the level of basic schooling.

The course of study to be followed in the twelve years of basic schooling should, therefore, be completely required, with only one exception. That exception is the choice of a second language. In addition to competence in the use of English as everyone's primary language, basic schooling should confer a certain degree of facility in the use of a second language. That second language should be open to elective choice.

The diagram on the opposite page depicts in three columns three distinct modes of teaching and learning, rising in successive gradations of complexity and difficulty from the first to the twelfth year. All three modes are essential to the overall course of study.

These three columns are interconnected, as the diagram indicates. The different modes of learning on the part of the students and the different modes of teaching on the part of the teaching staff correspond to three different ways in which the mind can be improved—(1) by the acquisition of organized knowledge; (2) by the development of intellectual skills; and (3) by the enlargement of understanding, insight, and aesthetic appreciation.

In addition to the three main Columns of Learning, the required course of study also includes a group of auxiliary subjects, of which one is physical education and care of the body. This runs through all twelve years. Of the other two auxiliary subjects, instruction in a variety of manual arts occupies a number of years, but not all twelve; and the third consists of an introduction to the world of work and its range of occupations and careers. It is given in the last two of the twelve years.

Column One: Acquisition of Knowledge

Here are three areas of subject matter indispensable to basic schooling—language, literature, and fine arts; mathematics and natural sciences; history, geography, and social studies.

Why these three? They comprise the most fundamental branches of learning. No one can claim to be educated who is not reasonably well acquainted with all three. They provide the learner with indispensable knowledge about nature and culture, the world in which we live, our social institutions, and ourselves.

	Column One	**Column Two**	**Column Three**
Goals	Acquisition of Organized Knowledge	Development of Intellectual Skills— Skills of Learning	Enlarged Understanding of Ideas and Values
	by means of	by means of	by means of
Means	Didactic Instruction Lectures and Responses Textbooks and Other Aids	Coaching, Exercise, and Supervised Practice	Maieutic or Socratic Questioning and Active Participation
	in three areas of subject-matter	in the operations of	in the
Areas *Operations* *and Activities*	Language, Literature, and the Fine Arts Mathematics and Natural Science History, Geography, and Social Studies	Reading, Writing, Speaking, Listening Calculating, Problem-Solving Observing, Measuring, Estimating Exercising Critical Judgment	Discussion of Books (not textbooks) and Other Works of Art and Involvement in Artistic Activities e.g., Music, Drama, Visual Arts

The three columns do not correspond to separate courses, nor is one kind of teaching and learning necessarily confined to any one class.

The traditional name for the mode of instruction here is "didactic," or "teaching by telling." It employs textbooks and other instructional materials and is accompanied by laboratory demonstrations. The mind here is improved by the acquisition of organized knowledge.

Instruction in language comprises the learning of grammar and syntax, the forms of discourse, and to some extent the history of our own language. Comparisons between English and other languages being studied in the program should be stressed. Whether mathematics is also a language and how it compares with a natural language such as English should be considered.

Instruction in mathematics, beginning with simple arithmetic in the first grade, should rise to at least one year of calculus. It should be integrated from the very beginning with instruction in the use of calculators and lead subsequently to at least introductory instruction in the use of, and programming for, computers.

Instruction in the natural sciences includes physics, chemistry, and biology. Their interconnectedness and interdependence are stressed. Such instruction does not begin formally in the early grades but preparation for it can be made in a variety of attractive ways from the beginning.

History and geography are to be understood as including our knowledge of human and social affairs, not only within the boundaries of our own nation, but with regard to the rest of the world. Preparation for the formal study of history should begin in the early grades by storytelling and biographical narratives but, when formal study begins, it should be sequential and systematic, combining a narration of events with knowledge of social, political, and economic institutions and diverse phases of cultural development.

The innovative aspect of the first column lies not in the choice of subject matter but in the concentration and continuity of the study required. Those who know how inadequate and fragmentary is the knowledge offered to a large majority of those now graduating from high school will recognize the importance of our emphasis on these requirements.

Column Two: Development of Skill

Here are the basic skills of learning—competence in the *use* of language, primarily English, aided by facility in a second language, as well as competence in dealing with a wide range of symbolic devices, such as calculators, computers, and scientific instruments.

The skills to be acquired are the skills of *reading, writing, speaking, listening, observing, measuring, estimating,* and *calculating.* They are linguistic, mathematical, and scientific skills. They are the skills that everyone needs in order to learn anything, in school or elsewhere. Without them, it is impossible to go on learning by one's self, whether for pleasure, or to qualify for a new job, or to be promoted in the present one.

It will be noted that language and mathematics appear in both Columns One and Two, but their significance is different in each. In Column One, *knowledge about* mathematics and language is acquired; in Column Two, the student learns *how to do* mathematical operations correctly and how to use language effectively for communication. "Know-how" consists in skilled performance. It differs from "knowledge about," which consists in knowing that something is the thus-and-so, and not otherwise.

The development of the Column Two skills clearly has close connections with the study of the three fundamental areas of subject matter in Column One. Only to the degree that pupils develop these skills, and form the habit of using them, can instruction in language and literature, mathematics and natural science, history and geography be successful.

Skills cannot be acquired in a vacuum. They must be practiced in the very study of the three basic areas of subject matter, as well as in the process of acquiring linguistic competence, competence in communication, competence in the handling of symbolic devices, and competence in critical thinking.

Since what is learned here is skill in performance, not knowledge of facts and formulas, the mode of teaching cannot be didactic. It cannot consist in the teacher telling, demonstrating, or lecturing. Instead, it must be akin to the coaching that is done to impart athletic skills. A coach does not teach simply by telling or giving the learner a rule book to follow. A coach trains by helping the learner to *do*, to go through the right motions, and to organize a sequence of acts in a correct fashion. He corrects faulty performance again and again and insists on repetition of the performance until it achieves a measure of perfection.

Only in this way can skill in reading, writing, speaking, and listening be acquired. Only in this way can a similar measure of skill be acquired in mathematical and scientific operations. Only in this way can the ability to think critically—to judge and to discriminate—be developed. When coaching is not adequately undertaken, little can be expected in the development of the basic skills.

Coaching involves a different teacher-pupil relationship and a different pupil-teacher ratio than does instruction by telling and by the use of textbooks.

The innovative aspect of Column Two in the basic course of study lies in the fact that nowadays effective coaching and drilling is much too frequently absent from basic schooling. The lack of coaching and drilling by itself accounts for the present deficiencies of many high school graduates in reading, writing, computing, and in following directions.

It is evident that Column Two is the backbone of basic schooling. Proficiency in all the skills that it lists—all of them the very means of learning itself—is indispensable to the efficient teaching and learning of the subject matters in Column One; and also indispensable to teaching and learning in Column Three.

Acquiring facility in the use of a second language is included in Column Two. Among modern languages, a choice can be made of French, German, Italian, Spanish, Russian, Chinese, and possibly others; it may even extend to Latin and Greek. A second language serves to enlarge the scope of the student's understanding of the culture in which English is the primary language by introducing him or her to the imagery and conceptual framework of the cultures that employ these other languages.

Column Three: Enlargement of the Understanding

Here we have a mode of teaching and learning that has all too rarely been attempted in the public schools. Columns One and Two have important innovative aspects when compared with what now goes on and is either largely or totally left out. Column Three is virtually all innovative.

The materials of learning in Column Three can be described by calling them, on the one hand, books—books that are *not* textbooks—and, on the other hand, products of human artistry. The books are of every kind—historical, scientific, philosophical, poems, stories, essays. The products of human artistry include individual pieces of music, of visual art, plays, and productions in dance, film, or television. The emphasis throughout is on the individual work.

The mode of learning in Column Three engages the mind in the study of individual works of merit, whether literary or otherwise, accompanied by a discussion of the ideas, the values, and the forms embodied in such products of human art.

The appropriate mode of instruction in Column Three is neither didactic nor coaching. It cannot be teaching by telling and by using textbooks. It cannot consist in supervising the activities involved in acquiring skills.

It must be the Socratic mode of teaching, a mode of teaching called "maieutic" because it helps the student bring ideas to birth. It is teaching by asking questions, by leading discussions, by helping students to raise their minds up from a state of understanding or appreciating less to a state of understanding or appreciating more.

The interrogative or discussion method of teaching to be employed in Column Three stimulates the imagination and intellect by awakening the creative and inquisitive powers. In no other way can children's understanding of what they know be improved, and their appreciation of cultural objects be enhanced.

The books in Column Three—fiction, poetry, essays, history, science, and philosophy—serve a twofold purpose.

On the one hand, discussion draws on the student's skills of reading, writing, speaking, and listening, and uses them to sharpen the ability to think clearly, critically, and reflectively. It teaches participants how to analyze their own minds as well as the thought of others, which is to say it engages students in disciplined conversation about ideas and values.

On the other hand, discussion introduces students to the fundamental ideas in the basic subject matters of Column One, and especially the ideas underlying our form of government and the institutions of our society.

To fulfill the objective of preparing all young people to become intelligent citizens requires the careful reading and discussion of at least the following documents: the Declaration of Independence, the Constitution, selections from the *Federalist Papers*, and the Gettysburg Address. Other books will fill this purpose out, but these few are basic to understanding our democracy.

For mutual understanding and responsible debate among the citizens of a democratic community, and for differences of opinion to be aired and resolved, citizens must be able to communicate with one another in a common language. "Language" in this sense involves a common vocabulary of ideas. This common intellectual resource is theirs only if they have read, discussed, and come to understand a certain number of books that deal with the ideas operative in the life of their time and place.

Music and other works of art can be dealt with in seminars in which ideas are discussed; but, like poetry and fiction, they need an additional treatment in order to be appreciated aesthetically—to be enjoyed and admired for their excellence. In this connection, exercises in the performance and composition of poetry, music, and visual works, as well as in the production of dramatic works, will help develop that appreciation in the most direct manner.

The best way to understand a play is to act in it, or at least to read it out loud. The best way to understand a piece of music is to sing or play it. The best way to understand a work of dance is to try to dance it. Participation in the creation of works of art is as important as viewing, listening to, and discussing them. All children should have such pleasurable experiences.

The Integration of the Three Columns

We have noted earlier the interplay between Columns One and Two. It can now be seen how Column Three supplements and reinforces the learning that is accomplished in the other two columns.

The reading of books throughout the twelve years of basic schooling, from easy books and mainly imaginative works in the early grades to more difficult books and expository as well as imaginative in the upper grades acquaints the growing mind with fundamental ideas in the subject matters of Column One, and at the same time employs and perfects all the linguistic skills of Column Two.

Without coaching, learners will lack the skills needed for the study of the basic subject matters. Without discussion, they may be memorizing machines, able to pass quizzes or examinations. But probe their minds and you will find that what they know by memory, they do not understand.

They have spent hours in classrooms where they were talked at, where they recited and took notes, plus hours (often too few) of homework poring over textbooks, extracting facts to commit to memory. But when have their minds been addressed, in what connection have they been called upon to think for themselves, to respond to important questions and to raise them themselves, to pursue an argument, to defend a point of view, to understand its opposite, to weigh alternatives?

There is little joy in most of the learning they are now compelled to do. Too much of it is make-believe, in which neither teacher nor pupil can take a lively interest. Without some joy in learning—a joy that arises from hard work well done and from the participation of one's mind in a common task—basic schooling cannot initiate the young into the life of learning, let alone give them the skill and the incentive to engage in it further. Only the student whose mind has been engaged in thinking for itself is an active participant in the learning process that is essential to basic schooling.

Without what is called for in Column Three, such participation cannot be accomplished to any satisfactory degree. It is not now accomplished at all for most of the students in our public schools, and it is accomplished to an insufficient degree for even the chosen few.

❦ Cultural Literacy: What Every American Needs to Know

E. D. Hirsch, Jr.

Edward Donald Hirsch, Jr., whose formal academic training is in literary studies, holds a chaired position in English at the University of Virginia. This excerpt is from his 1987 book Cultural Literacy: What Every American Needs to Know, a book that launched one of the most heated debates about education in this country in years.

The Decline of Literate Knowledge

This book explains why we need to make some very specific educational changes in order to achieve a higher level of national literacy. It does not anatomize the literacy crisis or devote many pages to Scholastic Aptitude Test scores. It does not document at length what has already been established, that Americans do not read as well as they should. It takes no position about methods of initial reading instruction beyond insisting that content must receive as much emphasis as "skill." It does not discuss teacher training or educational funding or school governance. In fact, one of its major purposes is to break away entirely from what Jeanne S. Chall has called "the great debate" about methods of reading instruction. It focuses on what I conceive to be the great hidden problem in American education, and I hope that it reveals this problem so compellingly that anyone who is concerned about American education will be persuaded by the book's argument and act upon it.

The standard of literacy required by modern society has been rising throughout the developed world, but American literacy rates have not risen to meet this standard. What seemed an acceptable level in the 1950s is no longer acceptable in the late 1980s, when only highly literate societies can prosper economically. Much of Japan's industrial efficiency has been credited to its almost universally high level of literacy. But in the United States, only two thirds of our citizens are literate, and even among those the average level is too low and should be raised. The remaining third of our citizens need to be brought as close to true literacy as possible. Ultimately our aim should be to attain universal literacy at a very high level, to achieve not only greater economic prosperity but also greater social justice and more effective democracy. We Americans have long accepted literacy as a paramount aim of schooling, but only recently have some of us who have done research in the field begun to realize that literacy is far more than a skill and that it requires large amounts of specific information. That new insight is central to this book.

Professor Chall is one of several reading specialists who have observed that "world knowledge" is essential to the development of reading and writing skills.[1] What she calls world knowledge I call cultural literacy, namely, the network of information that all competent

Preface and "Literacy and Cultural Literacy," CULTURAL LITERACY by E. D. Hirsch, Jr. Copyright © 1987 by Houghton Mifflin Company. Reprinted by permission of Houghton Mifflin Company. All rights reserved.

readers possess. It is the background information, stored in their minds, that enables them to take up a newspaper and read it with an adequate level of comprehension, getting the point, grasping the implications, relating what they read to the unstated context which alone gives meaning to what they read. In describing the contents of this neglected domain of background information, I try to direct attention to a new opening that can help our schools make the significant improvement in education that has so far eluded us. The achievement of high universal literacy is the key to all other fundamental improvements in American education.

Why is literacy so important in the modern world? Some of the reasons, like the need to fill out forms or get a good job, are so obvious that they needn't be discussed. But the chief reason is broader. The complex undertakings of modern life depend on the cooperation of many people with different specialties in different places. Where communications fail, so do the undertakings. (That is the moral of the story of the Tower of Babel.) The function of national literacy is to foster effective nationwide communications. Our chief instrument of communication over time and space is the standard national language, which is sustained by national literacy. Mature literacy alone enables the tower to be built, the business to be well managed, and the airplane to fly without crashing. All nationwide communications, whether by telephone, radio, TV, or writing are fundamentally dependent upon literacy, for the essence of literacy is not simply reading and writing but also the effective use of the standard literate language. In Spain and most of Latin America the literate language is standard written Spanish. In Japan it is standard written Japanese. In our country it is standard written English.

Linguists have used the term "standard written English" to describe both our written and spoken language, because they want to remind us that standard spoken English is based upon forms that have been fixed in dictionaries and grammars and are adhered to in books, magazines, and newspapers. Although standard written English has no intrinsic superiority to other languages and dialects, its stable written forms have now standardized the oral forms of the language spoken by educated Americans.[2] The chief function of literacy is to make us masters of this standard instrument of knowledge and communication, thereby enabling us to give and receive complex information orally and in writing over time and space. Advancing technology, with its constant need for fast and complex communications, has made literacy ever more essential to commerce and domestic life. The literate language is more, not less, central in our society now than it was in the days before television and the silicon chip.

The recently rediscovered insight that literacy is more than a skill is based upon knowledge that all of us unconsciously have about language. We know instinctively that to understand what somebody is saying, we must understand more than the surface meanings of words; we have to understand the context as well. The need for background information applies all the more to reading and writing. To grasp the words on a page we have to know a lot of information that isn't set down on the page.

Consider the implications of the following experiment described in an article in *Scientific American*.[3] A researcher goes to Harvard Square in Cambridge, Massachusetts, with a tape recorder hidden in his coat pocket. Putting a copy of the *Boston Globe* under his arm, he pretends to be a native. He says to passers-by, "How do you get to Central Square?" The passersby, thinking they are addressing a fellow Bostonian, don't even break their stride when they give their replies, which consist of a few words like "First stop on the subway."

The next day the researcher goes to the same spot, but this time he presents himself as a tourist, obviously unfamiliar with the city. "I'm from out of town," he says. "Can you tell me how to get to Central Square?" This time the tapes show that people's answers are much longer and more rudimentary. A typical one goes, "Yes, well you go down on the subway. You can see the entrance over there, and when you get downstairs you buy a token, put it in the slot, and you go over to the side that says Quincy. You take the train headed for Quincy, but you get off very soon, just the first stop is Central Square, and be sure you get off there. You'll know it because there's a big sign on the wall. It says Central Square." And so on.

Passers-by were intuitively aware that communication between strangers requires an estimate of how much relevant information can be taken for granted in the other person. If they can take a lot for granted, their communications can be short and efficient, subtle and complex. But if strangers share very little knowledge, their communications must be long and relatively rudimentary.

In order to put in perspective the importance of background knowledge in language, I want to connect the lack of it with our recent lack of success in teaching mature literacy to all students. The most broadly based evidence about our teaching of literacy comes from the National Assessment of Educational Progress (NAEP). This nationwide measurement, mandated by Congress, shows that between 1970 and 1980 seventeen-year-olds declined in their ability to understand written materials, and the decline was especially striking in the top group, those able to read at an "advanced" level.[4] Although these scores have now begun to rise, they remain alarmingly low. Still more precise quantitative data have come from the scores of the verbal Scholastic Aptitude Test (SAT). According to John B. Carroll, a distinguished psychometrician, the verbal SAT is essentially a test of "advanced vocabulary knowledge," which makes it a fairly sensitive instrument for measuring levels of literacy.[5] It is well known that verbal SAT scores have declined dramatically in the past fifteen years, and though recent reports have shown them rising again, it is from a very low base. Moreover, performance on the verbal SAT has been slipping steadily *at the top*. Ever fewer numbers of our best and brightest students are making high scores on the test.

Before the College Board disclosed the full statistics in 1984, antialarmists could argue that the fall in average verbal scores could be explained by the rise in the number of disadvantaged students taking the SATs. That argument can no longer be made. It's now clear that not only our disadvantaged but also our best educated and most talented young people are showing diminished verbal skills. To be precise, out of a constant pool of about a million test takers each year, 56 percent more students scored above 600 in 1972 than did so in 1984. More startling yet, the percentage drop was even greater for those scoring above 650–73 percent.[6]

In the mid 1980s American business leaders have become alarmed by the lack of communication skills in the young people they employ. Recently, top executives of some large U.S. companies, including CBS and Exxon, met to discuss the fact that their younger middle-level executives could no longer communicate their ideas effectively in speech or writing. This group of companies has made a grant to the American Academy of Arts and Sciences to analyze the causes of this growing problem. They want to know why, despite breathtaking advances in the technology of communication, the effectiveness of business communication has been slipping, to the detriment of our competitiveness in the world. The figures from NAEP surveys and the scores on the verbal SAT are solid evidence that literacy has been declining in this country just when our need for effective literacy has been sharply rising.

I now want to juxtapose some evidence for another kind of educational decline, one that is related to the drop in literacy. During the period 1970–1985, the amount of shared knowledge that we have been able to take for granted in communicating with our fellow citizens has also been declining. More and more of our young people don't know things we used to assume they knew.

A side effect of the diminution in shared information has been a noticeable increase in the number of articles in such publications as *Newsweek* and the *Wall Street Journal* about the surprising ignorance of the young. My son John, who recently taught Latin in high school and eighth grade, often told me of experiences which indicate that these articles are not exaggerated. In one of his classes he mentioned to his students that Latin, the language they were studying, is a dead language that is no longer spoken. After his pupils had struggled for several weeks with Latin grammar and vocabulary, this news was hard for some of them to accept. One girl raised her hand to challenge my son's claim. "What do they speak in Latin America?" she demanded.

At least she had heard of Latin America. Another day my son asked his Latin class if they knew the name of an epic poem by Homer. One pupil shot up his hand and eagerly said, "The Alamo!" Was it just a slip for *The Iliad*? No, he didn't know what the Alamo was, either. To judge from other stories about information gaps in the young, many American schoolchildren are less well informed than this pupil. The following, by Benjamin J. Stein, is an excerpt from one of the most evocative recent accounts of youthful ignorance.

I spend a lot of time with teenagers. Besides employing three of them part-time, I frequently conduct focus groups at Los Angeles area high schools to learn about teenagers' attitudes towards movies or television shows or nuclear arms or politicians. . . .

I have not yet found one single student in Los Angeles, in either college or high school, who could tell me the years when World War II was fought. Nor have I found one who could tell me the years when World War I was fought. Nor have I found one who knew when the Americans Civil War was fought. . . .

A few have known how many U.S. senators California has, but none has known how many Nevada or Oregon has. ("Really? Even though they're so small?") . . . Only two could tell me where Chicago is, even in the vaguest terms. (My particular favorite geography lesson was the junior at the University of California at Los Angeles who thought that Toronto must be in Italy. My second-favorite geography lesson is the junior at USC, a pre-law student, who thought that Washington, D.C. was in Washington State.). . .

Only two could even approximately identify Thomas Jefferson. Only one could place the date of the Declaration of Independence. None could name even one of the first ten amendments to the Constitution or connect them with the Bill of Rights. . . .

On and on it went. On and on it goes. I have mixed up episodes of ignorance of facts with ignorance of concepts because it seems to me that there is a connection. . . . The kids I saw (and there may be lots of others who are different) are not mentally prepared to continue the society because they basically do not understand the society well enough to value it.[7]

My son assures me that his pupils are not ignorant. They know a great deal. Like every other human group they share a tremendous amount of knowledge among themselves, much of it learned in school. The trouble is that, from the standpoint of their literacy and their ability to communicate with others in our culture, what they know is ephemeral and narrowly confined to their own generation. Many young people strikingly lack the information that writers of American books and newspapers have traditionally taken for granted among their readers from all generations. For reasons explained in this book, our children's lack of intergenerational information is a serious problem for the nation. The decline of literacy and the decline of shared knowledge are closely related, interdependent facts.

The evidence for the decline of shared knowledge is not just anecdotal. In 1978 NAEP issued a report which analyzed a large quantity of data showing that our children's knowledge of American civics had dropped significantly between 1969 and 1976.[8] The performance of thirteen-year-olds had dropped an alarming eleven percentage points. That the drop has continued since 1976 was confirmed by preliminary results from a NAEP study conducted in late 1985. It was undertaken both because of concern about declining knowledge and because of the growing evidence of a causal connection between the drop in shared information and in literacy. The Foundations of Literacy project is measuring some of the specific information about history and literature that American seventeen-year-olds possess.

Although the full report will not be published until 1987, the preliminary field tests are disturbing.[9] If these samplings hold up, and there is no reason to think they will not, then the results we will be reading in 1987 will show that two thirds of our seventeen-year-olds do not know that the Civil War occurred between 1850 and 1900. Three quarters do not know what *reconstruction* means. Half do not know the meaning of *Brown decision* and cannot identify either Stalin or Churchill. Three quarters are unfamiliar with the names of standard American and British authors. Moreover, our seventeen-year-olds have little sense of geography or the relative chronology of major events. Reports of youthful ignorance can no longer be considered merely impressionistic.[10]

My encounter in the seventies with this widening knowledge gap first caused me to recognize the connection between specific background knowledge and mature literacy. The research I was doing on the reading and writing abilities of college students made me realize two things.[11] First, we cannot assume that young people today know things that were known in the past by almost every literate person in the culture. For instance, in one experiment conducted in Richmond, Virginia, our seventeen- and eighteen-year-old subjects did not know who Grant and Lee were. Second, our results caused me to realize that we cannot treat reading and writing as empty skills, independent of specific knowledge. The reading skill of a person may vary greatly from task to task. The level of literacy exhibited in each task depends on the relevant background information that the person possesses.

The lack of wide-ranging background information among young men and women now in their twenties and thirties is an important cause of the illiteracy that large corporations are finding in their middle-level executives. In former days, when business people wrote and spoke to one another, they could be confident that they and their colleagues had studied many similar things in school. They could talk to one another with an efficiency similar to that of native Bostonians who speak to each other in the streets of Cambridge. But today's high school graduates do not reliably share much common information, even when they graduate from the same school. If young people meet as strangers, their communications resemble the uncertain, rudimentary explanations recorded in the second part of the Cambridge experiment.

My father used to write business letters that alluded to Shakespeare. These allusions were effective for conveying complex messages to his associates, because, in his day, business people could make such allusions with every expectation of being understood. For instance, in my father's commodity business, the timing of sales and purchases was all-important, and he would sometimes write or say to his colleagues, "There is a tide," without further elaboration. Those four words carried not only a lot of complex information, but also the persuasive force of a proverb. In addition to the basic practical meaning, "Act now!" what came across was a lot of implicit reasons why immediate action was important.

For some of my younger readers who may not recognize the allusion, the passage from *Julius Caesar* is:

There is a tide in the affairs of men
Which taken at the flood leads on to fortune;
Omitted, all the voyage of their life
Is bound in shallows and in miseries.
On such a full sea are we now afloat,
And we must take the current when it serves,
Or lose our ventures.

To say "There is a tide" is better than saying "Buy (or sell) now and you'll cover expenses for the whole year, but if you fail to act right away, you may regret it the rest of your life." That would be twenty-seven words instead of four, and while the bare message of the longer statement would be conveyed, the persuasive force wouldn't. Think of the demands of such a business communication. To persuade somebody that your recommendation is wise and well-founded, you have to give lots of reasons and cite known examples and authorities. My father accomplished that and more in four words, which made quoting Shakespeare as effective as any efficiency consultant could wish. The moral of this tale is not that reading Shakespeare will help one rise in the business world. My point is a broader one. The fact that middle-level executives no longer share literate background knowledge is a chief cause of their inability to communicate effectively.

The Nature and Use of Cultural Literacy

The documented decline in shared knowledge carries implications that go far beyond the shortcomings of executives and extend to larger questions of educational policy and social justice in our country. Mina Shaughnessy was a great English teacher who devoted her professional life to helping disadvantaged students become literate. At the 1980 conference dedicated to her memory, one of the speakers who followed me to the podium was the Harvard historian and sociologist Orlando Patterson. To my delight he departed from his prepared talk to mention mine. He seconded my argument that shared information is a necessary background to true literacy. Then he extended and deepened the ideas I had presented. Here is what Professor Patterson said, as recorded in the *Proceedings* of the conference.

Industrialized civilization [imposes] a growing cultural and structural complexity which requires persons to have a broad grasp of what Professor Hirsch has called cultural literacy: a deep understanding of mainstream culture, which no longer has much to do with white Anglo-Saxon Protestants, but with the imperatives of industrial civilization. It is the need for cultural literacy, a profound conception of the whole civilization, which is often neglected in talk about literacy.

Patterson continued by drawing a connection between background information and the ability to hold positions of responsibility and power. He was particularly concerned with the importance for blacks and other minorities of possessing this information, which is essential for improving their social and economic status.

The people who run society at the macro-level must be literate in this culture. For this reason, it is dangerous to overemphasize the problems of basic literacy or the relevancy of literacy to specific tasks, and more constructive to emphasize that blacks will be condemned in perpetuity to oversimplified, low-level tasks and will never gain their rightful place in controlling the levers of power unless they also acquire literacy in this wider cultural sense.

Although Patterson focused his remarks on the importance of cultural literacy for minorities, his observations hold for every culturally illiterate person in our nation. Indeed, as he observed, cultural literacy is not the property of any group or class.

To assume that this wider culture is static is an error; in fact it is not. It's not a WASP culture; it doesn't belong to any group. It is essentially and constantly changing, and it is open. What is needed is recognition that the accurate metaphor or model for this wider literacy is not domination, but dialectic; each group participates and contributes, transforms and is transformed, as much as any other group. . . . The English language no longer belongs to any single group or nation. The same goes for any other area of the wider culture.[12]

As Professor Patterson suggested, being taught to decode elementary reading materials and specific, job-related texts cannot constitute true literacy. Such basic training does not make a person literate with respect to newspapers or other writings addressed to a general public. Moreover, a directly practical drawback of such narrow training is that it does not prepare anyone for technological change. Narrow vocational training in one state of a technology will not enable a person to read manuals that explain new developments in the same technology. In modern life we need general knowledge that enables us to deal with new ideas, events, and challenges. In today's world, general cultural literacy is more useful than what Professor Patterson terms "literacy to a specific task," because general literate information is the basis for many changing tasks.

Cultural literacy is even more important in the social sphere. The aim of universal literacy has never been a socially neutral mission in our country. Our traditional social goals were unforgettably renewed for us by Martin Luther King, Jr., in his "I Have a Dream" speech. King envisioned a country where the children of former slaves sit down at the table of equality with the children of former slave owners, where men and women deal with each other as equals and judge each other on their characters and achievements rather than their origins. Like Thomas Jefferson, he had a dream of a society founded not on race or class but on personal merit.

In the present day, that dream depends on mature literacy. No modern society can hope to become a just society without a high level of universal literacy. Putting aside for the moment the practical arguments about the economic uses of literacy, we can contemplate the even more basic principle that underlies our national system of education in the first place—that people in a democracy can be entrusted to decide all important matters for themselves because they can deliberate and communicate with one another. Universal literacy is inseparable from democracy and is the canvas for Martin Luther King's picture as well as for Thomas Jefferson's.

Both of these leaders understood that just having the right to vote is meaningless if a citizen is disenfranchised by illiteracy or semiliteracy. Illiterate and semiliterate Americans are condemned not only to poverty, but also to the powerlessness of incomprehension. Knowing that they do not understand the issues, and feeling prey to manipulative oversimplifications, they do not trust the system of which they are supposed to be the masters. They do not feel themselves to be active participants in our republic, and they often do not turn out to vote. The civic importance of cultural literacy lies in the fact that true enfranchisement depends upon knowledge, knowledge upon literacy, and literacy upon cultural literacy.

To be truly literate, citizens must be able to grasp the meaning of any piece of writing addressed to the general reader. All citizens should be able, for instance, to read newspapers of substance, about which Jefferson made the following famous remark:

> Were it left to me to decide whether we should have a government without newspapers, or newspapers without a government, I should not hesitate a moment to prefer the latter. But I should mean that every man should receive those papers and be capable of reading them.[13]

Jefferson's last comment is often omitted when the passage is quoted, but it's the crucial one.

Books and newspapers assume a "common reader," that is, a person who knows the things known by other literate persons in the culture. Obviously, such assumptions are never identical from writer to writer, but they show a remarkable consistency. Those who write for a mass public are always making judgments about what their readers can be assumed to know, and the judgments are closely similar. Any reader who doesn't possess the knowledge assumed in a piece he or she reads will in fact be illiterate with respect to that particular piece of writing.

Here, for instance, is a rather typical excerpt from the *Washington Post* of December 29, 1983.

> A federal appeals panel today upheld an order barring foreclosure on a Missouri farm, saying that U.S. Agriculture Secretary John R. Block has reneged on his

responsibilities to some debt ridden farmers. The appeals panel directed the USDA to create a system of processing loan deferments and of publicizing them as it said Congress had intended. The panel said that it is the responsibility of the agriculture secretary to carry out this intent "not as a private banker, but as a public broker."

Imagine that item being read by people who are well trained in phonics, word recognition, and other decoding skills but are culturally illiterate. They might know words like *foreclosure*, but they would not understand what the piece means. Who gave the order that the federal panel upheld? What is a federal appeals panel? Where is Missouri, and what about Missouri is relevant to the issue? Why are many farmers debt ridden? What is the USDA? What is a public broker? Even if culturally illiterate readers bothered to look up individual words, they would have little idea of the reality being referred to. The explicit words are just surface pointers to textual meaning in reading and writing. The comprehending reader must bring to the text appropriate background information that includes knowledge not only about the topic but also the shared attitudes and conventions that color a piece of writing.

Our children can learn this information only by being taught it. Shared literate information is deliberately sustained by national systems of education in many countries because they recognize the importance of giving their children a common basis for communication. Some decades ago a charming book called *1066 and All That* appeared in Britain.[14] It dealt with facts of British history that all educated Britons had been taught as children but remembered only dimly as adults. The book caricatured those recollections, purposely getting the "facts" just wrong enough to make them ridiculous on their face. Readers instantly recognized that the book was mistaken in its theory about what Ethelred-the-Unready was unready for, but, on the other hand, they couldn't say precisely what he *was* unready for. The book was hilarious to literate Britons as a satire of their own vague and confused memories. But even if their schoolchild knowledge had become vague with the passage of time, it was still functional, because the information essential to literacy is rarely detailed or precise.

This haziness is a key characteristic of literacy and cultural literacy. To understand the *Washington Post* extract literate readers have to know only vaguely, in the backs of their minds, that the American legal system permits a court decision to be reversed by a higher court. They would need to know only that a judge is empowered to tell the executive branch what it can or cannot do to farmers and other citizens. (The secretary of agriculture was barred from foreclosing a Missouri farm.) Readers would need to know only vaguely what and where Missouri is, and how the department and the secretary of agriculture fit into the scheme of things. None of this knowledge would have to be precise. Readers wouldn't have to know whether an appeals panel is the final judicial level before the U.S. Supreme Court. Any practiced writer who feels it is important for a reader to know such details always provides them.

Much in verbal communication is necessarily vague, whether we are conversing or reading. What counts is our ability to grasp the general shape of what we are reading and to tie it to what we already know. If we need details, we rely on the writer or speaker to develop them. Or if we intend to ponder matters in detail for ourselves, we do so later, at our leisure. For instance, it is probably true that many people do not know what a beanball is in baseball. So in an article on the subject the author conveniently sets forth as much as the culturally literate reader must know.

> Described variously as the knockdown pitch, the beanball, the duster and the purpose pitch—the Pentagon would call it the peacekeeper—this delightful stratagem has graced the scene for most of the 109 years the major leagues have existed. It starts fights. It creates lingering grudges. It sends people to the hospital. . . . "You put my guy in the dirt, I put your guy in the dirt."[15]

To understand this text, we don't have to know much about the particular topic in advance, but we do require quite a lot of vague knowledge about baseball to give us a sense of the whole meaning, whether our knowledge happens to be vague or precise.

The superficiality of the knowledge we need for reading and writing may be unwelcome news to those who deplore superficial learning and praise critical thinking over mere information. But one of the sharpest critical thinkers of our day, Dr. Hilary Putnam, a Harvard philosopher, has provided us with a profound insight into the importance of vague knowledge in verbal communication.[16]

> Suppose you are like me and cannot tell an elm from a beech tree. . . . [I can nonetheless use the word "elm" because] *there is a division of linguistic labor. . . .* It is not at all necessary or efficient that everyone who wears a gold ring (or a gold cufflink, etc.) be able to tell with any reliability whether or not something is really gold. . . . Everyone to whom the word "gold" is important for any reason has to *acquire* the word "gold"; but he does not have to acquire the *method of recognizing* if something is or is not gold.

Putnam does acknowledge a limit on the degrees of ignorance and vagueness that are acceptable in discourse. "Significant communication," he observes, "requires that people know something of what they are talking about." Nonetheless, what is required for communication is often so vague and superficial that we can properly understand and use the word *elm* without being able to distinguish an elm tree from a beech tree. What we need to know in order to use and understand a word is an initial stereotype that has a few vague traits.

> Speakers are *required* to know something about (stereotypic) tigers in order to count as having acquired the word "tiger"; something about elm trees (or anyway about the stereotype thereof) to count as having acquired the word "elm," etc. . . . The nature of the required minimum level of competence depends heavily upon both the culture and the topic, however. In our culture speakers are not . . . required to know the fine details (such as leaf shape) of what an elm tree looks like. English speakers are *required by their linguistic community* to be able to tell tigers from leopards; they are not required to be able to tell beech trees from elm trees.

When Putnam says that Americans can be depended on to distinguish tigers and leopards but not elms and beeches, he assumes that his readers will agree with him because they are culturally literate. He takes for granted that one literate person knows approximately the same things as another and is aware of the probable limits of the other person's knowledge.

That second level of awareness—knowing what others probably know—is crucial for effective communication. In order to speak effectively to people we must have a reliable sense of what they do and do not know. For instance, if Putnam is right in his example, we should not have to tell a stranger that a leopard has spots or a tiger stripes, but we would have to explain that an elm has rough bark and a beech smooth bark if we wanted that particular piece of information conveyed. To know what educated people know about tigers but don't know about elm trees is the sort of cultural knowledge, limited in extent but possessed by all literate people, that must be brought into the open and taught to our children.

Besides being limited in extent, cultural literacy has another trait that it is important for educational policy—its national character. It's true that literate English is an international language, but only so long as the topics it deals with are international. The background knowledge of people from other English-speaking nations is often inadequate for complex and subtle communications within our nation. The knowledge required for national literacy differs from country to country, even when their national language is the same. It is no doubt true that one layer of cultural literacy is the same for all English-speaking nations. Australians, South Africans, Britons, and Americans share a lot of knowledge by virtue of their common language. But much of the knowledge required for literacy in, say, Australia is specific to that country, just as much of ours is specific to the United States.

For instance, a literate Australian can typically understand American newspaper articles on international events or the weather but not one on a federal appeals panel. The same holds true for Americans who read Australian newspapers. Many of us have heard "Waltzing Matilda," a song known to every Australian, but few Americans understand or need to understand what the words mean.

> Once a jolly swagman camped beside a billabong,
> Under the shade of a coolibah tree,
> And he sang as he sat and waited while his billy boiled,
> "You'll come a'waltzing Matilda, with me."

Waltzing Matilda doesn't mean dancing with a girl; it means walking with a kind of knapsack. A *swagman* is a hobo, a *billabong* is a pond, a *coolibah* is a eucalyptus, and a *billy* is a can for making tea.

The national character of the knowledge needed in reading and writing was strikingly revealed in an experiment conducted by Richard C. Anderson and others at the Center for the Study of Reading at the University of Illinois. They assembled two paired groups of readers, all highly similar in sexual balance, educational background, age, and social class.[17] The only difference between the groups was that one was in India, the other in the United States. Both were given the same two letters to read. The texts were similar in overall length, word-frequency distribution, sentence length and complexity, and number of explicit propositions. Both letters were on the same topic, a wedding, but one described an Indian wedding, the other an American wedding. The reading performances of the two groups—their speed and accuracy of comprehension—split along national lines. The Indians performed well in reading about the Indian wedding but poorly in reading about the American one, and the Americans did the opposite. This experiment not only reconfirmed the dependence of reading skill on cultural literacy, it also demonstrated its national character.

Although nationalism may be regrettable in some of its worldwide political effects, a mastery of national culture is essential to mastery of the standard language in every modern nation. This point is important for educational policy, because educators often stress the virtues of multicultural education. Such study is indeed valuable in itself; it inculcates tolerance and provides a perspective on our own traditions and values. But however laudable it is, it should not be the primary focus of national education. It should not be allowed to supplant or interfere with our schools' responsibility to ensure our children's mastery of American literate culture. The acculturative responsibility of the schools is primary and fundamental. To teach the ways of one's own community has always been and still remains the essence of the education of our children, who enter neither a narrow tribal culture nor a transcendent world culture but a national literate culture. For profound historical reasons, this is the way of the modern world.[18] It will not change soon, and it will certainly not be changed by educational policy alone.

The Decline of Teaching Cultural Literacy

Why have our schools failed to fulfill their fundamental acculturative responsibility? In view of the immense importance of cultural literacy for speaking, listening, reading, and writing, why has the need for a definite, shared body of information been so rarely mentioned in discussions of education? In the educational writings of the past decade, I find almost nothing on this topic, which is not arcane. People who are introduced to the subject quickly understand why oral or written communication requires a lot of shared background knowledge. It's not the difficulty or novelty of the idea that has caused it to receive so little attention.

Let me hazard a guess about one reason for our neglect of the subject. We have ignored cultural literacy in thinking about education—certainly I as a researcher also ignored it until recently—precisely because it was something we have been able to take for granted. We ignore the air we breathe until it is thin or foul. Cultural literacy is the oxygen of social intercourse. Only when we run into cultural illiteracy are we shocked into recognizing the importance of the information that we had unconsciously assumed.

To be sure, a minimal level of information is possessed by any normal person who lives in the United States and speaks elementary English. Almost everybody knows what is meant by *dollar* and that cars must travel on the right-hand side of the road. But this elementary level of information is not sufficient for a modern democracy. It isn't sufficient to allow us to read newspapers (a sin against Jeffersonian democracy), and it isn't sufficient to achieve economic fairness and high productivity. Cultural literacy lies *above* the everyday levels of knowledge that everyone possesses and *below* the expert level known only to specialists. It is that middle ground of cultural knowledge possessed by the "common reader." It includes information that we have traditionally expected our children to receive in school, but which they no longer do.

During recent decades Americans have hesitated to make a decision about the specific knowledge that children need to learn in school. Our elementary schools are not only dominated by the content-neutral ideas of Rousseau and Dewey, they are also governed by approximately sixteen thousand independent school districts. We have viewed this dispersion of educational authority as an insurmountable obstacle to altering the fragmentation of the school curriculum even when we have questioned that fragmentation. We have permitted school policies that have shrunk the body of information that Americans share, and these policies have caused our national literacy to decline.

At the same time we have searched with some eagerness for causes such as television that lie outside the schools. But we should direct our attention undeviatingly toward what the schools teach rather than toward family structure, social class, or TV programming. No doubt, reforms outside the schools are important, but they are harder to accomplish. Moreover, we have accumulated a great deal of evidence that faulty policy in the schools is the chief cause of deficient literacy. Researchers who have studied the factors influencing educational outcomes have found that the school curriculum is the most important controllable influence on what our children know and don't know about our literate culture.[19]

It will not do to blame television for the state of our literacy. Television watching does reduce reading and often encroaches on homework. Much of it is admittedly the intellectual equivalent of junk food. But in some respects, such as its use of standard written English, television watching is acculturative.[20] Moreover, as Herbert Walberg points out, the schools themselves must be held partly responsible for excessive television watching, because they have not firmly insisted that students complete significant amounts of homework, an obvious way to increase time spent on reading and writing.[21] Nor should our schools be excused by an appeal to the effects of the decline of the family or the vicious circle of poverty, important as these factors are. Schools have, or should have, children for six or seven hours a day, five days a week, nine months a year, for thirteen years or more. To assert that they are powerless to make a significant impact on what their students learn would be to make a claim about American education that few parents, teachers, or students would find it easy to accept.

Just how fragmented the American public school curriculum has become is described in *The Shopping Mall High School*, a report on five years of firsthand study inside public and private secondary schools. The authors report that our high schools offer courses of so many kinds that "the word 'curriculum' does not do justice to this astonishing variety." The offerings include not only academic courses of great diversity, but also courses in sports and hobbies and a "services curriculum" addressing emotional or social problems. All these courses are deemed "educationally valid" and carry course credit. Moreover, among academic offerings are numerous versions of each subject, corresponding to different levels of student interest and ability. Needless to say, the material covered in these "content area" courses is highly varied.[22]

Cafeteria-style education, combined with the unwillingness of our schools to place demands on students, has resulted in a steady diminishment of commonly shared information between generations and between young people themselves. Those who graduate from the same school have often studied different subjects, and those who graduate from different schools have often studied different material even when their courses have carried the same titles. The inevitable consequence of the shopping mall high school is a lack of shared knowledge across and within schools. It would be hard to invent a more effective recipe for cultural fragmentation.

The formalistic educational theory behind the shopping mall school (the theory that any suitable content will inculcate reading, writing, and thinking skills) has had certain political advantages for school administrators. It has allowed them to stay scrupulously neutral with regard to content.[23] Educational formalism enables them to regard the indiscriminate variety of school offerings as a positive virtue, on the grounds that such variety can accommodate the different interests and abilities of different students. Educational formalism has also conveniently allowed school administrators to meet objections to the traditional literate materials that used to be taught in the schools. Objectors have said that traditional materials are class-bound, white, Anglo-Saxon, and Protestant, not to mention racist, sexist, and excessively Western. Our schools have tried to offer enough diversity to meet these objections from liberals and enough Shakespeare to satisfy conservatives. Caught between ideological parties, the schools have been attracted irresistibly to a quantitative and formal approach to curriculum making rather than one based on sound judgments about what should be taught.

Some have objected that teaching the traditional literate culture means teaching conservative material. Orlando Patterson answered that objection when he pointed out that mainstream culture is not the province of any single social group and is constantly changing by assimilating new elements and expelling old ones.[24] Although mainstream culture is tied to the written word and may therefore seem more formal and elitist than other elements of culture, that is an illusion. Literate culture is the most democratic culture in our land: it excludes nobody; it cuts across generations and social groups and classes; it is not usually one's first culture, but it should be everyone's second, existing as it does beyond the narrow spheres of family, neighborhood, and region.

As the universal second culture, literate culture has become the common currency for social and economic exchange in our democracy, and the only available ticket to full citizenship. Getting one's membership card is not tied to class or race. Membership is automatic if one learns the background information and the linguistic conventions that are needed to read, write, and speak effectively. Although everyone is literate in some local, regional, or ethnic culture, the connection between mainstream culture and the national written language justifies calling mainstream culture _the_ basic culture of the nation.

The claim that universal cultural literacy would have the effect of preserving the political and social status quo is paradoxical because in fact the traditional forms of literate culture are precisely the most effective instruments for political and social change. All political discourse at the national level must use the stable forms of the national language and its associated culture. Take the example of _The Black Panther_, a radical and revolutionary newspaper if ever this country had one. Yet the _Panther_ was highly conservative in its language and cultural assumptions, as it had to be in order to communicate effectively. What could be more radical in sentiment but more conservative in language and assumed knowledge than the following passages from that paper?

> The present period reveals the criminal growth of bourgeoisdemocracy since the betrayal of those who died that this nation might live "free and indivisible." It exposes through the trial of the Chicago Seven, and its law and order edicts, its desperate turn toward the establishment of a police state. (January 17, 1970)
>
> In this land of "milk and honey," the "almighty dollar" rules supreme and is being upheld by the faithful troops who move without question in the name of "law and order." Only in this garden of hypocrisy and inequality can a murderer not be considered a murderer—only here can innocent people be charged with a crime and

be taken to court with the confessed criminal testifying against them. Incredible? (March 28, 1970)

In the United States, the world's most technologically advanced country, one million youths from 12 to 17 years of age are illiterate—unable to read as well as the average fourth grader, says a new government report. Why so much illiteracy in a land of so much knowledge? The answer is because there is racism. Blacks and other Nonwhites receive the worst education. (May 18, 1974)

The last item of the Black Panther Party platform, issued March 29, 1972, begins

10. WE WANT LAND, BREAD, HOUSING, EDUCATION, CLOTHING, JUSTICE, PEACE AND PEOPLE'S CONTROL OF MODERN TECHNOLOGY.

When in the course of human events it becomes necessary for one people to dissolve the political bands which have connected them with another, and to assume among the powers of the earth the separate and equal station to which the laws of nature and nature's God entitle them, a decent respect to the opinions of mankind requires that they should declare the causes which impel them to the separation.

And so on for the first five hundred of Jefferson's words without the least hint, or need of one, that this is a verbatim repetition of an earlier revolutionary declaration. The writers for *The Black Panther* had clearly received a rigorous traditional education in American history, in the Declaration of Independence, the Pledge of Allegiance to the Flag, the Gettysburg Address, and the Bible, to mention only some of the direct quotations and allusions in these passages. They also received rigorous traditional instruction in reading, writing, and spelling. I have not found a single misspelled word in the many pages of radical sentiment I have examined in that newspaper. Radicalism in politics, but conservatism in literate knowledge and spelling: to be a conservative in the *means* of communication is the road to effectiveness in modern life, in whatever direction one wishes to be effective.

To withhold traditional culture from the school curriculum, and therefore from students, in the name of progressive ideas is in fact an unprogressive action that helps preserve the political and economic status quo. Middle-class children acquire mainstream literate culture by daily encounters with other literate persons. But less privileged children are denied consistent interchanges with literate persons and fail to receive this information in school. The most straightforward antidote to their deprivation is to make the essential information more readily available inside the schools.

The Critical Importance of Early Schooling

Once we become aware of the inherent connection between literacy and cultural literacy, we have a duty to those who lack cultural literacy to determine and disclose its contents. To someone who is unaware of the things a literate person is expected to know, a writer's assumption that readers possess cultural literacy could appear to be a conspiracy of the literate against the illiterate, for the purpose of keeping them out of the club. But there is no conspiracy. Writers *must* make assumptions about the body of information their readers know. Unfortunately for the disadvantaged, no one ever spells out what that information is. But, as the Appendix illustrates, the total quantity of commonly shared information that the schools need to impart is less daunting than one might think, for the crucial background knowledge possessed by literate people is, as I have pointed out, telegraphic, vague, and limited in extent.

Preschool is not too early for starting earnest instruction in literate national culture. Fifth grade is almost too late. Tenth grade usually *is* too late. Anyone who is skeptical of this assertion should take a look at a heterogeneous class of fifth-graders engaged in summarizing a piece they have read. There are predictable differences between the summaries given by children with culturally adequate backgrounds and those given by children without. Although disadvantaged children often show an acceptable ability to decode and pronounce individual words, they are frequently unable to gain an integrated sense of a piece as a whole. They miss central implications and associations because they don't possess the background knowledge necessary to put the text in context. Hearing they hear not, and seeing they do not understand.[25]

Yet if you observe a kindergarten or first-grade class in which pupils have the same diversity of family background, you will not find a similar spread in the reading performances of pupils from different social classes. Disadvantaged first-graders do as well as middle class ones in sounding out letters and simple words.[26] What happens between first grade and fifth grade to change the equality of performance? The impression that something significant has occurred or has failed to occur in these early grades is confirmed by international comparisons of reading attainment at early ages in different countries. Before grade three, when reading skills are more mechanical than interpretive, the United States stands in the top group of countries. Later, when reading requires an understanding of more complex content, our comparative ranking drops.[27] Although our schools do comparatively well in teaching elementary decoding skills, they do less well than schools of some other countries in teaching the background knowledge that pupils must possess to succeed at mature reading tasks.

The importance of this evidence for improving our national literacy can scarcely be overemphasized. If in the early grades our children were taught texts with cultural content rather than "developmental" texts that develop abstract skills, much of the specific knowledge deficit of disadvantaged children could be overcome. For it is clear that one critical difference in the reading performances of disadvantaged fifth-graders as compared with advantaged pupils is the difference in their cultural knowledge. Background knowledge does not take care of itself. Reading and writing are cumulative skills; the more we read the more necessary knowledge we gain for further reading.

Around grade four, those who lack the initial knowledge required for significant reading begin to be left behind permanently. Having all too slowly built up their cultural knowledge, they find reading and learning increasingly toilsome, unproductive, and humiliating. It follows that teaching cultural information in the early grades would do more than just improve the reading performance of all our children. By removing one of the causes of failure, it would especially enhance the motivation, self-esteem, and performance of disadvantaged children.

Really effective reforms in the teaching of cultural literacy must therefore begin with the earliest grades. Every improvement made in teaching very young children literate background information will have a multiplier effect on later learning, not just by virtue of the information they will gain but also by virtue of the greater motivation for reading and learning they will feel when they actually understand what they have read.

Young children enjoy absorbing formulaic knowledge. Even if they did not, our society would still find it essential to teach them all sorts of traditions and facts. Critical thinking and basic skills, two areas of current focus in education, do not enable children to create out of their own imaginations the essential names and concepts that have arisen by historical accident. The Rio Grande, the Mason-Dixon line, "The Night Before Christmas,""and *Star Wars* are not products of basic skills or critical thought. Many items of literate culture are arbitrary, but that does not make them dispensable. Facts are essential components of the basic skills that a child entering a culture must have.

I'm not suggesting that we teach our children exactly what our grandparents learned. We should teach children current mainstream culture. It's obvious that the content of cultural literacy changes over the years. Today the term "Brown decision" belongs to cultural literacy, but in 1945 there hadn't been any Brown decision. The name Harold Ickes was current in 1945 but no longer is. Such mutability is the fate of most names and events of recent history. Other changes come through contributions of various subnational cultures. Ethnic words (like *pizza* and art forms (like *jazz*) are constantly entering and departing from mainstream culture. Other subnational cultures, including those of science and technology, also cause changes in the mainstream. DNA and quarks, now part of cultural literacy, were unknown in 1945. In short, terms that literate people know in the 1are different from those they knew in 1945, and forty years hence the literate culture will again be different.

The flux in mainstream culture is obvious to all. But stability, not change, is the chief characteristic of cultural literacy. Although historical and technical terms may follow the ebb and flow of events, the more stable elements of our national vocabulary, like George Washington, the tooth fairy, the Gettysburg Address, Hamlet, and the Declaration of Independence, have persisted for a long time. These stable elements of the national vocabulary are at the core of cultural literacy, and for that reason are the most important contents of schooling. Although the terms that ebb and flow are tremendously important at a given time, they belong, from an educational standpoint, at the periphery of culture. The persistent, stable elements belong at the educational core.

Let me give some concrete examples of the kinds of core information I mean. American readers are assumed to have a general knowledge of the following people (I give just the beginning of a list): John Adams, Susan B. Anthony, Benedict Arnold, Daniel Boone, John Brown, Aaron Burr, John C. Calhoun, Henry Clay, James Fenimore Cooper, Cornwallis, Davy Crockett, Emily Dickinson, Stephen A. Douglas, Frederick Douglass, Edwards, Ralph Waldo Emerson, Benjamin Franklin, Robert Fulton, Ulysses S. Grant, Alexander Hamilton, and Nathaniel Hawthorne. Most of us know rather little about these people, but that little is of crucial importance, because it allows writers and speakers to assume a starting point from which they can treat in detail what they wish to focus on.

Here is another list that no course in critical thinking skills, however masterful, could ever generate: Antarctic Ocean, Arctic Ocean, Atlantic Ocean, Baltic Sea, Black Sea, Caribbean Sea, Gulf of Mexico, Pacific Ocean, Red Sea. It has a companion list: Alps, Appalachians,

Himalayas, Matterhorn, Mount Everest, Mount Vesuvius, Rocky Mountains. Because literate people mention such names in passing, usually without explanation, children should acquire them as part of their intellectual equipment.

Children also need to understand elements of our literary and mythic heritage that are often alluded to without explanation, for example, Adam and Eve, Cain and Abel, Noah and the Flood, David and Goliath, the Twenty-third Psalm, Humpty Dumpty, Jack Sprat, Jack and Jill, Little Jack Horner, Cinderella, Jack and the Beanstalk, Mary had a little lamb, Peter Pan, and Pinocchio. Also Achilles, Adonis, Aeneas, Agamemnon, Antigone, and Apollo, as well as Robin Hood, Paul Bunyan, Satan, Sleeping Beauty, Sodom and Gomorrah, the Ten Commandments, and Tweedledum and Tweedledee.

Our current distaste for memorization is more pious than realistic. At an early age when their memories are most retentive, children have an almost instinctive urge to learn specific tribal traditions. At that age they seem to be fascinated by catalogues of information and are eager to master the materials that authenticate their membership in adult society. Observe for example how they memorize the rather complex materials of football, baseball, and basketball, even without benefit of formal avenues by which that information is inculcated.

The weight of human tradition across many cultures supports the view that basic acculturation should largely be completed by age thirteen. At that age Catholics are confirmed, Jews bar or bat mitzvahed, and tribal boys and girls undergo the rites of passage into the tribe. According to the anthropological record, all cultures whose educational methods have been reported in the *Human Relations Area Files* (a standard source for anthropological data) have used early memorization to carry on their traditions.[28]

In Korea, "numerous books must be memorized, including the five *Kyung*, and the four *Su*." In Tibet, "from eight to ten years of age, the boy spends most of his time reading aloud and memorizing the scriptures." In Chile, the Araucanian Indians use the memorization of songs as an educational technique to teach " the subtleties of the native tongue, and an insight into the customs and traditions of their tribe." In southern Africa, the children of the Kung bushmen listen for hours to discussions of which they understand very little until they "know the history of every object, every exchange between their families, before they are ten or twelve years old." In Indonesia, "memorization is the method commonly used." In Thailand, children "repeat their lessons until they know them by heart." In Arizona, the Papago Indians take children through the lengthy rituals "as many times as needed for the learner to say it all through, which may take a year."[29]

The new kind of teaching espoused by Rousseau and Dewey, which avoids rote learning and encourages the natural development of the child on analogy with the development of an acorn into an oak, has one virtue certainly: it encourages independence of mind. But the theory also has its drawbacks, one of which is that a child is not in fact like an acorn. Left to itself, a child will not grow into a thriving creature; Tarzan is pure fantasy. To thrive, a child needs to learn the traditions of the particular human society and culture it is born into.[30] Like children everywhere, American children need traditional information at a very early age.

A great deal is at stake in understanding and acting on this essential perception as soon as possible. The opportunity of acquiring cultural literacy, once lost in the early grades is usually lost for good. That is most likely to be true for children of parents who were not themselves taught the literate national culture.

Endnotes

1. For rising standards of literacy, see R. L. Thorndike, *Reading Comprehension Education in Fifteen Countries: An Empirical Study* (New York: Wiley, 1973). On the connection between high literacy and Japan's economic performance, see Thomas P. Rohlen, "Japanese Education: If They Can Do It, Should We?" *American Scholar 55, I* (Winter 1985–86): 29–44. For American literacy rates see Jeanne Chall, "Afterword," in R. C. Anderson et al., *Becoming a Nation of Readers: The Report of the Commission on Reading* (Washington, D. C.: National Institute of Education, 1985), 123–24. On "world knowledge" in literacy, see Jeanne S. Chall, *Stages of Reading Development* (New York: McGraw-Hill, 1983), 8.
2. The two classical discussions of the stabilizing effects of mass literacy on oral speech are Henry Bradley, *The Making of English*, revised edition by Simeon Potter (London: Macmillan, 1968), and Otto Jespersen, *Mankind, Nation, and Individual from a Linguistic Point of View*, Midland edition (Bloomington: Indiana University Press, 1964). Wider bibliographical references to this subject may be found in the first two chapters of my *Philosophy of Composition* (Chicago: University of Chicago Press, 1977).
3. The experiment is described in R. M. Krauss and S. Glucksberg, "Social and Nonsocial Speech," *Scientific American 236* (February 1977): 100–105.
4. National Assessment of Educational Progress, *Three National Assessments of Reading: Changes in Performance, 1970–1980* (Report II-R-01) (Denver: Education Commission of the States, 1981). The percentage of students scoring at the "advanced" level (4.9 percent) has climbed back to the very low levels of 1970. See *The Reading Report Card: Progress Toward Excellence in Our Schools, Trends in Reading Over Four National Assessments, 1971–1984* (Princeton, N.J.: Educational Testing Service No. 15-R-01, 1986).
5. John B. Carroll, "Psychometric Approaches to the Study of Language Abilities," in C. J. Fillmore, D. Kempler, and S.-Y. Wang, eds., *Individual Differences in Language Abilities and Language Behavior* (New York: Academic Press, 1979), 29.
6. The College Board, *College-Bound Seniors: Eleven Years of National Data from the College Board's Admission Testing Program, 1973–83* (New York, 1984). The College Board has sent me further details from an unpublished report that shows the breakdown of scores over 600 between 1972 and 1984. The percentage of students who scored over 600 was 7.3 percent in 1984 and 11.4 percent in 1972. The percentage scoring over 650 was 3.0 percent in 1984 and 5.29 percent in 1972.
7. Benjamin J. Stein, "The Cheerful Ignorance of the Young in L.A.," *Washington Post*, October 3, 1983. Reprinted with the kind permission of the author.
8. *Changes in Political Knowledge and Attitudes, 1969–76: Selected Results from the Second National Assessments of Citizenship and Social Studies* (Denver: National Assessment of Educational Progress, 1978).
9. The Foundations of Literacy Project under a grant from the National Endowment for the Humanities, has commissioned NAEP, now conducted by the Educational Testing Service of Princeton, to probe the literary and historical knowledge of American seventeen-year-olds.
10. I am breaking no confidences as a member of the NAEP panel in revealing these pretest figures. They were made public on October 8, 1985, in a press release by NEH Chairman John Agresto, which stated in part: "Preliminary findings indicate that two-thirds of the seventeen-year-old students tested could not place the Civil War in the correct half century; a third did not know that the Declaration of Independence was signed between 1750 and 1800; half could not locate the half century in which the First World War occurred; a third did not know that Columbus sailed for the New World 'before 1750'; three-fourths could not identify Walt Whitman or Thoreau or E. E. Cummings or Carl Sandburg. And one-half of our high school seniors did not recognize the names of Winston Churchill or Joseph Stalin."
11. See Chapter 2, pages 42–47.
12. Orlando Patterson, "Language, Ethnicity, and Change," in S. G. D'Eloia, ed., *Toward a Literate Democracy: Proceedings of the First Shaughnessy Memorial Conference, April 3, 1980*, special number of *The Journal of Basic Writing III (1980): 72–73*
13. Letter to Colonel Edward Carrington, January 16, 1787, taken from *The Life and Selected Writings of Thomas Jefferson*, ed. A. Koch and W. Peden (New York: Random House, 1944), 411–12.
14. W. C. Sellar and R. J. Yeatman, *1066 and All That: A Memorable History of England, Comprising All the Parts You Can Remember, Including 103 Good Things, 5 Bad Kings, and 2 Genuine Dates* (London: Methuen, 1947).
15. Melvin Durslag, "To Ban the Beanball," *TV Guide*, June 8–14, 1985, 9.
16. H. Putnam, "The Meaning of Meaning," in *Philosophical Papers, Volume 2: Mind, Language and Reality* (Cambridge: Cambridge University Press, 1975), 227–48.

17. See M. S. Steffensen, C. Joag-Des, and R. C. Anderson, "A Cross-Cultural Perspective on Reading Comprehension," *Reading Research Quarterly* 15, 1 (1979): 10–29.
18. This is fully discussed in Chapter 3.
19. See H. J. Walberg and T. Shanahan, "High School Effects on Individual Students," *Educational Researcher* 12 (August-September 1983): 4–9.
20. "Up to about ten hours a week, there is actually a slight positive relationship between the amount of time children spend watching TV and their school achievement, including reading achievement. Beyond this point, the relationship turns negative and, as the number of hours per week climbs, achievement declines sharply." R. C. Anderson et al., *Becoming a Nation of Readers*, 27.
21. Walberg and Shanahan, "High School Effects on Individual Students," 4–9.
22. Arthur G. Powell, Eleanor Farrar, and David K. Cohen, *The Shopping Mall High School: Winners and Losers in the Educational Marketplace* (Boston: Houghton Mifflin, 1985), 1–8.
23. The neutrality and avoidance of the schools are described in detail in *The Shopping Mall High School*.
24. Patterson, "Language, Ethnicity, and Change," 72–73.
25. Jeanne S. Chall, "Afterword," in R. C. Anderson et al., *Becoming a Nation of Readers*, 123–25.
26. J. S. Chall, C. Snow, et al., *Families and Literacy*, Final Report to the National Institute of Education, 1982.
27. R. L. Thorndike, *Reading Comprehension Education in Fifteen Countries: An Empirical Study* (New York: Wiley, 1973). There is also recent evidence that advanced reading skills have declined in the United States while elementary skills have risen. See J. S. Chall, "Literacy: Trends and Explanations, " *Educational Researcher* 12 (1983): 3–8, and R. C. Anderson et al., *Becoming a Nation of Readers*, 2.
28. *Human Relations Area Files*, microfiches (New Haven: Human Relations Area Files, 1899–1956).
29. Ibid. My examples are from more than two hundred entries, stretching from 1899 to 1949, under the topics "Educational Theories and Methods" and "Transmission of Beliefs."
30. L. A. Cremin, *The Transformation of the American School: Progressivism in American Education, 1876–1957*(New York: Knopf, 1964).

🍎 Literacy in Three Metaphors

Sylvia Scribner

Sylvia Scribner taught psychology on the graduate faculty of City University of New York. She conducted extensive fieldwork (with Michael Cole and others) among the Vai in West Africa. She continues to have an important impact on educational research and policy in the U.S. and other countries. This article originally appeared in the *American Journal of Education* in 1984.

Although literacy is a problem of pressing national concern, we have yet to discover or set its boundaries. This observation, made several years ago by a leading political spokesman (McGovern 1978), echoes a long–standing complaint of many policymakers and educators that what counts as literacy in our technological society is a matter "not very well understood" (Advisory Committee on National Illiteracy 1929).

A dominant response of scholars and researchers to this perceived ambiguity has been to pursue more rigorously the quest for definition and measurement of the concept. Many approaches have been taken (among them, Adult Performance Level Project 1975; Bormuth

"Literacy in Three Metaphors" by Sylvia Scribner. Taken from American Journal of Education, 93 (1984). Published by the University of Chicago Press. Used by permission.

1975; Hillerich 1976; Kirsch and Guthrie 1977–78; Miller 1973; Powell 1977), and at least one attempt (Hunter and Harman 1979) has been made to put forward an "umbrella definition." Each of these efforts has identified important parameters of literacy, but none has yet won consensual agreement (for a thoughtful historical and conceptual analysis of shifting literacy definitions, see Radwin [1978]).

The definitional controversy has more than academic significance. Each formulation of an answer to the question "What is literacy?" leads to a different evaluation of the scope of the problem (i.e., the extent of illiteracy) and to different objectives for programs aimed at the formation of a literate citizenry. Definitions of literacy shape our perceptions of individuals who fall on either side of the standard (what a "literate" or "nonliterate" is like) and thus in a deep way affect both the substance and style of educational programs. A chorus of clashing answers also creates problems for literacy planners and educators. This is clearly evident in the somewhat acerbic comments of Dauzzat and Deuzat (1977, p. 37), who are concerned with adult basic education: "In spite of all of the furor and the fervor for attaining literacy . . . few have undertaken to say what they or anyone else means by literacy. Those few professional organizations, bureaus and individuals who have attempted the task of explaining 'what is literacy?' generate definitions that conflict, contradict but rarely complement each other. . . . These 'champions of the cause of literacy' crusade for a national effort to make literacy a reality without establishing what that reality is."

What lies behind the definitional difficulties this statement decries? The authors themselves provide a clue. They suggest that literacy is a kind of reality that educators should be able to grasp and explain, or, expressed in more classical terms, that literacy has an "essence" that can be captured through some Aristotelian-like enterprise. By a rational process of discussion and analysis the "true" criterial components of literacy will be identified, and these in turn can become the targets of education for literacy.

Many, although by no means all, of those grappling with the problems of definition and measurement appear to be guided by such a search for the "essence"–for the "one best" way of conceptualizing literacy. This enterprise is surely a useful one and a necessary component of educational planning. Without denigrating its contribution, I would like to suggest, however, that conflicts and contradictions are intrinsic to such an essentialist approach.

Consider the following. Most efforts at definitional determination are based on a conception of literacy as an attribute of *individuals*; they aim to describe constituents of literacy in terms of individual abilities. But the single most compelling fact about literacy is that it is a *social* achievement; individuals in societies without writing systems do not become literate. Literacy is an outcome of cultural transmission; the individual child or adult does not extract the meaning of written symbols through personal interaction with the physical objects that embody them. Literacy abilities are acquired by individuals only in the course of participation in socially organized activities with written language (for a theoretical analysis of literacy as a set of socially organized practices, see Scribner and Cole [1981]). It follows that individual literacy is relative to social literacy. Since social literacy practices vary in time (Resmick [1983] contains historical studies) and space (anthropological studies are in Goody [1968]), what qualifies as individual literacy varies with them. At one time, ability to write one's name was a hallmark of literacy; today in some parts of the world, the ability to memorize a sacred text remains the modal literacy act. Literacy has neither a static nor a universal essence.

The enterprise of defining literacy, therefore, becomes of assessing what counts as literacy in the modern epoch in some given social context. If a nation–society is the context, this enterprise requires that consideration be given to the functions that the society in question has invented for literacy and their distribution throughout the populace. Grasping what literacy "is" inevitably involves social analysis: What activities are carried out with written symbols? What significance is attached to them, and what status is conferred on those who engage in them? Is literacy a social right or a private power? These questions are subject to empirical determination. But others are not: Does the prevailing distribution of literacy conform to standards of social justice and human progress? What social and educational policies might promote such standards? Here we are involved, not with fact but with considerations of value, philosophy, and ideology similar to those that figure prominently in debates about the purposes and goals of schooling. Points of view about literacy as a social good, as well as a social fact, form the ground of the definitional enterprise. We may lack consensus on how best to define literacy because we have differing views about literacy's social purposes and values.

These differing points of view about the central meaning of literacy warrant deeper examination. In this essay, I will examine some of them, organizing my discussion around three metaphors: literacy as adaptation, literacy as power, and literacy as a state of grace. Each of these metaphors is rooted in certain assumptions about the social motivations for literacy in this country, the nature of existing literacy practices, and judgments about which practices are critical for individual and social enhancement. Each has differing implications for educational policies and goals. I will be schematic in my discussion; my purpose is not to marshal supporting evidence for one or the other metaphor but to show the boundary problems of all. My argument is that any of the metaphors, taken by itself, gives us only a partial grasp of the many and varied utilities of literacy and of the complex social and psychological factors sustaining aspirations for and achievement of individual literacy. To illustrate this theme, I will draw on the literacy experiences of a Third World people who, although remaining at an Iron Age level of technology, have nevertheless evolved varied functions for written language; their experience demonstrates that, even in some traditional societies, literacy is a "many–meaninged thing."

Literacy as Adaptation

This metaphor is designed to capture concepts of literacy that emphasize its survival or pragmatic value. When the term "functional literacy" was originally introduced during World War I (Harman 1970), it specified the literacy skills required to meet the tasks of modern soldiering. Today, functional literacy is conceived broadly as the level of proficiency necessary for effective performance in a range of settings and customary activities.

This concept has a strong commonsense appeal. The necessity for literacy skills in daily life is obvious; on the job, riding around town, shopping for groceries, we all encounter situations requiring us to read or produce written symbols. No justification is needed to insist that schools are obligated to equip children with the literacy skills that will enable them to fulfill these mundane situational demands. And basic educational programs have a similar obligation to equip adults with the skills they must have to secure jobs or advance to better ones, receive the training and benefits to which they are entitled, and assume their civic and political responsibilities. Within the United States, as in other nations, literacy programs with these practical aims are considered efforts at human resource development and, as such, contributors to economic growth and stability.

In spite of their apparent commonsense grounding, functional literacy approaches are neither as straightforward nor as unproblematic as they first appear. Attempts to inventory "minimal functional competencies" have floundered on lack of information and divided perceptions of functionality. Is it realistic to try to specify some uniform set of skills as constituting functional literacy for all adults? Two subquestions are involved here. One concerns the choice of parameters for defining a "universe of functional competencies." Which literacy tasks (e.g., reading a newspaper, writing a check) are "necessary," and which are "optional"? The Adult Performance Level Project test (1975), one of the best conceptualized efforts to specify and measure competencies necessary for success in adult life, has been challenged on the grounds that it lacks content validity: "The APL test fails to meet this [validity] criterion . . . not necessarily because test development procedures were technically faulty, but because it is not logically possible to define this universe of behaviors [which compose functional competence] without respect to a value position which the test developers have chosen not to discuss" (Cervero 1980, p. 163).

An equally important question concerns the concept of uniformity. Do all communities and cultural groups in our class–based and heterogeneous society confront equivalent functional demands? If not, how do they differ? Some experts (e.g., Gray 1965; Hunter and Harman 1979) maintain that the concept of functional literacy makes sense only with respect to the proficiencies required for participation in the actual life conditions of particular groups or communities. But how does such a relativistic approach mesh with larger societal needs? If we were to consider the level of reading and writing activities carried out in small and isolated rural communities as the standard for functional literacy, educational objectives would be unduly restricted. At the other extreme, we might not want to use literacy activities of college teachers as the standard determining the functional competencies required for high school graduation. Only in recent years has research been undertaken on the range of literacy activities practiced in different communities or settings within the United States (e.g., Heath 1980, 1981; Scribner 1982a), and we still know little about how, and by whom, required literacy work gets done. Lacking such knowledge, public discussions fluctuate between narrow definitions of functional skills pegged to immediate vocational and personal to cope with college subject matter as the hallmark of literacy. On the other hand, adopting different criteria for different regions or communities would ensure the perpetuation of educational inequalities and the differential access to life opportunities with which these are associated.

Adapting literacy standards to today's needs, personal or social, would be shortsighted. The time–limited nature of what constitutes minimal skills is illustrated in the "sliding scale" used by the U.S. Bureau of Census to determine literacy. During World War I, a fourth–grade education was considered sufficient to render one literate; in 1947, a U.S. Census sample survey raised that figure to five years; and by 1952 six years of school was considered the minimal literacy threshold. Replacing the school–grade criterion with a functional approach to literacy does not eliminate the time problem. Today's standard for functional competency need to be considered in the light of tomorrow's requirements. But not all are agreed as to the nature or volume of literacy demands in the decades ahead. Some (e.g., Naisbitt 1962) argue that, as economic and other activities become increasingly subject to computerized techniques of production and information handling, even higher levels of literacy will be required of all. A contrary view, popularized by McLuhan (1962, 1964) is that new technologies and communication media are likely to reduce literacy requirements for all. A responding argument is that some of these technologies are, in effect, new systems of literacy. The ability to use minicomputers as information storage and retrieval devices requires mastery of symbol systems that build on natural language literacy; they are second–order literacies as it were. One possible scenario is that in coming decades literacy may be increased for some and reduced for others, accentuating the present uneven, primarily class–based distribution of literacy functions.

From the perspective of social needs, the seemingly well–defined concept of functional competency becomes fuzzy at the edges. Equally as many questions arise about functionality from the individual's point of view. Functional needs have not yet been assessed from the perspective of those who purportedly experience them. To what extent do adults whom tests assess as functionally illiterate perceive themselves as lacking the necessary skills to be adequate parents, neighbors, workers? Inner–city youngsters may have no desire to write letters to each other; raising one's reading level by a few grades may not be seen as a magic ticket to a job; not everyone has a bank account that requires the mastery of unusual forms (Heath 1980). Appeals to individuals to enhance their functional skills might founder on the different subjective utilities communities and groups attach to reading and writing activities.

The functional approach has been hailed as a major advance over more traditional concepts of reading and writing because it takes into account the goals and settings of people's activities with written language. Yet even tender probing reveals the many questions of fact, value, and purpose that complicate its application to educational curricula.

We now turn to the second metaphor.

Literacy as Power

While functional literacy stresses the importance of literacy to the adaptation of the individual, the literacy–as–power metaphor emphasizes a relationship between literacy and group or community advancement.

Historically, literacy has been a potent tool in maintaining the hegemony of elites and dominant classes in certain societies, while laying the basis for increased social and political participation in others (Resnick 1983; Goody 1968). In a contemporary framework, expansion of literary skills is often viewed as a means for poor and politically powerless groups to claim their place in the world. The International Symposium for Literacy, meeting in Persepolis, Iran (Bataille 1976), appealed to national governments to consider literacy as an instrument for human liberation and social change. Paulo Freire (1970) bases his influential theory of literacy education on the need to make literacy a resource for fundamental social transformation. Effective literacy education, in his view, creates a critical consciousness through which a community can analyze its conditions of social existence and engage in effective action for a just society. Not to be literate is a state of victimization.

Yet the capacity of literacy to confer power or to be the primary impetus for significant and lasting economic or social change has proved problematic in developing countries. Studies (Gayter, Hall, Kidd, and Shivasrava 1979; United Nations Development Program 1976) of UNESCO's experimental world literacy program have raised doubts about earlier notions that higher literacy rates automatically promote national development and improve the social and material conditions of the very poor. The relationship between social change and literacy education, it is now suggested (Harman 1977), may be stronger in the other direction. When masses of people have been mobilized for fundamental changes in social conditions—as in the USSR, China, Cuba, and Tanzania—rapid extensions of literacy have been accomplished (Gayter et al. 1979; Hammiche 1976; Scribner 1982b). Movements to transform social reality appear to have been effective in some parts of the world in bringing whole populations into participation in modern literacy activities. The validity of the converse proposition–that literacy per se mobilizes people for action to change their social reality–remains to be established

What does this mean for us? The one undisputed fact about illiteracy in America is its concentration among poor, black, elderly, and minority-language groups–groups without effective participation in our country's economic and educational institutions (Hunter and Harman 1979). Problems of poverty and political powerlessness are, as among some populations in developing nations, inseparably intertwined with problems of access to knowledge and levels of literacy skills. Some (e.g., Koxol 1980) suggest that a mass and politicized approach to literacy education such as that adopted by Cuba is demanded in these conditions. Others (e.g., Hunter and Harman 1979) advocate a more action-oriented approach that views community mobilization around practical, social, and political goals as a first step in creating the conditions for effective literacy instruction and for educational equity.

The possibilities and limits of the literacy-as-power metaphor within our present-day social and political structure are not at all clear. To what extent can instructional experiences and programs be lifted out of their social contexts in other countries and applied here? Do assumptions about the functionality and significance of literacy in poor communities in the United States warrant further consideration? Reder and Green's (1984) research and educational work among West Coast immigrant communities reveals that literacy has different meanings for members of different groups. How can these cultural variations be taken into account? How are communities best mobilized for literacy—around local needs and small-scale activism? Or as part of broader political and social movements? If literacy has not emerged as a priority demand, should government and private agencies undertake to mobilize communities around this goal? And can such efforts be productive without the deep involvement of community leaders?

Literacy as a State of Grace

Now we come to the third metaphor. I have variously called it literacy as salvation and literacy as a state of grace. Both labels are unsatisfactory because they give a specific religious interpretation to the broader phenomenon I want to depict—that is, the tendency in many societies to endow the literate person with special virtues. A concern with preserving and understanding scripture is at the core of many religious traditions, Western and non-Western alike. As studies by Resnick and Resnick (1977) have shown, the literacy-as-salvation metaphor had an almost literal interpretation in the practice of post-Luther Protestant groups to require of the faithful the ability to read and remember the Bible and other religious material. Older religious traditions—Hebraic and Islamic—have also traditionally invested the written word with great power and respect. "This is a perfect book. There is no doubt in it," reads a passage from the Qur'an. Memorizing the Qur'an—literally taking its words into you and making them part of yourself–is simultaneously a process of becoming both literate and holy.

The attribution of special powers to those who are literate has its ancient secular roots as well. Plato and Aristotle strove to distinguish the man of letters from the poet of oral tradition. In the perspective of Western humanism, literateness has come to be considered synonymous with being "cultured," using the term in the old-fashioned sense to refer to a person who is knowledgeable about the content and techniques of the sciences, arts, and humanities as they have evolved historically. The term sounds elitist and archaic, but the notion that participation in a literate—that is, bookish—tradition enlarges and develops a person's essential self is pervasive and still undergirds the concept of a liberal education (Steiner 1973). In the literacy-as-a-strate-of-grace concept, the power and functionality of literacy is not bounded by political or economic parameters but in a sense transcends them; the literate individual's life derives its meaning and significance from intellectual, aesthetic, and spiritual participation in the accumulated creations and knowledge of humankind, made available through the written word.

The self-enhancing aspects of literacy are often given a cognitive interpretation (Greenfield and Bruner 1969; Olson 1977). For centuries, and increasingly in this generation, appeals have been made for increased attention to literacy as a way of developing minds. An individual who is illiterate, a UNESCO (1972) publication states, is bound to concrete thinking and cannot learn new material. Some teachers of college English in the United States (e.g., Farrell 1977) urge greater prominence for writing in the curriculum as a way of promoting logical reasoning and critical thinking. Literate and nonliterate individuals presumably are not only in different states of grace but in different stages of intellectual development as well. Although evidence is accumulating (Scribner and Cole 1981) refuting this view, the notion that literacy per se creates a great divide in intellectual abilities between those who have and those who have not mastered written language is deeply entrenched in educational circles of industrialized countries.

The metaphor of literacy-as-grace, like the others, has boundary problems. For one thing, we need to know how widely dispersed this admiration of book knowledge is in our society. To what extent are beliefs about the value of literateness shared across social classes and ethnic and religious groups? How does book culture—more accurately, how do book cultures—articulate with the multiple and diverse oral cultures flourishing in the United States? Which people value literacy as a preserver of their history or endow their folk heroes with book learning? Are there broad cultural supports for book learning among wide sectors of the population? McLuhan and others have insisted that written literacy is a vestige of a disappearing "culture." Is this point of view defensible? And if so, what implications does it pose for our educational objectives?

I have described some current views of the meaning of literacy in terms of three metaphors. I have tried to indicate that each metaphor embraces a certain set of, sometimes unexamined, values; moreover, each makes assumptions about social facts in our society—the utilities of literacy and the conditions fostering individual attainment of literacy status. These metaphors are often urged on us as competitive; some choice of one or the other does in fact seem a necessary starting point for a definitional enterprise. But for purposes of social and educational planning, none need necessarily become paramount at the expense of the others; all may have validity. To illustrate this argument, I will briefly describe research on the social meaning of literacy among a West African people. Learning how literacy functions among a people far removed from us culturally and geographically may help us take a new look at its functions here at home.

Social Meaning of Literacy: A Case Study

My own consideration of the question "What is literacy?" was prompted by research experiences in a traditional West African society. Together with colleagues, I spent five years studying the social and intellectual consequences of literacy among the Vai people of West Africa (Scribner and Cole 1961). The material conditions of Vai life are harsh. Rural villages lack electricity and public water supplies; clinics and schools are scarce; dirt roads, often impassable in the rainy season, restrict social and economic exchanges. To the casual observer, Vai society is the very prototype of traditional nonliterate subsistence farming societies. Yet the Vai have practiced literacy for over 150 years, initially in a syllabic writing system of their own invention. The Vai script has been passed on from one generation to another in tutorial fashion without benefit of a formal institution such as a school and without the constitution of a professional teacher group. In addition to this indigenous script, literacy in the Arabic and Roman alphabets also flourishes in the countryside. The Vai are a Muslim people, and the Arabic script is the literacy for religious practice and theological learning. Missionaries and, more recently, the Liberian government have been disseminating English literacy, the official government literacy, through the establishment of Western-style schools. About one-third of the Vai male population is literate in one of these scripts, the majority in the Vai script. Many read and write both Vai and Arabic, and some outstanding scholars are literate in all three scripts. Since each writing system has a different orthography, represents a different language, and is learned in a different setting, becoming literate in two or more scripts is an impressive intellectual accomplishment. Why do people take the trouble to do it?

Certain obvious answers are ruled out. Literacy is not a necessity for personal survival. As far as we could determine, nonliteracy status does not exclude a person from full participation in economic activities or in town or society life. As we look around Vai country and see major activities and institutions continuing to function in the traditional oral mode, we are at a loss to define the literacy competencies that might be useful in everyday life. But Vai literates have not been at such a loss and have found no end of useful functions for writing. Commonly they engage in extensive personal correspondence, which for some involves the composition of thirty to forty letters per month. Since Vai society, like other traditional societies, maintains an effective oral grapevine system, reasons for the popularity of letter writing are not self-evident, especially since all letters must be personally sent and hand-delivered. Yet literates find the advantage of secrecy and guarantee of delivery more than compensation for the time and trouble spent in writing. Scholars (Hair 1963; Holsoe

1977) speculate that the usefulness of the Vai script in protecting secrets and allowing clandestine resistance to the central governing machinery of Liberia, whose official literacy was English, were important factors in its invention and longevity.

On closer study, we find that Vai script literacy also serves many personal and public record-keeping functions. Household heads keep albums for family births, deaths, and marriages; some maintain lists of dowry items and death feast contributions that help to regulate kinship exchanges. Records also enlarge the scope and planful aspects of commercial transactions. Artisans maintain lists of customers; farmers record the yield and income from cash-crop farming. The script also serves a variety of administrative purposes such as recording house tax payments and political contributions. Some fraternal and religious organizations maintain records in Vai script. All of these activities fit nicely into the metaphor of literacy as functional adaptation; the only surprising aspect is that so many varieties of pragmatic uses occur in an economic and social milieu in which modern institutions (schools, cash markets) still play a limited role.

Not all literacy uses are devoted to practical ends. Although the Vai script has not been used to produce public books or manuscripts, in the privacy of their homes, many Vai literates engage in creative acts of composition. Almost everyone keeps a diary; some write down maxims and traditional tales in copybooks; others maintain rudimentary town histories; some record their dreams and tales of advice to children; a few who might qualify as scholars produce extended family and clan histories. Townspeople, when questioned about the value of the script, will often cite its utilitarian functions, but will equally as often speak about its importance for self-education and knowledge. Vai script literates are known in the community, are accorded respect, and are sought out for their information and help as personal scribes or as town clerks. A Vai parable about the relative merits of money, power, and book learning for success in this world concludes with the judgment that the "man who knoweth book passeth all."

Why this excursion into a case of African literacy after our metaphoric discussion of the goals of literacy education in a technological society? Perhaps because Vai society, much simpler than ours in the range of literacy functions it calls for, nonetheless services to highlight unnecessary simplicities in our attempts to define the one best set of organizing principles for literacy education. If we were called on as experts to devise literacy education programs for the Vai people, which metaphor would dominate our recommendations? Would we emphasize the spread of functional competencies, urging all farmers to keep crop records and all carpenters to list customers? This would be an effective approach for some, but it would neglect the interests and aspirations of others. Should we appeal to the cultural pride of the populace, suggesting Vai script literacy be extended as an instrument for group cohesion and social change? We might count on support for this appeal, but resistance as well; Qur'amic schools and the network of Muslim teachers and scholars are a powerful counterforce to the Vai script and a countervailing center for cultural cohesion. Moreover, families participating in the Vai script tradition do not necessarily repudiate participation in English literacy; some find it prudent to have one or more children in English school as well as Qur'anic school. as for literacy as a state of grace, aspirations for self-improvement and social status clearly sustain many aspects of Vai literacy both in the Arabic religious and Vai secular traditions. A diversity of pragmatic, ideological, and intellectual factors sustains popular literacy among the Vai.

The sociohistorical processes leading to multiple literacies among the Vai are not unique. In their research in Alaska, Reder and Green (1983) found community members practicing literacy in any one (or, occasionally, a combination) of three languages. Some used the Cyrillic script, introduced by the Russian Orthodox Church, for reading and writing Russian; others used that script for literacy activities in their native Eskimo language; and still others participated in English literacy. Each of these literacies, they report, occurred through distinct socialization processes and in well-defined, nonoverlapping domains of activity, and each had a distinctive social meaning. Wagner (in press) similarly documents the multiple meanings of literacy in contemporary Moroccan Society, and other reports might be cited.

This is not to suggest, of course, that all cultural groups have elaborated rich functions for literacy, nor that all groups strive for participation in the official literacy of their state (as, for example, English in Alaska and throughout the United States). The value of the growing body of ethonographic studies for the "What is literacy?" question is twofold. First, it promotes skepticism of the "one best answer" approach to the improvement of literacy in our society. Second, it urges the need for understanding the great variety of beliefs and aspirations that various people have developed toward literacy in their particular historical and current life circumstances.

What implications does this analysis have for literacy policy and education? This is a question that calls for the continued, sustained, and thoughtful attention of educators and others in our society. One implication that I find compelling is the need to "disaggregate" various levels and kinds of literacy. If the search for an essence is futile, it might appropriately be replaced by serious attention to varieties of literacy and their place in social and educational programs. In this disentangling process, I would place priority on the need to extricate matters of value and policy from their hidden position in the definitional enterprise and to address them head on. The International Symposium for Literacy, closing UNESCO's Experimental World Literacy Program, declared that literacy is a fundamental human right (Betsile 1976). Literacy campaigns need no other justification. Setting long-range social and educational goals, however, pushes us farther toward an inquiry into the standard of literacy that is a desirable (valued) human right in our highly developed technological society, whose policies have such a powerful impact on the world's future. What is *ideal* literacy in our society? If the analysis by metaphor presented here contributes some approach to that question, it suggests that ideal literacy is simultaneously adaptive, socially empowering, and self-enhancing. Enabling youth and adults to progress toward that ideal would be a realization of the spirit of the symposium in Persepolis reflective of the resources and literacy achievements already available in our society. This suggests that long-term social and educational policies might be directed at maximal literacy objectives; minimal literacy standards would serve a useful function, not as goals but as indicators of our progress in equipping individuals and communities with the skills they need for "takeoff" in continuing literacy careers.

Recognition of the multiple meanings and varieties of literacy also argues for a diversity of educational approaches, informal and community-based as well as formal and school-based. As ethnographic research and practical experience demonstrate, effective literacy programs are those that are responsive to perceived needs, whether for functional skills, social power, or self-improvement. Individual objectives may be highly specific; to qualify for a promotion at work, to help children with their lessons, to record a family history. Anzalone and

McLaughlin (1982) have coined the term "specific literacies" to designate such special-interest or special-purpose literacy skills. The road to maximal literacy may begin for some through the feeder routes of a wide variety of specific literacies.

These are speculative and personal views; others will have different conceptions. The notions offered here of ideal and specific literacies do not simplify the educational issues nor resolve the definitional dilemmas. I hope, however, that these concepts and the metaphoric analysis from which they flowed suggest the usefulness of "dissecting literacy" into its many forms and, in the process, clarifying the place of fact and value in discussions of the social meaning of literacy.

Pedagogy of the Oppressed

Paulo Freire

Paulo Freire is a Brazilian educator who currently teaches at Catholic University in Sau Paulo. His work with and commitment to literacy education for the poor and disenfranchised are well known, and he has served as a national and international advisor on education and political reform. The following selection is from his 1972 book *The Pedagogy of the Oppressed*, probably his best known work.

A careful analysis of the teacher-student relationship at any level, inside or outside the school, reveals its fundamentally *narrative* character. This relationship involves a narrating Subject (the teacher) and patient, listening objects (the students). The contents, whether values or empirical dimensions of reality, tend in the process of being narrated to become lifeless and petrified. Education is suffering from narration sickness.

The teacher talks about reality as if it were motionless, static, compartmentalized, and predictable. Or else he expounds on a topic completely alien to the existential experience of the students. His task is to "fill" the students with the contents of his narration—contents which are detached from reality, disconnected from the totality that engendered them and could give them significance. Words are emptied of their concreteness and become a hollow, alienated, and alienating verbosity.

The outstanding characteristic of this narrative education, then, is the sonority of words, not their transforming power. "Four times four is sixteen; the capital of Pará is Belém." The student records, memorizes, and repeats these phrases without perceiving what four times four really means, or realizing the true significance of "capital" in the affirmation "the capital of Pará is Belém," that is, what Belém means for Pará and what Pará means for Brazil.

Narration (with the teacher as narrator) leads the students to memorize mechanically the narrated content. Worse yet, it turns them into "containers," into "receptacles" to be "filled"

Excerpt from Pedagogy of the Oppressed by Paulo Freire. Copyright 1993. Used by permission of The Continuum Publishing Company.

by the teacher. The more completely he fills the receptacles, the better a teacher he is. The more meekly the receptacles permit themselves to be filled, the better students they are.

Education thus becomes an act of depositing, in which the students are the depositories and the teacher is the depositor. Instead of communicating, the teacher issues communiqués and makes deposits which the students patiently receive, memorize, and repeat. This is the "banking" concept of education, in which the scope of action allowed to the students extends only as far as receiving, filing, and storing the deposits. They do, it is true, have the opportunity to become collectors or cataloguers of the things they store. But in the last analysis, it is men themselves who are filed away through the lack of creativity, transformation, and knowledge in this (at best) misguided system. For apart from inquiry, apart from the praxis, men cannot be truly human. Knowledge emerges only through invention and re-invention, through the restless, impatient, continuing, hopeful inquiry men pursue in the world, with the world, and with each other.

In the banking concept of education, knowledge is a gift bestowed by those who consider themselves knowledgeable upon those whom they consider to know nothing. Projecting an absolute ignorance onto others, a characteristic of the ideology of oppression, negates education and knowledge as processes of inquiry. The teacher presents himself to his students as their necessary opposite; by considering their ignorance absolute, he justifies his own existence. The students, alienated like the slave in the Hegelian dialectic, accept their ignorance as justifying the teacher's existence—but, unlike the slave, they never discover that they educate the teacher.

The *raison d'être* of libertarian education, on the other hand, lies in its drive towards reconciliation. Education must begin with the solution of the teacher-student contradiction, by reconciling the poles of the contradiction so that both are simultaneously teachers *and* students.

This solution is not (nor can it be) found in the banking concept. On the contrary, banking education maintains and even stimulates the contradiction through the following attitudes and practices, which mirror oppressive society as a whole:

- 🍎 the teacher teaches and the students are taught;
- 🍎 the teacher knows everything and the students know nothing;
- 🍎 the teacher thinks and the students are thought about;
- 🍎 the teacher talks and the students listen—meekly;
- 🍎 the teacher disciplines and the students are disciplined;
- 🍎 the teacher chooses and enforces his choice, and the students comply;
- 🍎 the teacher acts and the students have the illusion of acting through the action of the teacher;
- 🍎 the teacher chooses the program content, and the students (who were not consulted) adapt to it;
- 🍎 the teacher confuses the authority of knowledge with his own professional authority, which he sets in opposition to the freedom of the students;
- 🍎 the teacher is the Subject of the learning process, while the pupils are mere objects.

It is not surprising that the banking concept of education regards men as adaptable, manageable beings. The more students work at storing the deposits entrusted to them, the less they develop the critical consciousness which would result from their intervention in the world as transformers of that world. The more completely they accept the passive role imposed on them, the more they tend simply to adapt to the world as it is and to the fragmented view of reality deposited in them.

The capability of banking education to minimize or annul the students' creative power and to stimulate their credulity serves the interests of the oppressors, who care neither to have the world revealed nor to see it transformed. The oppressors use their "humanitarianism" to preserve a profitable situation. Thus they react almost instinctively against any experiment in education which stimulates the critical faculties and is not content with a partial view of reality but always seeks out the ties which link one point to another and one problem to another.

Indeed, the interests of the oppressors lie in "changing the consciousness of the oppressed, not the situation which oppresses them";[1] for the more the oppressed can be led to adapt to that situation, the more easily they can be dominated. To achieve this end, the oppressors use the banking concept of education in conjunction with a paternalistic social action apparatus, within which the oppressed receive the euphemistic title of "welfare recipients." They are treated as individual cases, as marginal men who deviate from the general configuration of a "good, organized, and just" society. The oppressed are regarded as the pathology of the healthy society, which must therefore adjust these "incompetent and lazy" folk to its own patterns by changing their mentality. These marginals need to be "integrated," "incorporated" into the healthy society that they have "forsaken."

The truth is, however, that the oppressed are not "marginals," are not men living "outside" society. They have always been "inside"—inside the structure which made them "beings for others." The solution is not to "integrate" them into the structure of oppression, but to transform that structure so that they can become "beings for themselves." Such transformation, of course, would undermine the oppressors' purposes; hence their utilization of the banking concept of education to avoid the threat of student *conscientização*.

The banking approach to adult education, for example, will never propose to students that they critically consider reality. It will deal instead with such vital questions as whether Roger gave green grass to the goat, and insist upon the importance of learning that, on the contrary, Roger gave green grass to the *rabbit*. The "humanism" of the banking approach masks the effort to turn men into automatons—the very negation of their ontological vocation to be more fully human.

Those who use the banking approach, knowingly or unknowingly (for there are innumerable well-intentioned bank-clerk teachers who do not realize that they are serving only to dehumanize), fail to perceive that the deposits themselves contain contradictions about reality. But, sooner or later, these contradictions may lead formerly passive students to turn against their domestication and the attempt to domesticate reality. They may discover through existential experience that their present way of life is irreconcilable with their vocation to become fully human. They may perceive through their relations with reality that reality is really a *process*, undergoing constant transformation. If men are searchers and their ontological vocation is humanization, sooner or later they may perceive the contradiction in which banking education seeks to maintain them, and then engage themselves in the struggle for their liberation.

But the humanist, revolutionary educator cannot wait for this possibility to materialize. From the outset, his efforts must coincide with those of the students to engage in critical thinking and the quest for mutual humanization. His efforts must be imbued with a profound trust in men and their creative power. To achieve this, he must be a partner of the students in his relations with them.

The banking concept does not admit to such partnership—and necessarily so. To resolve the teacher-student contradiction, to exchange the role of depositor, prescriber, domesticator, for the role of student among students would be to undermine the power of oppression and serve the cause of liberation.

Implicit in the banking concept is the assumption of a dichotomy between man and the world: man is merely *in* the world, not *with* the world or with others; man is spectator, not re-creator. In this view, man is not a conscious being (*corpo consciente*); he is rather the possessor of *a* consciousness: an empty "mind" passively open to the reception of deposits of reality from the world outside. For example, my desk, my books, my coffee cup, all the objects before me—as bits of the world which surrounds me—would be "inside" me, exactly as I am inside my study right now. This view makes no distinction between being accessible to consciousness and entering consciousness. The distinction, however, is essential: the objects which surround me are simply accessible to my consciousness, not located within it. I am aware of them, but they are not inside me.

It follows logically from the banking notion of consciousness that the educator's role is to regulate the way the world "enters into" the students. His task is to organize a process which already occurs spontaneously, to "fill" the students by making deposits of information which he considers to constitute true knowledge.[2] And since men "receive" the world as passive entities, education should make them more passive still, and adapt them to the world. The educated man is the adapted man, because he is better "fit" for the world. Translated into practice, this concept is well suited to the purposes of the oppressors, whose tranquility rests on how well men fit the world the oppressors have created, and how little they question it.

The more completely the majority adapt to the purposes which the dominant minority prescribe for them (thereby depriving them of the right to their own purposes), the more easily the minority can continue to prescribe. The theory and practice of banking education serve this end quite efficiently. Verbalistic lessons, reading requirements,[3] the methods for evaluating "knowledge," the distance between the teacher and the taught, the criteria for promotion: everything in this ready-to-wear approach serves to obviate thinking.

The bank-clerk educator does not realize that there is no true security in his hypertrophied role, that one must seek to live *with* others in solidarity. One cannot impose oneself, nor even merely co-exist with one's students. Solidarity requires true communication, and the concept by which such an educator is guided fears and proscribes communication.

Yet only through communication can human life hold meaning. The teacher's thinking is authenticated only by the authenticity of the students' thinking. The teacher cannot think for his students, nor can he impose his thought on them. Authentic thinking, thinking that is concerned about *reality*, does not take place in ivory tower isolation, but only in communication. If it is true that thought has meaning only when generated by action upon the world, the subordination of students to teachers becomes impossible.

Because banking education begins with a false understanding of men as objects, it cannot promote the development of what Fromm calls "biophily," but instead produces its opposite: "necrophily."

While life is characterized by growth in a structured, functional manner, the necrophilous person loves all that does not grow, all that is mechanical. The necrophilous person is driven by the desire to transform the organic into the inorganic, to approach life mechanically, as if all living persons were things. . . . Memory, rather than experience; having, rather than being, is what counts. The necrophilous person can relate to an object—a flower or a person—only if he possesses it; hence a threat to his possession is a threat to himself; if he loses possession he loses contact with the world. . . . He loves control, and in the act of controlling he kills life.[4]

Oppression—overwhelming control—is necrophilic; it is nourished by love of death, not life. The banking concept of education, which serves the interests of oppression, is also necrophilic. Based on a mechanistic, static, naturalistic, spatialized view of consciousness, it transforms students into receiving objects. It attempts to control thinking and action, leads men to adjust to the world, and inhibits their creative power.

When their efforts to act responsibly are frustrated, when they find themselves unable to use their faculties, men suffer. "This suffering due to impotence is rooted in the very fact that the human equilibrium has been disturbed."[5] But the inability to act which causes men's anguish also causes them to reject their impotence, by attempting

. . . to restore [their] capacity to act. But can [they], and how? One way is to submit to and identify with a person or group having power. By this symbolic participation in another person's life, [men have] the illusion of acting, when in reality [they] only submit to and become a part of those who act.[6]

Populist manifestations perhaps best exemplify this type of behavior by the oppressed, who, by identifying with charismatic leaders, come to feel that they themselves are active and effective. The rebellion they express as they emerge in the historical process is motivated by that desire to act effectively. The dominant elites consider the remedy to be more domination and repression, carried out in the name of freedom, order, and social peace (that is, the peace of the elites). Thus they can condemn—logically, from their point of view—"the violence of a strike by workers and [can] call upon the state in the same breath to use violence in putting down the strike."[7]

Education as the exercise of domination stimulates the credulity of students, with the ideological intent (often not perceived by educators) of indoctrinating them to adapt to the world of oppression. This accusation is not made in the naive hope that the dominant elites will thereby simply abandon the practice. Its objective is to call the attention of true humanists to the fact that they cannot use banking educational methods in the pursuit of liberation, for they would only negate that very pursuit. Nor may a revolutionary society inherit these methods from an oppressor society. The revolutionary society which practices banking education is either misguided or mistrusting of men. In either event, it is threatened by the specter of reaction.

Unfortunately, those who espouse the cause of liberation are themselves surrounded and influenced by the climate which generates the banking concept, and often do not perceive its true significance or its dehumanizing power. Paradoxically, then, they utilize this same instrument of alienation in what they consider an effort to liberate. Indeed, some "revolutionaries" brand as "innocents," "dreamers," or even "reactionaries" those who would challenge this educational practice. But one does not liberate men by alienating them. Authentic liberation—the process of humanization—is not another deposit to be made in men. Liberation is a praxis: the action and reflection of men upon their world in order to transform it. Those truly committed to the cause of liberation can accept neither the mechanistic concept of consciousness as an empty vessel to be filled, nor the use of banking methods of domination (propaganda, slogans—deposits) in the name of liberation.

Those truly committed to liberation must reject the banking concept in its entirety, adopting instead a concept of men as conscious beings, and consciousness as consciousness intent upon the world. They must abandon the educational goal of deposit-making and replace it with the posing of the problems of men in their relations with the world. "Problem-posing" education, responding to the essence of consciousness—*intentionality*—rejects communiqués and embodies communication. It epitomizes the special characteristic of consciousness: being *conscious of*, not only as intent on objects but as turned in upon itself in a Jasperian "split"— consciousness as consciousness *of* consciousness.

Liberating education consists in acts of cognition, not transferrals of information. It is a learning situation in which the cognizable object (far from being the end of the cognitive act) intermediates the cognitive actors—teacher on the one hand and students on the other. Accordingly, the practice of problem-posing education entails at the outset that the teacher-student contradiction be resolved. Dialogical relations—indispensable to the capacity of cognitive actors to cooperate in perceiving the same cognizable object—are otherwise impossible.

Indeed, problem-posing education, which breaks with the vertical patterns characteristic of banking education, can fulfill its function as the practice of freedom only if it can overcome the above contradiction. Through dialogue, the teacher-of-the-students and the students-of-the-teacher cease to exist and a new term emerges: teacher-student with students-teachers. The teacher is no longer merely the-one-who-teaches, but one who is himself taught in dialogue with the students, who in turn while being taught also teach. They become jointly responsible for a process in which all grow. In this process, arguments based on "authority" are no longer valid; in order to function, authority must be *on the side of freedom*, not *against* it. Here, no one teaches another, nor is anyone self-taught. Men teach each other, mediated by the world, by the cognizable objects which in banking education are "owned" by the teacher.

The banking concept (with its tendency to dichotomize everything) distinguishes two stages in the action of the educator. During the first, he cognizes a cognizable object while he prepares his lessons in his study or his laboratory; during the second, he expounds to his students about that object. The students are not called upon to know, but to memorize the contents narrated by the teacher. Nor do the students practice any act of cognition, since the object towards which that act should be directed is the property of the teacher rather than a medium evoking the critical reflection of both teacher and students. Hence in the name of the "preservation of culture and knowledge" we have a system which achieves neither true knowledge nor true culture.

The problem-posing method does not dichotomize the activity of the teacher-student: he is not "cognitive" at one point and "narrative" at another. He is always "cognitive," whether preparing a project or engaging in dialogue with the students. He does not regard cognizable objects as his private property, but as the object of reflection by himself and the students. In this way, the problem-posing educator constantly re-forms his reflections in the reflection of the students. The students—no longer docile listeners—are now critical co-investigators in dialogue with the teacher. The teacher presents the material to the students for their consideration, and re-considers his earlier considerations as the students express their own. The role of the problem-posing educator is to create, together with the students, the conditions under which knowledge at the level of the *doxa* is superseded by true knowledge, at the level of the *logos*.

Whereas banking education anesthetizes and inhibits creative power, problem-posing education involves a constant unveiling of reality. The former attempts to maintain the *submersion* of consciousness; the latter strives for the *emergence* of consciousness and *critical intervention* in reality.

Students, as they are increasingly posed with problems relating to themselves in the world and with the world, will feel increasingly challenged and obliged to respond to that challenge. Because they apprehend the challenge as interrelated to other problems within a total context, not as a theoretical question, the resulting comprehension tends to be increasingly critical and thus constantly less alienated. Their response to the challenge evokes new challenges, followed by new understandings; and gradually the students come to regard themselves as committed.

Education as the practice of freedom—as opposed to education as the practice of domination—denies that man is abstract, isolated, independent, and unattached to the world; it also denies that the world exists as a reality apart from men. Authentic reflection considers neither abstract man nor the world without men, but men in their relations with the world. In these relations consciousness and world are simultaneous: consciousness neither precedes the world nor follows it.

La conscience et le monde sont dormés d'un même coup: exté érieur par essence à la conscience, le monde est, par essence relatif à elle.[8]

In one of our culture circles in Chile, the group was discussing (based on a codification[9]) the anthropological concept of culture. In the midst of the discussion, a peasant who by banking standards was completely ignorant said: "Now I see that without man there is no world." When the educator responded: "Let's say, for the sake of argument, that all the men on earth were to die, but that the earth itself remained, together with trees, birds, animals, rivers, seas, the stars . . . wouldn't all this be a world?" "Oh no," the peasant replied emphatically. "There would be no one to say: 'This is a world'."

The peasant wished to express the idea that there would be lacking the consciousness of the world which necessarily implies the world of consciousness. I cannot exist without a *not-I*. In turn, the *not-I* depends on that existence. The world which brings consciousness into existence becomes the world *of* that consciousness. Hence, the previously cited affirmation of Sartre: *"La conscience et le monde sont dormés d'un même coup."* As men, simultaneously reflecting on themselves and on the world, increase the scope of their perception, they begin to direct their observations towards previously inconspicuous phenomena:

In perception properly so-called, as an explicit awareness [*Gewahren*], I am turned towards the object, to the paper, for instance. I apprehend it as being this here *and now. The apprehension is a singling out, every object having a background in experience. Around and about the paper lie books, pencils, ink-well, and so forth, and these in a certain sense are also "perceived", perceptually there, in the "field of intuition"; but whilst I was turned towards the paper there was no turning in their direction, nor any apprehending of them, not even in a secondary sense. They appeared and yet were not singled out, were not posited on their own account. Every perception of a thing has such a zone of background intuitions or background awareness, if "intuiting" already includes the state of being turned towards, and this also is a "conscious experience", or more briefly a "consciousness of" all indeed that in point of fact lies in the co-perceived objective background.*[10]

That which had existed objectively but had not been perceived in its deeper implications (if indeed it was perceived at all) begins to "stand out," assuming the character of a problem and therefore of challenge. Thus, men begin to single out elements from their "background awarenesses" and to reflect upon them. These elements are now objects of men's consideration, and, as such, objects of their action and cognition.

In problem-posing education, men develop their power to perceive critically *the way they exist* in the world *with which* and *in which* they find themselves; they come to see the world not as a static reality, but as a reality in process, in transformation. Although the dialectical relations of men with the world exist independently of how these relations are perceived (or whether or not they are perceived at all), it is also true that the form of action men adopt is to a large extent a function of how they perceive themselves in the world. Hence, the teacher-student and the students-teachers reflect simultaneously on themselves and the world without dichotomizing this reflection from action, and thus establish an authentic form of thought and action.

Once again, the two educational concepts and practices under analysis come into conflict. Banking education (for obvious reasons) attempts, by mythicizing reality, to conceal certain facts which explain the way men exist in the world; problem-posing education sets itself the task of demythologizing. Banking education resists dialogue; problem-posing education regards dialogue as indispensable to the act of cognition which unveils reality. Banking education treats students as objects of assistance; problem-posing education makes them critical thinkers. Banking education inhibits creativity and domesticates (although it cannot completely destroy) the *intentionality* of consciousness by isolating consciousness from the world, thereby denying men their ontological and historical vocation of becoming more fully human. Problem-posing education bases itself on creativity and stimulates true reflection and action upon reality, thereby responding to the vocation of men as beings who are authentic only when engaged in inquiry and creative transformation. In sum: banking theory and practice, as immobilizing and fixating forces, fail to acknowledge men as historical beings; problem-posing theory and practice take man's historicity as their starting point.

Problem-posing education affirms men as beings in the process of *becoming*—as unfinished, uncompleted beings in and with a likewise unfinished reality. Indeed, in contrast to other animals who are unfinished, but not historical, men know themselves to be unfinished; they are aware of their incompletion. In this incompletion and this awareness lie the very roots of education as an exclusively human manifestation. The unfinished character of men and the transformational character of reality necessitate that education be an ongoing activity.

Education is thus constantly remade in the praxis. In order to *be*, it must *become*. Its "duration" (in the Bergsonian meaning of the word) is found in the interplay of the opposites *permanence* and *change*. The banking method emphasizes permanence and becomes reactionary; problem-posing education—which accepts neither a "well-behaved" present nor a predetermined future—roots itself in the dynamic present and becomes revolutionary.

Problem-posing education is revolutionary futurity. Hence it is prophetic (and, as such, hopeful). Hence, it corresponds to the historical nature of man. Hence, it affirms men as beings who transcend themselves, who move forward and look ahead, for whom immobility represents a fatal threat, for whom looking at the past must only be a means of understanding more clearly what and who they are so that they can more wisely build the future. Hence, it identifies with the movement which engages men as beings aware of their incompletion—an historical movement which has its point of departure, its Subjects and its objective.

The point of departure of the movement lies in men themselves. But since men do not exist apart from the world, apart from reality, the movement must begin with the men-world relationship. Accordingly, the point of departure must always be with men in the "here and now," which constitutes the situation within which they are submerged, from which they emerge, and in which they intervene. Only by starting from this situation—which determines their perception of it—can they begin to move. To do this authentically they must perceive their state not as fated and unalterable, but merely as limiting—and therefore challenging.

Whereas the banking method directly or indirectly reinforces men's fatalistic perception of their situation, the problem-posing method presents this very situation to them as a problem. As the situation becomes the object of their cognition, the naive or magical perception which produced their fatalism gives way to perception which is able to perceive itself even as it perceives reality, and can thus be critically objective about that reality.

A deepened consciousness of their situation leads men to apprehend that situation as an historical reality susceptible of transformation. Resignation gives way to the drive for transformation and inquiry, over which men feel themselves to be in control. If men, as historical beings necessarily engaged with other men in a movement of inquiry, did not control that movement, it would be (and is) a violation of men's humanity. Any situation in which some men prevent others from engaging in the process of inquiry is one of violence. The means used are not important; to alienate men from their own decision-making is to change them into objects.

This movement of inquiry must be directed towards humanization—man's historical vocation. The pursuit of full humanity, however, cannot be carried out in isolation or individualism, but only in fellowship and solidarity; therefore it cannot unfold in the antagonistic relations between oppressors and oppressed. No one can be authentically human while he prevents others from being so. Attempting *to be more* human, individualistically, leads to *having more*, egotiscally: a form of dehumanization. Not that it is not fundamental to *have* in order *to be* human. Precisely because it *is* necessary, some men's *having* must not be allowed to constitute an obstacle to others' *having*, must not consolidate the power of the former to crush the latter.

Problem-posing education, as a humanist and liberating praxis, posits as fundamental that men subjected to domination must fight for their emancipation. To that end, it enables teachers and students to become Subjects of the educational process by overcoming authoritarianism and an alienating intellectualism; it also enables men to overcome their false perception of reality. The world—no longer something to be described with deceptive words—becomes the object of that transforming action by men which results in their humanization.

Problem-posing education does not and cannot serve the interests of the oppressor. No oppressive order could permit the oppressed to begin to question: Why? While only a revolutionary society can carry out this education in systematic terms, the revolutionary leaders need not take full power before they can employ the method. In the revolutionary process, the leaders cannot utilize the banking method as an interim measure, justified on grounds of expediency, wills the intention of *later* behaving in a genuinely revolutionary fashion. They must be revolutionary—that is to say, dialogical—from the outset.

Endnotes

1. Simone de Beauvoir, *La Pensée de Droite, Aujord'hui* (Paris); ST, *El Pensamiento Político de la Derecha* (Buenos Aires, 1963), p. 34.
2. This concept corresponds to what Sartre calls the "digestive" or "nutritive" concept of education, in which knowledge is "fed" by the teacher to the students to "fill them out." See Jean-Paul Sartre, "Une idée fundamentale de la phénomenologie de Husserl: L'intentionalité," *Situations 1* (Paris, 1947).
3. For example, some professors specify in their reading lists that a book should be read from pages 10 to 15—and do this to "help" their students!
4. Fromm, *op. cit.*, p. 41.
5. *Ibid.*, p. 31.
6. *Ibid.*
7. Reinhold Niebuhr, *Moral Man and Immoral Society* (New York, 1960), p. 130.
8. Sartre, *op. cit.*, p. 32.
9. See Chapter 3.—Translator's note.
10. Edmund Husserl, *Ideas—General Introduction to Pure Phenomenology* (London, 1969), pp. 105–106.

Literacy and Schooling in Subordinate Cultures

John U. Ogbu

John U. Ogbu came to the U.S. from Nigeria and earned his bachelor's master's, and doctoral degrees at the University of California, Berkeley, where he continues to conduct research and teach anthropology. He is considered to be one of the world's leading educational anthropologists. This piece originally appeared in *Literacy in Historical Perspective*, edited by Daniel Resnick, published in 1983.

The Case of Black Americans

L iteracy is currently receiving a good deal of attention from researchers, policy-makers, and professional educators. Common concerns are the development of literacy among children and the problem of literacy competence or functional literacy among adults. In industrialized nations like the United States these problems are regarded as particularly acute among the lower class and subordinate minorities.

The literacy problem of subordinate minorities, the focus of this paper, is threefold and relative, the latter because it derives partly from comparing minorities with the dominant group. One aspect of the problem is that a larger proportion of minorities has not successfully learned to read, write, and compute. Another is that a greater proportion of minorities is not functionally literate. That is, they are unable to demonstrate the ability to read, write, or compute in social and economic situations that require these skills; for example, they cannot fill out job applications and income-tax forms or read and comprehend instructional manuals and utilize the information. Third, school children among subordinate minorities lag behind their dominant-group peers in reading and computation as judged by classroom grades and scores on standardized tests.

Our research since the late 1960s has been on this lag in minority student's performance, and we have compared the situation in the United States with those in other countries like Britain, India, Israel, Japan, and New Zealand. For this paper, we will limit our discussion to black Americans, beginning with the current hypothesis that black children fall disproportionately in school because they come from a predominantly oral culture which engenders a discontinuity in their participation in the literate culture of the school. We will then suggest an alternative interpretation of the disproportionate school failure of black children in its historical and structural context.

Literacy and Schooling in Subordinate Cultures by John Ogbu. Reprinted by permission of the author.

Oral Culture, Literate Culture, and School Performance

Shifting Theories of Language Research

Over the past two decades, there has been a continuing shift in theories generated by language studies to explain the disproportionate failure among blacks to learn to read. A brief review of these theories, as provided by Simons (1976), will take us to the current hypothesis that school failure among blacks, especially in reading, is due to the fact that they come from an essentially oral culture.

Initially, the field of language studies was dominated by a deficit perspective, whose hypothesis (which still survives in some quarters) is that black dialect is inferior to standard English and constitutes a handicap in the thinking and learning of blacks. Ethnographic studies by Labov (1972) and others showed that this model was false, and it was replaced by the difference perspective, whose initial hypothesis asserted that black dialect is different from standard English but still constitutes a viable system of thinking and learning. Black children failed, especially in reading, because a "mismatch between children's language and the language used in school and in the reading texts interfered with black children's acquisition of reading skills" (Simons 1976:3). That is, schools did not use black dialect as a medium of teaching and learning.

Efforts to use black dialect in texts and in the classroom, while teaching standard English, did not, however, improve reading achievement among black children. Critics charged that the difference hypothesis focused too much on materials and teachers and failed to specify the mechanisms by which the interference or mismatch occurred. Critics proposed two types of interference, the first of which was phonological. It was thought that differences in pronunciation "might interfere with the acquisition of word recognition skills," but this was subsequently shown not to be a significant factor (Simons 1976:8; see also Rentel and Kennedy 1972). The second hypothesized interference was grammatical; that is, a "mismatch between black child's syntax and the standard English syntax of the texts used by the teacher" (Baratz 1969; Stewart 1969). But reading achievement among black children who read materials written in black dialect grammar did not significantly improve. It was concluded from these studies that black dialect was not the source of the failure of children to learn to read (Simons 1976:11).

In the early 1970s a new hypothesis moved beyond language *per se* to the broader area of communication strategies, speculating that school failure is caused by a mismatch between communicative etiquettes of teachers and students, especially during reading. The hypothesis holds that teachers and minority students who come from different cultures have different communicative strategies and interpretations of situated meanings that lead to miscommunication during reading activities. This interferes with children's acquisition of reading skills.

What is at issue is what is *communicated* by the classroom environment, not the differences in the cultural backgrounds or languages of the teacher and students. The goal of research is to isolate the processes that are meaningful to the participants in classroom communication. Philip's notion of participant structure (1972) provides the conceptual framework for this research. Basically, a participant structure is "a constellation of norms, mutual rights and obligations that shape social relationships, determine participants' perceptions about what is going on, and influence learning" (Simons 1976). Subordinate minority-group children have different participant structures at home than at school, and their generally poor school performance is attributed to this discontinuity.

I have criticized this mismatch hypothesis (Ogbu 1980s), on three grounds. First, it does not warrant generalization about minority school failure because it is based primarily on research into only one type of minority group, namely, castelike minorities. It does not explain why other minorities, who also have different participant structures at home than at school, learn to read in the same classrooms where blacks and similar groups fail. Second, the mismatch model ignores historical and societal forces which may actually generate the pattern of classroom processes. And third, although data and insights from studies based on the mismatch model can be used for remedial efforts (Simons 1976; Erickson 1978), they cannot lead to social change that would eventually eliminate the need for remedial efforts.

Oral Culture and Literacy

The most recent development in language studies focuses on literacy and attributes the disproportionate school failure of blacks and similar minorities to a discontinuity between their essentially oral cultures and the literate culture of the white middle-class represented by the public schools. This hypothesis is based on studies of literacy and its consequences in traditional or small-scale societies (Goody 1977; Luria 1976); on studies of language and communicative styles in minority communities (Labov 1969; Abrahams 1970; Kochman 1973); and on microethnographic studies of teacher-pupil interactions in classrooms (Erickson and Mohatt 1977, cited in Koehler 1978; Gumperz 1979; Philips 1972).

Reviewing studies of both nonliterate, small-scale societies and literate Western societies, Lewis (1979) argues that participants in oral cultures differ significantly from participants in literate cultures, whose sensory orientations are aural rather than oral. She cites a large body of evidence that these two sensory orientations generate contrasting notions of time, causality, space, and the self "which affect the way children are raised and interact with adults" (p. 2). Although the contrast is primarily between non-Western nonliterate populations and Western middle-class populations, she coins the term "residual oral cultures" or "residual oral peoples" to designate segments of Western societies (e.g., subordinate minorities and the lower class) in which many people have minimal knowledge of reading and writing, arguing that these populations resemble in many respects those of nonliterate small-scale societies. Lewis claims that the disproportionate school failure of minority and lower-class children in the United States is due to their participation in those essentially oral cultures. As she puts it,

[In] our society, the schools as key institutions of literate culture tend to reject the oral tradition. As a result, the relatively illiterate find their assumptions about reality in conflict with school expectations. This conflict insures failure and exacerbates other experiences of race and class exclusion (p. 2).

One difficulty with Lewis's formulation is the questionable extent to which one can generalize from small-scale Asian and African societies to groups historically subordinated by their class, ethnic, and racial backgrounds in complex industrial societies. Furthermore, the introduction of literacy or schooling in the small-scale societies does not usually result in the same types of problems it often creates among subordinate minorities and the lower class in the United States (Heyneman 1979; van den Berghe 1979). To the contrary, the introduction of schooling in small-scale societies tends to increase cognitive and linguistic or communicative similarities to the pattern of middle-class populations of industrialized societies (Cole and Scribner 1973; Greenfield 1976; Luria 1976). Why, then, after generations of school attendance by blacks and centuries of interaction with whites, haven't their cognitive and communicative strategies changed to those of the white middle class?

Finally, we know that descendants of illiterate Asian and European immigrants (who might be regarded as "residual oral peoples") have achieved greater success in American public schools than subordinate minorities. For example, studies of Chinese peasant villages in the 1930s (Pepper 1971: 199; Snow 1961: 69) showed that illiteracy rates were often as high as 90 percent. But children of illiterate Chinese peasant immigrants have done quite well in American schools. Gumperz and Cook-Gumperz have proposed a sociolinguistic formulation of the problem (1979). Drawing from the work of Goody (1977) and Luria (1976), they contrast oral and literate cultures in terms of (1) storage and transmission of knowledge, (2) decontextualization of knowledge, and (3) cognitive strategies in communication and learning. They argue (1) that in oral cultures stored knowledge is static and its transmission inaccurate, whereas in literate cultures change is built into knowledge and its transmission is accurate; (2) that knowledge acquisition and transmission in literate cultures, unlike oral cultures, are decontextualized; and (3) that in literate cultures a distinctive mode of reasoning emerges that is separate from everyday activities. Using these three domains of change as criteria, the authors contend that the *home*, in contrast to *school*, is a place of oral culture, and they suggest the changes children must make in their cognitive and communicative strategies in order to learn and use written language effectively. They summarize the process involved in the transition from oral to written culture for all children as follows:

> Developmentally the transition from speaking to writing as a medium for learning about the world of others requires a change from the interpretative strategies of oral cultures in which children grow up, to the interpretative principles of discursive written language. The move into literacy requires children to make some basic adjustments to the way they socially attribute meaning to events and the processes of every day world in order to be able to loosen their dependence upon contextually specific information and to adopt a decontextualized perspective. Among other things, they must learn to rely on an incrementally acquired knowledge rather than on what is said within any one context. In another dimension the move into literacy requires children linguistically to change their process of interpretation (p. 16).

Gumperz and Cook-Gumperz imply that literacy problems began in the present century with industrialization, bureaucratization, and other socioeconomic changes which have tended to (a) erase the boundaries between elite and popular education; (b) increase the dichotomy between speaking and writing; (c) make literacy prerequisite to economic survival; and (d) institute evaluation of literacy competence through methods which take no account of the socioeconomic changes (Gumperz and Cook-Gumperz 1979: 11–12).

If this twentieth-century situation creates problems for all children, why do some children make the transition to literacy more easily than others? According to the authors, some oral cultures prepare children better than others: "The argument we have been developing," they state, "is that for all children the literacy experience requires essential changes in the processing of verbal information. For some children, however, the shift of understanding of written language is sometimes facilitated by early language experience; the child is able early in life to gain processing experience of the written word" (p. 27). Elsewhere, after reviewing several microethnographic studies of communicative interaction between teachers and children of subordinate groups (e.g., Native Americans, blacks, Native Hawaiians, rural Appalachians, and working-class British), Gumperz sums up the underlying cause of their disproportionate school failure as follows:

> This work highlights the point that children's responses to school tasks are directly influenced by values and presuppositions learned in the home. It demonstrates moreover that classroom equipments, spatial arrangements or social groupings of teachers and students are not the primary determinants of learning. What is important is what is *communicated* in the classroom as a result of complex processes of interaction between educational goals, background knowledge and what various participants perceive over time as taking place (1960:5).

The authors have certainly made an important contribution to our understanding of the cognitive and linguistic changes all children make in learning to use written language. But their implicit and explicit explanations of the special problem of minorities is essentially one of mismatch of communicative etiquettes which we previously criticized. Furthermore, in looking at the problem historically, we find that the educational experiences of blacks and other subordinate minorities in the United States (e.g., Chicanos, Indians) do not conform to the nineteenth century situation described by the authors (Ogbu 1978). Though many Americans idealize education for its own sake, for most Americans, and for blacks in particular, it has been aimed at developing marketable skills. We shall return to this point later.

The oral culture-literate culture discontinuity hypothesis seems inadequate to explain the disproportionate school failure of subordinate minority children. We shall suggest an adequate hypothesis which considers both historical and macro-structural forces that shape classroom processes under which children acquire their literacy. But first we wish to distinguish subordinate minorities from other minorities who do not necessarily share similar problems in school and from lower-class people for the same reason.

Stratification as a Context: Castelike and Class

We define a given population as a minority group if it is in a subordinate power relation to another population in the same society. A minority status is not determined by mere number because the subordinate group might outnumber the dominant group, as the Bantu in South

Africa outnumber whites by more than 2 to 1. For some purposes, such as education, it is useful to distinguish different types of minorities, and in our work we have classified minorities into autonomous, castelike and immigrant types.

Autonomous minorities, which are represented in the United States by Jews and Mormons, are also found in most developing Asian and African nations. They are primarily numerical minorities who may be victims of prejudice but are not totally subordinated in systems of stratification, and their separateness is not based on specialized denigrated economic, political, or ritual roles. Moreover, they often have a cultural frame of reference which demonstrates and encourages success in education and other areas as defined by the larger society.

Castelike minorities—those we have referred to as subordinate minorities—are either incorporated into a society more or less involuntarily and permanently or are forced to seek incorporation and then relegated to inferior status. In America, for example, blacks were incorporated through slavery; Chicanos and Indians through conquest.

Castelike minorities are generally regarded as inherently inferior by the dominant group, who thus rationalize their relegation to inferior social, political, economic, and other roles. Until recently it was (and in many instances still is) more difficult for castelike minority-group members than for dominant-group members to advance on the basis of individual training and ability. The concept of a job ceiling (Ogbu 1978) at best describes the circumscribed occupational and economic opportunities historically faced by castelike minorities. A job ceiling is set by the pressures and obstacles that consign minorities to jobs at the lowest levels of status, power, dignity, and income and meanwhile allow the dominant group to acquire the jobs and rewards above those levels. As we shall argue, the access of castelike minorities to schooling and their perceptions of and responses to schooling have historically been shaped by the job ceiling and related barriers.

Immigrant minorities are those who have come more or less voluntarily unless they are refugees) to their new society for economic, political, and social self-betterment. Immigrants may be subject to pillory and discrimination but have usually not internalized their effects. That is, at least in the first generation, they have not experienced such treatment as an ingrained part of their culture and thus have not been disillusioned to the same extent as castelike minorities. This is true even when the two minority types are faced with the same job ceiling and other barriers. Immigrants also tend to measure their success or failure against that of their peers in their homeland and not against the higher classes of their host society. (See Ogbu 1978, for further elaboration of these and other factors that differentiate immigrants from castelike minorities).

Minority groups do not usually accept subordination passively, though their responses vary. Some groups reduce or eliminate aspects of their subordination; others may actually reinforce some aspects of that subordination. Moreover, different types of minorities respond differently. Except for political emigres, the immigrants have the symbolic option of returning to their homeland or re-emigrating elsewhere. This option may, in fact, motivate the acquisition of education and literacy because immigrants can transfer these skills elsewhere for greater rewards. Because this option is usually not open to castelike minorities, they tend to develop various gross and subtle devices to raise, eliminate or circumvent the job ceiling and other barriers. We shall explore the important implications that these devices have for schooling and literacy.

Lower-Class and Castelike Minorities

Current discussion tends strongly to equate the education and literacy problems of caste-like minorities with those of the lower class. But the differences between them appear in the attempt to distinguish castelike stratification from class stratification. "Caste" or "castelike" in this essay is a purely methodological reference to the structural form underlying the history of minority subordination in America and similar societies.

In a class stratification people are ranked by their education, their jobs, their behavior and how much money they make; that is, by achieved criteria. Lower-class individuals have difficulty advancing into higher classes by achieving more wealth and education or better jobs and social positions because they lack requisite training (education), ability, or proper connections. But class stratification, at least in the United States, has a built-in ideology which encourages lowerclass people to strive for social and economic self-betterment that would put them and/or their children into higher classes. This social mobility occurs enough among white Americans that they view America as a land of great opportunity and success as a matter of ability, perseverance, and education (Berreman 1972; Warner *et al.* 1945).

In a castelike stratification people are, by contrast, assigned to their respective groups at birth or by ascribed criteria such as skin color, and they have few options to escape that designation. Each caste group (e.g., blacks in America) has its own class system but less opportunity for class differentiation and mobility than the dominant class system. For example, the job ceiling in the United States affects black-white racial stratification but not the stratification of social classes within the white group or within the black group. Caste thus gives class in the minority population added disadvantages: a white lower-class American is only lower class; a black lower-class American is also faced with a job ceiling and other caste barriers.

There is current debate over whether and to what extent class stratification has replaced racial or castelike stratification in America (Willie 1979; Wilson 1978). Since the 1960s, civil rights legislation and other efforts have raised the job ceiling and somewhat reduced other racial barriers, but they have not eliminated these barriers altogether. No one knows the extent to which blacks are now employed in more desirable jobs as a matter of compliance with the law. What is certain is that the number of blacks in top jobs more than doubled after affirmative action legislation went into effect in 1966 and 1972; that there is a strong white resistance to these laws; and that blacks are still underrepresented in desirable jobs and overqualified for the jobs that they do (Brimmer 1974; U.S. Commission on Civil Rights 1978).

Furthermore, the positive changes have not reached far enough to affect significantly the social and economic conditions of the black lower class; nor have they been consistent through the years because of economic recessions, white backlash, and changes in political climate. Statistics easily conceal the single most important indication that castelike stratification persists in America: the extraordinary supports (affirmative action, Equal Employment Opportunities Commission Appeals, Special Programs) that blacks need, but that whites do not, in order to move into the middle class. The pattern of change is significant for the problem of education and literacy in that black perceptions of American racial stratification and their opportunities within it have not grown to resemble the perceptions of the white population.

A Cultural Ecological Explanation of Black School Failure

The Framework

Cultural ecology provides a more adequate framework for understanding the literacy problems of black and similar minorities, whether we focus on school completion, functional literacy, or performance on classroom and standardized tests. This framework enables us to study the connections between the school or learning processes *and* societal forces (such as economic patterns and opportunities, intergroup relations, and status mobility in a given society) which affect school curricula, classroom attitudes and efforts, and various activities of school personnel and other members of the educational system.

Cultural ecology is the study of institutionalized and socially transmitted patterns of behavior interdependent with features of the environment (Netting 1968:11; see also Geertz 1962; Goldschmidt 1971; Bennett 1969). It does not deal with the over-all physical environment but with the effective environment, that is, those aspects that directly affect subsistence quest (techno-economic activities) and physical survival. In modern societies the effective environment is primarily the bureaucratized industrial economy. A given population's effective environment generally consists, however, of its resources, its ability to exploit these resources, and its level of technology. The principal economic activities or subsistence strategies depend upon the effective environment. And each mode of exploitation calls for specific skills, knowledge, and other attributes which facilitate subsistence and survival under the specific condition. Ecological adaptation for a given population consists of the congruence or fit between the population's strategies for subsistence, survival, and status and the instrumental competencies and related behaviors of its members. Adaptation for an individual consists of learning about resources and exploitative strategies and acquiring appropriate instrumental competencies and rules of behaviors for achievement as it is defined by for his or her social group.

Childrearing and formal education are culturally organized to insure that children in a given population meet these criteria for adaptation (Ogbu 1980). In modern societies the school is the principal institution adapting children to bureaucratized industrial economy in four ways: teaching them the basic practical skills of reading, writing, and computation essential for almost every subsistence activity in the economy; preparing them for more specialized job training when they later enter the labor force (Wilson 1973); socializing them by means of organizational features (teacher-pupil authority relations, the grading system, etc.) to develop social-emotional attributes essential for participation in the work force (Scrupski 1975; Wilcox 1978); and providing the credentials young adults need to enter the work force (Jencks 1972). In the latter role, schooling is more or less a culturally institutionalized device for allocating and rewarding individuals in society's status system, particularly in the economy (Ogbu 1979 a, b; 1980).

While ideologically most Americans do not see their schools this way, it is a reasonable analysis based on our own study of school and economic behaviors in Stockton, California. In our research, we asked people why they go to school; why they send their children to school; and why they pay taxes to support schools; we listened to public and private discussions and gossip about schooling, jobs, and related matters; we examined documents from local school systems and from city and county planning departments, as well as from employment and welfare agencies. These sources suggest that Stocktonians do not seek education for its own sake, to satisfy their curiosity, or for self-fulfillment, but in order to get jobs as adults and thereby achieve full adult status as defined by their community. Not only do Stocktonians believe that more and better schooling leads to more desirable jobs, higher income, and other social and economic benefits, but local statistics also tend to support their belief—for the majority whites: In Stockton, as elsewhere in the nation, whites with high school diplomas generally have a better chance at more desirable jobs and greater lifetime earning power than their peers with only elementary school diplomas; however they have less chance at desirable jobs and less earning power than their peers with college degrees.

The belief that economic opportunities are commensurate with educational achievement is a part of local white epistemology and is borne out historically by the actual experiences of most whites in the job market. The belief is communicated to local white children and reinforced in a variety of ways. These observations lead us to conclude that the school efforts of local whites are greatly influenced by their experiences in and perceptions of the connection between schooling and adult economic participation.

A major ecological consequence of castelike stratification and job ceiling is that blacks in Stockton and elsewhere in the United States have traditionally occupied economic positions characterized by scarce, dead-end, peripheral, or unstable jobs and by low wages, few chances for advancement on the job, and little social credit as measured by values of the larger society. Some ghetto blacks occupy economic positions that are almost devoid of any wage labor but that contain social resources such as other ghetto residents and caretaker institutions (Harrison 1972; Ross and Hill 1967). Equally important is the fact that the blacks' effective environment contains, in addition to these conventional resources, a subeconomy or "street economy" defined as "a market for the distribution of goods and services which are in demand but have been outlawed officially for social and moral reasons" (Bullock 1973: 100, see also Foster 1974; Heard 1968; Milner 1970; Wolfe 1970).

Educational Consequences

What are the educational consequences of the black effective environment? Because the traditional social and economic positions of blacks have not required much formal education or rewarded educational accomplishments highly, the pattern of schooling which has evolved for blacks generally prepares them for inferior roles. It does not qualify blacks for the more desirable social and economic positions open to whites, nor does it encourage blacks to achieve their maximum. These combined factors have traditionally affected black literacy as measured by school completion, functional literacy, and performance on classroom and standardized tests. We now want to suggest four specific ways in which these factors sustain the lag in black school performance by (a) promoting certain treatment or experiences of blacks in school and classroom and (b) fostering certain classroom attitudes, orientations, and behavior.

White Perceptions of Blacks and Black Access to Education. Blacks have had some access to formal schooling ever since they were brought to America in the early seventeenth century. Although formal education was available to only a few in the South (where most blacks lived before emancipation), and although there was strong opposition to black education in both the South and the North, actual legal prohibitions against black education were instituted in the South only from 1832 to about 1861 after Nat Turner's Revolt (Bond 1966:21; Bullock 1970). Black access to the public schools increased after emancipation, and, as the following table shows, their illiteracy rates steadily declined.

However, factors important to understanding the present situation are concealed by the table. First, blacks have had to fight for almost every increase in their access to public schools; in neither the South nor the North have they been free as a matter of right to attend their community public schools (Bond 1966; Bullock 1970; Kluger 1977; Ogbu 1978). Second, black education in both the South and North has usually been inferior, often separate, and generally based on white perceptions and stereotypes of black status in society and especially in the economy. Third, because blacks do not share white perceptions of their status, they tend not to accept white standards of education for them. Consequently, since the second half of the nineteenth century, blacks have been fighting whites against both inferior and separate education (Kluger 1977).

Let us briefly summarize how white perceptions of black status have shaped black education historically and affected the quality of black literacy. (See table 14.1).

Before emancipation, blacks received occasional biblical education because their masters believed it would make them more obedient and faithful. After the Civil War, when blacks were relegated to peon-like status as sharecroppers or were limited to "Negro jobs" in domestic service and unskilled labor, education followed suit. The ruling white elites believed the tenant farming system would break down if black children received the same education as white children. They would, for example, learn to question the high rates of interest and the exploitative accounting methods the planters imposed on illiterate tenants. Thus, black education was starved of funds.

As the South urbanized, blacks at first received some "industrial" education, chiefly in cooking and low grade building skills. But when many desirable factory jobs began to require special training, black school curricula began, ironically, to emphasize classical and academic rather than industrial education, which was now offered in white schools (Bond 1966: 404, Myrdal 1944: 897–98; Ogbu 1978: 117).

We can conclude that, historically, if blacks did not qualify for desirable jobs it was because their education was designed to disqualify them, not because they were incompetent. Until perhaps the 1960s, American society never seriously intended blacks to achieve social and occupational equality with whites through education.

Even now, "subtle mechanisms" continue to adapt black and white graduates to different futures. One such mechanism for lowering the job ceiling is the disproportionate labeling of black children as educationally "handicapped." For example, in a recent court case brought by blacks against the San Francisco School District, evidence showed that blacks made up only 31.1 percent of the school enrollment in 1976–77, but constituted 53.8 percent of those categorized as educable mentally retarded and relegated to special classes. In the same year, in the twenty California school districts which enrolled 80 percent of black children, black students comprised about 27.5 percent of the school population but 62 percent of those labeled educable mentally retarded. In his decision favoring blacks the judge concluded that

The statistical analyses of the statewide and district-by-district figures indicate the obvious. Their (i.e., black) apparent overenrollment could not be the result of

chance. For example, there is less than one in a million chance that the overenrollment of black children and the underenrollment of non-black children in the E.M.R. classes in 1976–77 would have resulted under a color-blind system of placement (U.S. District Court for Northern California, 1979: 21–22).

The figures are similar to those of other large American cities, including Chicago and New York (see, for example, U.S. Commission on Civil Rights, 1974).

Black Responses. We pointed out earlier that castelike minorities do not usually accept their subordination passively and that blacks have been fighting since emancipation for more and better schooling and against the job ceiling. Those responses, as they relate to schooling and jobs, may in fact contribute to the lag in the school performance, as we shall demonstrate. *A. Black School Conflict and Mistrust:* History has left blacks with a feeling that whites and their institutions cannot be trusted to benefit blacks equitably. Public schools, particularly in the ghetto, are generally not trusted by blacks to provide black children with the "right education." This mistrust of schools arises partly from black perceptions of past and current discriminatory treatment by public schools. This treatment is fully documented in several studies (see Bond 1966, 1969; Kluger 1977; Weinberg 1977).

For over a century, having first "fought" against total exclusion from the public schools, blacks have been "fighting" against inferior education in both segregated and integrated schools. In the totally segregated Southern school systems, blacks of course identified

TABLE 1   Black and White Illiteracy, 14 Years Old and Over, by Region for Selected Years, 1890–1969 (Numbers in thousands)

Area and year	Black Illiterate			White Illiterate		
	Total	*Number*	*Percent*	*Total*	*Number*	*Percent*
United States:						
1890	4259	2607	61	35818	2880	8
1910	823	91	11	43091	1944	5
1930	8027	1445	18	77357	2350	3
1947	10471	1152	11	95952	1919	2
1959	12210	910	7	109163	1709	2
1969	14280	509	4	127449	891	1
South:						
1890	3769	2462	65	7755	1170	15
1910	5308	1906	36	12790	1087	8
1930	6116	1351	22	18390	780	4
North and West:						
1890	631	208	33	28063	1710	6
1910	823	91	11	43091	1944	5
1930	1911	94	5	58967	1570	3

Source: U.S. Department of Commerce, Bureau of the Census. *Current Population Reports, Special Studies, Series p. 23, No. 80, The Social and Economic Status of the Black Population in the United States: An Historical View, 1790–1978.* Table 68, p. 91.

strongly and therefore cooperated with "black schools." But their effectiveness was under-mined by their simultaneous rejection of these same schools as inferior to white schools and thus their need to "fight" for school desegregation. Their attention, commitment, and efforts were diverted from maximizing achievement in black schools to the pursuit of equal resources and an ideal learning setting, namely, desegregated schools.

But in desegregated schools throughout the nation disaffection and mistrust also abound because blacks see inferior education perpetuated through many subtle devices they sus-pected the schools of using (e.g., biased testing, misclassification, tracking, biased textbooks, biased counseling, etc.), and because they doubt that these schools understand black children and their needs.

This doubt is particularly widespread at the moment: it was openly expressed by many blacks at public meetings and in ethnographic interviews during our fieldwork in Stockton. In a study of a desegregated high school, Slawski and Scherer (1977) also found that local blacks tended to attribute low school performance of black males to the school's inability to "relate to black males in ways that will help them learn." The point we would like to stress is that black mistrust and conflict with schools reduce the degree to which black parents and their children can accept as legitimate the schools' goals, standards, and instructional approaches. As a result they tend not to experience a need to cooperate with the schools or to follow their rules and requirements for achievement.

The same conflicts and mistrust also force the schools into defensive approaches to black education—control, paternalism, or actual "contests"—which divert the attention of both blacks and schools from the real task of educating black children. This contrasts sharply with the experience of white middle-class parents and their children, who tend to see the comple-tion of school tasks and conformity with school standards as necessary, desirable, and com-patible with their own goals. Ghetto blacks tend sometimes to interpret the same demands as deceptions or as unnecessary impositions incompatible with their "real educational goals." Perseverance at academic tasks thus becomes difficult for black children.

B. Disillusionment Over Job Ceiling and Academic Efforts: Throughout history a greater propor-tion of blacks than whites have been educationally better qualified or overqualified for their jobs yet underpaid for their educational achievements (Henderson 1967; Norgren and Hill 1964; Newman *et al.* 1978; Sharp 1970; U.S. Commission on Civil Rights 1978). Even in recent years their gradual penetration into more desirable jobs has been accomplished mainly through collective struggle for civil rights (Newman *et al.* 1978; Scott 1976; Ogbu 1978). Job opportunities remain the primary concern of black Americans today.

The job ceiling and related discriminatory practices shape black operations, which in turn influence their perceptions of and responses to schooling. Blacks are generally bitter, frus-trated, and resentful at the job ceiling and other barriers to the full benefits of their education. The extent of this bitterness is evident in the time and resources they expend in efforts to break or circumvent the job ceiling (see Davis, Gardner and Gardner 1965; Dollard 1957; Drake and Cayton 1970; Ogbu 1974; Powdermaker 1968; Newman *et al.* 1978; Scott 1976) as are their strategies for achieving their objectives, such as "uncle tomming," boycotting white businesses, protesting, rioting, and appealing to the courts, to Fair Employment Practices Commissions, to the Equal Employment Opportunity Commission, and the like (see Drake and Cayton 1970:745; National Advisory Commission on Civil Disorders, *Report* 1968:61; Newman *et al.* 1978:10–26; Ogbu 1978; Powdermaker 1968:107, 100, 112; Schemer 1965:85).

When civil rights effectively expand black employment opportunities and other rewards for education, as they appeared to be doing in the 1960s, this encourages black students to work hard in school (Ginsberg *et al.* 1967). But a discouraging message is also communicated, namely, that without such a collective civil rights struggle, blacks automatically have fewer opportunities than whites to benefit from education.

Black children learn about the job ceiling and other barriers quite early in life, though not necessarily from explicit statements by their parents and other adults in their community. In our ethnographic research in Stockton, California, we have found, however, that black parents communicate contradictory attitudes toward schooling. They emphasize the need for their children to get more education than they did, and they insist that their children work hard to order to get good grades and to graduate from high school and college. However, the same parents, by being unemployed, underemployed, and discriminated against, and by gossiping about the similar experiences of relatives and other adults in the community, imply that even if the children succeed in school their chances at good jobs and other societal rewards are not as good as those of their white peers. It is also a part of local black epistemology that a black person must be "twice as good" or "twice as qualified" as the white in order to compete successfully in any situation where whites are judges. Thus the actual example of the lives of black parents can undercut their stated encouragements.

Black children also learn about the job ceiling from public demonstrations calling for more jobs and better wages and from mass media reports of these and related events. These sources convey to black children that the connection between school success and one's ability to get ahead is not as good for blacks as for whites. As black children get older and experience personal failures and frustrations in looking for part-time jobs and summer jobs, these negative messages are reinforced. Some perceptions of young blacks, such as their impression of unlimited employment opportunities for their white peers, may not be accurate (Ogbu 1974); they nonetheless lead to increasing disillusionment among blacks about their future and to doubts about the value of schooling (Ogbu 1974:100; see also Frazier 1940:134–47; Schulz 1969:159; Powdermaker 1968:321).

Not only do these perceptions discourage black children from developing serious attitudes toward school and from persevering in their schoolwork; they also teach them to "blame the system" rather than themselves for their failures. In our research in Stockton we have found that black children learn very early to blame the school system for their failures, just as their parents and black adults in general blame their failures on the larger "system." A resulting paradox is that black students may express high educational aspirations coupled with low academic effort and perseverance and thus low school performance.

C. Survival Strategies and Competencies Incongruent with Demands of Schooling: Another black response to the job ceiling is the evolution of "survival strategies." This effects even children much too young to understand the labor market and other barriers and has serious implications for school performance and classroom processes. There are two kinds of survival strategies. The purpose of the first kind is to increase conventional economic and social resources of the black community and to make available conventional jobs and other societal rewards. These strategies include collective struggles or civil rights activities (Newman *et al.* 1978; Scott 1976), clientship or uncle tomming (Dollard 1957; Myrdal 1944; Farmer 1968; Ogbu 1978). Civil rights strategy is well known to most people; but clientship also arises from the job ceiling and other barriers. Blacks learned long ago that one key to self-betterment within the caste system is through white patronage (i.e., favoritism, not merit alone), which can be solicited through some version of the old "Uncle Tom" role, that is, through compliance, dependence, and manipulation. More recently the reverse strategy of "shuckin' and jivin' " has been adopted, which is another defensive way to manipulate white patronage. The second kind of survival strategy, which includes hustling, pimping, and the like, exploits nonconventional economic and social resources or "the street economy" (Bullock 1973; Foster 1974; Heard 1968; Milner 1970; Wolfe 1970).

Thus within the black community success in terms of conventional jobs and resources often requires collective struggles and/or clientship *in addition to educational credentials*. Nonconventional forms of success and ways of making a living are also open to blacks. Thus "successful people" are not only those who succeed in conventional terms either with school credentials alone or with clientship and collective struggle as well, but also those who make it in the street through hustling and related strategies. They are admired, and they influence the efforts of others, including children, to succeed.

We have suggested that survival strategies may require knowledge, attitudes, and skills that are not wholly compatible with white middle-class teaching and learning behavior. We have also suggested that children learn the survival strategies during preschool years as a normal part of their cultural learning: consequently, the potential for learning difficulties may already exist when children enter school. Whether and to what extent those difficulties arise depends on the individual child's experience in school and the classroom. We suspect that insofar as children have become competent in these survival strategies they may lack serious attitudes toward schooling and toward academic tasks in general, including test taking.

Conclusion

In this paper we have argued that the disproportionate school failure of black children is not because they come from an oral culture, though we have not challenged the assertion that black culture is an oral culture. We have only noted that members of the so-called oral cultures of small-scale societies and immigrants into the United States from residual cultures of more complex societies do not manifest the same learning problems in school that are found among black and similar castelike minorities.

We have suggested an alternative view of the problem within an ecological framework in which school is a culturally organized means of preparing children for adult roles in the social and economic life of their society or social group. Within this framework the traditional social and economic positions of blacks have not required much education nor rewarded blacks highly for educational accomplishments. Black menial positions enforced by castelike or racial stratification has influenced how the dominant whites who control their schooling perceive them and define their educational needs. It has also influenced how blacks themselves perceive their opportunities and the importance of schooling.

The perceptions of whites have led them to provide blacks with inadequate schooling and to communicate attitudes in school settings that do not encourage blacks to maximum efforts. Black perceptions generate disillusionment about schooling and a lack of perseverance toward schoolwork; they lead to survival strategies that require knowledge, attitudes, and skills which may be incompatible with school requirements. Furthermore, it is likely that perennial conflict and mistrust between blacks and the schools interfere with the willingness of blacks to comply with school rules and standards and place the schools in a defensive posture toward blacks. Closer study is needed to determine how these factors contribute, singly and in combination, to the learning difficulties observed in classrooms.

Since the 1960s some efforts have been made to change black status and schooling, for example, through legislative and administrative channels noted earlier in the essay. The magnitude and quality of these changes, however, have not broken the job ceiling or significantly altered black expectations, especially among the lower segments of the black community.

During the same period, efforts have also been made to improve black schooling and raise academic achievement levels through school desegregation, compensatory education, preschool (Headstart) educations, parent education and training. Follow-Through, special admissions, special scholarships, and many others (Ogbu 1978). These programs have helped many blacks to complete higher levels of schooling, to achieve greater functional literacy, and to improve their performance in classroom and on standardized tests. But the number benefiting from such programs remains small and many who do benefit probably do not come from the lower segments of the community. These programs remain ineffective for or unavailable to the majority. Moreover, they are essentially remedial and often based on misconceptions of the underlying causes of black school problems (Obgu 1978). Preventing learning problems before they develop will require a strategy that will simultaneously have to (a) consider the economic expectations of blacks as a root cause rather than a consequence of the school failure and literacy problem; (b) eliminate the gross and subtle mechanisms which differentiate black schooling from white schooling; and (c) examine black perceptions and "adaptive" responses, including the problem of mistrust and conflict in black relations with the schools.

🍎 Women's Ways of Knowing

Mary Field Belenky, Blythe McVicker Clinchy, Nancy Rule Goldberger, and Jill Mattuck Tarule

The following excerpt is from the book *Women's Ways of Knowing: The Development of Self, Voice, and Mind* written by Mary Field Belenky, Blythe Clinchy, Nancy Goldberger, and Jill Tarule, and published in 1986. This book has been influential in discussions of education generally and, specifically, feminist approaches to learning. The research reported in this work was supported by the Fund for Improvement of Post-secondary Education.

A better understanding of women's experience would permit, even force, a far-reaching revision of the broader fields of higher education and intellectual life in the United States.

—Patricia Palmieri, 1979

Toward an Education for Women

Most of the institutions of higher education in this country were designed by men, and most continue to be run by men. In recent years feminist teachers and scholars have begun to question the structure, the curriculum, and the pedagogical practices of these institutions; and they have put forth useful proposals for change (for example, Bowles and Duelli-Klein 1983; Martin 1985; Nicholson 1980; Rich 1979; Spanier, Bloom, and Boroviak 1984; Tarule 1980). But, as the scholar Patricia Palmieri (1979, p. 541) suggests, in order to design an education appropriate for women we must learn about the academic experiences of ordinary women.

All of the individuals we interviewed were ordinary women. Most of them were neither teachers nor scholars nor even feminists but simply students. We asked each woman what she thought would stay with her about her experiences in the school or program she attended. We asked her to tell us about specific academic and nonacademic experiences, about good and bad teachers, good and bad assignments, good and bad programs or courses. We asked her whether she thought that her participation in the program changed the way she thought about herself or the world. We asked, "In your learning here, have you come across an idea that made you see things differently? What has been most helpful to you about this place? Are there things it doesn't provide that are important to you? Things you would like to learn that you can't learn here?" Finally, we asked, "Looking back over your whole life, can you tell us about a really powerful learning experience that you've had, in or out of school?"

The women responded, of course, in diverse ways; but as we examined their accounts of what they learned and failed to learn, of how they liked to learn and how they were forced to

Chapters 9 and 10 from WOMEN'S WAYS OF KNOWING by MARY FIELD BELENKY ET AL. Copyright © 1986 by Basic Books, Inc. Reprinted by permission of BasicBooks, a division of HarperCollins Publishers, Inc.

learn, some common themes emerged, themes that are distinctively, although surely not exclusively, feminine.

Reminiscences of College

We begin with the reminiscences of two ordinary women, each recalling an hour during her first year at college. One of them, now middle aged, remembered the first meeting of an introductory science course. The professor marched into the lecture hall, placed upon his desk a large jar filled with dried beans, and invited the students to guess how many beans the jar contained. After listening to an enthusiastic chorus of wildly inaccurate estimates the professor smiled a thin, dry smile, revealed the correct answer, and announced, "You have just learned an important lesson about science. Never trust the evidence of your own senses."

Thirty years later, the woman could guess what the professor had in mind. He saw himself, perhaps, as inviting his students to embark upon an exciting voyage into a mysterious underworld invisible to the naked eye, accessible only through scientific method and scientific instruments. But the seventeen-year-old girl could not accept or even hear the invitation. Her sense of herself as a knower was shaky, and it was based on the belief that she could use her own firsthand experience as a source of truth. This man was saying that this belief was fallacious. He was taking away her only tool for knowing and providing her with no substitute. "I remember feeling small and scared," the woman says, "and I did the only thing I could do. I dropped the course that afternoon, and I haven't gone near science since."

The second woman, in her first year at college, told a superficially similar but profoundly different story about a philosophy class she had attended just a month or two before the interview. The teacher came into class carrying a large cardboard cube. She placed it on the desk in front of her and asked the class what it was. They said it was a cube. She asked what a cube was, and they said a cube contained six equal square sides. She asked how they knew that this object contained six equal square sides. By looking at it, they said. "But how do you know?" the teacher asked again. She pointed to the side facing her and, therefore, invisible to the students; then she lifted the cube and pointed to the side that had been face down on the desk, and, therefore, also invisible. "We can't look at all six sides of a cube at once, can we? So we can't exactly *see* a cube. And yet, you're right. You know it's a cube. But you know it not just because you have eyes but because you have intelligence. You invent the sides you cannot see. You use your intelligence to create the 'truth' about cubes."

The student said to the interviewer,

> It blew my mind. You'll think I'm nuts, but I ran back to the dorm and I called my boyfriend and I said, "Listen, this is just incredible," and I told him all about it. I'm not sure he could see why I was so excited. I'm not sure I understand it myself. But I really felt, for the first time, like I was really in college, like I was—I don't know— sort of *grown up.*

Both stories are about the limitations of firsthand experience as a source of knowledge— we cannot simply see the truth about either the jar of beans or the cube—but there is a difference. We can know the truth about cubes. Indeed, the students did know it. As the science professor pointed out, the students were wrong about the beans; their senses had deceived them. But, as the philosophy teacher pointed out, the students were right about the cube; their minds had served them well.

The science professor was the only person in the room who knew how many beans were in that jar. Theoretically, the knowledge was available to the students; they could have counted the beans. But faced with that tedious prospect, most would doubtless take the professor's word for it. He is authority. They had to rely upon his knowledge rather than their own. On the other hand, every member of the philosophy class knew that the cube had six sides. They were all colleagues.

The science professor exercised his authority in a benign fashion, promising the students that he would provide them with the tools they needed to excavate invisible truths. Similarly, the philosophy teacher planned to teach her students the skills of philosophical analysis, but she was at pains to assure them that they already possessed the tools to construct some powerful truths. They had built cubes on their own, using only their own powers of inference, without the aid of elaborate procedures or fancy apparatus or even a teacher. Although a teacher might have told them once that a cube contained six equal square sides, they did not have to take the teacher's word for it; they could have easily verified it for themselves.

The lesson the science professor wanted to teach is that experience is a source of error. Taught in isolation, this lesson diminished the student, rendering her dumb and dependent. The philosophy teacher's lesson was that although raw experience is insufficient, by reflecting upon it the student could arrive at truth. It was a lesson that made the student feel more powerful ("sort of grown up").

No doubt it is true that, as the professor in May Sarton's novel *The Small Room* says, the "art" of being a student requires humility. But the woman we interviewed did not find the science lesson humbling; she found it humiliating. Arrogance was not then and is not now her natural habitat. Like most of the women in our sample she lacked confidence in herself as a thinker; and the kind of learning the science teacher demanded was not only painful but crippling.

In thinking about the education of women, Adrienne Rich writes, "Suppose we were to ask ourselves, simply: What does a woman need to know?" (1979, p. 240). A woman, like any other human being, does need to know that the mind makes mistakes; but our interviews have convinced us that every woman, regardless of age, social class, ethnicity, and academic achievement, needs to know that she is capable of intelligent thought, and she needs to know it right away. Perhaps men learn this lesson before going to college, or perhaps they can wait until they have proved themselves to hear it; we do not know. We do know that many of the women we interviewed had not yet learned it.

Confirmation of the Self as Knower

In the masculine myth, confirmation comes not at the beginning of education but at the end. "Welcome to the community of scholars," the president announces at the Harvard commencement. ("That sure sounded weird to me," said a woman graduate. "He says 'Welcome.' Then he shows us the door.") Confirmation as a thinker and membership in a community of thinkers come as the climax of Perry's story of intellectual development in the college years.

The student learns, according to Perry, that "we must all stand judgment" and that he must earn "the privilege of having [his] ideas respected" (1970, p. 33). Having proved beyond reasonable doubt that he has learned to think in complex, contextual ways, the young man is admitted to the fraternity of powerful knowers. Certified as a thinker, he becomes one of "them" (now dethroned to lower-case "them"). Doubt precedes belief; separation leads to connection. The weak become powerful, and the inferiors join their superiors. This scenario may capture the "natural" course of men's development in traditional, hierarchical institutions, but it does not work for women. For women, confirmation and community are prerequisites rather than consequences of development.

Most of the women reported that they had often been treated as if they were stupid. This was especially (although by no means exclusively) true of the less privileged. Consider, for example, the case of Lillian, a student at one of the "invisible colleges." When Lillian's infant son suffered an attack of projectile vomiting, she called her pediatrician. "Don't worry about it," he said. Instead of respecting her concern, he dismissed it. Lillian wanted respect, and she wanted information.

I wasn't asking for the complete history of projectile vomiting. I just really wanted an explanation, simple, something like you would give a child if they asked you a question like where do babies come from. You don't give them a whole routine, just a piece of it, and let them deal with that. You don't say, "Never mind." You don't patronize them. I don't do that with my own child, so I don't like to be treated like that. I really wanted to be dealt with as a person, not just a hysterical mother, not even as a mother, as just another person who was halfway intelligent.

Lillian's encounters with authority (teachers, bosses, doctors, priests, bureaucrats, and policemen) taught her that "experts" usually tried to assert dominance over less knowledgeable people either by assaulting them with information or by withholding information. But her experience as a mother provided her with a different model, a model we call "connected teaching," in which the expert (parent) examines the needs and capacities of the learner (child) and composes a message that is, in the psychologist Jerome Bruner's felicitous term, "courteous" to the learner (1963, p. 52). Although Lillian knew more than her son knew, she did not think she was better than he. She did not want to exert power over him. She wanted to help him on his own terms, and she needed experts who would do the same for her.

Fortunately a public health clinic for children, run on the connected teaching model, opened up in Lillian's area. The elite of the clinic defined the clinic's job not as "teaching mothers how to raise children" but as "trying to help mothers do what they need to do." Lillian, having placed her child under the clinic's care, exclaimed, "What a difference!" Members of the clinic staff never patronized her, nor did they patronize her son. 'They've always seemed to deal with me and, now that Shaun's older, with him on equal levels." To allay Shaun's fears of examinations, the nurse practitioner carried out an entire examination on the little boy's teddy bear, explaining "very sincerely," in terms the child could understand, what she was doing and why. Lillian marveled at the staff's patience, as did Ann, another client whom we met in earlier chapters of this book. Ann's private pediatrician always made her feel rushed. Embarrassed to ask for clarification, she pretended she understood his directions. Afraid of "wasting his time," she hesitated to raise issues that were bothering her. At the clinic, on the other hand, they "take time to explain things"; they "spell it all out."

Having been subjected to the usual view of health care professionals that parents are incompetent, mothers who used the clinic were astonished to discover that members of the staff, nearly all of them women, believed in them. As Lillian said, "They seemed to have trust in me. I hadn't had that in a long time, that feeling like my parents gave me, that I was—no questions asked—trusted."

What these women needed and what the clinic provided, perhaps more clearly, consistently, and sincerely than any other institution we sampled, was confirmation that they could be trusted to know and to learn. Given confirmation, they felt they could "just do anything." Lacking it, as one woman said, they were "crippled" and "just can't function." Most of the women we interviewed made it clear that they did not wish to be told merely that they had the capacity or the potential to *become* knowledgeable or wise. They needed to know that they already knew something (although by no means everything), that there was something good inside them. They worried that there was not. "Suppose one woke and found oneself a fraud?" wrote Virginia Woolf. "It was part of my madness that horror" (1980, p. 138).

The worry was especially acute among older women returning to college or entering it for the first time. Some of these women found the confirmation they needed in an adult education program. A fifty-four-year-old widow, having raised six children, said, "I had reached a point in my life where I wasn't sure I had any worth as a human being. As the kids grew up and left, that kicked out any props I had. If I had any worth at all it was as their mother. What was I going to be for the rest of my life? A shell of what I had been?" But in the program, she found, "I'm accepted for what I am, the ability to be me. I came here and discovered I'm not a shell. I've got a lot of stuff in me."

A younger adult in the same program said that her teachers and fellow students made her realize that the knowledge she gained through her life experiences "is important and real and valuable." At the urging of a teacher, she wrote a paper about her escape to the Arctic in search of self. The paper was accepted for credit and circulated among members of the community. The woman said, "It validated who I was, that something that was real personal to me, that I carried around alone—that I could share that in writing and get credit for it. That I was recognized and respected." And a twenty-seven-year-old single parent, who "needed people to believe me," found them in the same program: "The people just accepted that of course I was a person, that I had something to say. They didn't look down on me at all. It was a whole different environment than I was used to. There was no oppression."

Even the most privileged women in our sample expressed the need to be accepted as a "person," as opposed to being oppressed or patronized. Privilege does not ensure freedom from oppression—incest, for instance, occurs in the "best" of families—achievement does not guarantee self-esteem. Indeed, highly competent girls and women are especially likely to underestimate their abilities. Most of the women who attended the more prestigious colleges in the sample had a history of privilege and achievement, but most felt uncertain about their abilities. Several suspected that they had been admitted through a fluke.

Some women found the confirmation they needed in these colleges. Faith, for example, said that although she had always done well in school, no one had ever told her that she was intelligent until she came to college. There, Faith said, "people say, 'Well, you know, you're a pretty smart person.' If people say that to you enough you have to figure that they know at least a little of what they're talking about."

A classmate, however, interviewed toward the end of her first year, told a different story. Although she had entered college with SAT scores in the high 600s, she felt that she was "the dumbest girl here." Her high school teachers doled out constant praise but in college the teachers were silent.

> You need a little bit of praise to keep you going. If you get an idea that the teacher likes what you're doing, it helps you go on more, whereas most of my courses the teachers are kind of—They don't say "bad," they don't say "good," so you start having doubts and thinking, "Well, if he doesn't say something nice, he must not like it." And you just get into such a rut where you can't do anything. There's just an extreme lack of praise around here.

In high school she and her friends had been stars; in this highly competitive college they were just average.

> We all had a lot of self-esteem, and we didn't really think about it, we just knew we could do it. Whereas now, it's totally different. If I could just think to myself that I've done something really exceptionally good, 'cause sometimes I feel like I'm getting lost in the crowd. If I could just write maybe one paper and have a teacher say, "Hey, that was really, really good," I think that would help a lot.

We asked her if the approval had to come from a teacher. Could it not come from within her? "Not at this point," she said. "It's been so far pushed down it couldn't come back up by itself."

Some women were so consumed with self-doubt that they found it difficult to believe a teacher's praise, especially when the teacher was a man. One young woman told us that she never felt sure a male professor would take her seriously. The women worried that professors who praised their minds really desired their bodies. Elizabeth "got suspicious" of a male professor because he praised her so much.

> I got to know him personally, and it then became hard for me. I learned that evaluation is subjective, that there's not such a thing as an objective evaluation of things like work. I realized the guy liked me, so he's going to like my papers. Then I said, "This is really screwed up."

Elizabeth went on to describe a woman teacher who encouraged and helped her with her writing without babying her. "She was the only one who said, 'Yeah, that's good,'" "But," said the interviewer, "I thought you said [the male professor] was encouraging." "He was encouraging," Elizabeth replied, "but I think I felt that there were strings attached."

Several women spoke of the ambiguity inherent in male professors' praise for women students, of the "games" that male professors and female students fell into. Stella, an artist, said, "That's something every woman deals with, going to college: Am I a student or a flirtation? Why is the teacher giving them attention? Why does he draw on your pad and not hers?" The teacher may have to draw the lines very carefully in order to avoid ambiguity.

The problem was exacerbated—and the need for clear boundaries especially acute—for the many women who arrived at college having already suffered sexual abuse at the hands of a male in a position of authority, such as Elizabeth, whose father had repeatedly molested her. Whenever powerful men praised relatively powerless women, the women started looking for "the strings," especially when, as many admitted, they knew that they, themselves, had used their sexuality in the past to elicit praise.

Knowing the Realities: The Voice of Experience

In considering how to design an education appropriate for women, suppose we were to begin by simply asking: What does a woman know? Traditional courses do not begin there. They begin not with the student's knowledge but with the teacher's knowledge. The courses are about the culture's questions, questions fished out of the "mainstream" of the disciplines. If the student is female, her questions may differ from the culture's questions, since women, paddling in the bywaters of the culture, have had little to do with positing the questions or designing the agendas of the disciplines. (See, for example, Harding and Hintikka 1983; Reinharz 1984; Sherman and Beck 1979; Smith 1974.) Indeed, as writer Mary Jacobus points out, although nineteenth- and twentieth-century feminists have sought access to education as a means of liberation, "this access to a male dominated culture may equally be felt to bring with it alienation, repression, division—a silencing of the 'feminine,' a loss of women's inheritance" (1979, p. 10).

Most women students do not expect colleges to honor their concerns. One young woman who had always relied heavily on authorities as the source of truth told us that she hesitated before signing up for a women's studies course at her university, fearing that the course would not be respected; but it turned out to be the best course she'd ever taken. For the first time, she said, she was really interested in what she was studying. Two women team-taught the course, and it fascinated her that two people thought it was important enough to teach. The authorities' sanction enabled her to respect her own interests.

Cynthia, the alumna whose mother digested her experiences for her during college and told her what she felt, said that although she enjoyed the "austerity" of the college curriculum and did well, she felt lonely and sad throughout the four years. At the time, she thought her problems were "just personal," but lately she had begun to wonder if the curriculum contributed to her depression. She had been reading an essay by E. B. White about a battle between an old gander and a younger, stronger gander.

They have this heroic battle. And the older goose at the end of the story is seen leaping off to lick his wounds somewhere in a patch of sun in a field. And it struck me that E. B. White saw everything in terms of great struggles—these great clashes between opposing forces—and that's what life was like, this—uh—sort of larger-than-life thing.

The larger-than-life knowledge contained in the college curriculum seemed to her at the time the only respectable form of knowledge; but now that she had more sense of herself as a woman, it struck her as a distinctively masculine perspective.

You know, it's not a battle between the gods that concerns women. Women are concerned with how you get through life from minute to minute. What each little teeny tiny incident—how it can affect everything else you do. Women see things close at hand and are more concerned with minutiae.

This feminine mode seemed "realer, somehow," to Cynthia. It was a real way of knowing, an embryonic form, perhaps, of the close-up mothering eye that won for Barbara McClintock, belatedly, a Nobel prize (Keller 1983).

Although Cynthia's grades in college suggest that she mastered the masculine mode, she felt that it really never quite "took." Someday she hopes to master it. "I guess ultimately I would like to balance them. I would like to have a larger picture, too. I would like to be able to study history the way men can study history and see patterns in the development of the world and of civilization." But not right now. Right now she wants to put her ear to the ground, listen to the squirrel's heart beat, as George Eliot put it, and prowl among the webs of little things.

At this point I want to explore those things that are more womanlike, the kinds of sensations and response that I have to things on a very day-to-day small scale. I like playing with my impressions of the silliest things. I think I haven't ever seen things in quite this way, been quite as aware of the fun I could have with introspection and observation of daily life.[2]

Most of the women we interviewed were drawn to the sort of knowledge that merges from firsthand observation, and most of the educational institutions they attended emphasized abstract "out-of-context learning" (Cole, Gay, Glick, and Sharp 1971). We asked a young woman from such an institution to tell us about a good paper that she had written. She said she had not written many good papers, but there was one that she really liked.

It was for a writing course. We were allowed to write about whatever we wanted. And I just described a place where I had worked—the social structure and all the cattiness—and I really enjoyed that. I was just so excited about what I was writing, and I thought it was just the greatest thing to read, and I sent copies to friends I had worked with, and they just loved it. [But the teacher] didn't think it was an important issue. He said it was well written but lacked content, whatever that means. [Laughs.] ("How about a bad paper?" the interviewer asked.) There was one I wrote analyzing a book that I hadn't finished. That wasn't too good. You know, it's really easy, though, to read part of a book and then pick up a few sources and annotate everything. I just thought it was horrible. I just knew that I didn't know what I was talking about, and I think it showed.

But apparently it did not; the teacher liked the paper. The student's standards were in conflict with the teacher's. When she wrote out of her own experience, she felt she knew what she was talking about, but the teacher felt the paper was not about anything. When she pasted together a mess of undigested, secondhand information, he was satisfied.

The women we interviewed nearly always named out-of-school experiences as their most powerful learning experiences. The mothers usually named childbearing or child rearing. The kind of knowledge that is used in child rearing is typical of the kind of knowledge women value and schools do not. Much of it comes not from words but from action and observation, and much of it has never been translated into words, only into actions. As a single parent of nine children said, "There are things I have up here [taps her temple] that I can't put down on paper. I know I use a lot of it in my daily life, like in trying to help my children."

This kind of knowledge does not necessarily lead to general propositions. Good mothering requires adaptive responding to constantly changing phenomena; it is tuned to the concrete and particular. A response that works with a particular child at a particular moment may not work with a different child or with the same child at a different moment. Mothers expect change, Ruddick says, and "change requires a kind of learning in which what one learns cannot be applied exactly, and often not even by analogy, to a new situation" (1980, p. 111). In this sense "maternal thinking" differs from scientific thinking, which considers an experimental result to be real—a fact—only if it can be replicated. As the philosopher Carol McMillan says, mothers are understandably "extremely hesitant about concocting theories about how other people should bring up their children and are sceptical about the advice thrust upon them by the 'experts' " (1982, p. 54).

Many of the women we interviewed—mothers or not—remarked upon the discrepancy between the kind of thinking required in school and the kind required in dealing with people. A college junior, for example, said she found academics much easier than personal life.

> I'm very good at doing tasks. You know, you just compartmentalize something. It's time to sit down and write a paper and think about what someone said. And you do it. But when you're dealing with people you can't always compartmentalize— you know, sort of wrap them up in little packets and put them on the shelf and then you know how to deal with them from then on. Because everyone is always in an amorphous state. And they're all changing so much all the time. What may have worked with one person five days ago isn't going to work with them tomorrow.

Most of these women were not opposed to abstraction as such. They found concepts useful in making sense of their experiences, but they balked when the abstractions preceded the experiences or pushed them out entirely. Even the women who were extraordinarily adept at abstract reasoning preferred to start from personal experience. Mary Lou was one of them.

> I think women care about things that relate to their lives personally. I think the more involvement they have in something that affects them personally, the more they're going to explore it and the more they're going to be able to give and to get out of it. I think that men—because they're male they haven't been put down all the time for their sex, so they can go into any subject with confidence, saying,

"I can learn about this" or "I have the intellect to understand this." Whereas I think women don't deal with things that way. I think they break down an issue and pick out what it is about it that has happened to them or they can relate to in some way, and that's how they start to explore it.

After graduating from high school Mary Lou took an entry-level job in day care, and worked her way up to be director of a center, designing and administering a program for children with minimal brain damage. Entering college at thirty-three, she did not regret the years spent in the field.

I think the way I've learned in the past it's always been a very experiential kind of thing. That's how I learned about day care and about children to begin with. It was doing it. It was having to do it every single day for eight hours a day. I think that's where I got the wealth of my knowledge. I feel more comfortable knowing that. I like to know the realities. I like to know what's going on, so it's hard for me to explore something on the theory aspect and then go out and get the practical. I like to have the practical first, so I know what's going on and what it's really like, and then look at the theories that way.

Mary Lou was driven to reenter college by the need to organize the observations of women and children she had accumulated over the years.

Things weren't sinking in. They were just all there, and there was no connection. Then when I came here and lived in the women's dorm and started having discussions about feminist theory and philosophy, everything just kind of fell into place. There was a lot that I had seen going on and I had observed, but I didn't have anything really to relate it to. I feel much more knowledgeable now. I have words. I know reasons.

Judith, a staff member at the children's health clinic and one of our most highly educated and cerebral informants, said, "I don't like getting things totally out of a book. I really like having some real experience of it myself." Judith felt that much of what people thought they knew, they knew only in the form of "general concepts"; they did not really know it. "In the most exciting kind of learning, people are allowed to go right down to rock bottom and really look at these concepts and find out what their experience has been with it, what they know about it." Judith has had this sort of intense conversation in informal meetings with friends but never in school. In school, she said, people are "supposed to learn it the way somebody else sees it."

Usually, we are supposed to learn it the way men see it. Men move quickly to impose their own conceptual schemes on the experience of women, says French feminist writer Marguerite Duras. These schemes do not help women make sense of their experience; they extinguish the experience. Women must find their own words to make meaning of their experiences, and this will take time. Meanwhile, "men must renounce their theoretical rattle" (1973, p. 111).

Duras says that men have all the old words on the tips of their tongues, and so they can speak right out, while

> Women have been in darkness for centuries. They don't know themselves. Or only poorly. And when women write, they translate this darkness. Men don't translate. They begin from a theoretical platform that is already in place, already elaborated. The writing of women is really translated from the unknown, like a new way of communicating, rather than an already formed language. (1975, p. 174)

It should come as no surprise that the courses most often mentioned as powerful learning experiences were, as with Mary Lou, courses in feminist theory, which helped the women translate their ideas from the darkness of private experience into a shared public language.

Women also described as "powerful" the opportunities for experiential learning provided by their institutions. Mary Lou, studying to be a midwife, said that she and her classmates were "terrified" before giving their first pelvic exams. The teacher prepared them by taking them through a fantasy exercise in which they imagined performing the exam. "She guided us through it and told us exactly what we would be feeling for and how it would feel. We had our eyes closed and were moving our hands along with her directions, like 'Now you move four inches this way.' " Initially cynical about the value of the exercise, Mary Lou found that it worked. When she performed her first real exam she found herself "saying the same things the teacher did. 'Okay, now we move over to the spine and then we go up and feel for the sacriatic curve.' That was something that was concrete, and it was there."

Freedom, Structure, and the Tyranny of Expectation

Probably the most pervasive theme we found in our interviews with women of all sorts was one we called "inner-outer," encompassing issues women raised concerning the source and types of control and validation they had experienced in their lives. In analyzing each woman's interview, we asked ourselves, who or what, in this woman's eyes, defines the goals, sets the pace, and evaluates the outcomes of her behavior? In terms of education, we asked, to what degree does she perceive the tasks, the timetable, and the standards as imposed by the institution, to what degree by herself, and with what consequences?

The Need for Structure

All of the women we interviewed, even the most rebellious, wanted some structure in their educational environments. Those who relied most heavily upon received knowledge favored the most clear-cut externally imposed pattern. Some of the students at the community college, for example, appreciated the college's precisely articulated curriculum. "I need to follow something structured," said one of them. "I like to know what I have to do." Overburdened by responsibilities at home and at work, she had neither the energy nor the time to map out her own structure. She was irritated when teachers and students departed from the structure of the lesson. "I'm not good in math, and I need to listen to an instructor from the beginning of the session through to the end. I don't want to hear about his kids or his wife or his prob-lems, right? Or the students who come in late. I don't want to hear that. I just want to listen to the instructor."

Some of the women at purportedly progressive institutions complained that the absence of structure served as an excuse for self-indulgence and led to a lack of seriousness among both students and faculty. A first-year student complained that in most of her seminars, although the material was excellent, both teachers and students were unprepared. Instead of helping the students focus their attention upon the material, the teacher drew attention to himself: "My experience with free-form classes has been the professor free-forming it. He does all the talking." In general, the student said,

> This place has no expectations as an institution. None. It's almost impossible to flunk out. Anything socially that you do is probably acceptable. There are no social guidelines. Some very basic expectations should be set up so that people have an obligation to their peers and to the faculty and to the administration.

Other students at this college and at the early college also complained that their class-mates' irresponsibility corroded both academic and social life; but still others believed that the very absence of rules conveyed the message, as one early college student said, that "you're respected until proven irresponsible." She and several classmates appreciated the fact that the college, instead of pointing them in a particular direction and insisting that they stay on a prescribed path, allowed them "freedom to go through changes," floundering down blind alleys and into dead ends and changing course without penalty.

The Tyranny of Expectation

In general, we heard more complaints about excessive control than about lack of structure. Students from the most prestigious and academically "demanding" institutions were most eloquent in their complaints. Some alumnae of the women's college, for instance, said that they had never learned to make choices; the college made the choices for them. Cheryl, an alumna who majored in chemistry, was happy that she had attended this college but found it a painful experience also. It was hard, but in another sense, it was easy. To "keep up" was "a never-ending struggle," but the structure was clear-cut. if you did the assignments, you made the grade. But when she graduated, Cheryl encountered a more ambiguous world. "You don't know quite what to do to succeed in your job. It's not clear-cut. You have to make sense of a lot of things that are not well organized. You have to find out what's important. You have to establish priorities. And I didn't know how to do that."

Cheryl's first job was with a physician who asked her to set up a research project. Having no idea how to do it, she looked to him for direction, but he was as ignorant as she. Ultimately, she organized and executed the project, experiencing a depth of satisfaction she never felt in completing her assigned tasks in college.

Bridget's story illustrates what can happen when "good" girls go to good colleges. Like most girls in our society, Bridget was raised to be "nice." Two years out of college, niceness remained a problem.

I'm constantly having to fight this natural tendency I have to be "a nice person." I've been mad at myself for being too nice for a long time, and yet, at the same time, I know I can get away with murder sometimes, because I'm so nice. I'm still very afraid of not being nice, very afraid.

Nice girls fulfill other people's expectations. Bridget thought that the women's college was wrong for her because it expected too much: "It was too competitive and too demanding. I'm a very conscientious person, and I found myself always trying to do the work."

In high school Bridget consistently achieved top marks without working very hard. At college she continued to take it easy, and her grades at the end of the first semester were terrible. In the second semester she tried a new approach.

I worked my butt off. I have never been so intense and disciplined working before. I ended up getting the second highest grade in the economics final, coming up from the bottom of the class. I memorized every goddamn picture there was in art history. I spent three hours every day going over those pictures. For three hours every day I studied French; for three hours every day I studied art; and for three hours every day I ground myself through economics.

At the end of each day she went swimming to loosen her constipated brain.

I swam a mile every day, and it wasn't until the end of that mile that I finally felt my muscles begin to loosen up, and my head was finally clear of all this crap that I was stuffing it full of. That was probably the peak of my career at the college in terms of beating the system.

Bridget portrayed herself during the next three terms as a drudge, motivated by duty rather than desire (Weil 1951), slogging through dull courses in order to fulfill various "distribution requirements" and prepare herself for a successful career. But, although she worked constantly, she was always "behind" and she got mediocre grades.

In her third year she moved off campus and enrolled for two terms at an Ivy League college, where, she found, "You don't have to do that much work to keep up." She found time to carry a part-time job, to study dance, and to maintain a communal household. Returning to the women's college for her final semester, although continuing to live off campus, Bridget felt that everything had changed. She no longer worried about "getting caught up with things."

I hardly did any of the reading I was supposed to do in most of my classes and still did very well. I don't know how it happened. I did loads of extra reading for the Women in American History course and loved it. I was so into the subject. I promised I would give myself the gift of no economics classes as a senior. I promised myself I'd only take classes that interested me. I did, and my grade point average just soared. It was incredible. I was so detached from the campus. It's as *though I was walking through that place and felt no reality. I felt as though I was looking through a glass window at the whole thing. I was totally out of touch with that school. That was my overriding impression of the last semester, besides enjoying my work for the first time. Finally feeling as though I was making that school work for me, extracting from it what I wanted, no longer feeling pressured that I must be career-oriented and any number of the other things I felt.*

Bridget and other women who attended the women's college and other equally "demanding" institutions felt in retrospect that their intellectual development was stunted rather than nourished by the incessant academic pressure. "Ever since leaving college," Bridget says, "my joy in reading and my desire to read has increased incredibly. I'm absolutely thrilled to be learning what I want to learn. It's been like a rennaissance."

The teachers in these colleges do not intend, of course, to inhibit their students' intellectual development. Some are especially kind and concerned and accessible, but this only makes it worse. It is especially difficult for good girls to disobey good parents. Teachers, as well as students, yearn for an atmosphere less academic and more intellectual, but the teachers are unable to reduce the pressure and the students are unable to resist it, except on rare occasions. One undergraduate blushed as if about to confess to a crime and said,

Last weekend—I don't know why I did it—I decided to read a book, a fun book. This is the first time since I've come here I've read a fun book from cover to cover—no worries if it was read with complete comprehension. I read it perfectly. It was mine.

Both teachers and students are proud of the institution's "high standards," and many see the standards as luring the students into performing at the top of their capacities. These standards play a major role in Perry's (1970) account of development. It is in attempting to discern the standards and to meet them that the student is propelled into independent contextual thinking. But for nice girls like Bridget, the standards act more as impediments than as goads to independent thinking, distracting their attention from the intellectual substance of the work and transforming their efforts to learn into efforts to please.

Women may benefit especially from systems in which the teaching function and the assessing function are separated. Teaching and certification of competence, at least as usually practiced, are quite different and often opposing functions; and, where certification is deemed necessary, it should be detached from teaching by, for example, using external examiners to evaluate the students' performance.

Some educators (for example, Elbow 1979) advocate competency-based programs in which the student must exhibit mastery of a set of clearly articulated objectives. Traditional professors, Elbow says, because they "contain the thing to be learned inside them . . . stand up in front of students and say, in effect, 'Get what is inside me inside you. Look at me; listen to me; be like me. I am important'" (p. 107). In competency-based programs the teacher no longer acts as the embodiment of knowledge or the container of secret criteria and so becomes less "important," less the authority, more a "coach" or an "ally" in Elbow's terms, more a "partner" in the language of Paulo Freire (1971). The teacher's attempts to "believe" the student, to confirm her as a knower, are not undermined by the inevitable "doubt" expressed in impersonal assessment.

It is not evaluation per se that subverts the aims of instruction but evaluation in the separate (impersonal, objective) mode. Evaluation in the connected mode requires that the standards of evaluation be constructed in collaboration with the students. Where impersonal standards are used, the students are turned into objects, and the connection between teacher and student is broken. The "feminine world of subjectness" is abandoned in favor of the "masculine world of objectness" (Noddings 1984, p. 196). As Noddings says, "Many of the practices embedded in the masculine curriculum masquerade as essential to the maintenance of standards," but in fact "they accomplish quite a different purpose: the systematic dehumanization of both female and male children through the loss of the feminine" (pp. 192–93). In an educational institution that placed care and understanding of persons rather than impersonal standards at its center, human development might take a different course, and women's development, in particular, might proceed with less pain.

But at traditional, hierarchically organized institutions run by powerful judges charged with enforcing the high standards of their disciplines and administering justice through blind evaluation of the students' work without respect for the students' persons, images of being watched ("God with His movie camera," as Bridget put it) flood the minds of women students. The women search the eyes that watch them for reflections of themselves. They cannot get back behind their own eyes. "Turn a pair of eyes on me," Alice Koller writes, "and instantly I begin looking into them for myself" (1983, p. 94). Ironically, Bridget managed to meet the standards only when she became able to ignore them. She produced what They wanted only when she became able to do what she wanted.

Being Bad and Breaking Out

Several women described moments of rebellion that produced turning points in their education. The moment often occurred late at night when an unwritten paper was due the next day. Saying, "Oh, the hell with it," the student wrote a "bad" paper, using her own voice, that broke the rules. Sometimes, she was punished. But sometimes she was rewarded with an "A," indicating that the teacher preferred the student's private voice to her public voice. The problem of "standards" for women, then, is a double problem. Nice women cannot help trying to produce what They want, but sometimes they are wrong about what They want.

The student's discovery that teachers respect her authentic voice is gratifying, of course, but for many of the women we interviewed, it came late. Much time had been wasted being good; and for many women the relentless effort to be good had prevented the development of a more authentic voice.

Women like Bridget, still struggling to formulate their own and their own standards, although eager for formal graduate training in order to pursue professional careers, are fearful of entering another institution that may try and may succeed in shaping them according to its standards. Deborah had derided in high school that she would become a clinical psychologist, but after graduating from college she worked for three years before applying to graduate school.

> One of the reasons I took the years in between was so that I would be very certain that when I went I'd be able to do what I wanted to do there, and that I wouldn't feel I had to follow what they were setting up for me to do.

But, on the eve of entering graduate school, she did not sound so certain.

I'm afraid of some clashes between what I want to do and what they want me to do, and I'm not sure how those will be resolved, not understanding the system. It may take me a semester to find out how you don't do what they're asking you to do.

Deborah was determined not to repeat the experience of her first year in college during her first year in graduate school. Instead of being good—doing everything she was supposed to do—she would figure out how to be bad and do what she wanted to do.

When we interviewed Gretchen in her senior year, she had already been accepted at a prestigious medical school but had decided to defer enrollment for a year.

I have to find myself absolutely alone for a while. I don't feel as if I'm gonna *last* through another five years of school unless I sit back and find for myself or remind myself that I am an independent person and I am defined by my own standards and not by these external standards. Right now I feel sort of very wishy-washy about myself, and that's because I've been getting different sorts of signals from different people or institutions which have been evaluating me. And I've been letting these things sort of cloud over my own feelings about myself. Sort of refractional crystallization. Sort of getting rid of the dirt and the garbage and just sort of crystallizing out what is me. I want to spend a year not letting myself be evaluated by other people's standards.

Judith was eager to improve her skills as a therapist, but she dreaded a repetition of her graduate school experience.

I worry about getting further analytic training, 'cause you're supposed to learn it the way that somebody else sees it. It would be different if I could find something—a program—where I was helped to see things in my own way. That would be gold.

The Need for Freedom

Some of the women we interviewed discovered "gold" in their institutions. We asked a twenty-seven-year-old mother of two what was most helpful to her about the adult program she was attending.

The faculty not being above us, not being the boss. Making our own decisions and writing our own curriculum. And it's real hard at first, when you're not used to it. You expect, "Well, what do we do next?" It developed me a lot more in thinking, "What is it that I want?" instead of listening to what people tell me.

Another student described the program as operating according to a model like the one physician Mary Howell calls "housewifery," with the teacher respecting the student's own rhythms rather than imposing an arbitrary timetable.

> When I would get stuck in the middle of my studies—as I always did—I never got any silly notes from the teacher saying, "Now, now, you must produce your stuff on time, otherwise blah blah blah." He would just say, "Well, I guess you're stuck. You'll get over it." He gave me a lot of space and a lot of guidance.

For Stella, the progressive college, seen by some as lacking in standards, was Utopia.

> It was this plot of land where I could talk to these teachers or hear them lecture and read and write and really grow. It was this time for me to be away from my family, some place I felt safe, and just sort of feel out different things.

The freedom and support the college offered helped Stella feel her way toward becoming a painter and developing her "own sort of natural working habit."

> I choke under pressure, but I do very well under pressures that I've created, goals that I establish, so the college is perfect for me, because there's not a lot of pressure, and there's a tremendous amount of time to work on your own.

The college exempted her from formal classes during her senior year and provided her with a studio: "I'm able to work all day and all night on my own. If I was meeting with classes all the time, and if there was a different attitude about work and grades and competition, I'd hate painting." The college put little emphasis on grades.

> When something really attracts you, you can really get obsessive about it. There's a lot of freedom, trusting that people are going to want to work, that people have instincts and will find out what they want to do and how they're going to go about doing it. But with teachers that are knowledgeable and can give you guidance and support and believe in you.

A student at one of the more highly structured, high-pressure colleges gave a dramatically different account. "How much time do you really have," she asked, "to think about the material you're studying?"

> I remember last semester getting *really* almost terrified when I was studying for finals, because all of a sudden I got so wrapped up in the material. I hadn't put it down for a while. And I just realized, you know, that it was really exciting to do all this stuff. But if you did that all semester long, you'd go crazy. It seems that they require a lot more automated responses from you. Just turn in this paper now. It seems that you don't have a chance to reflect. I don't try and figure out anything

while I'm at school. As soon as I get away from my books, then everything gets complex; but as long as I'm looking at a book, then I tend to open it up and read it and just do what's required of me.

Some of the students at this women's college feared that without the pressure they would "go bad," as one put it, or "go dead," as another said. They would sleep late, cut classes, and stop working. Bridget and others who moved temporarily into less pressured environments did indeed go bad. They cut more classes and they spent less time on assigned work. But they did not go dead; they emerged as more active agents in their own learning. The late psychologist Jeanne Block (1984) argued that because girls in our society are raised to accommodate to existing structures, they need colleges that will help set them free. But, for the same reason, women also need strong support in moving toward freedom.

We once heard a professor from a women's college remark that the students were passive because the teachers were "too nurturant" and that a more impersonal approach might produce more independent, responsible, and active learners. Presumably she meant that in "taking care" of students we rob them of responsibility; and there may be some truth in this. But surely there are forms of taking care that make the ones we care for stronger rather than weaker. Taking care need not mean taking over. The children's health clinic, the most nurturant institution in our sample, empowers its clients by fostering their expertise. Remember the client who said, "I feel like they could hire me. That's how much knowledge they've given me." And, indeed, it is the clinic's policy to make use of its clients' wisdom and even on occasion to invite them to join the staff.

The more traditional, formal educational institutions we sampled operated more in terms of bureaucracy than housewifery. Although teachers and staff in these colleges paid close personal attention to individual students, the system itself was relatively impersonal. All students were expected to perform certain tasks and deliver certain products at specified uniform dates to be evaluated according to objective criteria. Their work was compared not with their own past work but with other students' work. Students had duties and obligations; they had little choice and less responsibility than is required in the institutions that allow or insist that students participate in these decisions. At the other end of the continuum, institutions that do none of the defining clearly abdicate their own responsibility for helping students formulate their own agendas for learning; they rob women students of the support most of them need in order to break free.

Endnotes

1. For research showing that girls with higher scores on intelligence tests than other girls express unrealistically low expectations of success, see Crandall (1969) and Stipek and Hoffman (1980).
2. We must beg to differ with Cynthia. The late E. B. White taught us quite a lot about how to hear the squirrel's heart beat.
3. Shulamit Reinharz writes, "If we *start* with labels, we have excluded experience altogether." She urges researchers to "describe and analyze with as few assumptions, presuppositions, or definitions beforehand as possible. . . . Try to see things as they are without blinders, labels, or intermediaries" (1984, pp. 359, 363).

Ideas for Discussion, Writing and Research

1. Contrast "banking education" with "liberatory education." What sorts of classroom activities would attend each kind of education? What larger assumptions (about culture, about individuals, about the relation between schools and society) underlie each approach to education? Brainstorm a list of experiences in your own educational background that you would characterize as "education as banking" or "education as liberation." Compare your list to those of your classmates. Can you find any common patterns?

2. Work in groups to research the "cultural literacy" of undergraduates at your university. First, small groups should construct eight to ten questions that you think any "culturally literate" undergraduate should be able to answer. Note ways in which this is difficult, and bring them up in class discussion later. Next, combine your questions with those of other groups to come up with a 25 to 30 item "test" of cultural literacy, and administer this test to a number of your friends, classmates, and dormmates. Discuss your "findings" in class.[1]

3. Using the results of your research project (in 2, above), evaluate the state of undergraduate education at your university in a short position paper. One half of the class can use the findings to argue positively for the knowledge of the students; the other can use them to make a negative evaluation. Discuss your evaluations in class.

4. Working in groups of two or three, design a writing course for first year students at your university as you think either Freire or Hirsch would. (One half of the groups could use the work of each scholar as the basis of their course.) Think specifically about the issues a teacher of writing would need to attend to: objectives, reading and writing assignments, in-class exercises, grades, classroom management, etc. What would each scholar identify as the basic goals for a freshman writing course? What sorts of assignments would each design? How would students be evaluated? Compare your course designs with those of the other groups: did the groups using Freire (or Hirsch) agree on what he would expect of a freshman course? How much common ground can you find between Hirsch and Freire as you work through this exercise? Which course would you rather take and why?

5. Now, use Adler's proposal for education to evaluate the courses you designed in #4 (above). Which course(s) would meet with Adler's approval and why? Defend your course design against critiques that Adler might make of it. Do the same from the perspective of Selenky et al., defending your course design against critiques they might make.

6. Examine the diagram of Adler's three kinds of teaching/learning on page 159. Furnish examples from your own educational experience to flesh out this chart. Has one kind of teaching/learning been emphasized at the expense of others? Should all courses include all three kinds? Should one take primacy over others? Use Adler's scheme to evaluate a specific educational experience you have had. Or, conversely, evaluate Adler's proposal based on your own experience as a learner.

---

[1]This activity, and the one following, are adaptations of ones used by Jennifer Frank of the English Department at Penn State. We are grateful to Jenn for allowing us to include them here.

7. Using your library's on-line databases, find and read six to eight articles on "literacy" that have been published in the last five years. Use Scribner's conceptual triad of literacy as adaptation/power/state of grace to discuss the dominant metaphors in the articles you found. Use the results of your research (and that of your classmates) to write an analysis of how our culture (or some segment of it) views literacy.

8. As Helen Fox (1994) has noted, Ogbu uses a controlled academic tone to discuss a very volatile educational issue. Examine Ogbu's prose (at the level of word choice and syntactic arrangement) to determine how he manages this task. Try rewriting a paragraph or two of Ogbu's text using a different tone or voice: strident, disgusted, angry, disheartened. Compare your rewritten versions with those of your classmates.

9. Select one section of Ogbu's piece and identify the major claim or claims and types of evidence used. Discuss what you find with your classmates, who have examined other sections of the article. Discuss how the claims and evidence Ogbu uses are related to his tone, as you described it in #8 above.

10. Examine the table Ogbu presents on page 213; identify as many claims as you can that are supported by the data in this table. Does any of this information surprise you? How does Ogbu use it to support his larger point? At another level, discuss whether or not the numbers "speak for themselves." That is, is the chart easy or difficult to read, understand, and use?

11. Use Belenky et als.' themes of "need for structure," "tyranny of expectation," "being bad/breaking out," and the "need for freedom":

    a) to analyze the information you gathered for Discussion Question #4 in Chapter Two. How do their four themes add to or complicate your conclusions about the kinds of learning that students are expected to demonstrate in secondary school and/or in college?

    b) to analyze several of the personal narratives in Chapter One. How do Belenky et als.' themes add to your understanding of the stories you read?

CHAPTER 4

Exploring Issues in Testing and Measuring Learning

🍎 The Mismeasure of Man

Stephen Jay Gould

Stephen Jay Gould is currently professor of Zoology at Harvard and Director of the university's Museum of Comparative Zoology. He is a prolific writer of both scholarly and popular treatments of paleontology and evolutionary biology. This selection is from his book The Mismeasure of Man, *which won the National Book Critics Award for general nonfiction in 1981.*

The Hereditarian Theory of IQ

An American Invention

Alfred Binet and the Original Purposes of the Binet Scale

Binet Flirts with Craniometry

When Alfred Binet (1857–1911), director of the psychology laboratory at the Sorbonne, first decided to study the measurement of intelligence, he turned naturally to the favored method of a waning century and to the work of his great countryman Paul Broca. He set out, in short, to measure skulls, never doubting at first the basic conclusion of Broca's school:

> The relationship between the intelligence of subjects and the volume of their head . . . is very real and has been confirmed by all methodical investigators, without exception. . . . As these works include observations on several hundred subjects, we conclude that the preceding proposition [of correlation between head size and intelligence] must be considered as incontestable (Binet, 1898, pp. 294–295).

During the next three years, Binet published nine papers on craniometry in *L'Année psychologique,* the journal he had founded in 1895. By the end of this effort, he was no longer so sure. Five studies on the heads of school children had destroyed his original faith.

Binet went to various schools, making Broca's recommended measurements on the heads of pupils designated by teachers as their smartest and stupidest. In several studies, he increased his sample from 62 to 230 subjects. "I began," he wrote, "with the idea, impressed upon me by the studies of so many other scientists, that intellectual superiority is tied to superiority of cerebral volume" (1900, p. 427).

Binet found his differences, but they were much too small to matter and might only record the greater average height of better pupils (1.401 vs. 1.378 meters). Most measures did favor the better students, but the average difference between good and poor amounted to a mere

The Mismeasure of Man by Stephen Jay Gould, published by W.W. Norton & Company. Copyright 1981. Reprinted by permission.

millimeter—"extrêmement petite" as Binet wrote. Binet did not observe larger differences in the anterior region of the skull, where the seat of higher intelligence supposedly lay, and where Broca had always found greatest disparity between superior and less fortunate people. To make matters worse, some measures usually judged crucial in the assessment of mental worth favored the poorer pupils—for anteroposterior diameter of the skull, poorer students exceeded their smarter colleagues by 3.0 mm. Even if most results tended to run in the "right" direction, the method was surely useless for assessing individuals. The differences were too small, and Binet also found that poor students varied more than their smarter counterparts. Thus, although the smallest value usually belonged to a poor pupil, the highest often did as well.

Binet also fueled his own doubts with an extraordinary study of his own suggestibility, an experiment in the primary theme of this book—the tenacity of unconscious bias and the surprising malleability of "objective," quantitative data in the interest of a preconceived idea. "I feared," Binet wrote (1900, p. 323), "that in making measurements on heads with the intention of finding a difference in volume between an intelligent and a less intelligent head, I would be led to increase, unconsciously and in good faith, the cephalic volume of intelligent heads and to decrease that of unintelligent heads." He recognized the greater danger lurking when biases are submerged and a scientist believes in his own objectivity (1900, p. 324): "Suggestibility . . . works less on an act of which we have full consciousness, than on a half-conscious act—and this is precisely its danger."

How much better off we would be if all scientists submitted themselves to self-scrutiny in so forthright a fashion: "I want to state very explicitly," Binet wrote (1900, p. 324), "what I have observed about myself. The details that follow are those that the majority of authors do not publish; one does not want to let them be known." Both Binet and his student Simon had measured the same heads of "idiots and imbeciles" at a hospital where Simon was in intern. Binet noted that, for one crucial measurement, Simon's values were consistently less than his. Binet therefore returned to measure the subjects a second time. The first time, Binet admits, "I took my measures mechanically, without any other preconception than to remain faithful to my methods." But the second time "I had a different preconception. . . . I was bothered by the difference" between Simon and myself. "I wanted to reduce it to its true value. . . . This is self-suggestion. Now, capital fact, the measures taken during the second experiment, under the expectation of a diminution, are indeed smaller than the measures taken [on the same heads] during the first experiment." In fact, all but one head had "shrunk" between the two experiments and the average diminution was 3 mm—a good deal more than the average difference between skulls of bright and poor students in his previous work.

Binet spoke graphically of his discouragement:

I was persuaded that I had attacked an intractable problem. The measures had required travelling, and tiring procedures of all sorts; and they ended with the discouraging conclusion that there was often not a millimeter of difference between the cephalic measures of intelligent and less intelligent students. The idea of measuring intelligence by measuring heads seemed ridiculous. . . . I was on the point of abandoning this work, and I didn't want to publish a single line of it (1900, p. 403).

At the end, Binet snatched a weak and dubious victory from the jaws of defeat. He looked at his entire sample again, separated out the five top and bottom pupils from each group, and eliminated all those in the middle. The differences between extremes were greater and more consistent—3 to 4 mm on average. But even this difference did not exceed the average potential bias due to suggestibility. Craniometry, the jewel of nineteenth-century objectivity, was not destined for continued celebration.

Binet's Scale and the Birth of IQ

When Binet returned to the measurement of intelligence in 1904, he remembered his previous frustration and switched to other techniques. He abandoned what he called the "medical" approaches of craniometry and the search for Lombroso's anatomical stigmata, and decided instead on "psychological" methods. The literature on mental testing, at the time, was relatively small and decidedly inconclusive. Galton, without notable success, had experimented with a series of measurements, mostly records of physiology and reaction time, rather than tests of reasoning. Binet decided to construct a set of tasks that might assess various aspects of reasoning more directly.

In 1904 Binet was commissioned by the minister of public education to perform a study for a specific, practical purpose: to develop techniques for identifying those children whose lack of success in normal classrooms suggested the need for some form of special education. Binet chose a purely pragmatic course. He decided to bring together a large series of short tasks, related to everyday problems of life (counting coins, or assessing which face is "prettier," for example), but supposedly involving such basic processes of reasoning as "direction (ordering), comprehension, invention and censure (correction)" (Binet, 1909). Learned skills like reading would not be treated explicitly. The tests were administered individually by trained examiners who led subjects through the series of tasks, graded in their order of difficulty. Unlike previous tests designed to measure specific and independent "faculties" of mind, Binet's scale was a hodgepodge of diverse activities. He hoped that by mixing together enough tests of different abilities he would be able to abstract a child's general potential with a single score. Binet emphasized the empirical nature of his work with a famous dictum (1911, p. 329): "One might almost say, 'It matters very little what the tests are so long as they are numerous.' "

Binet published three versions of the scale before his death in 1911. The original 1905 edition simply arranged the tasks in an ascending order of difficulty. The 1908 version established the criterion used in measuring the so-called IQ ever since. Binet decided to assign an age level to each task, defined as the youngest age at which a child of normal intelligence should be able to complete the task successfully. A child began the Binet test with tasks for the youngest age and proceeded in sequence until he could no longer complete the tasks. The age associated with the last tasks he could perform became his "mental age," and his general intellectual level was calculated by subtracting this mental age from his true chronological age. Children whose mental ages were sufficiently behind their chronological ages could then be identified for special educational programs, thus fulfilling Binet's charge from the ministry. In 1912 the German psychologist W. Stern argued that mental age should be divided by chronological age, not subtracted from it, and the intelligence *quotient*, or IQ, was born.

IQ testing has had momentous consequences in our century. In this light, we should investigate Binet's motives, if only to appreciate how the tragedies of misuse might have been avoided if its founder had lived and his concerns been heeded.

In contrast with Binet's general intellectual approach, the most curious aspect of his scale is its practical, empirical focus. Many scientists work this way by deep conviction or explicit inclination. They believe that theoretical speculation is vain and that true science progresses by induction from simple experiments pursued to gather basic facts, not to test elaborate theories. But Binet was primarily a theoretician. He asked big questions and participated with enthusiasm in the major philosophical debates of his profession. He had a long-standing interest in theories of intelligence. He published his first book on the "Psychology of Reasoning" in 1886, and followed in 1903 with his famous "Experimental Study of Intelligence," in which he abjured previous commitments and developed a new structure for analyzing human thinking. Yet Binet explicitly declined to award any theoretical interpretation to his scale of intelligence, the most extensive and important work he had done in his favorite subject. Why should a great theoretician have acted in such a curious and apparently contradictory way?

Binet did seek "to separate natural intelligence and instruction" (1905, p. 42) in his scale: "It is the intelligence alone that we seek to measure, by disregarding in so far as possible, the degree of instruction which the child possesses. . . . We give him nothing to read, nothing to write, and submit him to no test in which he might succeed by means of rote learning" (1905, p. 42). "It is a specially interesting feature of these tests that they permit us, when necessary, to free a beautiful native intelligence from the trammels of the school" (1908, p. 259).

Yet, beyond this obvious desire to remove the superficial effects of clearly acquired knowledge, Binet declined to define and speculate upon the meaning of the score he assigned to each child. Intelligence, Binet proclaimed, is too complex to capture with a single number. This number, later called IQ, is only a rough, empirical guide constructed for a limited, practical purpose:

> The scale, properly speaking, does not permit the measure of the intelligence, because intellectual qualifies are not superposable, and therefore cannot be measured as linear surfaces are measured (1905, p. 40).

Moreover, the number is only an average of many performances, not an entity unto itself. Intelligence, Binet reminds us, is not a single, scalable thing like height. "We feel it necessary to insist on this fact," Binet (1911) cautions, "because later, for the sake of simplicity of statement, we will speak of a child of 8 years having the intelligence of a child of 7 or 9 years; these expressions, if accepted arbitrarily, may give place to illusions." Binet was too good a theoretician to fall into the logical error that John Stuart Mill had identified—"to believe that whatever received a name must be an entity or being, having an independent existence of its own."

Binet also had a social motive for his reticence. He greatly feared that his practical device, if reified as an entity, could be perverted and used as an indelible label, rather than as a guide for identifying children who needed help. He worried that schoolmasters with "exaggerated zeal" might use IQ as a convenient excuse: "They seem to reason in the following way: 'Here is an excellent opportunity for getting rid of all the children who trouble us,' and without the true critical spirit, they designate all who are unruly, or disinterested in the school" (1905, p.

169). But he feared even more what has since been called the "self-fulfilling prophesy." A rigid label may set a teacher's attitude and eventually divert a child's behavior into a predicted path:

> It is really too easy to discover signs of backwardness in an individual when one is forewarned. This would be to operate as the graphologists did who, when Dreyfus was believed to be guilty, discovered in his handwriting signs of a traitor or a spy" (1905, p. 170).

Not only did Binet decline to label IQ as inborn intelligence; he also refused to regard it as a general device for ranking all pupils according to mental worth. He devised his scale only for the limited purpose of his commission by the ministry of education: as a practical guide for identifying children whose poor performance indicated a need for special education—those whom we would today call learning disabled or mildly retarded. Binet wrote (1908, p. 263): "We are of the opinion that the most valuable use of our scale will not be its application to the normal pupils, but rather to those of inferior grades of intelligence." As to the causes of poor performance, Binet refused to speculate. His tests, in any case, could not decide (1905, p. 37):

> Our purpose is to be able to measure the intellectual capacity of a child who is brought to us in order to know whether he is normal or retarded. We should therefore study his condition at the time and that only. We have nothing to do either with his past history or with his future; consequently, we shall neglect his etiology, and we shall make no attempt to distinguish between acquired and congenital idiocy. . . . As to that which concerns his future, we shall exercise the same abstinence; we do not attempt to establish or prepare a prognosis, and we leave unanswered the question of whether this retardation is curable, or even improvable. We shall limit ourselves to ascertaining the truth in regard to his present mental state.

But of one thing Binet was sure: whatever the cause of poor performance in school, the aim of his scale was to identify in order to help and improve, not to label in order to limit. Some children might be innately incapable of normal achievement, but all could improve with special help.

The difference between strict hereditarians and their opponents is not, as some caricatures suggest, the belief that a child's performance is all inborn or all a function of environment and learning. I doubt that the most committed antihereditarians have ever denied the existence of innate variation among children. The differences are more a matter of social policy and educational practice. Hereditarians view their measures of intelligence as markers of permanent, inborn limits. Children, so labeled, should be sorted, trained according to their inheritance and channeled into professions appropriate for their biology. Mental testing becomes a theory of limits. Antihereditarians, like Binet, test in order to identify and help. Without denying the evident fact that not all children, whatever their training, will enter the company of Newton and Einstein, they emphasize the power of creative education to increase the achievements of all children, often in extensive and unanticipated ways. Mental testing becomes a theory for enhancing potential through proper education.

Binet spoke eloquently of well-meaning teachers, taught in the unwarranted pessimism of their invalid hereditarian assumptions (1909, pp. 16–17):

> As I know from experience,. . . they seem to admit implicitly that in a class where we find the best, we must also find the worst, and that this is a natural and inevitable phenomenon, with which a teacher must not become preoccupied, and that it is like the existence of rich and poor within a society. What a profound error.

How can we help a child if we label him as unable to achieve by biological proclamation?

> If we do nothing, if we don't intervene actively and usefully, he will continue to lose time . . . and will finally become discouraged. The situation is very serious for him, and since his is not an exceptional care (since children with defective comprehension are legion), we might say that it is a serious question for all of us and for all of society. The child who loses the taste for work in class strongly risks being unable to acquire it after he leaves school (1909, p. 100).

Binet railed against the motto "stupidity is for a long time" ("*quand on est bête, c'est pour longtemps*"), and upbraided teachers who "are not interested in students who lack intelligence. They have neither sympathy nor respect for them, and their intemperate language leads them to say such things in their presence as 'This is a child who will never amount to anything . . . he is poorly endowed . . . he is not intelligent at all.' How often have I heard these imprudent words" (1909, p. 100). Binet then cites an episode in his own baccalaureate when one examiner told him that he would never have a "true" philosophical spirit: "Never! What a momentous word. Some recent thinkers seem to have given their moral support to these deplorable verdicts by affirming that an individual's intelligence is a fixed quantity, a quantity that cannot be increased. We must protest and react against this brutal pessimism; we must try to demonstrate that it is founded upon nothing" (1909, p. 101).

The children identified by Binet's test were to be helped, not indelibly labeled. Binet had definite pedagogical suggestions, and many were implemented. He believed, first of all, that special education must be tailored to the individual needs of disadvantaged children: it must be based on "their character and their aptitudes, and on the necessity for adapting ourselves to their needs and their capacities" (1909, p. 15). Binet recommended small classrooms of fifteen to twenty students, compared with sixty to eighty then common in public schools catering to poor children. In particular, he advocated special methods of education, including a program that he called "mental orthopedics":

> What they should learn first is not the subjects ordinarily taught, however important they may be; they should be given lessons of will, of attention, of discipline; before exercises in grammar, they need to be exercised in mental orthopedics; in a word they must learn how to learn (1908, p. 257).

Binet's interesting program of mental orthopedics included a set of physical exercises designed to improve, by transfer to mental functioning, the will, attention, and discipline that

Binet viewed as prerequisites for studying academic subjects. In one, called *"l'exercise des stat-ues,"* and designed to increase attention span, children moved vigorously until told to adopt and retain an immobile position. (I played this game as a kid in the streets of New York; we also called it "statues.") Each day the period of immobility would be increased. In another, designed to improve speed, children filled a piece of paper with as many dots as they could produce in the allotted time.

Binet spoke with pleasure about the success of his special classrooms (1909, p. 104) and argued that pupils so benefited had not only increased their knowledge, but their intelligence as well. Intelligence, in any meaningful sense of the word, can be augmented by good educa-tion; it is not a fixed and inborn quantity:

> It is in this practical sense, the only one accessible to us, that we say that the intel-ligence of these children has been increased. We have increased what constitutes the intelligence of a pupil: the capacity to learn and to assimilate instruction.

The Dismantling of Binet's Intentions in America

In summary, Binet insisted upon three cardinal principles for using his tests. All his caveats were later disregarded, and his intentions overturned, by the American hereditarians who translated his scale into written form as a routine device for testing all children.

1. The scores are a practical device; they do not buttress any theory of intellect. They do not define anything innate or permanent. We may not designate what they measure as "intelligence" or any other reified entity.
2. The scale is a rough, empirical guide for identifying mildly retarded and learning-dis-abled children who need special help. It is not a device for ranking normal children.
3. Whatever the cause of difficulty in children identified for help, emphasis shall be placed upon improvement through special training. Low scores shall not be used to mark chil-dren as innately incapable.

If Binet's principles had been followed, and his tests consistently used as he intended, we would have been spared a major misuse of science in our century. Ironically, many American school boards have come full cycle, and now use IQ tests only as Binet originally recommended: as instruments for assessing children with specific learning problems. Speaking personally, I feel that tests of the IQ type were helpful in the proper diagnosis of my own learning-disabled son. His average score, the IQ itself, meant nothing, for it was only an amalgam of some very high and very low scores; but the pattern of low values indicated his areas of deficit.

The misuse of mental tests is not inherent in the idea of testing itself. It arises primarily from two fallacies, eagerly (so it seems) embraced by those who wish to use tests for the main-tenance of social ranks and distinctions: reification and hereditarianism. The next chapter shall treat reification—the assumption that test scores represent a single, scalable thing in the head called general intelligence.

The hereditarian fallacy is not the simple claim that IQ is to some degree "heritable." I have no doubt that it is, though the degree has dearly been exaggerated by the most avid heredi-tarians. It is hard to find any broad aspect of human performance or anatomy that has no heritable component at all. The hereditarian fallacy resides in two false implications drawn from this basic fact:

1. The equation of "heritable" with "inevitable." To a biologist, heritability refers to the passage of traits or tendencies along family lines as a result of genetic transmission. It says little about the range of environmental modification to which these traits are subject. In our vernacular, "inherited" often means "inevitable." But not to a biologist. Genes do not make specific bits and pieces of a body; they code for a range of forms under an array of environmental conditions. Moreover, even when a trait has been built and set, environmental intervention may still modify inherited defects. Millions of Americans see normally through lenses that correct innate deficiencies of vision. The claim that IQ is so-many percent "heritable" does not conflict with the belief that enriched education can increase what we call, also in the vernacular, "intelligence." A partially inherited low IQ might be subject to extensive improvement through proper education. And it might not. The mere fact of its heritability permits no conclusion.

2. The confusion of within- and between-group heredity. The major political impact of hereditarian theories does not arise from the inferred heritability of tests, but from a logically invalid extension. Studies of the heritability of IQ, performed by such traditional methods as comparing scores of relatives, or contrasting scores of adopted children with both their biological and legal parents, are all of the "within-group" type—that is, they permit an estimate of heritability *within* a single, coherent population (white Americans, for example). The common fallacy consists in assuming that if heredity explains a certain percentage of variation among individuals within a group, it must also explain a similar percentage of the difference in average IQ between groups—whites and blacks, for example. But variation among individuals within a group and differences in mean values between groups are entirely separate phenomena. One item provides no license for speculation about the other.

A hypothetical and noncontroversial example will suffice. Human height has a higher heritability than any value ever proposed for IQ. Take two separate groups of males. The first, with an average height of 5 feet 10 inches, live in a prosperous American town. The second, with an average height of 5 feet 6 inches, are starving in a third-world village. Heritability is 95 percent or so in each place—meaning only that relatively tall fathers tend to have tall sons and relatively short fathers short sons. This high within-group heritability argues neither for nor against the possibility that better nutrition in the next generation might raise the average height of third-world villagers above that of prosperous Americans. Likewise, IQ could be highly heritable within groups, and the average difference between whites and blacks in America might still only record the environmental disadvantages of blacks.

I have often been frustrated with the following response to this admonition: "Oh well, I see what you mean, and you're right in theory. There may be no necessary connection in logic, but isn't it more likely all the same that mean differences between groups would have the same causes as variation within groups?" The answer is still "no." Within- and between-group heredity are not tied by rising degrees of probability as heritability increases within groups and differences enlarge between them. The two phenomena are simply separate. Few arguments are more dangerous than the ones that "feel" right but can't be justified.

Alfred Binet avoided these fallacies and stuck by his three principles. American psychologists perverted Binet's intention and invented the hereditarian theory of IQ. They reified Binet's scores, and took them as measures of an entity called intelligence. They assumed that intelligence was largely inherited, and developed a series of specious arguments confusing cultural differences with innate properties. They believed that inherited IQ scores marked people and groups for an inevitable station in life. And they assumed that average differences between groups were largely the products of heredity, despite manifest and profound variation in quality of life.

This chapter analyzes the major works of the three pioneers of hereditarianism in America: H. H. Goddard, who brought Binet's scale to America and reified its scores as innate intelligence; L. M. Terman, who developed the Stanford-Binet scale, and dreamed of a rational society that would allocate professions by IQ scores; and R. M. Yerkes, who persuaded the army to test 1.75 million men in World War I, thus establishing the supposedly objective data that vindicated hereditarian claims and led to the Immigration Restriction Act of 1924, with its low ceiling for lands suffering the blight of poor genes.

The hereditarian theory of IQ is a home-grown American product. If this claim seems paradoxical for a land with egalitarian traditions, remember also the jingoistic nationalism of World War I, the fear of established old Americans facing a tide of cheap (and sometimes politically radical) labor immigrating from southern and eastern Europe, and above all our persistent, indigenous racism.

H. H. Goddard and the Menace of the Feeble-Minded

Intelligence as a Mendelian Gene

Goddard Identifies the Moron

> It remains now for someone to determine the nature of feeble-mindedness and complete the theory of the intelligence quotient.
> —H. H. Goddard, 1917, in a review of Terman, 1916

Taxonomy is always a contentious issue because the world does not come to us in neat little packages. The classification of mental deficiency aroused a healthy debate early in our century. Two categories of a tripartite arrangement won general acceptance: idiots could not develop full speech and had mental ages below three; imbeciles could not master written language and ranged from three to seven in mental age. (Both terms are now so entrenched in the vernacular of invectives that few people recognize their technical status in an older psychology.) Idiots and imbeciles could be categorized and separated to the satisfaction of most professionals, for their affliction was sufficiently severe to warrant a diagnosis of true pathology. They are not like us.

But consider the nebulous and more threatening realm of "high-grade defectives"—the people who could be trained to function in society, the ones who established a bridge between pathology and normality and thereby threatened the taxonomic edifice. These people, with mental ages of eight to twelve, were called débile (or weak) by the French.

Americans and Englishmen usually called them "feeble-minded," a term mired in hopeless ambiguity because other psychologists used feeble-minded as a genetic term for all mental defectives, not just those of high grade.

Taxonomists often confuse the invention of a name with the solution of a problem. H. H. Goddard, the energetic and crusading director of research at the Vineland Training School for Feeble-Minded Girls and Boys in New Jersey, made this crucial error. He devised a name for "high-grade" defectives, a word that became entrenched in our language through a series of jokes that rivaled the knock-knock or elephant jokes of other generations. The metaphorical whiskers on these jokes are now so long that most people would probably grant an ancient pedigree to the name. But Goddard invented the word in our century. He christened these people "morons," from a Greek word meaning foolish.

Goddard was the first popularizer of the Binet scale in America. He translated Binet's articles into English, applied his tests, and agitated for their general use. He agreed with Binet that the tests worked best in identifying people just below the normal range—Goddard's newly christened morons. But the resemblance between Binet and Goddard ends there. Binet refused to define his scores as "intelligence," and wished to identify in order to help. Goddard regarded the scores as measures of a single, innate entity. He wished to identify in order to recognize limits, segregate, and curtail breeding to prevent further deterioration of an endangered American stock, threatened by immigration from without and by prolific reproduction of its feeble-minded within.

A Unilinear Scale of Intelligence. The attempt to establish a unilinear classification of mental deficiency, a rising scale from idiots to imbeciles to morons, embodies two common fallacies pervading most theories of biological determinism discussed in this book: the reification of intelligence as a single, measurable entity; and the assumption, extending back to Morton's skulls (pp. 50–69) and forward to Jensen's universal scaling of general intelligence (pp. 317–320), that evolution is a tale of unilinear progress, and that a single scale ascending from primitive to advanced represents the best way of ordering variation. The concept of progress is a deep prejudice with an ancient pedigree (Bury, 1920) and a subtle power, even over those who would deny it explicitly (Nisbet, 1980).

Can the plethora of causes and phenomena grouped under the rubric of mental deficiency possibly be ordered usefully on a single scale, with its implication that each person owes his rank to the relative amount of a single substance—and that mental deficiency means having less than most? Consider some phenomena mixed up in the common numbers once assigned to defectives of high grade: general low-level mental retardation, specific learning disabilities caused by local neurological damage, environmental disadvantages, cultural differences, hostility to testers. Consider some of the potential causes: inherited patterns of function, genetic pathologies arising accidentally and not passed in family lines, congenital brain damage caused by maternal illness during pregnancy, birth traumas, poor nutrition of fetuses and babies, a variety of environmental disadvantages in early and later life. Yet, to Goddard, all people with mental ages between eight and twelve were morons, all to be treated in roughly the same way: institutionalized or carefully regulated, made happy by catering to their limits, and, above all, prevented from breeding.

Goddard may have been the most unsubtle hereditarian of all. He used his unilinear scale of mental deficiency to identify intelligence as a single entity, and he assumed that everything important about it was inborn and inherited in family lines. He wrote in 1920 (quoted in Tuddenham, 1962, p. 491):

> Stated in its boldest form, our thesis is that the chief determiner of human conduct is a unitary mental process which we call intelligence: that this process is conditioned by a nervous mechanism which is inborn: that the degree of efficiency to be attained by that nervous mechanism and the consequent grade of intellectual or mental level for each individual is determined by the kind of chromosomes that come together with the union of the germ cells: that it is but little affected by any later influences except such serious accidents as may destroy part of the mechanism.

Goddard extended the range of social phenomena caused by differences in innate intelligence until it encompassed almost everything that concerns us about human behavior. Beginning with morons, and working up the scale, he attributed most undesirable behavior to inherited mental deficiency of the offenders. Their problems are caused not only by stupidity per se, but by the link between deficient intelligence and immorality. High intelligence not only permits us to do our sums; it also engenders the good judgment that underlies all moral behavior.

> The intelligence controls the emotions and the emotions are controlled in proportion to the degree of intelligence. . . . It follows that if there is little intelligence the emotions will be uncontrolled and whether they be strong or weak will result in actions that are unregulated, uncontrolled and, as experience proves, usually undesirable. Therefore, when we measure the intelligence of an individual and learn that he has so much less than normal as to come within the group that we call feeble-minded, we have ascertained by far the most important fact about him (1919, p. 272).

Many criminals, most alcoholics and prostitutes, and even the "ne'er-do-wells" who simply don't fit in, are morons: "We know what feeble-mindedness is, and we have come to suspect all persons who are incapable of adapting themselves to their environment and living up to the conventions of society or acting sensibly, of being feeble-minded" (1914, p. 571).

At the next level of the merely dull, we find the toiling masses, doing what comes naturally. "The people who are doing the drudgery," Goddard writes (1919, p. 246), "are, as a rule, in their proper places."

> We must next learn that there are great groups of men, laborers, who are but little above the child, who must be told what to do and shown how to do it; and who, if we would avoid disaster, must not be put into positions where they will have to act upon their own initiative or their own judgment. . . . There are only a few leaders, most must be followers (1919, pp. 243–244).

At the upper end, intelligent men rule in comfort and by right. Speaking before a group of Princeton undergraduates in 1919, Goddard proclaimed:

> Now the fact is, that workmen may have a 10 year intelligence while you have a 20. To demand for him such a home as you enjoy is as absurd as it would be to insist that every laborer should receive a graduate fellowship. How can there be such a thing as social equality with this wide range of mental capacity?

"Democracy," Goddard argued (1919, p. 237), "means that the people rule by selecting the wisest, most intelligent and most human to tell them what to do to be happy. Thus Democracy is a method for arriving at a truly benevolent aristocracy."

Breaking the Scale into Mendelian Compartments. But if intelligence forms a single and unbroken scale, how can we solve the social problems that beset us? For at one level, low intelligence generates sociopaths, while at the next grade, industrial society needs docile and dull workers to run its machinery and accept low recompense. How can we convert the unbroken scale into two categories at this crucial point, and still maintain the idea that intelligence is a single, inherited entity? We can now understand why Goddard lavished so much attention upon the moron. The moron threatens racial health because he ranks highest among the undesirable and might, if not identified, be allowed to flourish and propagate. We all recognize the idiot and imbecile and know what must be done; the scale must be broken just above the level of the moron.

> The idiot is not our greatest problem. He is indeed loathsome. . . . Nevertheless, he lives his life and is done. He does not continue the race with a line of children like himself. . . . It is the moron type that makes for us our great problem (1912, pp. 101–102).

Goddard worked in the first flourish of excitement that greeted the rediscovery of Mendel's work and the basic deciphering of heredity. We now know that virtually every major feature of our body is built by the interaction of many genes with each other and with an external environment. But in these early days, many biologists naïvely assumed that all human traits would behave like the color, size, or wrinkling of Mendel's peas: they believed, in short, that even the most complex parts of a body might be built by single genes, and that variation in anatomy or behavior would record the different dominant and recessive forms of these genes. Eugenicists seized upon this foolish notion with avidity, for it allowed them to assert that all undesirable traits might be traced to single genes and eliminated with proper strictures upon breeding. The early literature of eugenics is filled with speculations, and pedigrees laboriously compiled and fudged, about the gene for *Wanderlust* traced through the family lines of naval captains, or *the* gene for temperament that makes some of us placid and others domineering. We must not be misled by how silly such ideas seem today; they represented orthodox genetics for a brief time, and had a major social impact in America.

Goddard joined the transient bandwagon with a hypothesis that must represent an ultimate in the attempted reification of intelligence. He tried to trace the pedigrees of mental defectives in his Vineland School and concluded that "feeble-mindedness" obeyed Mendelian rules of inheritance. Mental deficiency must therefore be a definite thing, and it must be governed by a single gene, undoubtedly recessive to normal intelligence (1914, p. 539). "Normal intelligence," Goddard concluded, "seems to be a unit character and transmitted in true Mendelian fashion" (1914, p. ix).

Goddard claimed that he had been compelled to make this unlikely conclusion by the press of evidence, not by any prior hope or prejudice.

> Any theories or hypotheses that have been presented have been merely those that were suggested by the data themselves, and have been worked out in an effort to understand what the data seem to comprise. Some of the conclusions are as surprising to the writer and as difficult for him to accept as they are likely to be to many readers (1914, p. viii).

Can we seriously view Goddard as a forced and reluctant convert to a hypothesis that fit his general scheme so well and solved his most pressing problem so neatly? A single gene for normal intelligence removed the potential contradiction between a unilinear scale that marked intelligence as a single, measurable entity, and a desire to separate and identify the mentally deficient as a category apart. Goddard had broken his scale into two sections at just the right place: morons carried a double dose of the bad recessive; dull laborers had at least one copy of the normal gene and could be set before their machines. Moreover, the scourge of feeble-mindedness might now be eliminated by schemes of breeding easily planned. One gene can be traced, located, and bred out. If one hundred genes regulate intelligence, eugenic breeding must fail or proceed with hopeless sloth.

The Proper Care and Feeding (but not breeding) of Morons. If mental deficiency is the effect of a single gene, the path to its eventual elimination lies evidently before us: do not allow such people to bear children:

> If both parents are feeble-minded all the children will be feeble-minded. It is obvious that such matings should not be allowed. It is perfectly clear that no feeble-minded person should ever be allowed to marry or to become a parent. It is obvious that if this rule is to be carried out the intelligent part of society must enforce it (1914, p. 561).

If morons could control their own sexual urges and desist for the good of mankind, we might permit them to live freely among us. But they cannot, because immorality and stupidity are inexorably linked. The wise man can control his sexuality in a rational manner: "Consider for a moment the sex emotion, supposed to be the most uncontrollable of all human instincts; yet is notorious that the ingredient man controls even this" (1919, p. 273). The moron cannot behave in so exemplary and abstemious a fasion:

They are not only lacking in control but they are lacking often in the perception of moral qualities; if they are not allowed to marry they are nevertheless not hindered from becoming parents. So that if we are absolutely to prevent a feeble-minded person from becoming a parent, something must be done other than merely prohibiting the marrying. To this end there are two proposals: the first is colonization, the second is sterilization (1914, p. 566).

Goddard did not oppose sterilization, but he regarded it as impractical because traditional sensibilities of a society not yet wholly rational would prevent such widespread mayhem. Colonization in exemplary institutions like his own at Vineland, New Jersey, must be our preferred solution. Only here could the reproduction of morons be curtailed. If the public balked at the great expense of building so many new centers for confinement, the cost could easily be recouped by its own savings:

If such colonies were provided in sufficient number to take care of all the distinctly feeble-minded cases in the community, they would very largely take the place of our present almshouses and prisons, and they would greatly decrease the numbers in our insane hospitals. Such colonies would save an annual loss in property and life, due to the action of these irresponsible people, sufficient to nearly, or quite, offset the expense of the new plant (1912, pp. 105–106).

Inside these institutions, morons could operate in contentment at their biologically appointed level, denied only the basic biology of their own sexuality. Goddard ended his book on the causes of mental deficiency with this plea for the care of institutionalized morons: "Treat them as children according to their mental age, constantly encourage and praise, never discourage or scold; and *keep them happy*" (1919, p. 327).

Preventing the Immigration and Propagation of Morons

Once Goddard had identified the cause of feeble-mindedness in a single gene, the cure seemed simple enough: don't allow native morons to breed and keep foreign ones out. As a contribution to the second step, Goddard and his associates visited Ellis Island in 1912 "to observe conditions and offer any suggestions as to what might be done to secure a more thorough examination of immigrants for the purpose of detecting mental defectives" (Goddard, 1917, p. 253).

As Goddard described the scene, a fog hung over New York harbor that day and no immigrants could land. But one hundred were about ready to leave, when Goddard intervened: "We picked out one young man whom we suspected was defective, and, through the interpreter, proceeded to give him the test. The boy tested 8 by the Binet scale. The interpreter said, 'I could not have done that when I came to this country,' and seemed to think the test unfair. We convinced him that the boy was defective" (Goddard, 1913, p. 105).

Encouraged by this, one of the first applications of the Binet scale in America, Goddard raised some funds for a more thorough study and, in the spring of 1913, sent two women to

Ellis Island for two and a half months. They were instructed to pick out the feeble-minded by sight, a task that Goddard preferred to assign to women, to whom he granted innately superior intuition:

> After a person has had considerable experience in this work, he almost gets a sense of what a feeble-minded person is so that he can tell one afar off. The people who are best at this work, and who I believe should do this work, are women. Women seem to have closer observation than men. It was quite impossible for others to see how these two young women could pick out the feeble-minded without the aid of the Binet test at all (1913, p. 106).

Goddard's women tested thirty-five Jews, twenty-two Hungarians, fifty Italians, and forty-five Russians. These groups could not be regarded as random samples because government officials had already "culled out those they recognized as defective." To balance this bias, Goddard and his associates "passed by the obviously normal. That left us the great mass of 'average immigrants.' " (1917, p. 244). (I am continually amazed by the unconscious statements of prejudice that slip into supposedly objective accounts. Note here that average immigrants are below normal, or at least not obviously normal—the proposition that Goddard was supposedly testing, not asserting a priori.)

Binet tests on the four groups led to an astounding result: 83 percent of the Jews, 80 percent of the Hungarians, 79 percent of the Italians, and 87 percent of the Russians were feeble-minded—that is, below age twelve on the Binet scale. Goddard himself was flabbergasted: could anyone be made to believe that four-fifths of any nation were morons? "The results obtained by the foregoing evaluation of the data are so surprising and difficult of acceptance that they can hardly stand by themselves as valid" (1917, p. 247). Perhaps the tests had not been adequately explained by interpreters? But the Jews had been tested by a Yiddish-speaking psychologist, and they ranked no higher than the other groups. Eventually, Goddard monkeyed about with the tests, tossed several out, and got his figures down to 40 to 50 percent, but still he was disturbed.

Goddard's figures were even more absurd than he imagined for two reasons, one obvious, the other less so. As a nonevident reason, Goddard's original translation of the Binet scale scored people harshly and made morons out of subjects usually regarded as normal. When Terman devised the Stanford-Binet scale in 1916, he found that Goddard's version ranked people well below his own. Terman reports (1916, p. 62) that of 104 adults tested by him as between twelve and fourteen years mental age (low, but normal intelligence), 50 percent were morons on the Goddard scale.

For the evident reason, consider a group of frightened men and women who speak no English and who have just endured an oceanic voyage in steerage. Most are poor and have never gone to school; many have never held a pencil or pen in their hand. They march off the boat; one of Goddard's intuitive women takes them aside shortly thereafter, sits them down, hands them a pencil, and asks them to reproduce on paper a figure shown to them a moment ago, but now withdrawn from their sight. Could their failure be a result of testing conditions, of weakness, fear, or confusion, rather than of innate stupidity? Goddard considered the possibility, but rejected it:

The next question is 'drawing a design from memory,' which is passed by only 50 percent. To the uninitiated this will not seem surprising since it looks hard, and even those who are familiar with the fact that normal children of 10 pass it without difficulty may admit that persons who have never had a pen or pencil in their hands, as was true of many of the immigrants, may find it impossible to draw the design (1917, p. 250).

Permitting a charitable view of this failure, what but stupidity could explain an inability to state more than sixty words, any words, in one's own language during three minutes?

What shall we say of the fact that only 45 percent can give 60 words in three minutes, when normal children of 11 years sometimes give 200 words in that time! It is hard to find an explanation except lack of intelligence or lack of vocabulary, and such a lack of vocabulary in an adult would probably mean lack of intelligence. How could a person live even 15 years in any environment without learning hundreds of names of which he could certainly think of 60 in three minutes? (1917, p. 251)

Or ignorance of the date, or even the month or year?

Must we again conclude that the European peasant of the type that immigrates to America pays no attention to the passage of time? That the drudgery of life is so severe that he cares not whether it is January or July, whether it is 1912 or 1906? Is it possible that the person may be of considerable intelligence and yet, because of the peculiarity of his environment, not have acquired this ordinary bit of knowledge, even though the calendar is not in general use on the continent, or is somewhat complicated as in Russia? If so what an environment it must have been! (1917, p. 250)

Since environment, either European or immediate, could not explain such abject failure, Goddard stated: "We cannot escape the general conclusion that these immigrants were of surprisingly low intelligence" (1917, p. 251). The high proportion of morons still bothered Goddard, but he finally attributed it to the changing character of immigration: "It should be noted that the immigration of recent years is of a decidedly different character from the early immigration. . . . We are now getting the poorest of each race" (1917, p. 266). "The intelligence of the average 'third class' immigrant is low, perhaps of moron grade" (1917, p. 243). Perhaps, Goddard hoped out loud, things were better on the upper decks, but he did not test these wealthier customers.

What then should be done? Should all these morons be shipped back, or prevented from starting out in the first place? Foreshadowing the restrictions that would be legislated within a decade, Goddard argued that his conclusions "furnish important considerations for future actions both scientific and social as well as legislative" (1917, p. 261). But by this time Goddard had softened his earlier harsh position on the colonization of morons. Perhaps there were not enough merely dull workers to fill the vast number of frankly undesirable jobs. The moron might have to be recruited: "They do a great deal of work that no one else will do. . . . There is an immense amount of drudgery to be done, an immense amount of work for which we do not wish to pay enough to secure more intelligent workers. . . . May it be that possibly the moron has his place" (1917, p. 269).

Nonetheless, Goddard rejoiced in the general tightening of standards for admission. He reports that deportations for mental deficiency increased 350 percent in 1913 and 570 percent in 1914 over the average of the five preceding years:

> This was due to the untiring efforts of the physicians who were inspired by the belief that mental tests could be used for the detection of feeble-minded aliens. . . . If the American public wishes feeble-minded aliens excluded, it must demand that congress provide the necessary facilities at the ports of entry (1917, p. 271).

Meanwhile, at home, the feeble-minded must be identified and kept from breeding. In several studies, Goddard exposed the menace of moronity by publishing pedigrees of hundreds of worthless souls, charges upon the state and community, who would never have been born had their feeble-minded forebears been debarred from reproduction. Goddard discovered a stock of paupers and ne'er-do-wells in the pine barrens of New Jersey and traced their ancestry back to the illicit union of an upstanding man with a supposedly feeble-minded tavern wench. The same man later married a worthy Quakeress and started another line composed wholly of upstanding citizens. Since the progenitor had fathered both a good and a bad line, Goddard combined the Greek words for beauty (*kallos*) and bad (*kakos*), and awarded him the pseudonym Martin Kallikak. Goddard's Kallikak family functioned as a primal myth of the eugenics movement for several decades.

Goddard's study is little more than guesswork rooted in conclusions set from the start. His method, as always, rested upon the training of intuitive women to recognize the feeble-minded by sight. Goddard did not administer Binet tests in pine-barren shacks. Goddard's faith in visual identification was virtually unbounded. In 1919 he analyzed Edwin Markham's poem "The Man With The Hoe":

> Bowed by the weight of centuries he leans
> Upon his hoe and gazes at the ground,
> The emptiness of ages in his face
> And on his back the burden of the world. . . .

Markham's poem had been inspired by Millet's famous painting of the same name. The poem, Goddard complained (1919, p. 239), "seems to imply that the man Millet painted came to his condition as the result of social conditions which held him down and made him like the clods that he turned over." Nonsense, exclaimed Goddard; most poor peasants suffer only from their own feeble-mindedness, and Millet's painting proves it. Couldn't Markham see that the peasant is mentally deficient? "Millet's Man With The Hoe is a man of arrested mental development—the painting is a perfect picture of an imbecile" (1919, pp. 239–240). To Markham's searing question: "Whose breath blew out the light within this brain," Goddard replied that mental fire had never been kindled.

Since Goddard could determine degrees of mental deficiency by examining a painting, he certainly anticipated no trouble with flesh and blood. He dispatched the redoubtable Ms. Kite, soon to see further service on Ellis Island, to the pine barrens and quickly produced the sad pedigree of the kakos line. Goddard describes one of Ms. Kite's identifications (1912, pp. 77–78):

Used as she was to the sights of misery and degradation, she was hardly prepared for the spectacle within. The father, a strong, healthy, broad-shouldered man, was sitting helplessly in a corner. . . . Three children, scantily clad and with shoes that would barely hold together, stood about drooping jaws and the unmistakable look of the feeble-minded. . . . The whole family was a living demonstration of the futility of trying to make desirable citizens from defective stock through making and enforcing compulsory education laws. . . . The father himself, though strong and vigorous, showed by his face that he had only a child's mentality. The mother in her filth and rags was also a child. In this house of abject poverty, only one sure prospect was ahead, that it would produce more feeble-minded children with which to clog the wheels of human progress.

If these spot identifications seem a bit hasty or dubious, consider Goddard's method for inferring the mental state of the departed, or otherwise unavailable (1912, p. 15):

After some experience, the field worker becomes expert in inferring the condition of those persons who are not seen, from the similarity of the language used in describing them to that used in describing persons she has seen.

It may be a small item in the midst of such absurdity, but I discovered a bit of more conscious skulduggery two years ago. My colleague Steven Selden and I were examining his copy of Goddard's volume of the Kallikaks. The frontispiece shows a member of the kakos line, saved from depravity by confinement in Goddard's institution at Vineland. Deborah, as Goddard calls her, is a beautiful woman (Fig. 5.1). She sits calmly in a white dress, reading a book, a cat lying comfortably on her lap. Three other plates show members of the kakos line, living in poverty in their rural shacks. All have a depraved look about them (Fig. 5.2). Their mouths are sinister in appearance; their eyes are darkened slits. But Goddard's books are nearly seventy years old, and the ink has faded. It is now clear that all the photos of non institutionalized kakos were phonied by inserting heavy dark lines to give eyes and mouths their diabolical appearance. The three plates of Deborah are unaltered.

Selden took his book to Mr. James H. Wallace, Jr., director of Photographic Services at the Smithsonian Institution. Mr. Wallace reports (letter to Selden, 17 March 1980):

There can be no doubt that the photographs of the Kallikak family members have been retouched. Further, it appears that this retouching was limited to the facial features of the individuals involved—specifically eyes, eyebrows, mouths, nose and hair.

By contemporary standards, this retouching is extremely crude and obvious. It should be remembered, however, that at the time of the original publication of the book, our society was far less visually sophisticated. The widespread use of photographs was limited, and casual viewers of the time would not have nearly the comparative ability possessed by even pre-teenage children today. . . .

The harshness clearly gives the appearance of dark, staring features, sometimes evilness, and sometimes mental retardation. It would be difficult to understand why any of this retouching was done were it not to give the viewer a false impression of the characteristics of those depicted. I believe the fact that no other areas of the photographs, or the individuals have been retouched is significant in this regard also. . . .

I find these photographs to be an extremely interesting variety of photographic manipulation.

Goddard Recants

By 1928 Goddard had changed his mind and become a latter-day supporter of the man whose work he had originally perverted, Alfred Binet. Goddard admitted, first of all, that he had set the upper limit of moronity far too high:

It was for a time rather carelessly assumed that everybody who tested 12 years or less was feeble-minded. . . . We now know, of course, that only a small percentage of the people who test 12 are actually feeble-minded—that is, are incapable of managing their affairs with ordinary prudence or of competing in the struggle for existence (1928, p. 220).

But genuine morons still abound at their redefined level. What shall be done with them? Goddard did not abandon his belief in their inherited mentality, but he now took Binet's line and argued that most, if not all, could be trained to lead useful lives in society:

The problem of the moron is a problem of education and training. . . . This may surprise you, but frankly when I see what has been made out of the moron by a system of education, which as a rule is only half right, I have no difficulty in concluding that when we get an education that is entirely right there will be no morons who cannot manage themselves and their affairs and compete in the struggle for existence. If we could hope to add to this a social order that would literally give every man a chance, I should be perfectly sure of the result (1928, pp. 223–224).

But if we let morons live in society, will they not marry and bear children; is this not the greatest danger of all, the source of Goddard's previous and passionate warnings?

Some will object that this plan neglects the eugenic aspect of the problem. In the community, these morons will marry and have children. And why not? . . . It may still be objected that moron parents are likely to have imbecile or idiot children.

There is not much evidence that this is the case. The danger is probably negligible. At least it is not likely to occur any oftener than it does in the general population. I assume that most of you, like myself, will find it difficult to admit that the foregoing may be the true view. We have worked too long under the old concept (1928, pp. 223–224).

Goddard concluded (1928, p. 225) in reversing the two bulwarks of his former system:

1. Feeble-mindedness (the moron) is *not incurable* [Goddard's italics].
2. The feeble-minded do not generally need to be segregated in institutions.

"As for myself," Goddard confessed (p. 224), "I think I have gone over to the enemy."

Endnotes

1. Division is more appropriate because it is the relative, not the absolute, magnitude of disparity between mental and chronological age that matters. A two-year disparity between mental age two and chronological age four may denote a far severer degree of deficiency than a two-year disparity between mental age fourteen and chronological age sixteen. Binet's method of subtraction would give the same result in both cases, while Stern's IQ measures 50 for the first case and 88 for the second. (Stern multiplied the actual quotient by 100 to eliminate the decimal point.)
2. The link of morality to intelligence was a favorite eugenical theme. Thorndike (1940, pp. 264–265), refuting a popular impression that all monarchs are reprobates, cited a correlation coefficient of 0.56 for the estimated intelligence vs. the estimated morality of 269 male members of European royal families!

Myths about Test Score Comparisons

Iris C. Rotberg

Iris Rotberg lives in Potomac, Maryland. This article appeared in *Science*, volume 270, December, 1995.

📖

In recent years, our expectations about what we can learn from testing students have become increasingly unrealistic. We use tests for inappropriate purposes and draw inaccurate conclusions from the results. To fix the perceived problem—low test scores—we administer more tests. In the process, we ignore real problems.

Testing has become an integral part of the public policy dialogue about major national issues. Scores on standardized tests are blamed for perceived failures in our economy and in international competition. They drive the debate on school reform. When educators express concern about the focus on standardized tests, we create new and, inevitably, more time-consuming tests that do not address the basic problem: Test score comparisons are highly misleading indicators of the quality of education and are irrelevant to decisions about the wisdom of any particular school reform.

I will address here a set of myths that surround standardized testing. Let me acknowledge at the outset, however, that tests can be valuable for some purposes. They have been used effectively to measure student progress, predict future performance, diagnose learning problems, encourage changes in curriculum and teaching methods, and describe national trends. However, the current use of tests has gone well beyond the reality of what they can accomplish.

Myth 1: Test score comparisons between nations, states, or schools provide valid measures of the quality of education. The international science and mathematics comparisons: demonstrate the fallacy of equating test scores with school quality. These comparisons are methodologically flawed and have little to do with the quality of education. The basic problem is student selectivity: The fewer the students who take the test, the higher the average score. That score is not a valid measure of the overall quality of the education system. It simply reflects the fact that the students represented in the test comparisons have been much more highly selected in some countries than in others.

In addition, the test results reflect differences among nations in the proportion of low-income children in the test-taking population. The United States, for example, has a large proportion of low-income students as compared with many other industrialized countries. There is a strong association between poverty and low test scores. We tend to hold the education system responsible for test results reflecting broad societal problems.

Test score rankings also reflect differences in curriculum emphases among nations; for example, the proportion of 12th-grade students who study calculus, the degree of subject-

"Myths about Test Score Comparisons" by Iris C. Rotberg. Reprinted with permission from Science. Copyright 1995 American Association for the Advancement of Science.

matter specialization after age 16 and the amount of time devoted to cram courses in addition to regular schooling. The decision about whether or not to adopt a particular educational practice should be based on a careful consideration of the merits of the proposed change, not on rankings on standardized tests that compare quite different systems.[1]

Sampling problems found in international studies also apply to state rankings on the Scholastic Aptitude Test (SAT). The states with the highest proportions of students taking the SAT tend to have the lowest average SAT scores.[2]

Comparisons of schools within a school system are similarly biased by sampling problems. The fewer and more highly selected the students who take the test, the higher the average score. That score has little to do with the quality of the school.

Schools can raise their scores by excluding low-performing students. After an elementary school was put on probation for low test scores, the third graders made major gains within a single school year because the "officials simply stopped testing most of the third graders . . . . [Four years later], only 28 percent of the class took the standardized test . . ."[3]

Schools also inflate their scores by encouraging students to drop out of school before the examination or by retaining them in their grade. An educator put it this way: "I'm concerned because we have fewer students after grade 9 and it looks like it's to a school's advantage to get a kid to drop out rather than to keep him on the rolls and have poor test scores at grade 12".[4]

This technique is not limited to the United States. A World Bank study described primary schools in Kenya that increased test scores by encouraging low achieving students to drop out before the test was administered. And as many as 20% of Chinese students may be retained in grade in upper-middle school in order to increase that school's scores—and, therefore, its reputation—on university entrance examinations.[5]

Myth 2: The quality of our schools has declined; that is why we are no longer competitive. We incorrectly conclude from the flawed test comparisons that our schools or our parents or our students have failed. We overestimate the quality and rigor of education in previous generations. We ignore the strides that have been made in educating a large proportion of the population. In 1940, 38.1% of 25- to 29-year-olds in the United States had graduated from high school. By 1993, that percentage had risen to 88.2%. In the same time period, graduation rates from 4-year colleges rose from 5.9% to 23.7%.[6] Moreover, out educational accomplishments equal and in many cases surpass those of previous years. A recent study by the RAND Corporation found that students' reading and mathematics performance improved for all racial and ethnic groups between 1970 and 1990.[7]

Clearly, the United States faces serious educational problems, but they are not the problems identified by the public rhetoric. In the 1950s, we responded to Sputnik by blaming the schools for a perceived inferiority to the Soviet Union in science and technology. Later, we predicted a shortage of scientists and engineers in the 1990s—again due to the failures of our education system. Both concerns were unjustified.

We continue, however, to hear about problems in international competitiveness. The conventional wisdom is that U.S. economic competitiveness has declined because our schools produce a poorly trained work force. Yet, the evidence shows that the problems are caused by quite different factors, such as the realities of the global economy, business practices, and government policies—for example, financial incentives that encourage offshore manufacturing: differential wage rates, profit margins, and government subsidies; licensing practices; exchange rates; and trade policy.

Myth 3: We can fix our schools by administering more tests. Or, if we hold teacher accountable for students' standardized test scores our schools will improve. The evidence shows the opposite.

Testimony before the U.S. House of Representatives put it this way: "[Test-based accountability] has been tried many times over a period of centuries in numerous countries, and its track record is unimpressive . . . . It was the linchpin of the educational reform movement of the 1980s. The failure of which provides much of the impetus for the current wave of reform . . . Holding people accountable for performance on tests tends to narrow the curriculum. It inflates test scores, leading to phony accountability. It can have pernicious effects on instruction, such as substitution of cramming for teaching . . . . It can adversely affect students already at risk—for example, increasing the dropout rate and producing more egregious cramming for the tests in schools with large minority enrollments".[8]

Test comparisons do not provide a valid basis for an accountability system. The results do not control for changes in student population, for incentives to encourage certain students to take or not take the test, or for consistency between the test and the instructional program. We can raise test scores if we teach to the test or if we exclude low-achieving students from taking the test, but the higher scores gained under those circumstances do not reflect improved education.

The RAND study referred to above concluded: "Comparisons of simple, unadjusted test scores from one year to the next or across different schools or districts do not provide a valid indicator of the performance of the teachers, schools, or school districts unless the differences in scores are very large compared to what might be accounted for by changing demographic or family characteristics. This is rarely the case; so, any use of unadjusted test scores to judge or reward teachers or schools will inevitably misjudge which teachers and schools are performing better."[9]

A key question is whether we can alleviate the problem by using alternative measures, such as attendance rates, graduation rates, or the proportion of students going to college. Clearly, these measures provide communities with valuable information about educational accomplishments and problems. However, they do not provide an equitable basis for measuring teacher accountability. The basic problem remains: The effects of teacher quality cannot be separated from the wide range of other factors that influence school outcomes.

Myth 4: The problems in current standardized testing programs can be solved by development of new and improved tests. It is argued that innovative tests, called performance tests or portfolio assessments, will take care of flaws in current testing programs. However, little attention is paid to how long such tests take to develop, how much they cost, whether they can be administered on a large scale, the amount of instructional time they displace, and the validity of the resulting comparisons.

Studies of state testing programs show that the new tests do not reduce methodological problems, they increase them. The scoring is unreliable and measures of validity (for example, whether the tests predict students' future academic performance) are lacking.[10,11] Some state testing programs have tried to use complex statistical formulas to control for student background variables that might affect scores. The attempt has not worked. Indeed, it has resulted in a scoring system that is incomprehensible even to educators working within the system.[12]

Although the new tests may draw teachers' attention toward writing and problem-solving skills and away from rote learning, this benefit, could be obtained by incorporating performance tests or portfolio assessments into a school's instructional program without attempting to make comparisons that provide spurious information.

Moreover, the testing programs are extremely costly and time consuming. Researchers estimate the potential cost of national testing in five subject areas in only three grades to be more than $3 billion per year.[13] In Kentucky's testing program, fourth-grade teachers were "overwhelmed" by the administration and grading of writing and mathematics portfolios.[14] In Vermont, teachers spent an average of 30 hours per month, excluding training, working on mathematics portfolios—time taken from instruction children otherwise would receive.[10]

Perhaps the best example of what happens to testing programs comes from England. In 1988, Parliament mandated national curricula and assessments. The assessments of 7-year-olds took 2 to 4 weeks out of the school year. The marking and reporting form for 14-year-olds in mathematics was 112 pages long. As a result, teachers, with strong parental support, boycotted administration of the tests and reporting of test scores. They cited a range of concerns similar to those emerging from testing programs in the United States—overwork, bureaucracy, disruption of regular schooling, flawed tests, invalid comparisons of schools, and opposition to a national curriculum.[15] The program has been abandoned.

Myth 5: We can compensate for the inadequate resources spent on poor children by increasing testing requirements. Or, put another way, money does not matter. Research shows, however, that per pupil expenditure, teacher expertise, and class size do make a difference in student achievement.[16] Increasing testing requirements does not buy better teachers or the attention children can receive in small schools or classes. Tests do not provide low-income inner city or rural students with science laboratories, computers, or decent facilities, amenities that affluent students take for granted.

Nor will tests reduce school finance inequities that relegate low-income children to the most poorly funded schools. For example, the 100 poorest districts in Texas spend an average of just under $3000 per student. The 100 wealthiest districts spend about $7200 per student. In Illinois, school districts spend between $2400 and $8300 per student.[17]

We cannot improve our schools by giving more tests. The danger is that myths about testing will lead to policies that are irrelevant and counterproductive in addressing the nation's most pressing educational problems; the large proportion of children who live in poverty and the vast differences in educational resources between rich and poor schools. My greatest concern is that a focus on test scores takes attention away from our most troubled schools, the work that needs to be done to resolve the problems, and the resources needed to do it.

References and Notes

1. The first set of international comparisons, conducted 25 years ago, did not take into account in the percentage of the age group actually enrolled in upper secondary school. At the time the tests were administered, only about 20% of the age group in Europe attended upper secondary school—the highest achieving 20%—compared with 80% of the age group in the United States (18). More recent studies have tried to deal with the sampling problem by testing only those 12th-grade students who are in an academic track and taking mathematics or advanced science (19). These changes do not address the problem. Consider, for example, a recent assessment of mathematics students in Hungary and England. Hungary ranks near the top in the eighth-grade comparison. By the 12th grade, when Hungary retains more students in mathematics than any other country, Hungary ranks among the bottom countries. England, by contrast, scores in the bottom half in most of the eighth-grade comparisons, but

ranks among the top countries by the 12th grade, when only a highly select group of students there takes the test, students who have studied science and mathematics almost exclusively since the age of 16. When a country's rank can change so dramatically between the eighth and 12th grades, it simply shows that the test comparisons are meaningless as a measure of school quality (20). Another example of the methodological problems comes from a comparison of 11th-grade students at several different sites: Minneapolis, MN; Fairfax County, VA; the province of Alberta in Canada; Beijing, China:; Taipei, Taiwan; and Sendal, Japan (21). Clearly, these sites are not representative of their nations as a whole, nor were the students selected within each site representative of the age group in their communities. The comparison between China and Japan shows how biases in the sample lead to misleading findings. China ranked first even though we know that Japan educates a much higher proportion of its young people, and Japanese students often spend up to 20 hours a week in cram courses in addition to their regular schooling. The reality is that the test score rankings reflected student selectivity, not the overall performances of the education system. Like many other developing countries with scarce resources, China has an elitist education system that provides upper secondary education to only a small proportion of its young people. Although most Japanese students complete high school, a majority of Chinese students already have left school by the 11th grade. As a result, only a small proportion of the age group in China is represented in the test results. They are the highest achieving students, in the capital city, in a country with particularly wide disparities between urban and rural education. A recent study showed no significant difference between U.S. and Chinese ninth-grade scores when students were selected from both urban and rural areas. Although these samples are more representative then those in the study described above, selectivity remains a problem because a large number of Chinese students have already left school by the ninth grade and therefore are not tested (22).

2. *College-Bound Seniors: The Class of 1990* (College Board, New York, August 1990); I. C. Rotberg, Phi Delta Kappan 65, 10 (1984).

3. B. Ziatos, "Scores That Don't Add Up," *New York Times*, 11 November 1994, p. 28.

4. R. F. Elmore, C. H. Abelmann, S. H. Fuhrman, paper presented at the Brookings Institution conference on Performance-Based Approaches to School Reform, Washington, DC, 6 and 7 April 1995, p. 34.

5. V. Greaney and T. Kellaghan, *Equity Issues in Public Examinations in Developing Countries*, Technical Paper No. 272 (World Bank, Washington, DC, 1995).

6. *Digest of Education Statistics: 1994*, National Center for Education Statistics 94–115 (U.S. Department of Education, Washington, DC, 1994), p. 17.

7. D. W. Grissmer, S. N. Kirby, M. Berends, S. Williamson, *Student Achievement and the Changing American Family*, MR-488-LE (RAND Institute on Education and Training, Santa Monica, CA, 1994).

8. D. M. Koretz, G. F. Madaus, E. Heartel, A. E. Beaton, *National Educational Standards and Testing*: A Response to the Recommendations of the National Council on Education Standards and Testing, CT-100 (RAND Corp., Santa Monica, CA, 1992), p. 9.

9. D. W. Grissmer, *ibid.*, p. XXXV.

10. See, for example. D. Koretz, B. Stecher, S. Klein, D. McCaffrey, *The Vermont Portfolio Assessment Program*, RP-366 (RAND Corp., Santa Monica, CA, 1995).

11. See, for example. R. K. Hambleton *et al., Review of the Measurement Quality of the Kentucky Instructional Results Information System, 1991–1994* (Office of Educational Accountability, Kentucky General Assembly, Frankfort, KY, June 1995).

12. R. F. Elmore. C. H. Abelmann, S. H. Fuhrman, paper presented at the Brookings Institution conference on Performance-Based Approaches to School Reform. Washington, DC, 6 and 7 April 1995.

13. D. M. Koretz, G. F. Madaus, E. Haertel, A. E. Beaton. *National Educational Standards and Testing: A Response to the Recommendations of the National Council on Education Standards and Testing*, CT-100 (RAND Corp., Santa Monica, CA, 1992).

14. R. F. Elmore, in (11), p. 43.

15. "Massive Teacher Boycott Derails British National Tests," reprinted from *Fair Test Examiner* (Summer 1993).

16. See, for example, R. F. Ferguson, *Harvard J. Legis.* 28, 465 (1991); L. V. Hedges, R. D. Lalne, R. Greenwald, *Educ. Res.* 23, 3 (1994); R. J. Murnane. *Harvard J. Legis.* 28, 457 (1991).

17. I. C. Rotberg and J. J. Harvey, *Federal Policy Options for Improving the Education of Low-Income Students, Volume I: Findings and Recommendations.* MR-209-LE (RAND Corp., Santa Monica, CA. 1993).

18. T. Husen, *Phi Delta Kappan 64*, 7 (1983).

19. *The Underachieving Curriculum: Assessing U.S. School Mathematics from an International Perspective* (International Association for the Evaluation of Education Achievement. University of Illinois, Champaign, IL, 1987).

20. Adapted from a more detailed analysis by I. C. Rotberg in *Phi Delta Kappan 72*, 4 (1990).

21. *Stevenson Study of Mathematics Achievement in Alberta Schools*, Summary Report based on a presentation by Harold Stevenson, Alberta Education Department. Edmonton, Alberta, Canada, 24 October 1993.

22. J. Wang, paper presented at the 76th Annual Meeting of the American Educational Research Association, San Francisco, CA, 18 to 22 April 1995.

23. This paper is based on remarks presented at the North Central Alberta Teachers' Convention, Edmonton, Alberta, Canada, 8 to 10 February 1995, and the American Youth Policy Forum, Institute for Educational Leadership. Washington, DC, 2 June 1995.

Reasoning about Testing

Gregory J. Cizek

Gregory Cizek has worked for the American College Testing Program, the organization that produces the ACT college entrance exam. This article originally appeared in *Education Week*, volume 9, no. 28, 1990.

Criticism of testing has lately been widespread and multifaceted. Recently, we have learned of a movement to abolish assessment in early grades and of a coalition formed to combat standardized testing. We have also been offered arguments for reconsidering standards and assessments altogether.

There may be solid grounds for such reappraisal. But the rationale advanced in recent discussions is ill-conceived and poorly defended—the product of sloppy logic. The American public has actually yet to be presented by anyone with a substantial, well-conceived argument for abandoning testing.

Sloppy reasoning has at least three characteristics: It employs grandiose but vacuous rhetoric, makes careless inferences regarding cause and effect, and mistakes faith for fact. While the mere presence of this unholy trinity in this debate is worrisome, more troubling is the possibility that it could actually influence a reform movement.

Emotional Appeal

The abolitionists' use of rhetoric is most noticeable in attempts to capture the moral high ground through emotional appeal. On first glance, what right-thinking person would not want "schools with high standards," an "attitude of excellence," "genuine accountability," more "quality than quantity," "authentic evaluation," or "empowerment for teachers"?

But what does all this jargon really mean? Are any of these phrases meant for any purpose except to make us *feel* bad about evaluation and to make us *feel* good about poorly defined alternatives? I don't think so. In fact, all of the moaning and gloom-saying about current

The 'Sloppy' Logic of Test Abolitionists by Gregory J. Cizek. Taken from Education Week, April 4, 1990. Reprinted with permission of Gregory J. Cizek, Associate Professor of Educational Research and Measurement, College of Education and Allied Professions, University of Toledo, Toledo, OH.

practice suggests a new moniker around which the abolitionists can rally: "genuwhine assessment."

In fairness to the movement, we must ask if the whining is justified. Unfortunately, the argumentation offered in support of this position is mired in careless inferences about cause and effect.

Generally, abolitionists rightly note that testing is not the cause of higher achievement. No one seriously contends that it is. But neither is it logical to argue that testing causes lower achievement. Assessment is simply an attempt to gauge the current state of affairs. The too-frequently invoked medical analogy remains useful in this context, especially given a widespread perception that the education system is ailing: We take the patient's temperature more frequently when there appears to be reason to believe that something is wrong. Such monitoring, we think, will provide a hint about why the patient is sick and tell us whether appropriate therapy is leading to better health.

The cause-and-effect mistake runs even deeper. Researcher Grant Wiggins, for example, has commented that "in the last 20 years, the most massive investment in testing ever undertaker has coincided with a palpable decrease in the quality of education." Sure. And also in the last 20 years, average cholesterol levels have risen, Communist governments have begun to fall, and Nelson Mandela has been freed. Ah, the power of testing!

Teachers Favor Standardized Testing

Studies prove that teachers are for standardized testing: As a report from the University of Pittsburgh concluded, "Feeling strongly that they know their own students, teachers think of the tests as yet one more piece of evidence, one further measure of how a child is doing in school. The tests are particularly helpful, the study noted, in assisting teachers in identifying those students who do better on the tests than the teacher had predicted based on his or her observations and experiences with the child."

Sally D. Reed, *A Parent's Survival Guide to the Public Schools, 1991.*

The most plausible cause-and-effect inference regarding testing and educational quality has been overlooked by abolitionists: that the patient's temperature is being taken more frequently because other data suggest that there is a problem. To hypothesize that testing could undermine reform efforts is to wholly misunderstand the problem.

Interestingly, the same abolitionists who claim that a love of testing is the root of all educational evils propose as an alternative merely to substitute different kinds of testing. The newest is "performance assessment," which, we are told, is more "authentic" or "genuine." Or maybe it's "higher order," or "holistic." In any event, opponents of standardized assessment are urging testing companies and the public to read the handwriting on the wall and support the use of something else, something "more real." Indeed. If anything, the public has already read the handwriting on the wall and is reacting negatively because it contains misspellings and poor grammar.

Faith for Fact

Which brings us to the third characteristic of sloppy reasoning: mistaking faith for fact. If this sort of thinking isn't acceptable in teaching about matters as significant as the origin of the world, it shouldn't be permitted in areas of arguably lesser importance, either.

The abolitionists would ask us to be educationally healed by faith in their dogma. While promoting higher standards for education, they suggest that "students with high standards are diligent, thoughtful, engaged, persistent, and thorough—no matter what they learn." Such emotive language might compel the reader to accept blindly the underlying assumption that it doesn't matter what students learn. Are we to accept this premise on faith? Is it sound?

A. Graham Down, executive director of the Council for Basic Education, asserts that alternatives are needed because the traditional tests measure only "knowledge." Now, I suppose I could be accused of being old fashioned, but somehow I'm fixated on the notion that knowledge is still fundamental to learning.

Serious Charges

What about allegations that testing has been particularly harmful for children in the early grades and that, in the words of one abolitionist, "in some schools they spend more time in testing than they do in actual classrooms"? These are serious charges—if true. Such claims must be supported if we are to believe them; we can't simply take them on faith.

Perhaps all of these lapses in reasoning can be explained by the spread of what might be called "evalophobia." In proposing that testing be banned, abolitionists are also implicitly suggesting that we renounce any means of exploring the link between quality of instruction and quality of performance. Of course, standardized tests don't measure *everything* that is valuable or interesting about student achievement. But they do measure some of what is valuable and interesting in an extremely efficient and accurate way.

Reasonable inferences from high scores on a standardized test include the following: High-scoring students seem to be grasping what is taught; they are performing better on the tested material than some other students; and the instruction has been appropriate. Reliance on the proposed "genuine," "empowering" assessments would render such conclusions as the first two tenuous and the third impossible. In fact, much rhetoric surrounding alternative assessment leaves individual students entirely culpable for their educational shortcomings. We should not, for fear of the information provided by testing, deprive ourselves and our students of one of the few sources of objective data for evaluating our own performance.

Keep Standardized Tests

We should all recognize that we have not achieved technical perfection in assessment; we must also admit that existing instruments address only a portion of what is useful for both our students and ourselves. But we should not jettison the tests we have because they don't do everything we wish they could. At minimum, tests do provide important information about *some* aspects of learning, as everyone should acknowledge. And we should develop new devices to assess other facets of students' intellectual growth.

● Standardized Testing: Helpful . . . or Harmful?

Ramsay Selden

Ramsay Selden has been the director of the State Education Assessment Center in Washington D.C. His article appeared in the March 1989 issue of PTA Today.

Standardized testing means administering the same test in the same way to two or more pupils. It is a very broad class of uniform testing activities.

Standardized testing is the kind of testing we must use to look at education beyond the context of an individual student. We need such testing whenever we want to get a sense of how two or more entities in the educational process are doing relative to one another. The entities can be children, schools or states. This is for fairness: if we wish to examine *relative* performance, we must use standard procedures that give each child or school or other entity an equal chance to do well.

Is it important to compare? Some believe it is not appropriate to evaluate the performance of children or another entity on a relative scale. They say the child, school or school system should be evaluated and encouraged in terms of his or her (or its) own unique characteristics. Others disagree. They feel that it is desirable to review performances in relation to one another for a variety of purposes, such as to know which are doing well or not so well and to select one.

Value of Testing

The vast majority of teachers and parents find some merit in measuring the relative performance of students. Students are given grades by teachers, and millions of parents encourage their children to participate in testing for college admission and to determine their relative achievement.

Most members of the public as well as the policymakers who represent them feel it is valuable to monitor and evaluate the academic performance of their schools and school districts as well as their states and the nation. This enables them to tell, for example, if their school systems are doing better or worse over time and if they are doing better or worse than schools, districts, states or nations whose performance they feel should be similar. If we are willing to decide on goals or values, we can even use test results to tell how our school systems are doing in relation to them.

Let's look at the arguments against standardized testing. First, some critics assert that the failure of some standardized tests to tap important and complex educational skills or the cultural bias of some tests are reasons not to test at all. That premise is based on a view that these shortcomings in tests are rampant and unremediable. But if that perception is wrong it would

Standardized Testing: Helpful . . . or Harmful? by Ramsay Selden. Taken from PTA Today, March, 1989. Reprinted by permission.

leave us unnecessarily without any objective information upon which to judge the relative strength of our school systems.

Tests are generally developed or chosen to measure as well as possible the skills that are deemed important for the school system. Many states have conscientiously increased the sophistication of the skills their testing programs measure to reflect deeper goals. Also, the creativity of methods used to test in areas such as writing, reading comprehension and science has been improved dramatically in recent years, permitting more effective testing in these areas.

Standardized Tests Assesss Effectiveness

Along with other evaluations and measures, tests can be used for assessing the effectiveness of teaching and learning. Results of tests can be used to compare schools, school districts, colleges, states, and even countries in assessing how effective they are in educating students. In making such comparisons, it is clear that tests can be used to hold individuals accountable for leadership, teaching, or learning—or the lack of leadership, teaching, or learning.

Kenneth H. Ashworth. *The College Board Review*, Winter 1989—90.

Good test designers customarily review their programs for cultural bias and stereotyping, and items are regularly eliminated if they reflect large group differences in background characteristics that affect performance on them. Now, group differences have been reduced largely to differences in knowledge or experience that are important educationally and that are difficult to "unconfound" from instruction.

As consumers of education, and as those responsible for the quality of their children's schooling, parents should have and use test results, as long as they are sound. Testing must be done as well as we know how, and we must avoid the shortcomings of poor or expedient testing. There is undoubtedly room to improve, but fair and valid testing is not beyond us. Current tests are not so bad that they should be thrown out while we wait for ideal ones to be developed. We need test data now to know whether our schools are on course.

Test Content

Another criticism expressed by opponents of standardized testing is that the content of tests drives instruction inappropriately. This was of special concern when the Council of Chief State School Officers began to push toward comparative achievement testing among states. The question was whether comparing states would result in an overbearing influence on curriculum from the national level. Or, would state comparisons result in watering down the tests to what could be tested easily?

For state comparisons, states agreed on a comprehensive, forward-looking framework for mathematics—the first subject to be tested comparatively—in the National Assessment of Educational Progress (NAEP) for 1990. This framework represents a broad consensus of teachers, policymakers and school administrators who determined what *should* be tested in mathematics, not a least-common denominator. It does not appear to exclude major areas of the subject that some states might wish to emphasize. It allows for great flexibility in what is emphasized and how and when it is taught.

A final argument is that attention to test scores will ignore differences in the conditions under which schools operate and that it will detract from constructive support and improvement of the schools. The chief state school officers have insisted adamantly that states should not be compared simply with other states, but with other states with similar circumstances and needs. They have also called for reporting of achievement indicators in relation to indicators of school processes and inputs, so people can begin to see where to place their efforts to make things better.

States Must Know

In many ways states have become the level of government with the most responsibility for education. They are raising and spending the money, setting many of the standards and spear-heading many of the efforts to reform. For states *not* to know how well they are doing in education relative to other states would be like a business not knowing its relative profit margin.

The results of standardized achievement testing should not be the be-all and end-all of educational accountability. But knowing how we are doing—from the individual student to the nation as a whole—in terms of a comparative reference point is appropriate. The relative results of achievement testing programs must be collected through the best-constructed tests we can assemble. There are shortcomings with many of our testing programs, but this does not eliminate the necessity of having them. And, fortunately, the technology for producing them and improving them is already within our grasp.

● Ideas for Discussion, Writing and Research

1. In class discussion, summarize the narratives or stories of Binet and Goddard, as Gould tells them. What reaction do you have to these narratives? What claims were Binet and Goddard making, and what evidence were they using to support these claims? Now, consider Gould's larger point: What claim is Gould himself making in this piece? How does he use the narratives of Goddard and Binet to support this claim? How might readers' reactions to the stories of Binet and Goddard work for Gould?

2. Brainstorm a list of instances of standardized testing (that is, tests in which you have been assigned a rank or score relative to other students) that you have encountered in your schooling. What were the goals of these tests, as you understood them? How would you characterize the testing experience? Are there tests (or types of tests) that differ in fundamental ways from other tests; either in goals or in the testing experience? Are there ways to distinguish between means of assessment that are more or less useful, more or less humane, more or less reliable, more or less fair, more or less unpleasant? Write an argument in which you either 1) make a claim about the nature of a specific kind of test, or 2) argue for a means of distinguishing between types of tests.

3. Write a rhetorical analysis of the Rotberg piece. What are the major claims and how is each supported? What varieties of evidence are used to support the claims? Can you think of kinds of evidence that Rotberg doesn't use? Construct a visual diagram of Rotberg's argument (that is, her claims and evidence). Conduct a similar analysis of Cizek, Selden, and/or Gould. Use your visual diagrams to construct a comparison of the arguments of these writers.

4. Now, look at the ethos or authorial voice of two or more of the writers in this section. What kind of "voice" does the author "speak" with (impassioned, reasoned, ironic, indignant, amused, etc.)? What words, phrases, or other language structures contribute to each author's voice? Identify several such textual structures for each author. Can you rewrite a paragraph or two from one author's piece in the "voice" of another? Discuss the difficulties of this exercise in class.

5. Note the metaphors that Cizek and Selden use in their pieces: Cizek sets up testing as like "taking a patient's temperature"; Selden equates testing with assessing the relative profit margin of a company. What aspects of testing do these metaphors illuminate or emphasize? What is the effect on the reader of these metaphors? Are there ways in which the metaphors might be harmful or misleading? Can you and your classmates generate other metaphors for testing?

6. Research the procedure at your university whereby students are "placed" into (or out of) freshman writing, introductory math or another university required course. What sort of procedure or instrument is used? How was it developed? Who administers it? What proportions of students are placed into or out of a course based on these procedures? Have the proportions changed in recent years? Do teachers of these courses feel that the procedures are useful and fair? Do students? Write an evaluation of your institution's practices based on this research, the readings in this section, and class discussions. Alternatively, write a

proposal (to a specific audience with the power to effect change) arguing for a change in policy.

7. Research the use of standardized tests in assessing what students know. To what extent have those making up these tests responded to the charge that the tests are "culturally biased," as Victor Villanueva suggests in Chapter One?

CHAPTER 5

Defining Problems and Proposing Solutions

● A Nation At Risk

A Report by the National Commission on Excellence in Education _____

A Nation at Risk is a report prepared by the National Commission on Excellence in Education. Published in 1983, it was intended to serve as a wake-up call "to all who care about America and its future . . . to concerned citizens everywhere." According to its authors, "the educational foundations of our society are presently being eroded by a rising tide of mediocrity that threatens our very future as a Nation and a people." This alarming report became the springboard for many discussions about reforming education in the United States.

Our Nation is at risk. Our once unchallenged preeminence in commerce, industry, science, and technological innovation is being overtaken by competitors throughout the world. This report is concerned with only one of the many causes and dimensions of the problem, but it is the one that undergirds American prosperity, security, and civility. We report to the American people that while we can take justifiable pride in what our schools and colleges have historically accomplished and contributed to the United States and the well-being of its people, the educational foundations of our society are presently being eroded by a rising tide of mediocrity that threatens our very future as a Nation and a people. What was unimaginable a generation ago has begun to occur—others are matching and surpassing our educational attainments.

If an unfriendly foreign power had attempted to impose on America the mediocre educational performance that exists today, we might well have viewed it as an act of war. As it stands, we have allowed this to happen to ourselves. We have even squandered the gains in student achievement made in the wake of the Sputnik challenge. Moreover, we have dismantled essential support systems which helped make those gains possible. We have, in effect, been committing an act of unthinking, unilateral educational disarmament.

Our society and its educational institutions seem to have lost sight of the basic purposes of schooling, and of the high expectations and disciplined effort needed to attain them. This report, the result of 18 months of study, seeks to generate reform of our educational system in fundamental ways and to renew the Nation's commitment to schools and colleges of high quality throughout the length and breadth of our land.

That we have compromised this commitment is, upon reflection, hardly surprising, given the multitude of often conflicting demands we have placed on our Nation's schools and colleges. They are routinely called on to provide solutions to personal, social, and political problems that the home and other institutions either will not or cannot resolve. We must understand that these demands on our schools and colleges often exact an educational cost as well as a financial one.

On the occasion of the Commission's first meeting, President Reagan noted the central importance of education in American life when he said: "Certainly there are few areas of

A report by the National Commission on Excellence in Education, April, 1983. U.S. Department of Education.

American life as important to our society, to our people, and to our families as our schools and colleges." This report, therefore, is as much an open letter to the American people as it is a report to the Secretary of Education. We are confident that the American people, properly informed, will do what is right for their children and for the generations to come.

The Risk

History is not kind to idlers. The time is long past when America's destiny was assured simply by an abundance of natural resources and inexhaustible human enthusiasm, and by our relative isolation from the malignant problems of older civilizations. The world is indeed one global village. We live among determined, well-educated, and strongly motivated competitors. We compete with them for international standing and markets, not only with products but also with the ideas of our laboratories and neighborhood workshops. America's position in the world may once have been reasonably secure with only a few exceptionally well-trained men and women. It is no longer.

The risk is not only that the Japanese make automobiles more efficiently than Americans and have government subsidies for development and export. It is not just that the South Koreans recently built the world's most efficient steel mill, or that American machine tools, once the pride of the world, are being displaced by German products. It is also that these developments signify a redistribution of trained capability throughout the globe. Knowledge, learning, information, and skilled intelligence are the new raw materials of international commerce and are today spreading throughout the world as vigorously as miracle drugs, synthetic fertilizers, and blue jeans did earlier. If only to keep and improve on the slim competitive edge we still retain in world markets, we must dedicate ourselves to the reform of our educational system for the benefit of all—old and young alike, affluent and poor, majority and minority. Learning is the indispensable investment required for success in the "information age" we are entering.

Our concern, however, goes well beyond matters such as industry and commerce. It also includes the intellectual, moral, and spiritual strengths of our people which knit together the very fabric of our society. The people of the United States need to know that individuals in our society who do not possess the levels of skill, literacy, and training essential to this new era will be effectively disenfranchised, not simply from the material rewards that accompany competent performance, but also from the chance to participate fully in our national life. A high level of shared education is essential to a free, democratic society and to the fostering of a common culture, especially in a country that prides itself on pluralism and individual freedom.

For our country to function, citizens must be able to reach some common understandings on complex issues, often on short notice and on the basis of conflicting or incomplete evidence. Education helps form these common understandings, a point Thomas Jefferson made long ago in his justly famous dictum:

> I know no safe depository of the ultimate powers of the society but the people themselves; and if we think them not enlightened enough to exercise their control with a wholesome discretion, the remedy is not to take it from them but to inform their discretion.

Part of what is at risk is the promise first made on this continent: All, regardless of race or class or economic status, are entitled to a fair chance and to the tools for developing their individual powers of mind and spirit to the utmost. This promise means that all children by virtue of their own efforts, competently guided, can hope to attain the mature and informed judgment needed to secure gainful employment, and to manage their own lives, thereby serving not only their own interests but also the progress of society itself.

Indicators of the Risk

The educational dimensions of the risk before us have been amply documented in testimony received by the Commission. For example:

● International comparisons of student achievement, completed a decade ago, reveal that on 19 academic tests American students were never first or second and, in comparison with other industrialized nations, were last seven times.

● Some 23 million American adults are functionally illiterate by the simplest tests of everyday reading, writing, and comprehension.

● About 13 percent of all 17-year-olds in the United States can be considered functionally illiterate. Functional illiteracy among minority youth may ran as high as 40 percent.

● Average achievement of high school students on most standardized tests is now lower than 26 years ago when Sputnik was launched.

● Over half the population of gifted students do not match their tested ability with comparable achievement in school.

● The College Board's Scholastic Aptitude Tests (SAT) demonstrate a virtually unbroken decline from 1963 to 1980. Average verbal scores fell over 50 points and average mathematics scores dropped nearly 40 points.

● College Board achievement tests also reveal consistent declines in recent years in such subjects as physics and English.

● Both the number and proportion of students demonstrating superior achievement on the SATs (i.e., those with scores of 650 or higher) have also dramatically declined.

● Many 17-year-olds do not possess the "higher order" intellectual skills' we should expect of them. Nearly 40 percent cannot draw inferences from written material; only one-fifth can write a persuasive essay; and only one-third can solve a mathematics problem requiring several steps.

● There was a steady decline in science achievement scores of U.S. 17-year-olds as measured by national assessments of science in 1969, 1973, and 1977.

● Between 1975 and 1980, remedial mathematics courses in public 4-year colleges increased by 72 percent and now constitute one-quarter of all mathematics courses taught in those institutions.

● Average tested achievement of students graduating from college is also lower.

● Business and military leaders complain that they are required to spend millions of dollars on costly remedial education and training programs in such basic skills as reading, writing, spelling, and computation. The Department of the Navy, for example, reported to the Commission that *one-quarter* of its recent recruits cannot read at the *ninth grade level*, the minimum needed simply to *understand written safety instructions*. Without remedial work they cannot even begin, much less complete, the sophisticated training essential in much of the modern military.

These deficiencies come at a time when the demand for highly skilled workers in new fields is accelerating rapidly. For example:

🍎 Computers and computer-controlled equipment are penetrating every aspect of our lives—homes, factories, and offices.

🍎 One estimate indicates that by the turn of the century millions of jobs will involve laser technology and robotics.

🍎 Technology is radically transforming a host of other occupations. They include health care, medical science, energy production, food processing, construction, and the building, repair, and maintenance of sophisticated scientific, educational, military, and industrial equipment.

Analysts examining these indicators of student performance and the demands for new skills have made some chilling observations. Educational researcher Paul Hurd concluded at the end of a thorough national survey of student achievement that within the context of the modern scientific revolution, "We are raising a new generation of Americans that is scientifically and technologically illiterate." In a similar vein, John Slaughter, a former Director of the National Science Foundation, warned of "a growing chasm between a small scientific and technological elite and a citizenry ill-informed, indeed uninformed, on issues with a science component."

But the problem does not stop there, nor do all observers see it the same way. Some worry that schools may emphasize such rudiments as reading and computation at the expense of other essential skills such as comprehension, analysis, solving problems, and drawing conclusions. Still others are concerned that an over-emphasis on technical and occupational skills will leave little time for studying the arts and humanities that so enrich daily life, help maintain civility, and develop a sense of community. Knowledge of the humanities, they maintain, must be harnessed to science and technology if the latter are to remain creative and humane, just as the humanities need to be informed by science and technology if they are to remain relevant to the human condition. Another analyst, Paul Copperman, has drawn a sobering conclusion. Until now, he has noted:

Each generation of Americans has outstripped its parents in education, in literacy, and in economic attainment. For the first time in the history of our country, the educational skills of one generation will not surpass, will not equal, will not even approach, those of their parents.

It is important, of course, to recognize that *the average citizen* today is better educated and more knowledgeable than the average citizen of a generation ago—more literate, and exposed to more mathematics, literature, and science. The positive impact of this fact on the well-being of our country and the lives of our people cannot be overstated. Nevertheless, *the average graduate* of our schools and colleges today is not as well-educated as the average graduate of 25 or 35 years ago, when a much smaller proportion of our population completed high school and college. The negative impact of this fact like wise cannot be overstated.

Hope and Frustration

Statistics and their interpretation by experts show only the surface dimension of the difficulties we face. Beneath them lies a tension between hope and frustration that characterizes current attitudes about education at every level.

We have heard the voices of high school and college students, school board members, and teachers; of leaders of industry, minority groups, and higher education; of parents and State officials. We could hear the hope evident in their commitment to quality education and in their descriptions of outstanding programs and schools. We could also hear the intensity of their frustration, a growing impatience with shoddiness in many walks of American life, and the complaint that this shoddiness is too often reflected in our schools and colleges. Their frustration threatens to overwhelm their hope.

What lies behind this emerging national sense of frustration can be described as both a dimming of personal expectations and the fear of losing a shared vision for America.

On the personal level the student, the parent, and the caring teacher all perceive that a basic promise is not being kept. More and more young people emerge from high school ready neither for college nor for work. This predicament becomes more acute as the knowledge base continues its rapid expansion, the number of traditional jobs shrinks, and new jobs demand greater sophistication and preparation.

On a broader scale, we sense that this undertone of frustration has significant political implications, for its cuts across ages, generations, races, and political and economic groups. We have come to understand that the public will demand that educational and political leaders act forcefully and effectively on these issues. Indeed, such demands have already appeared and could well become a unifying national preoccupation. This unity, however, can be achieved only if we avoid the unproductive tendency of some to search for scape goats among the victims, such as the beleaguered teachers.

On the positive side is the significant movement by political and educational leaders to search for solutions—so far centering largely on the nearly desperate need for increased support for the teaching of mathematics and science. This movement is but a start on what we believe is a larger and more educationally encompassing need to improve teaching and learning in fields such as English, history, geography, economics, and foreign languages. We believe this movement must be broadened and directed toward reform and excellence throughout education.

Excellence in Education

We define "excellence" to mean several related things. At the level of the *individual learner*, it means performing on the boundary of individual ability in ways that test and push back personal limits, in school and in the workplace. Excellence characterizes a *school or college* that sets high expectations and goals for all learners, then tries in every way possible to help students reach them. Excellence characterizes a *society* that has adopted these policies, for it will then be prepared through the education and skill of its people to respond to the challenges of a rapidly changing world. Our Nation's people and its schools and colleges must be committed to achieving excellence in all these senses.

We do not believe that a public commitment to excellence and educational reform must be made at the expense of a *strong public commitment to the equitable treatment* of our *diverse population*. The twin goals of equity and high-quality schooling have profound and practical meaning for our economy and society, and we cannot permit one to yield to the other either in principle or in practice. *To do so would deny young people their chance to learn and live according to their aspirations and abilities.* It also would lead to a *generalized accommodation* to mediocrity in our society on the one hand or the creation of an undemocratic elitism on the other.

Our goal must be to develop the talents of all to their fullest. Attaining that goal requires that we expect and assist all students to work to the limits of their capabilities. We should expect schools to have genuinely high standards rather than minimum ones, and parents to support and encourage their children to make the most of their talents and abilities.

The search for solutions to our educational problems must also include a commitment to life-long learning. The task of rebuilding our system of learning is enormous and must be properly understood and taken seriously: Although a million and a half new workers enter the economy each year from our schools and colleges, the adults working today will still make up about 75 percent of the workforce in the year 2000. These workers, and new entrants into the workforce, will need further education and retraining if they— and we as a Nation— are to thrive and prosper.

The Learning Society

In a world of ever-accelerating competition and change in the conditions of the workplace, of ever-greater danger, and of ever-larger opportunities for those prepared to meet them, educational reform should focus on the goal of creating a Learning Society. At the heart of such a society is the commitment to a set of values and to a system of education and affords all members the opportunity to stretch their minds to full capacity, from early childhood through adulthood, learning more as the world itself changes. Such a society has as a basic foundation the idea that education is important not only because of what it contributes to one's career goals but also because of the value it adds to the general quality of one's life. Also at the heart of the Learning Society are educational opportunities extending far beyond the traditional institutions of learning, our schools and colleges. They extend into homes and workplaces; into libraries, art galleries, museums, and science centers; indeed, into every place where the individual can develop and mature in work and life. In our view, formal schooling in youth is the essential foundation for learning throughout one's life. But without life-long learning, one's skills will become rapidly dated.

In contrast to the ideal of the Learning Society, however, we find that for too many people education means doing the minimum work necessary for the moment, then coasting through life on what may have been learned in its first quarter. But this should not surprise us because we tend to express our educational standards and expectations largely in terms of "minimum requirements." And where there should be a coherent continuum of learning, we have none, but instead an often incoherent, outdated patchwork quilt. Many individual, sometimes heroic, examples of schools and colleges of great merit do exist. Our findings and testimony confirm the vitality of a number of notable schools and programs, but their very distinction stands out against a vast mass shaped by tensions and pressures that inhibit systematic academic and vocational achievement for the majority of students. In some metropolitan areas basic literacy has become the goal rather than the starting point. In some colleges maintaining enrollments is of greater day-to-day concern than maintaining rigorous academic standards. And the ideal of academic excellence as the primary goal of schooling seems to be fading across the board in American education.

Thus, we issue this call to all who care about America and its future: to parents and students; to teachers, administrators, and school board members; to colleges and industry; to union members and military leaders; to governors and State legislators; to the President; to members of Congress and other public officials; to members of learned and scientific societies; to the print and electronic media; to concerned citizens everywhere America is at risk.

We are confident that America can address this risk. If the tasks we set forth are initiated now and our recommendations are fully realized over the next several years, we can expect reform of our Nation's schools, colleges, and universities. This would also reverse the current declining trend—a trend that stems more from weakness of purpose, confusion of vision, underuse of talent, and lack of leadership, than from conditions beyond our control.

The Tools at Hand

It is our conviction that the essential raw materials needed to reform our educational system are waiting to be mobilized through effective leadership:

🍎 the natural abilities of the young that cry out to be developed and the undiminished concern of parents for the well-being of their children;

🍎 the commitment of the Nation to high retention rates in schools and colleges and to full access to education for all;

🍎 the persistent and authentic American dream that superior performance can raise one's sate in life and shape one's own future;

🍎 the dedication, against all odds, that keeps teachers serving in schools and colleges, even as the rewards diminish;

🍎 our better understanding of learning and teaching and the implications of this knowledge for school practice, and the numerous examples of local success as a result of superior effort and effective dissemination;

🍎 the ingenuity of our policymakers, scientists, State and local educators, and scholars in formulating solutions once problems are better understood;

🍎 the traditional belief that paying for education is an investment in ever-renewable human resources that equipment, and the availability in this country of sufficient financial means to invest in education;

🍎 the equally sound tradition, from the Northwest Ordinance of 1787 until today, that the Federal Government should supplement State, local, and other resources to foster key national educational goals; and

🍎 the voluntary efforts of individuals, businesses, and parent and civic groups to cooperate in strengthening educational programs.

These raw materials, combined with the unparalleled array of educational organizations in America, offer us the possibility to create a Learning Society, in which public, private, and parochial schools; colleges and universities; vocational and technical schools and institutes; libraries; science centers, museums, and other cultural institutions; and corporate training and retraining programs offer opportunities and choices for all to learn throughout life.

The Public's Commitment

Of all the tools at hand, the public's support for education is the most powerful. In a message to a National Academy of Sciences meeting in May 1982, President Reagan commented on this fact when he said:

This public awareness—and I hope public action—is long overdue. . . . This country was built on American respect for education. . . Our challenge now is to create a resurgence of that thirst for education that typifies our Nation's history.

The most recent (1982) Gallup Poll of the *Public's Attitudes Toward the Public Schools* strongly supported a theme heard during our hearings: People are steadfast in their belief that education is the major foundation for the future strength of this country. They even considered education more important than developing the best industrial system or the strongest military force perhaps because they understood education as the cornerstone of both. They also held that education is "extremely important" to one's future success, and that public education should be the top priority for additional Federal funds. Education occupied first place among 12 funding categories considered in the survey—above health care, welfare, and military defense, with 55 percent selecting public education as one of their first three choices. Very dearly, the public understands the primary importance of education as the foundation for a satisfying life, an enlightened and civil society, a strong economy, and a secure Nation.

At the same time, the public has no patience with undemanding and superfluous high school offerings. In another survey, more than 75 percent of all those questioned believed every student planning to go to college should take 4 years of mathematics, English, history/U.S. government, and science, with more than 50 percent adding 2 years each of a foreign language and economics or business. The public even supports requiring much of this curriculum for students who do not plan to go to college. These standards far exceed the strictest high school graduation requirements of any State today, and they also exceed the admission standards of all but a handful of our most selective colleges and universities.

Another dimension of the public's support offers the prospect of constructive reform. The best term to characterize it may simply be the honorable word "patriotism." Citizens know intuitively what some of the best economists have shown in their research, that education is one of the chief engines of a society's material well-being. They know, too, that education is the common bond of a pluralistic society and helps tie us to other cultures around the globe. Citizens also know in their bones that the safety of the United States depends principally on the wit, skill, and spirit of a self-confident people, today and tomorrow. It is, therefore, essential—especially in a period of long-term decline in educational achievement—for government at all levels to affirm its responsibility for nurturing the Nation's intellectual capital.

And perhaps most important, citizens know and believe that the meaning of America to the rest of the world must be something better than it seems to many today. Americans like to think of this Nation as the preeminent country for generating the great ideas and material benefits for all mankind. The citizen is dismayed at a steady 15-year decline in industrial productivity, as one great American industry after another falls to world competition. The citizen wants the country to act on the belief, expressed in our hearings and by the large majority in the Gallup Poll, that education should be at the top of the Nation's agenda.

Findings

We conclude that declines in educational performance are in large part the result of disturbing inadequacies in the way the educational process itself is often conducted. The findings that follow, culled from a much more extensive list, reflect four important aspects of the educational process: content, expectations, time, and teaching.

Findings Regarding Content

By content we mean the very "stuff" of education, the curriculum. Because of our concern about the curriculum, the Commission examined patterns of courses high school students took in 1964–69 compared with course patterns in 1976–81. On the basis of these analyses we conclude:

- 🍎 Secondary school curricula have been homogenized, diluted, and diffused to the point that they no longer have a central purpose. In effect, we have a cafeteria-style curriculum in which the appetizers and desserts can easily be mistaken for the main courses. Students have migrated from vocational and college preparatory programs to "general track" courses in large numbers. The proportion of students taking a general program of study has increased from 12 percent in 1964 to 42 percent in 1979.
- 🍎 This curricular smorgasbord, combined with extensive student choice, explains a great deal about where we find ourselves today. We offer intermediate algebra, but only 31 percent of our recent high school graduates complete it; we offer French I, but only 13 percent complete it: and we offer geography, but only 16 percent complete it. Calculus is available in schools enrolling about 60 percent of all students, but only 6 percent of all students complete it.
- 🍎 Twenty-five percent of the credits earned by general track high school students are in physical and health education, work experience outside the school, remedial English and mathematics, and personal service and development courses, such as training for adulthood and marriage.

Findings Regarding Expectations

We define expectations in terms of the level of knowledge, abilities, and skills school and college graduates should possess. They also refer to the time, hard work, behavior, self-discipline, and motivation that are essential for high student achievement. Such expectations are expressed to students in several different ways:

- by grades, which reflect the degree to which students demonstrate their mastery of subject matter;
- through high school and college graduation requirements, which tell students which subjects are most important;
- by the presence or absence of rigorous examinations requiring students to demonstrate their mastery of content and skill before receiving a diploma or a degree;
- by college admissions requirements, which reinforce high school standards; and
- by the difficulty of the subject matter students confront in their texts and assigned readings.

Our analyses in each of these areas indicate notable deficiencies:

- The amount of homework for high school seniors has decreased (two-thirds report less than 1 hour a night) and grades have risen as average student achievement has been declining.
- In many other industrialized nations, courses in mathematics (other than arithmetic or general mathematics), biology, chemistry, physics, and geography start in grade 6 and are required of *all* students. The time spent on these subjects, based on class hours, is about three times that spent by even the most science-oriented U.S. students, i.e., those who select 4 years of science and mathematics in secondary school.
- A 1980 State-by-State survey of high school diploma requirements reveals that only eight States require high schools to offer foreign language instruction, but none requires students to take the courses. Thirty-five States require only 1 year of mathematics, and 36 require only 1 year of science for a diploma.
- In 13 States, 50 percent or more of the units required for high school graduation may be electives chosen by the student. Given this freedom to choose the substance of half or more of their education, many students opt for less demanding personal service courses, such as bachelor living.
- "Minimum competency" examinations (now required in 37 States) fall short of what is needed, as the "minimum" tends to become the "maximum," thus lowering educational standards for all.
- One-fifth of all 4-year public colleges in the United States must accept every high school graduate within the State regardless of program followed or grades, thereby serving notice to high school students that they can expect to attend college even if they do not follow a demanding course of study in high school or perform well.
- About 23 percent of our more selective colleges and universities reported that their general level of selectivity declined during the 1970s, and 29 percent reported reducing the number of specific high school courses required for admission (usually by dropping foreign language requirements, which are now specified as a condition for admission by only one-fifth of our institutions of higher education).
- Too few experienced teachers and scholars are involved in writing textbooks. During the past decade or so a large number of texts have been "written down" by their publishers to ever-lower reading levels in response to perceived market demands.

• A recent study by Education Products Information Exchange revealed that a majority of students were able to master 80 percent of the material in some of their subject-matter texts before they had even opened the books. Many books do not challenge the students to whom they are assigned.

• Expenditures for textbooks and other instructional materials have declined by 50 percent over the past 17 years. While some recommend a level of spending on texts of between 5 and 10 percent of the operating costs of schools, the budgets for basal texts and related materials have been dropping during the past decade and a half to only 0.7 percent today.

Findings Regarding Time. Evidence presented to the Commission demonstrates three disturbing facts about the use that American schools and students make of time: (1) *compared to other nations, American students spend much less time on school work;* (2) *time spent in the classroom and on homework is often used ineffectively;* and (3) *schools are not doing enough to help students develop either the study skills required to use time well or the willingness to spend more time on school work.*

• In England and other industrialized countries, it is not unusual for academic high school students to spend 8 hours a day at school, 220 days per year. In the United States, by contrast, the typical school day lasts 6 hours and the school year is 180 days.

• In many schools, the time spent learning how to cook and drive counts as much toward a high school diploma as the time spent studying mathematics, English, chemistry, U.S. history, or biology.

• A study of the school week in the United States found that some schools provided students only 17 hours of academic instruction during the week, and the average school provided about 22.

• A California study of individual classrooms found that because of poor management of classroom time, some elementary students received only one-fifth of the instruction others received in reading comprehension.

• In most schools, the teaching of study skills is haphazard and unplanned. Consequently, many students complete high school and enter college without disciplined and systematic study habits.

Findings Regarding Teaching. The Commission found that not enough of the academically able students are being attracted to teaching; that teacher preparation programs need substantial improvement; that the professional working life of teachers is on the whole unacceptable; and that a serious shortage of teachers exists in key fields.

• Too many teachers are being drawn from the bottom quarter of graduating high school and college students.

• The teacher preparation curriculum is weighted heavily with courses in "educational methods" at the expense of courses in subjects to be taught. A survey of 1,350 institutions training teachers indicated that 41 percent of the time of elementary school teacher candidates is spent in education courses, which reduces the amount of time available for subject matter courses.

- The average salary after 12 years of teaching is only $17,000 per year; and many teachers are required to supplement their income with part-time and summer employment. In addition, individual teachers have little influence in such critical professional decisions as, for example, textbook selection.
- Despite widespread publicity about an overpopulation of teachers, severe shortages of certain kinds of teachers exist: in the fields of mathematics, science, and foreign languages; and among specialists in education for gifted and talented, language minority, and handicapped students.
- The shortage of teachers in mathematics and science is particularly severe. A 1981 survey of 45 States revealed shortages of mathematics teachers in 43 States, critical shortages of earth sciences teachers in 33 States, and of physics teachers everywhere.
- Half of the newly employed mathematics, science, and English teachers are not qualified to teach these subjects; fewer than one-third of U.S. high schools offer physics taught by qualified teachers.

Recommendations

In light of the urgent need for improvement, both immediate and long term, this Commission has agreed on a set of recommendations that the American people can begin to act on now, that can be implemented over the next several years, and that promise lasting reform. The topics are familiar, there is little mystery about what we believe must be done. Many schools, districts, and States are already giving serious and constructive attention to these matters, even though their plans may differ from our recommendations in some details.

We wish to note that we refer to public, private, and parochial schools and colleges alike. All are valuable national resources. Examples of actions similar to those recommended below can be found in each of them.

Better Schools

Theodore Sizer

Theodore Sizer is chair of the Education Department at Brown University and formerly Dean of the Graduate School of Education at Harvard. "Better Schools" is one of the final chapters from his book *Horace's Compromise: The Dilemma of the American High School,* a book-length study of American high schools published in 1984 as part of a five-year inquiry into secondary education called A Study of High Schools, cosponsored by the National Association of Secondary School Principals and the Commission on Educational Issues of the National Association of Independent Schools.

Theodore Sizer, Horace's Compromise: The Dilemma of the American School. Copyright © 1984 by Houghton Mifflin Company. Reprinted with permission.

There are five imperatives for better schools:

1. Give room to teachers and students to work and learn in their own, appropriate ways.
2. Insist that students clearly exhibit mastery of their school work.
3. Get the incentives right, for students and for teachers.
4. Focus the students' work on the use of their minds.
5. Keep the structure simple and thus flexible.

Giving teachers and students room to take full advantage of the variety among them implies that there must be substantial authority in each school. For most public and diocesan Catholic school systems, this means the decentralization of power from central headquarters to individual schools. For state authorities, it demands the forswearing of detailed regulations for how schools should be operated. It calls for the authorities to trust teachers and principals—and believe that the more trust one places in them, the more their response will justify that trust. This trust can be tempered by judicious accreditation systems, as long as these do not reinfect the schools with the blight of standardized required practice.

The purpose of decentralized authority is to allow teachers and principals to adapt their schools to the needs, learning styles, and learning rates of their particular students. The temptation in every school will be to move toward orderly standardization: such is the instinct, it seems, of Americans, so used as we are to depending on structure. Good schools will have to resist this appeal of standardization: the particular needs of each student should be the only measure of how a school gets on with its business. Greater authority is an incentive for teachers, one that will attract and hold the kind of adults which high schools absolutely need on their staffs.

The requirement for *exhibitions of mastery* forces both students and teachers to focus on the substance of schooling. It gives the state, the parents, prospective employers, and the adolescents themselves a real reading of what a student can do. It is the only sensible basis for accountability.

Effective exhibitions will be complicated to construct and time-consuming to administer. To be fair, they need to be flexible: not all students show themselves off well in the same way. They cannot, then, merely be standardized, machine-graded, paper-and-pencil tests.

The process of constructing and overseeing these exhibitions can be threatening, because it will force teachers to see and to deal with the gaps and redundancies that arise from the traditional curriculum. Teachers find it safe to work in the privacy of their classrooms, delivering the credits their courses bestow on each student. A commonly constructed exhibition invades this privacy—a step that is as necessary as it may be intimidating.[7]

The existence of specific exhibitions is itself a strong *incentive* for both students and teachers. Exhibitions clarify ends. The student knows what she or has to do in order to progress and graduate. If pursuit of that high school graduation diploma is voluntary, the adolescent is left on his or her own; the games attendant on compulsory attendance can no longer be used as excuses. To the young person who has met the minimal competencies in literary, numeracy, and civic understanding, the high school says, "Here is what our diploma means; join us and we'll help you master the knowledge it represents, but the work is basically yours to do." The challenge of such an arrangement is powerful. There is self-esteem to be gained from being the key worker, and if wise teachers appropriately adjust the study to the pace of each student, success will breed success. The personalization inherent in such adjusted pacing is also rewarding; it signals to the student that he or she is important as an individual.

Not all adolescents will find any one school setting congenial. Some students respond well to judicious prodding. Others wilt under it, but flourish in gentler places. The claim for personalization extends to a variety of school settings (separate schools or schools-within-schools), and the opportunity for choice among them itself is a spur to energy. Loyalty roots only with difficulty, if at all, in places forced on us; commitment readily follows from free choice.

The focus of high school should be on *the use of the mind*. Although young citizens need to learn about and be exposed to many sides of life, the mind is central, and the school is the principal institution that society has for assisting adolescents in its use. High schools cannot be comprehensive and should not try to be comprehensive; there are some aspects of an adolescent's life in which a school has no right to intrude, and helping students to use their minds well is a large enough assignment, in any case.

The only way to learn to think well and usefully is by practice. The way a teacher assists this learning is by coaching. What a student chooses or is asked to think about is important, obviously, but secondary to the skills of observing and imaginatively using knowledge. A self-propelled learner is the goal of a school, and teachers should insist that students habitually learn on their own. Teacher-delivered knowledge that is never used is temporary.

Issues concerning values inevitably arise in every school, and learning to use one's mind involves making decisions of conduct and belief. How one uses one's mind, and how one accordingly behaves, raise questions about character: Is this fair? Is it thoughtful? Is it generous? Is it *decent*? Schools should not teach merely pure thinking; they must also promote thoughtfulness, at core the qualities of decency. Schools should accept that obligation, not only because it is important, but because it is inescapable. A school *will* affect its students' character, willy-nilly. It should do so carefully, in a principled way.

Personalization of learning and instruction requires a flexible school structure. A flexible structure implies *a simple structure*. A school day segmented into seven or eight time units, each with its own set of imperatives, is almost impossible to bend. A curriculum represented by six or seven autonomous subjects quickly freezes hard: if each gets what its teacher feels is its due, all lose substantial freedom. Furthermore, such a fractionated and specialized set of subjects distorts knowledge for young minds; a simpler, more cogent organization of subject matter is wise.

Any effort to simplify the curriculum will be as threatening to teachers as will be the creation of general graduation exhibitions. We have been trained in our specializations, and we step outside them with trepidation. Our university mentors may often mock these forays, too; for many of them "specialization" and "standards" are synonymous—a false equation, but one that they will nonetheless scathingly defend. Reconstituting the shape of the curriculum—strengthening it by simplifying it and making it cogent to adolescents—will be a lonely, politically rocky effort. Fortunately, each of these five imperatives governs the work of one or another existing school. There is no novelty here. However, pressing them ahead *together* would be novel, a school reconstruction effort of considerable scope and risk.

We hope that many schools will find one or more of these imperatives persuasive enough to push them vigorously. We also hope that some will have the courage to embrace them all, simultaneously. We need new model schools, ones resting on imperatives, like these five, that appear to serve well modern conditions and adolescents. The imperatives interlock, and as they are engineered into practical forms, their interconnection will become a source of strength—and of efficiency. The financial costs of better schools can be justified if the pretentious practices of comprehensiveness are stalwartly eliminated.

Better schools will come when better structures are built. Those structures have no inherent merit, however: their sole function will be to provide apt and nurturing conditions that will attract students and teachers and make their work together worthwhile and efficient.

America 2000: An Education Strategy—A Sourcebook

U.S. Department of Education _____

The following selection is an excerpt from *America 2000: An Education Strategy—A Sourcebook*, published in 1991 by the United States Department of Education. It opens with a speech presented by then President George Bush, outlining the goals of the "America 2000 national strategy" for improving education.

The White House, April 18, 1991

Remarks by the President at the Presentation of the National Education Strategy

Thank you all for joining us here in the White House today. Let me thank the Speaker for being with us, and the Majority Leader, other distinguished members, committee heads and ranking members and very important education committees here with us today. I want to salute the governors, the educators, the business and the labor leaders, and especially want to single out the National Teachers of the Year. I believe we have 10 of the previous 11 Teachers of the Year with us here today, and that's most appropriate and most fitting.

But together, all of us, we will underscore the importance of a challenge destined to define the America that we'll know in the next century.

For those of you close to my age, the 21st century has always been a kind of shorthand for the distant future—the place we put our most far-off hopes and dreams. And today, that 21st century is racing toward us—and anyone who wonders what the century will look like can find the answer in America's classrooms.

Nothing better defines what we are and what we will become than the education of our children. To quote the landmark case, *Brown* v. *Board of Education*, "It is doubtful that any child may reasonably be expected to succeed in life if he is denied the opportunity of an education."

Education has always meant opportunity. Today, education determines not just which students will succeed, but also which nations will thrive in a world united in pursuit of freedom in enterprise. Think about the changes transforming our world. The collapse of communism

U.S. Department of Education.

and the Cold War. The advent and acceleration of the Information Age. Down through history, we've defined resources as soil and stones, land and the riches buried beneath. No more. Our greatest national resource lies within ourselves—our intelligence, ingenuity—the capacity of the human mind.

Nations that nurture ideas will move forward in years to come. Nations that stick to stale old notions and ideologies will falter and fail. So I'm here today to say, America will move forward. The time for all the reports and rankings, for all the studies and the surveys about what's wrong in our schools is passed. If we want to keep America competitive in the coming century, we must stop convening panels that report on ourselves. We must stop convening panels to report the obvious. And we must accept responsibility for educating everyone among us, regardless of background or disability.

If we want America to remain a leader, a force for good in the world, we must lead the way in educational innovation. And if we want to combat crime and drug abuse, if we want to create hope and opportunity in the bleak corners of this country where there is now nothing but defeat and despair, we must dispel the darkness with the enlightenment that a sound and well-rounded education provides.

Think about every problem, every challenge we face. The solution to each starts with education. For the sake of the future, of our children and of the nation's, we must transform America's schools. The days of the status quo are over.

Across this country, people have started to transform the American school. They know that the time for talk is over. Their slogan is: Don't dither, just do it. Let's push the reform effort forward. Use each experiment, each advance to build for the next American century. New schools for a new world.

As a first step in this strategy, we must challenge not only the methods and the means that we've used in the past, but also the yardsticks that we've used to measure our progress. Let's stop trying to measure progress in terms of money spent.

We spent 33 percent more per pupil in 1991 than we did in 1981—33 percent more in real, constant dollars—and I don't think there's a person anywhere who would say—anywhere in the country—who would say that we've seen a 33 percent improvement in our schools' performance.

Dollar bills don't educate students. Education depends on committed communities determined to be places where learning will flourish; committed teachers, free from the noneducational burdens; committed parents, determined to support excellence; committed students, excited about school and learning. To those who want to see real improvement in American education, I say: There will be no renaissance without revolution.

We who would be revolutionaries must accept responsibilities for our schools. For too long, we've adopted a "no fault" approach to education. Someone else is always to blame. And while we point fingers out there, trying to assign blame, the students suffer. There's no place for a no-fault attitude in our schools. It's time we held our schools—and ourselves—accountable for results.

Until now, we've treated education like a manufacturing process, assuming that if the gauges seemed right, if we had good pay scales, the right pupil-teacher ratios, good students would just pop out of our schools. It's time to turn things around to focus on students, to set standards for our schools—and let teachers and principals figure out how best to meet them.

We've made a good beginning by setting the nation's sights on six ambitious national education goals—and setting for our target the year 2000. Our goals have been forged in partnership with the nation's governors, several of whom are with us here today in the East Room. And those who have taken a leadership role are well-known to everyone in this room. And for those who need a refresher course—there may be a quiz later on—let me list those goals right now.

By 2000, we've got to, first, ensure that every child starts school ready to learn; second one, raise the high school graduation rate to 90 percent; the third one, ensure that each American student leaving the 4th, 8th and 12th grades can demonstrate competence in core subjects; four, make our students first in the world in math and science achievements; fifth, ensure that every American adult is literate and has the skills necessary to compete in a global economy and exercise the rights and responsibilities of citizenship; and sixth, liberate every American school from drugs and violence so that schools encourage learning.

Our strategy to meet these noble national goals is founded in common sense and common values. It's ambitious and, yet, with hard work, it's within our reach. And I can outline our strategy in one paragraph, and here it is:

For today's students, we must make existing schools better and more accountable. For tomorrow's students, the next generation, we must create a New Generation of American Schools. For all of us, for the adults who think our school days are over, we've got to become a Nation of Students recognize learning is a lifelong process. Finally, outside our schools we must cultivate communities where learning can happen. That's our strategy.

People who want Washington to solve our educational problems are missing the point. We can lend appropriate help through such programs as Head Start. But what happens here in Washington won't matter half as much as what happens in each school, each local community and, yes, in each home. Still, the federal government will serve as a catalyst for change in several important ways.

Working closely with the governors, we will define new World Class Standards for schools, teachers and students in the five core subjects: math and science, English, history and geography.

We will develop voluntary—let me repeat it—we will develop voluntary national tests for 4th, 8th and 12 graders in the five core subjects. These American Achievement Tests will tell parents and educators, politicians and employers, just how well our schools are doing. I'm determined to have the first of these tests for 4th graders in place by the time that school starts in September of 1993. And for high school seniors, let's add another incentive—a distinction sure to attract attention of colleges and companies in every community across the country— a Presidential Citation to students who excel on the 12th grade test.

We can encourage educational excellence by encouraging parental choice. The concept of choice draws its fundamental strength from the principle at the very heart of the democratic idea. Every adult American has the right to vote, the right to decide where to work, where to live. It's time parents were free to choose the schools that their children attend. This approach will create the competitive climate that stimulates excellence in our private and parochial schools as well.

But the centerpiece of our National Education Strategy is not a program, it's not a test. It's a new challenge: to reinvent American education—to design New American Schools for the year 2000 and beyond.

The idea is simple but powerful: Put America's special genius for invention to work for America's schools. I will challenge communities to become what we will call AMERICA 2000 Communities. Governors will honor communities with this designation if the communities embrace the national education goals, create local strategies for reaching these goals, devise report cards for measuring progress, and agree to encourage and support one of the new generation of America's Schools.

We must also foster educational innovation. I'm delighted to announce today that America's business leaders, under the chairmanship of Paul O'Neill, will create the New American Schools Development Corporation—a private-sector research and development fund of at least $150 million to generate innovation in education.

This fund offers an open-end challenge to the dreamers and the doers eager to reinvent— eager to reinvigorate our schools. With the results of this R & D in hand, I will urge Congress to provide $1 million in start-up funds for each of the 535 New American Schools—at least one in every congressional district—and have them up and running by 1996.

The New American Schools must be more than rooms full of children seated at computers. If we mean to prepare our children for life, classrooms also must cultivate values and good character, give real meaning to right and wrong.

We ask only two things of these architects of our New American Schools: that their students meet the new national standards for the five core subjects and that outside of the costs of the initial research and development, the schools operate on a budget comparable to conventional schools. The architects of the New American Schools should break the mold. Build for the next century. Reinvent—literally start from scratch and reinvent the American school. No question should be off limits, no answers automatically assumed. We're not after one single solution for every school. We're interested in finding every way to make schools better.

There's a special place in inventing the New American School for the corporate community, for business and labor. And I invite you to work with us not simply to transform our schools, but to transform every American adult into a student.

Fortunately, we have a secret weapon in America's system of colleges and universities— the finest in the entire world. The corporate community can take the lead by creating a voluntary private system of World Class Standards for the workplace. Employers should set up skill centers where workers can seek advice and learn new skills. But most importantly, every company and every labor union must bring the worker into the classroom and bring the classroom into the workplace.

We'll encourage every federal agency to do the same. And to prove no one's ever too old to learn, Lamar, with his indefatigable determination and leadership, has convinced me to become a student again myself. Starting next week, I'll begin studying. And I want to know how to operate a computer. Very candidly—I don't expect this new tutorial to teach me how to set the clock on the VCR or anything complicated. But I want to be computer literate, and I'm not. There's a lot of kids, thank God, that are. And I want to learn, and I will.

The workplace isn't the only place we must improve opportunities for education. Across this nation, we must cultivate communities where children can learn. Communities where the school is more than a refuge, more than a solitary island of calm amid chaos. Where the school is the living center of a community where people care—people care for each other and their futures. Not just in the school but in the neighborhood. Not just in the classroom, but in the home.

Our challenge amounts to nothing less than a revolution in American education. A battle for our future. And now, I ask all Americans to be points of light in the crusade that counts the most: the crusade to prepare our children and ourselves for the exciting future that looms ahead.

What I've spoken about this afternoon are the broad strokes of this National Education Strategy. Accountable schools for today, a new generation of schools for tomorrow. A nation of students committed to a lifetime of learning and communities where all our children can learn.

There are four people here today who symbolize each element of this strategy and point the way forward for our reforms. Esteban Pagan, Steve, an award winning eighth grade student in science and history at East Harlem Tech, a choice school.

Mike Hopkins. "Lead Teacher" in the Saturn School in St. Paul, Minnesota, where teachers have already helped reinvent the American school.

David Kelley. A high-tech troubleshooter at the Michelin Tire plant in Greenville, South Carolina. David has spent the equivalent of one full year of his four years at Michelin back at his college expanding his skills.

Finally, Michelle Moore, of Missouri. A single mother, active in Missouri's Parents as Teachers program. She wants her year-old son, Alston, to arrive for his first day of school ready to learn.

So, to sum it up, for these four people and for all the others like them, the revolution in American education has already begun. Now I ask all Americans to be points of light in the crusade that counts the most: the crusade to prepare our children and ourselves for the exciting future that looms ahead. At any moment in every mind, the miracle of learning beckons us all.

Between now and the year 2000, there is not one moment or one miracle to waste.

Thank you all. Thank you for your interest, for your dedication. And may God bless the United States of America. Thank you very much.

America 2000: An Education Strategy

Overview

AMERICA 2000 is a long-term strategy to help make this land all that it should be—a nine-year crusade to move us toward the six ambitious national education goals that the president and the governors adopted in 1990 to close our skills-and-knowledge gap.

The strategy anticipates major change in our 110,000 public and private schools, change in every American community, change in every American home, change in our attitude about learning.

This strategy is bold, complex and long-range. It will start quickly, but results won't come quickly. It will occupy us at least for the rest of this decade.

It will spur far-reaching changes in weary practices, outmoded assumptions and long-assumed constraints on education. It will require us to make some lifestyle changes, too. Yet few elements of this strategy are unprecedented. Today's best ideas, dedicated education reforms, impressive innovations and ambitious experiments already point the way. We already know the direction in which we must go; the AMERICA 2000 strategy will help us get there.

AMERICA 2000 is a national strategy, not a federal program. It honors local control, relies on local initiative, affirms states and localities as the senior partners in paying for education and recognizes the private sector as a vital partner, too. It recognizes that real education reform happens community by community, school by school, and only when people come to understand what they must do for themselves and their children and set about to do it.

The federal government's role in this strategy is limited as wisely—its part in education always has been. But that role will be played vigorously. Washington can help by setting standards, highlighting examples, contributing some funds, providing flexibility in exchange for accountability and pushing and prodding—then pushing and prodding some more.

The AMERICA 2000 strategy has four parts that will be pursued simultaneously. They can be visualized as four giant trains—big enough for everyone to find a place on board—departing at the same time on parallel tracks on the long journey to educational excellence. All four must move swiftly and determinedly if the nation is to reach its destination:

1. **For today's students**, we must radically improve today's schools, all 110,000 of them—make them better and more accountable for results.
2. **For tomorrow's students**, we must invent new schools to meet the demands of a new century—a New Generation of American Schools, bringing at least 535 of them into existence by 1996 and thousands by decade's end.
3. **For those of us already out of school and in the work force**, we must keep learning if we are to live and work successfully in today's world. A "Nation at Risk" must become a "Nation of Students."
4. **For schools to succeed**, we must look beyond their classrooms to our communities and families. Schools will never be much better than the commitment of their communities. Each of our communities must become a place where learning can happen.

Our vision is of four big trains, moving simultaneously down four parallel tracks: Better and more accountable schools; a New Generation of American Schools; a Nation of Students continuing to learn throughout our lives; and communities where learning can happen.

The Challenge: America's Skills and Knowledge Gap

Eight years after the National Commission on Excellence in Education declared us a "Nation at Risk," we haven't turned things around in education. Almost all our education trend lines are flat. Our country is idling its engines, not knowing enough nor being able to do enough to make America all that it should be.

Yet we're spending far more money on education. Total spending for elementary and secondary schools has more than doubled since 1980 while the number of students has remained about the same. In real terms, education spending has increased approximately 33 percent more per public school student. As a nation, we now invest more in education than in defense. But the results have not improved, and we're not coming close to our potential or what is needed.

Nor is the rest of the world sitting idly by, waiting for America to catch up. Serious efforts at education improvement are under way by most of our international competitors and trading partners. Yet while we spend as much per student as almost any country in the world, American students are at or near the back of the pack in international comparisons. If we don't make radical changes, that is where we are going to stay.

Meanwhile, our employers cannot hire enough qualified workers. Immense sums are spent on remedial training, much of it at the college level. Companies export skilled work—or abandon projects that require it.

Shortcomings are not limited to what today's students are learning in school. The fact is that close to 85 percent of America's work force in the year 2000 is already in the work force today. These people are the products of the same education system.

Perhaps 25 million adults are functionally illiterate. As many as 25 million more adult workers need to update their skills or knowledge.

While more than 4 million adults are taking basic education courses outside the schools, there is no systematic means of matching training to needs; no uniform standards measure the skills needed and the skills learned.

While the age of technology, information and communications rewards those nations whose people learn new skills to say ahead, we are still a nation that groans at the prospect of going back to school. At best, we are reluctant students in a world that rewards learning.

And there is one more big problem: Today's young Americans spend barely 9 percent of their first eighteen years in school, on average. What of the other 91 percent, the portion spent elsewhere—at home, on playgrounds, in front of the television?

● For too many of our children, the family that should be their protector, advocate and moral anchor is itself in a state of deterioration.
● For too many of our children, such a family never existed.
● For too many of our children, the neighborhood is a place of menace, the street a place of violence.
● Too many of our children start school unready to meet the challenges of learning.
● Too many of our children arrive at school hungry, unwashed and frightened.
● And other modern plagues touch our children: drug use and alcohol abuse, random violence, adolescent pregnancy, AIDS and the rest.

No civil society or compassionate nation can neglect the plight of these children who are, in almost every case, innocent victims of adult misbehavior.

But few of those problems are amenable to solution by government alone, and none by schools alone. Schools are not and cannot be parents, police, hospitals, welfare agencies or drug treatment centers. They cannot replace the missing elements in communities and families.

Schools can contribute to the casing of these conditions. They can sometimes house additional services. They can welcome tutors, mentors and caring adults. But they cannot do it alone.

At one level, everybody knows this. Yet few Americans think it has much to do with them. We tend to say that "the nation is at risk, but I'm okay." Complacency is widespread with regard to one's own school, one's own children, one's own community.

This leaves us stuck at far too low a level, a level we ought not tolerate. One of the lessons of the education reform movement of the 1980s was that little headway can be made if few of us see the need to change our own behavior. Yet few of us can imagine what a really different education system would look like. Few of us are inclined to make big changes in familiar institutions and habits.

Until last year, few could even describe our education goals. As a nation, we didn't really have any.

In 1990, the president and the governors adopted six ambitions education goals. AMERICA 2000 is a strategy to achieve them.

America's Education Goals

By the year 2000:

1. All children in America will start school ready to learn.
2. The high school graduation rate will increase to at least 90 percent.
3. American students will leave grades four, eight, and twelve having demonstrated competency in challenging subject matter including English, mathematics, science, history, and geography; and every school in America will ensure that all students learn to use their minds well, so they may be prepared for responsible citizenship, further learning, and productive employment in our modern economy.
4. U.S. students will be first in the world in science and mathematics achievement.
5. Every adult American will be literate and will possess the knowledge and skills necessary to compete in a global economy and exercise the rights and responsibilities of citizenship.
6. Every school in America will be free of drugs and violence and will offer a disciplined environment conducive to learning.

The four-part AMERICA 2000 Education Strategy will enable us to achieve these goals.

Sins of Omission in "America 2000"

Harold Howe II _____

Harold Howe II is Senior Lecturer Emeritus at Harvard Graduate School of Education and a former U.S. Commissioner of Education. "Sins of Omission in 'America 2000' " originally appeared in the journal *The Education Digest,* Feb. 1992, and was condensed from *Phi Delta Kappan,* 73 (November 1991), 192–203.

The origins of President Bush's "America 2000" plan for education are not available to the public. This is important when its strategies are judged by many thoughtful educators and analysts of public education to be inadequate or unwise. My own surmise about how this document was prepared is as follows:

The staff of the White House Domestic Policy Council met with the Secretary of Education and selected advisors to establish what the President might do and say to become an Education

Sins of Omission in America 2000 by Harold Howe, from Education Digest, February, 1992. Reprinted with permission.

President—without doing any violence to his political commitments on other fronts. From this meeting came lists of positions to be taken and issues to be avoided. With this material in hand—probably reviewed by White House Chief of Staff John Sununu and perhaps even by the President—writers were put to work, their drafts reviewed repeatedly before the high priests of rhetoric polished the organization, flow, and emotional appeal of the document, probably also producing the "four trains" on "four tracks": today's students, tomorrow's students, workers out of school, and families/communities. But three major topics failed to make any of the four trains:

School Finance

The basic posture of America 2000 is that there is plenty of money in the schools; its reforms require no significant new revenue from local, state, or national governments. It doesn't mention a central fact of life: maldistribution of education revenues from state to state, district to district, school to school.

Is the unavoidable fact of differing capacities of the states to raise funds for schools not even of passing interest? If school districts with very low per-pupil expenditures tend to serve large numbers of students from poor, black, and Hispanic families and if white and middle-class families predominate in districts that spend more, shouldn't we expect some concern about this disparity and the educational harm wrought by our current system of financing education? What did the authors of America 2000 mean when they defined the continuing federal role in education as "assuring equal opportunity"?

Two positions apparently explain why school finance must have been put on my hypothetical "issues to be avoided" list: that additional taxation for any purpose is bad policy (and bad politics); and that providing more money for schools would be counterproductive and simply encourage ineffective education.

Such notions must be set against the fact that the current recession has combined with a 10-year process of shifting the burden for supporting major social programs from the federal government to the states, thus creating significant problems for school funding. The crisis has been exacerbated in some states by legislation imposing ceilings on tax rates. The powerful role of business in supporting tax ceilings is seldom mentioned, but there is no question of the damage done to children by such recent developments, which are totally ignored by America 2000. The least the President could do is appoint a national group to study and report on the unfair outcomes of our disorderly, unsystematic arrangements for supporting schools.

Our current nonsystem is sustained in part by the American belief in local control of schools, which allows communities to have both good and bad schools, sometimes in the same district. It's about time we decided that every child has a *right* to a decent education and abandoned the shabby idea that funding has no influence on the quality of schools. Adequate funds for schooling are one of the main considerations on the road to excellence—but not the only one.

Poverty

America 2000 never says a word about the overwhelming fact that communities and families differ immensely in capacity to generate effective efforts on behalf of children and youth.

It invites both Scarsdale and Harlem to help themselves. It totally ignores the effects of vast economic disparities among families and communities, and it implies that equal opportunity is served regardless of these differences. America 2000 offers communities, including the ones that are barefoot, only the challenge to pick themselves up by their own bootstraps.

There is not even a whisper to suggest that the troubles of children and youth are closely related to the rapid growth of poverty in our society in the last two decades. The number of children in poverty in the U.S. has grown from one child in seven in 1970, to one child in six in 1980, to one child in five in 1990. And it is headed for one child in four in 2000. The unstated expectation of America 2000 is that poverty-stricken youngsters will take the new tests, meet the new standards, benefit from the new model schools, and use the leverage of choice to find schools that will best serve their interests and needs. This is a pipe dream.

A high percentage of these youngsters face serious health problems with limited access to health care. Another substantial proportion started life at very low birth weight and confront serious emotional or physical handicaps as a result. The neighborhoods in which they live are often destructive; so are many of their peer associations. Poverty is the parent of school failure, job failure, emotional imbalance, and social rejection. Yet our new education initiative offers no suggestions for how the government might lessen the effects of poverty on children.

Dodging the Issue

Poverty was almost certainly one of the "issues to be avoided" when this exercise was planned. Poverty is complicated and expensive. Although there would be a good payoff some years down the road for dealing with this issue, that's too far away to make it worth our while. Indeed, this is exactly what the Domestic Policy Council decided more than a year ago in considering options for dealing with the circumstances of disadvantaged children.

Most countries that threaten America's competitive edge in the international marketplace expect some of their population to be at risk of unemployment. They believe that giving these people support for decent, healthy lives and training them for employment are necessary to sustain democratic and economic goals of the society. Could it be that this view and attendant policies enhance a nation's competitiveness by increasing the productivity of the poor?

Cultural and Racial Diversity

An issue close to being most important in American life is how to make the social and cultural diversity of American society work. Diversity must become a strength upon which our nation's future can depend, rather than a reason for reviving ancient animosities or inventing new ones.

Given the serious, daily incidents awakened by interracial and intercultural tensions and the direct involvement of children and youth (and sometimes schools) in these events, how could a wide-ranging plan for the future of our schools and students fail even to mention this topic? I assume this was simply fenced out of the conversation from the beginning. Or perhaps the authors thought this entirely a local concern that deserved comment only at that level. If so, again, what did they mean when they claimed a federal responsibility for "assuring equal opportunity"?

Diversity of student backgrounds is probably the most serious and difficult issue with which our schools now struggle—partly because their transition to a many-cultured community has been more rapid than that of adult society as a whole. There are no easy answers to this growing social complexity. If we don't find ways to deal constructively with it, all four trains bound for educational excellence are apt to be derailed.

Everything America 2000 comments on is affected by racial and ethnic diversity. When standards are being discussed, diversity cannot be denied. The same is true for choice. Diversity is a basic issue in training and retraining teachers. Correlative to diversity are major issues of school desegregation—another subject on which America 2000 is silent. Have the authors really lived in this country for the last 20 years, or have they made only a brief visit from another planet and missed the essential landscape?

The four trains now leaving for educational excellence, flying the flag of America 2000, are scheduled to arrive in nine years. They are not likely to reach their destination, mainly because, along the way, fuel, supplies, maintenance, and salaries for the crew will cost money. And these trains brought very little money with them, on the mistaken assumption it could be found lying along the tracks.

America 2000 identifies some aspects of schooling that need attention, but these are clouded by questionable policies, inadequate funding, and a tendency to talk the game of localism while pursuing a strategy of federalism from the top. The entire proposal lacks a sense of reality about the situation of children and youth in America. Their growing diversity is ignored, their growing poverty is not even mentioned, and muddled thinking about their motivation suggests that forcing them to fail tests will awaken their desire to learn.

The authors of America 2000 rightly perceived that the family and community are significant sources of learning and supports for schooling that must be enlisted to help children mature successfully. But they failed to recognize that a growing proportion of families and communities in the U.S. need substantial assistance—just as schools do—to perform their roles adequately. The assistance America 2000 offers takes two forms: noble rhetoric and prizes from the President. Neither will improve our schools.

🍎 A Crisis Created by Education Myths

Education Digest _____

"A Crisis Created by Education Myths" was originally published in The Education Digest Oct. 1995 where it was condensed from Virginia Journal of Education, 88 (May 1995), 6–11. As stated in its introduction, this article summarizes research and data regarding seven "education myths" based on a research paper by David C. Berliner, a professor of Curriculum and Instruction at Arizona State University.

Much criticism of public schools today is based on assumptions that gained credibility over the past decade or so, often accepted as fact by the public, political decision-makers, the media—and some educators. Let's look at seven of those myths about education in the light of research, data, and the truth, provided courtesy of David C. Berliner, Arizona State University professor of curriculum and instruction, upon whose research paper, *Educational Reform in an Era of Disinformation*, this article is based. On the same subject is Berliner's new book, *The Manufactured Crisis: Myths, Fraud, and the Attack on America's Public Schools*, co-authored by Bruce J. Biddle. available for $25.00 from Addison-Wesley Publishing, 170 Fifth Avenue, New York, NY 10010; phone: 1–212–463–8440.

MYTH 1: Today's youth are not as smart as students used to be. Reality: U.S. intelligence test scores are up dramatically.

- 🍎 Since 1932, the mean IQ of white Americans aged 2 to 75 has risen about 0.3 points per year. Today's students actually average about 14 IQ points higher than their grandparents, about 7 points higher than their parents.
- 🍎 The number of students who have IQs of 130 or more—a cutoff for giftedness—is about seven times greater for today's students than for their grandparents. The number of students above 145 IQ is now about 18 times greater for today's students than two generations ago.
- 🍎 The increases in IQ throughout the industrialized world have been most pronounced in the abstract, problem-solving areas of the tests, the parts that are purer measures of general intelligence. Studies in the United States and Israel have concluded that the skills measured on intelligence tests and the processes underlying test performance are learned in school (i.e., the more schooling, the higher the intelligence score). Estimates of the magnitude of this influence range as high as six IQ points lost per year of schooling missed. Thus, the growing number of children in poverty, who have less access to

A Crisis Created by Education Myths from Education Digest, October, 1995. Reprinted with permission.

quality day care and K-12 education, is likely to stop the rise in intelligence test scores, and the cause is not in schools, but in society.

🍎 Between 1978 and 1990, the number of high-schoolers taking Advanced Placement (AP) tests for college credit jumped 255 percent, from 90,000 to 481,000. The mean score dropped eleven one-hundredths of a point (0.11) over this period, during which the number of Asians taking the AP tests tripled, the percentage of African-Americans taking the tests doubled, and the percentage of Hispanics quadrupled.

MYTH 2: The Scholastic Aptitude Test (SAT) has shown a marked decrease in mean score in the last 25 years, indicating failure of schools and teachers to do their jobs. Reality: Since 1965, average SAT score decline has been 3.3 percent of the raw total score—about five fewer items answered correctly over 25 years.

🍎 The reason for the decline should make teachers proud: A much greater number of students from the bottom 60 percent of their class has been taking the test since the 1960s.

🍎 The decline (most of which took place between 1965 and 1975) is an indication of two facts: a higher high-school graduation rate, particularly for minority students, and increased access to higher education for everyone. Again, both should be sources of pride for teachers.

🍎 And while SAT scores may have declined slightly overall between 1975 and 1990, they have gone up for white, African-American, Asian-American, Native-American, Mexican-American, and Puerto Rican students.

🍎 Every one of the subgroups for whom there is data increased its average SAT score over the period when the mean dropped.

🍎 If we consider only those students from 1975 to 1990 who match those who took the SAT in 1975 in terms of demographics variables (rank in high school class, gender, etc.), the scores actually rose significantly.

🍎 Educational Testing Service, developers of the SAT, says today's test is more difficult than in 1975.

MYTH 3: Despite extra efforts and expenditures, the performance of American students on standardized achievement tests reveals gross inadequacies. Reality: According to the National Assessment of Educational Progress (NAEP), which provides tests in math, science, reading, writing, geography, and computer skills to 9-, 13-, and 17-year-olds, scores have registered modest gains since the 1970s.

🍎 NAEP states unequivocally that "the national data on student performance does not indicate a decline in any area." (Emphasis in original.) NAEP concludes that "students today appear to be as well educated as previously educated students."

🍎 It takes a high score now to hit the fiftieth percentile rank in every major assessment test. "Composite achievement in 1984–85 was at an all-time high in nearly all test areas," according to the Iowa Test of Basic Skills. The same trend was found in the Stanford Achievement Test, the Metropolitan Achievement Test, and the Comprehensive Test of Basic Skills.

● As for schools scoring below the national average, because the tests are scored on a bell-curve, 50 percent of schools must fall below the average.

MYTH 4: Money doesn't matter. There is no relationship between amount spent on education and productivity of schools. Reality: Although data correlating SAT scores with money spent by states indicate that the lowest-spending states seem to out perform the highest-spending, the highest spenders have, on average, 11 times higher percentages of their students taking the SAT than the lowest spenders.

● Working with a greater at-risk population, the highest-spending states lost up to 10 items, or about 7 percent of the raw score points on the SAT. But they also posted a 1,150 percent increase in the percent of high school seniors thinking about going to college.

● A 1990 study, examining whether current income could be predicted from characteristics of the public school systems where men received their education during the first half of the century, found that teachers' salaries, class size, and length of the school year were significant predictors of future earnings. States that spent the most produced citizens who earned the most. Another study found that higher salaries attract and retain teaching candidates with higher academic ability.

● Texas study, comparing test data of millions of students in 900 districts, concluded that teachers' academic proficiency explains 20 to 25 percent of variations in achievement test scores, and that teachers with greater experience have students with higher test scores, lower dropout rates, and higher rates of taking the SAT. Teacher experience accounts for about 10 percent of score variations, according to the study. An increase of 10 percent in the number of teachers with nine or more years' experience was predicted to reduce dropout rates by about 4 percent and increase the percentage of students taking the SAT by 3 percent. In grades 1–7, each additional student in excess of 18 caused achievement to fall between 10 and 20 percent of a standard deviation. Also, student scores are positively affected by larger numbers of teachers with master's degrees.

● Thus, research shows that academically more proficient teachers, who are experienced, better educated, and work with smaller classes, are associated with students who demonstrate significantly higher school achievement. It costs money to attract, retain, and provide ongoing professional development for these teachers. And it costs money to maintain effective class size.

MYTH 5: American schools are too expensive. We spend more on education than any other country. Reality: This charge was made by several persons attached to the Bush Administration, but a study of their claims by the Economic Policy Institute of Washington found the figures used to be false.

● According to UNESCO data, the U.S. is tied with Canada and the Netherlands, and all three fall behind Sweden in amount spent per pupil for education in K-12 and higher education.

🍎 Our relatively high rank is because we spend much more than most nations on higher education and have two or three times more people per 100,000 population enrolled in higher education than most other countries. When only pre-primary, primary, and secondary education are considered, however, we actually spend much less than the average industrialized nation.

🍎 We rank ninth among 16 industrialized nations in per-pupil K-12 expenditures, spending 14 percent less than Germany, 30 percent less than Japan, and 51 percent less than Switzerland.

🍎 In terms of percent of per-capita income spent on education, the U.S. is fourteenth among 16 industrialized nations.

🍎 To come up just to the average percentage expended per-capita on education in the 15 other nations, we would have to invest an additional $20 billion per year in K-12 education.

MYTH 6: Our high schools, colleges, and universities are not supplying us with enough mathematicians and scientists to maintain our competitiveness in world markets. Reality: A study by Sandia National Laboratories, using data from the National Science Foundation, shows that from the 1960s to the 1990s, the percent of 22-year-olds receiving science and engineering degrees has remained steady. And, while the actual members continue to be small, more women and minorities now have access to technical jobs.

🍎 According to data from the Graduate Record Examination (GRE), the test taken by most students contemplating post-graduate education, today's college graduates know as much as their predecessors. In fact, the 1980s saw college graduates with higher math skills than ever.

🍎 Since 1982, the measure of analytical and logical reasoning on the GRE, assessing thinking skills, has increased about a third of a standard deviation. And it has gone up while the number of those taking the test has increased 16 percent.

🍎 The Sandia report estimates that even with no increase in the rate of supply, we will accumulate a surplus of about one million engineers and scientists by the year 2010. Continuing military cutbacks could easily increase this figure.

🍎 According to surveys from Michigan and New York, it is the affective and motivational characteristics of workers that employers worry about most. They do not find the technical ability of the work force to be a problem.

MYTH 7: The U.S. is an enormous failure in international comparisons of educational achievement. Reality: In the first International Assessment of Educational Achievement, from which we learned how "awful" the U.S. was doing, the average performance of 75 percent of the American group was compared with average scores of the top 9 percent of students in West Germany, the top 13 percent in the Netherlands, and the top 45 percent in Sweden.

🍎 In the most recent international comparisons of science and math achievement, the U.S. did not do as well as Korea and Taiwan. But about 10 percent of the U.S. students had a year or two less schooling than their Korean and Taiwanese counterparts (accounted for, partially, by longer school years in the latter two nations). Thus, the samples were not equivalent.

- A researcher examining the data behind the Second International Mathematics Study, in which U.S. students fared poorly against the Japanese, found that 75 percent of the students in the U.S. sample had not been exposed to the same level of math instruction as the Japanese students. Adjusting for this discrepancy by comparing the top 20 percent of American students in terms of math ability with the top 20 percent of the Japanese sample, he found the scores of U.S. students as good as or better than those of their Japanese counterparts. The American students were broken out into four groups—remedial, those with typical math backgrounds, those with pre-algebra, and those with algebra. The latter two groups did as well as or better than their Japanese counterparts, all of whom had full exposure to algebra.

- Thus, the differences in achievement between nations are based mainly on differences in national curricula rather than differences in the effectiveness of a particular education system.

- As David C. Berliner points out, "Because we are a nation that is rich enough and democratic enough to attempt to retain our youngsters longer in school, and because we send a comparatively large number of them on to college, we often look poorly in international comparisons. Many of our students learn what they need to learn later than in other countries."

- Student motivation is also a factor. Korean students are taking the test for the honor of their country. In the United States, our students know that neither they, their parents, nor their teacher will ever see the scores they make. It is not an honor to take the test, but an inconvenience.

Equitable Treatment of Girls and Boys in the Classroom

American Association of University Women

"Equitable Treatment of Girls and Boys in the Classroom" is an "issue brief" published by American Association of University Women in 1989. According to its stated goals, "AAUW promotes equity for women, education and self-development over the life span, and positive societal change."

The More Things Change . . .

The major federal statute prohibiting sex discrimination in education, Title IX of the Education Amendments of 1972, was signed into law more than 15 years ago. In following years, Congress authorized funding for model sex equity programs through the Women's Educational Equity Act (WEEA, 1974) and required states to work to eliminate sex bias from their vocational education programs (1976).

Women's education advocates anticipated that these programs would encourage both girls and boys to explore nontraditional fields and place a high priority on school performance and career preparation. They foresaw that the range of occupations considered appropriate for both sexes would be broadened and that, as a result, occupational sex segregation would decline and the pay gap between men and women would narrow in the long run.

Although Title IX has increased women's access to education and many excellent model programs have been created under WEEA and the Vocational Education Act, sex differences in educational preparation and occupational choice persist. For example, even though all vocational programs must now be open to both sexes, 70 percent of all girls in vocational high schools study traditionally female fields.[1] And while women made up 53 percent of all college students by 1987, they still received less than 15 percent of all engineering degrees.[2]

The limited impact of the educational equity programs begun in the 1970s has been due largely to inadequate funding and lack of enforcement, particularly after the U.S. Supreme Court's ruling in *Grove City College v. Bell* in 1984 limited the application of Title IX to specific programs.[3] But perhaps a major factor in blunting their impact are girls' everyday interactions with teachers and other students in the classroom. Too often, classroom dynamics are laced with unconscious sex stereotyping, as when teachers spend more time with boys in math classes and more time with girls in reading classes. Such subtle but powerful messages have been shown to circumscribe girls' and women's choices regarding academic preparation, achievement, and careers.

In the past two years, AAUW and the AAUW Educational Foundation have launched twin initiatives—*Choices for Tomorrow's Women* and the Eleanor Roosevelt Fund for Women

"Equitable Treatment of Girls and Boys in the Classroom," taken from American Association of University Women, June, 1989. Reprinted by permission.

and Girls: Intergenerational Partnerships, respectively—to address the ways women and girls make choices about education, family life, and careers (see "What We Can Do," page 5). This brief, an introductory instrument of those efforts, discusses various theories about the causes of sex differences in academic performance, reviews recent research on sex differences in classroom interaction, and suggests ways to change stubborn patterns of sex discrimination.

Girls, Boys, and Brains

Extensive research shows that girls and boys perform differently on most standardized academic tests. In the U.S. administration of the Second International Science Study test in 1983, for instance, fifth-grade boys scored 6.2 percent higher than the girls. Similarly, in the 1981–1982 National Assessment of Educational Progress high-school girls scored higher in reading, but lower in math and science, than boys.[4]

The test results don't tell us why such differences exist; they could be caused by differential ability, preparation, motivation, or expectations about the probability of success. Theories attempting to explain academic performance differences between girls and boys can be divided roughly into two categories: biological and sociological.

Some researchers have suggested that differences in intellectual functioning are caused by inherited, sex-linked genes or by the effect of sex-linked hormones on brain development before birth and at puberty. Although links have been shown between hormones and brain development, no link to intelligence has been proven. Similarly, there is no physical evidence that intelligence genes exist, whether sex-linked or not. Studies claiming to establish such a biological link typically hypothesize cause based on correlation.

For instance, a much-publicized 1980 study by Camilla Benbow and Julian Stanley was widely reported as proving the existence of "male" math genes. During a John Hopkins University study, groups of mathematically gifted junior-high students were administered the math sections of the Scholastic Aptitude Test. The boys in the study consistently outscored the girls and Benbow and Stanley argued that, since all students take the same sequence of math courses from elementary through junior high school, the difference must be due largely to inherited ability.

But critics were quick to point out that Benbow and Stanley had ignored the informal ways boys and girls learn about math, and had assumed that their experiences with math in the classroom were the same. Other researchers in the same study had investigated the students' backgrounds and found that the boys' parents gave them more encouragement and more math- and science-related experiences.[5]

A boy took some playdough in a pot to the stove, and announced he was cooking. 'Daddies don't cook,' two little girls told him. He backed away, saying, 'My poppy cooks. . .' and looking uncertain. The teacher then told the two girls that daddies sometimes do cook. The boy immediately returned to the stove and started.[42]

One difficulty with research of this sort is finding a measure that will distinguish learned skills from innate ability. In 1974, psychologists Eleanor Maccoby and Carol

Jacklin surveyed this research and concluded that while girls showed slightly more verbal ability, boys had more quantitative and spatial-visualization abilities.[6] But a 1981 study by Janet Hyde pointed out that although those differences were present in the studies reviewed, their magnitude was very small. Sex accounted for less than 5 percent of the differences between boys and girls in verbal, quantitative, and spatial-visualization abilities.[7] In other words, the variation between individuals of either sex is greater than that between the sexes.

Other researchers suggest that gender-role socialization accounts for most of the differences between girls' and boys' academic performance. Gender roles are the range of activities, attitudes, and emotions considered socially appropriate for men and women, and they are learned through interactions with parents, peers, teachers, and other adults, as well as from the print and electronic media. Although children acquire extensive knowledge of gender roles, there are great differences in the extent to which individuals internalize and act out those roles as a part of their identity (masculinity or femininity). One study of math achievement, for instance, found that for students who had enrolled in the same sequence of math courses the difference between girls' and boys' performance on achievement tests was very small; it disappeared altogether when sociocultural factors like parents' attitudes toward the subject and participation in math-related activities—such as building things—were taken into account.[8]

Research suggests that gender-role socialization mediates intellectual achievement in several ways:

● Children learn from parents, teachers, and peers that some activities are inappropriate for their gender, and so they do not consider achievement in those areas possible or desirable. Research shows that parents typically believe that boys do better than girls in advanced math and that they attribute boys' successes in math to talent, but girls' to effort.

● Some of the psychological traits that are differentially acquired during gender-role socialization may be helpful for certain types of learning. In science education, for instance, it is important to explore, to learn by experience, and to take risks—behaviors that are more encouraged in boys than girls.

● Because they are differently socialized, boys and girls follow a different pattern of intellectual development and develop different learning styles, so they respond differently to the same classroom climate. For example, various studies have shown that girls respond better to a cooperative, rather than a competitive, classroom environment, perhaps because their moral development focuses on what psychologist Carol Gilligan calls the "ethic of care."[9]

● Some researchers suggest that these differences are so deeply entrenched that they amount to different sex-role cultures.[10]

Research has also shown that ideas about appropriate gender roles vary between cultures. A 1987 study revealed that girls scored higher than boys in math achievement tests in Hawaii, for instance. The results were most pronounced for Japanese-American, Filipino-American, and native Hawaiian students, suggesting the math achievement is not seen as inimical to the feminine role in those cultures.[11] Other studies found that Asian-American girls receive more parental encouragement and less negative male peer pressure about preparing for math and science careers.[12]

Different cultures may also produce different learning styles. In Asian-American cultures, for instance, it is typically assumed that everyone can learn if they work hard enough: lack of "natural" ability is not an acceptable excuse for failure.

Other researchers have suggested that low-income and minority cultures stress group interaction and cooperation more than white middle-class cultures, which tend to stress individualism and competition.[13] This puts minority girls at a double disadvantage in the classroom.

Teaching the Hidden Curriculum

Research conducted in the past decade has shown that the structure of lessons and the dynamics of classroom interaction all too often create an environment alien, if not hostile, to girls (again, doubly so for girls from certain ethnic groups and social classes). Patterns of differential treatment sometimes are so deeply ingrained that even teachers who strive to be fair and impartial are not aware of all of them. And even when treatment is identical, there may be a negative impact on girls because they may experience it differently than boys.

Schoolrooms

Particularly at the pre-school and kindergarten level, rooms often are arranged into highly gender-stereotyped play areas, such as a cooking corner for girls and a building-blocks corner for boys. This both reinforces the idea that such activities are incompatible and makes crossing over to "gender-inappropriate" activities more difficult.[14]

Teacher-student Interaction

The interaction between teachers and students is interladen with subtle messages that affect girls' self-esteem and sense of identity. Research shows that

- 🍎 minority students of both sexes receive less attention from the teacher, which decreases self-esteem.[15]
- 🍎 teachers believe that the ideal pupil is orderly, conforming, and dependent, traits that are also identified with the "feminine" gender role. A first glance, this would seem to work to the advantage of female students. In fact, it works against them because teachers tend to give less attention to those they think are ideal pupils. Also, teachers' positive reinforcement of this identification discourages girls from more active, assertive learning styles that tend to get students farther in the long run.[16]
- 🍎 boys who do not conform to the ideal pupil role are disciplined, but girls are ignored; this means boys get yet more attention when they misbehave.[17] When both boys and girls are misbehaving, teachers are three times as likely to discipline the boys: this conveys that boys are more important even though the context is negative.[18] This pattern holds true across racial and ethnic lines.

A 1987 study revealed that girls scored higher than boys in math achievement tests in Hawaii. The results were most pronounced for Japanese-American, Filipino-American, and native Hawaiian students, suggesting that math achievement is not seen as inimical to the feminine role in those cultures.[11]

- 🍎 teachers initiate 10 percent more communication with boys in the classroom, again strengthening their sense of dominance and importance.[19]
- 🍎 teachers ask boys more complex, abstract, and open-ended questions, which provide better opportunities for active learning.[20]
- 🍎 regarding class projects and assignments, teachers are more likely to give detailed instructions to boys and more likely to take over and finish the task for girls, again depriving them of active learning.[21]
- 🍎 teachers spend more time with girls in reading classes and more time with boys in math classes.[22]
- 🍎 ninety percent of the praise for boys' schoolwork is directed at the intellectual content and quality of their work, rather than form or neatness, compared to 80 percent for girls.[23]
- 🍎 nearly 90 percent of the criticism of girls' schoolwork is directed at the intellectual content and quality of their work, compared to 50 percent for boys.[24] (See chart on page 2).
- 🍎 when teachers criticize boys, they often tell them that their failings are due to lack of effort. Girls are not given this message, the absence of which implies that effort would not improve their results.[25]

Student-Student Interaction

The social relationships between students—patterns of work and play that reflect their understanding of appropriate and desirable behavior—are typically much more gender-stereotyped than teacher-student relationships. Students' social relationships often reinforce the messages that girls are less capable and have fewer career choices than boys. Research shows that

- 🍎 classroom interaction between boys and girls is highly infrequent from preschool through junior high school; thus, stereotypes about sex-segregated activities are reinforced.[26]
- 🍎 during high school, girls typically increase their motivation to form relationships and decrease their motivation to achieve academically, which affects crucial education and career choices they make at that time.[27]
- 🍎 when classes are divided into groups by ability, boys with high math achievement scores are more likely than girls with similar scores to be assigned to the high-ability group.[28]
- 🍎 within math groups, girls who ask questions of their peers are answered only by other girls; boys who ask questions are answered by both boys and girls.[29]
- 🍎 when boys and girls work together on science projects, girls spend four times as much time watching and listening, and 25 percent less time manipulating the equipment involved, than boys.[30]

This web of relationships, reflecting unconscious and largely unexamined assumptions about the different capabilities and appropriate roles of men and women, has been called the "hidden curriculum."

Lifelong Lessons

The hidden curriculum encourages boys to be more autonomous, to find out things for themselves, and to develop their own abilities and resources. On the other hand, it encourages girls to be more dependent, to wait to hear answers rather than discover them, and to rely on the teacher for guidance. These patterns have far-reaching consequences.

Self-esteem

One result of these patterns is that girls are much more likely to believe that lack of ability causes inadequacies in their school performance, while boys are more likely to believe lack of effort causes their failures. Whereas effort is something a child can control, ability is seen as immutable. Thus, girls' self-esteem and motivation to succeed are undercut.

Girls are particularly likely to believe that they lack ability in areas stereotyped as more appropriate for boys. Girls tend to attribute failures in math and science tasks to lack of ability, for instance, while attributing failures in language arts to inadequate effort.[31]

Independence

Girls do not have as much opportunity to work independently as boys do, and therefore lose the chance to develop habits and skills critical to academic and professional success: taking the initiative, problem-solving, taking risks, persisting despite setbacks, manipulating tools and equipment, and leading groups. These habits and skills are particularly important for science careers.

The children were making paper baskets; the handles had to be stapled in place. The teacher moved around the room, showing the boys how to use the stapler and holding the handle while the boys used the stapler. When the girls asked for assistance, the teacher took the basket and stapled it for them.[43]

Achievement motivation

Girls interest in higher education and nontraditional careers peaks when they are 13 years old. Throughout high school, boys' ambitions steadily increase while girls' decline.[32] Research suggests that the motivation to achieve depends at least partly on an expectation of success. The low self-esteem created when girls believe they are less able than boys, particularly in male-dominated fields, also reduces their motivation to succeed. In addition, girls recognize that lingering sex discrimination in higher education and the workplace means that the cost of success will be higher for them, which further reduces the incentive to try.[33]

Occupational choices

Children learn occupational segregation as young as two or three, and these ideas are continuously reinforced by schoolbooks and the media, as well as by teachers' expectations and patterns of interaction at school.[34] By high school, girls' career choices are highly sex-segregated compared with boys'.[35] Because female-dominated occupations are typically paid much less than male-dominated ones, this pattern of occupational choice contributes to the cycle of poverty for women.

Rewriting the Script

Guaranteeing access to education and employment is not enough to end gender stereotyping and provide girls with opportunities for success. The subtle, discouraging messages girls receive everyday about their roles and potential choices must be changed to ones of possibility and achievement. This is especially true for minority and immigrant girls, who will be 29 percent of the new workers in the work force between now and the year 2000.[36]

To foster girls' self-confidence and serious consideration of a range of career choices, parents need to encourage their daughters to be independent, to explore, and to experiment—even if it means they will occasionally get dirty or hurt. Girls need to be provided with toys such as building blocks, erector sets, and chemistry sets, which encourage facility with spatial relationships and mechanics, as well as with traditional girls' toys.

Schools must provide equal access to all resources for girls and boys. This may involve rearranging classrooms, placing, for example, building blocks and cooking toys in the same area. It also means providing a variety of role models in everything from faculty and staff hiring to textbook selection to the designation of speakers at assemblies.

Schools can also provide special programs to help girls make wise choices. The Hispanic Mother-Daughter Program at Arizona State University in Tempe, Arizona, for instance, brings mothers and daughters together for visits to local colleges and universities, classroom exercises in career choices, and presentations by professionals from the community.

Teachers can help by providing opportunities in class lessons and discussions for girls and boys to learn to identify gender-role stereotypes and how those stereotypes limit their lives. Teachers can also thwart the informal structures of sex segregation by encouraging girls to play with equipment that is *de facto* reserved for boys, and vice versa.

Structuring group projects in ways that ensure girls an equal opportunity to participate is another way teachers can defeat the insidious effects of the hidden curriculum. Although boys typically dominate mixed-sex groups, research has shown that when teachers are trained to set up equitable group projects, girls and boys spend roughly equal amounts of time actively engaged in manipulating the equipment involved.[37]

Researchers have suggested that girls might do better work in classrooms that use cooperative learning techniques, particularly in math.[38] In cooperative learning, students are divided into small groups that work together on a particular subject. Individual students are tested regularly, and groups compete for prizes based on overall group improvement.[39]

Teachers also need to be trained to be sensitive to girls' special needs regarding conflicts between "appropriate" gender roles and wise career choices. Minority and immigrant girls may be struggling with other cultural norms as well. In addition, teachers must learn to praise and criticize the same behaviors by girls and boys consistently, and encourage girls to develop intellectual independence. Such habits and skills can be developed through in-service training such as the Gender-Ethnic Expectations and Student Achievement program initiated in 1984 by the Los Angeles, California, school system. This program trains selected teachers in equity concepts and strategies for overcoming bias in the classroom and sends them back to their school districts as peer trainers for other teachers.

Training in equitable teaching techniques should be included in every teacher education program and required for certification, but many schools of education have dropped sex equity from their agendas. One good resource in this area is the *Sex Equity Handbook for Schools*, a textbook on non-sexist teaching. The handbook was published under the aegis of the Non-Sexist Teacher Education Project, which was funded under the WEEA in 1978–79 to develop teacher education materials on sex-equitable treatment.

What We Can Do

Help to ensure our daughters' futures by joining in these recent AAUW initiatives.

Choices for Tomorrow's Women aims to empower women and girls to make appropriate life choices. Under *Choices for Tomorrow's Women*. AAUW branches and divisions across the country are working with broad coalitions of allies to break down the institutional barriers that limit the choices of women and girls and provide second chances when inadequate choices were made the first time around.

The AAUW Educational Foundation's **Eleanor Roosevelt Fund for Women and Girls: Intergenerational Partnerships** was established to encourage original research and action to eliminate barriers to girls' and women's participation in education, promote the value of diversity and cross-cultural communication, and gain and disseminate a greater understanding of how women and girls think, learn, work, and play. As its first action project, the fund is sponsoring Teacher Enrichment Sabbaticals that will provide elementary and secondary school teachers the opportunity to improve their effectiveness with at-risk girls and with girls in math and science courses. Within a couple of years, AAUW branches and divisions will be helping to put research conducted under the fund's auspices into practice in schools in their communities.

Within these initiatives you can

- plan a branch program on changing the patterns of differential treatment of girls and boys in the classroom. Invite teachers, administrators, school board members, professors from schools of education, and/or students to participate in the meeting.
- build broad coalitions—including AAUW college/university member institutions that conduct teacher training and/or pedagogical research—in your community around issues of equal access and treatment in education. Use this brief as an initial resource.
- present information on these issues at a Parent-Teacher Association (PTA) meeting. A

student-teacher forum on differential treatment in the classroom is one way to approach the subject.

● present information on these issues to the school board, and ask to work with them on strategies for attacking the problem.

● support the Fund for Women and Girls and encourage teachers in your community to apply for a Teacher Enrichment Sabbatical (for application information, please contact the Fund for Women and Girls, AAUW Educational Foundation, address below: 202/728–7603).

● sponsor a conference or workshop—for teachers, students, or the entire community—presenting research on differential treatment in the classroom, especially that conducted by Fund for Women and Girls sabbatical research awardees. Invite local university and public school faculty as speakers.

● donate materials on gender-role stereotyping and sex bias—including this brief—to the schools for use in curriculum development and the classroom. Provide training materials in sex-equitable teaching techniques to your school system.

● present awards to teachers who use sex-equitable teaching techniques.

During a first-grade testing period, each child was instructed to find the correct page in a seven-page testing booklet and fold the booklet back so only that page showed. When girls who had finished the task saw classmates who were having trouble doing it, they got up, did the task for them, and sat back down. No boys offered to help another child, and no one thanked the girls for their help.[44]

● work to have sex-equitable teaching techniques added to the curriculum of your *alma mater* and teacher treatment training institutions in your area and to requirements for teacher certification in your state. Contact your state board of education for information on those requirements and how they may be changed.

● seek support for your efforts by applying for an AAUW Educational Foundation Research & Projects (R&P) Grant. Funding available for 1989–90 includes Issue Focus Grants for projects emphasizing math and science enrichment for girls, mentoring for girls and women, or parenting and family education. For application information, please contact R&P Grants, AAUW Educational Foundation: 202/728–7609. (Please note that not all of the ideas listed above are necessarily R&P Grant-eligible activities.)

● apply for a WEEA project grant from the U.S. Department of Education. This grants program aims to promote equity for girls and women at all levels of education, preschool through adult. The 28 projects funded this year include efforts to develop and evaluate educational materials, establish model programs for educational personnel, perform research and development activities, and provide guidance and counseling services. Contact your state board of education for further information.

● support funding for WEEA, which must be appropriated by the U.S. Congress annually. To keep informed of federal action, subscribe to *Action Alert*, AAUW's legislative newsletter ($20/AAUW members, $25/nonmembers; send check or money order to *Action Alert* Subscription).

In one science class, children were divided into groups to work on constructing an electrical switch. When some of the girls had difficulty assembling their equipment, the teacher repeatedly told them to 'go and ask the boys for help.'[45]

A Different Equity

In a pluralistic society such as ours there are many different cultures—defined by intersections of gender, class, ethnicity, location, and other affiliations—which foster different learning styles. Too often, classrooms and teaching techniques are geared to meet the strengths of only one learning style; the learning styles of boys are accommodated over those of girls, just as the intellectual habits of some cultural minorities are catered to more than others by our schools.

Already, 45 percent of our work force is female, including 51 percent of mothers of children under the age of 3.[40] And by 2020, almost 40 percent of our citizens will be minorities.[41] Clearly, the future of the United States will rest largely on our ability to create learning environments that provide equal encouragement, resources, and opportunities to girls and boys from all backgrounds. This brief was prepared by Kathy Vandell, Research Associate, Program and Policy Department, and Lauren Fishbein, Senior Editor, Communications Department, with special thanks to Janice Earle, Director, Center on Education Equity, National Association of State Boards of Education.

Endnotes

1. National Commission on Working Women, "Women, Work and the Future," (Washington, DC: Wider Opportunities for Women, 1988). n.p.
2. National Center for Education Statistics, *1988Education Indicators* (Washington, DC: Government Printing Office, 1988), p. 122: National Center for Education Statistics, *Digest of Education Statistics 1987* (Washington, DC: Government Printing Office, 1988), p. 176.
3. *The Grove City College* v. *Bell* ruling eventually was vitiated by the U.S. Congress' passage (and override of President Ronald Reagan's veto) of the Civil Rights Restoration Act in February 1988, and the Department of Justice is once again accepting for review complaints filed under Title IX.
4. National Center for Education Statistics, *Digest of Education Statistics 1988* (Washington, DC: Government Printing Office, 1989), pp. 102–107: Dyanne Tracy. "Toys, Spatial Ability, and Science and Mathematics Achievement," *Sex Roles* 17 (August 1987), p. 132
5. Camilla Benbow and Julian Stanley, "Sex Differences in Mathematical Ability: Fact or Artifact?" *Science* 210 (1980), pp. 1262–64: Anne Fausto-Sterling, *Myths of Gender* (New York: Basic Books, 1985), Chapter 2.
6. Eleanor Maccoby and Carol Nagy Jacklin, *The Psychology of Sex Differences* (Stanford, CA: Stanford University Press, 1974), Chapter 3.
7. Janet Hyde, "How Large Are Cognitive Gender Differences?" *American Psychologist* 36 (August 1981), p. 894.
8. Elizabeth Fennema and Julia Sherman, "Sex-Related Differences in Mathematics Achievements: Spatial Visualization and Affective Factors," *American Educational Research Journal* 14 (Winter 1977), pp. 65–66.
9. Kirsten Goldberg, "Among Girls,'Ethic of Caring' May Stifle Classroom Competitiveness, Study Shows," *Education Week*, April 27, 1988, pp.1, 24.
10. Patrick Lee and Nancy Gropper, "Sex-Role Culture and Educational Practice." *Harvard Educational Review* 44 (August 1974), pp. 370–371.
11. P.R. Brandon, et al., "Children's Mathematics Achievement in Hawaii: Sex Differences Favoring Girls," *American Education Research Journal* 24 (1987), p. 457.
12. James Campbell and Charlene Connolly, {Deciphering the Effects of Socialization,"*Journal of Educational Equity and Leadership* 7 (Fall 1987), pp. 221–222.

13. Dionne Jones, "Cognitive Styles: Sex and Ethnic Differences," paper presented at the Annual Meeting of the American Educational Research Association, Washington DC., November 13–15 1986; "Self-Interest and the Common Weal," *Education Week*, April 27, 1988, p. 18.
14. Lee and Gropper, pp. 390–392.
15. Myra and David Sadker, *Sex Equity Handbook for Schools* (New York: Longman, 1982), p. 105.
16. Lee and Gropper, op. cit., p. 389.
17. Idid., pp. 389–390.
18. Sadker and Sadker, op. cit., p. 103.
19. Jacquelynne Eccles and Phylis Blumenfield, "Classroom Experience and Student Gender: Are There Differences and Do They Matter?" In *Gender Influences in Classroom Interaction*, eds. Louise Cherry Wilkinson and Cora B. Marret (Orlando: Academic Press, 1985), p. 84.
20. Sadker and Sadker, op. cit., p. 105.
21. Ibid. p. 105.
22. Gaea Leinhardt, Andrea Seewalk, and Mary Engel, "Learning What's Taught: Sex Differences in Instruction." *Journal of Educational Psychology*, 71 (1979), p. 437.
23. Sadker and Sadker, op. cit., pp. 108–109.
24. Ibid.
25. Ibid. p. 109.
26. Marlaine Lockheed and Abigaile Harris, "Cross-Sex Collahorative Learning in Elementary Classrooms." *American Education Research Journal* 221 (Summer 1984), p. 279.
27. Lee and Gropper, op. cit., pp. 383–4.
28. Maureen Hallinen and Aage Sorensen, "Ability Grouping and Sex Differences in Mathematics Achievement," *Sociology of Education* 60 (1987), p. 67.
29. Lockheed and Harris, op. cit., p. 291.
30. Leonie Rennie and Lesley Parker, "Detecting and Accounting for Gender Differences in Mixed-Sex and Single-Sex Grouping in Science Lessons," *Educational Review* 39 (1987), pp. 67–68.
31. David Ryckman and Percy Peckham, "Gender Differences in Attributions for Success and Failure Situations Across Subject Areas," *Journal of Educational Research* 81 (December 1987), pp. 123–124.
32. Margaret Marini, "Sex Differences in the Determination of Adolescent Aspiration: A Review of Research," *Sex Rules* 4 (October 1978), p. 728.
33. Jacquelynne Eccles, "Gender Roles and Women's Achievement Related Decisions," *Psychology of Women Quarterly* 11 (1987).
34. Linda Gettys and Arnie Cann, "Children's Perceptions of Occupational Stereotypes," *Sex Roles*, 7 (1981), pp. 303–4.
35. Marini, op. cit., p. 729.
36. National Commission on Working Women, op. cit.
37. Rennie and Parker, op. cit., pp. 67–8.
38. Eccles, op. cit., pp. 158–9.
39. Robert Slavin, "Cooperative Learning and the Cooperative School," *Educational Leadership* (November 1987).
40. U.S. Department of Labor, Bureau of Labor Statistics, *Projections 2000* (Washington DC: Government Printing Office, March 1988); National Commission on Working Women, op.cit.
41. American Council on Education and Education Commission of the States, *One-Third of a Nation: A Report of the Commission on Minority Participation in Education and American Life* (Washington, DC: May 1988), p. 3.
42. Lee and Gropper, op. cit., pp. 402–403.
43. Sadker and Sadker, op. cit., p. 105.
44. Raphaela Best, *We've All Got Scars: What Boys and Girls Learn in Elementary School* (Bloomington: Indiana University Press, 1983), p.89.
45. Rennie and Parker, op. cit., p. 72.

This brief was prepared by Kathy Vandell, Research Associate, Program and Public Policy Department, and Layren Fishbein, Senior Editor, Communications Department, with special thanks to Janice Earle, Director, Center on Education Equality, National Association of State Boards of Education.

Toward the Improvement of Education

David C. Berliner and Bruce J. Biddle _____

David C. Berliner is a professor of Curriculum and Instruction at Arizona State University, and Bruce J. Biddle is a professor at the University of Missouri. The following selection contains excerpts from a chapter from their book, *The Manufactured Crisis: Myths, Fraud, and the Attack on America's Public Schools*, 1995. In the preface to their book, Berliner and Biddle explain, "we profoundly hope that this effort will . . . encourage the reemergence of more humane and honest dialogues concerning American education."

On Dignity and Hope

Principle: Schooling in America can be improved by according parents more dignity and their children more hope.

Where there is no vision, the people perish.

—Proverbs 29:18

In his book *Savage Inequalities* Jonathan Kozol wrote about a New York City school in terrible distress. One of us had a very personal response to the conditions he described. Tears came to that reader's eyes because it was the school he had attended from kindergarten through ninth grade. It was always an ugly school, serving the poor, and that certainly has not changed. But now, because of worse poverty and more unemployment, lawlessness in the neighborhood, and reduced funding for social services and education, the school that had served so many, so well, for so many years, is now barely functioning at all. Two features of this sad situation stand out: the tragic loss of dignity among families in the area; and the decline of hope among the students who now attend this school.

People in the neighborhood around this school have always been poor. Indeed, few adults who grew up in this working-class area would say they had a glorious past, although their memories of childhood are often quite positive. This is possible because through the decades of the forties and fifties the average working-class family near this school functioned in ways that provided most parents with a modicum of dignity. Jobs were available for the men (the primary wage earners in those days), and those jobs paid enough for families to afford a basic

D. C. Berliner/B. J. Biddle, THE MANUFACTURED CRISIS, © 1995 David C. Berliner & Bruce J. Biddle. Reprinted by permission of Addison-Wesley Publishing Company, Inc.

apartment. Also, women were able to stretch their husbands' dollar incomes by doing a good deal of unpaid labor. Thus, in spite of their limited finances, these families were able to provide food, shelter, clothing, and medical care for their families. Furthermore, the growth of the economy gave them some optimism about their lives and their families' futures.

Streets were also a lot safer for children in those days, and children in those families were led to believe that they would do better in life than their parents had. Almost everyone in the neighborhood thought that better days were ahead. Affordable higher education, better jobs and higher incomes, improved housing, and a secure if not luxurious retirement—all of this seemed to be within the reach of people who strived and persevered. In those days, then, parents had dignity and their children had hope, and this meant that children in the neighborhood had good reason to attend school and to work hard there. Educating those children was actually an easy task (although teachers in the school may not have thought so at the time). But what is it like in the neighborhood today?

Today, there are very few job opportunities in the area; the few jobs now available are likely to be part-time, to pay low wages, to provide few fringe benefits, and to offer no opportunities for advancement. Single mothers struggle to provide for their children and, in the absence of affordable child-care facilities, are sometimes forced to leave their children unattended in order to go to work. Even two employed parents find it difficult to make ends meet and often have to make do without health or retirement benefits. Well-maintained apartments near the school are difficult to find, and even the most neglected apartments are very expensive. Recreational, health, and other support facilities are rare in the neighborhood, and few people can afford the cost of transportation to find them elsewhere. But these people are *Americans*, and like everyone else in the country, they have been exposed repeatedly to media images of successful living. Thus, because their community lacks the social services, the job opportunities, and the standard of living that are found elsewhere, the parents of school-children in this neighborhood have very little dignity.

Young people in the neighborhood also have little hope. Some have no legal source of income and, as a result, get involved in theft, prostitution, violence, and drug pushing. Since their parents have little dignity, family ties are weak, and these young people often turn to gangs for social support. And since sport and recreational facilities are rarely available, they lead boring lives and are attracted to illegal activities. Also, their school is miserably funded, most of their academic records are mediocre, and few care about finishing high school— never mind going on to college. Most youths in the neighborhood also believe, correctly, that the cost of a college education is beyond their means and that scholarships for needy students are very rare. Thus, the everyday activities of their lives provide no vision of a better life for these young people, and they find it difficult to think of paths by which they might "make it" in the mainstream of American society. So they become angry, embittered, alienated—and too often they end up in prison or the morgue. And since parents who now live in the neighborhood have little dignity and their children lack hope, motivating those children in school is a much, much harder task.

For decades social scientists have studied what happens to families when they lose dignity and hope. Unexpected loss of jobs in the family can generate lowered self-esteem, disruption of respect and commitment, alcoholism, spouse and child abuse, divorce, crime, vandalism, lower achievement in schools, and other symptoms of dysfunction. Researchers have also found that when previously stable families from Eastern Europe or Puerto Rico came as impoverished immigrants to our country they had a very difficult time.[3] In fact, it has often taken a generation or more for such immigrant groups to regain a sense of personal dignity and family stability, although these processes have also been affected by the ethnic stereotypes, discriminatory practices, educational opportunities, and socio-economic conditions prevailing when they arrived.[4]

As our example from New York City suggests, these serious problems afflict not only individuals and families today but neighborhoods and whole communities in our country. Unfortunately, this fact is ignored by many critics and politicians, who like to pretend that problems in our schools and communities result solely from a "lack of family values." They contend that families no longer seem to be working. This is, in fact, a favorite theme of former Vice President Dan Quayle, who has often decried a "loss of family values" throughout the nation. Critics like Quayle are partly right—families are *not* working in America, that is, literally, *not working*. In too many American families, *no* member of the family has been able to find meaningful, legal, remunerative work—or, if someone is employed, that person works only on a part-time basis or at a job that pays less than the minimum wage, provides no health-care or retirement benefits, and offers only a bleak future. In addition, in too many cases the children of those families have few reasons to expect their lives to improve. These harsh realities are *real* causes of educational failure in our nation.

The achievement levels of our poorest and most alienated students will not be raised by lectures about responsibility from the critics, setting higher standards, or developing better tests (as recommended by our federal government and by many state legislatures). And school vouchers, another vacuous "solution" now being touted by Speaker of the House of Representatives Newt Gingrich, will not rescue impoverished families from despair. Rather, a decent standard of living, social services, jobs, and reasons to hope for the future are needed to improve the lives of those families and their students' educational achievements.

Hope and School Achievement

The importance of dignity and hope for educational achievement has recently been demonstrated in findings from a massive research project, the National Education Longitudinal Study (NELS). NELS researchers examined changes in achievement and a host of other factors for about 25,000 nationally representative students who were in the eighth grade in 1988. The students were followed through twelfth grade (in 1992), but to the best of our knowledge only the data for eighth and tenth grades have been reported so far.

One recent analysis of NELS data explored factors in families and among students that might predict student achievement.[5] When a host of such factors were examined, the *largest* effect found was for a characteristic called "student ambition and plans for the future." Students who had hopeful but realistic visions for themselves as successful in the future achieved well; those who had weaker visions did not. (Some associated factors also predicted student achievement: parental expectations for achievement, time spent doing home work, parental monitoring of friends and activities, and school-attendance rate; but these were weaker effects. Whether the student did or did not attend a private school or came from a single-parent family did *not* predict achievement.) Essentially, then, when children have strong visions for their futures, they achieve more. A strong vision for the future—hope—is a major predictor of learning!

Doing Something About It

As we know, poverty is now a *lot* worse in America than in other Western countries, and the problem of poverty has become much worse in the past decade. Thus, in all too many American neighborhoods parents have indeed lost dignity and children have little hope. From the small towns of Appalachia to inner-city ghettos and barrios—from depressed rural communities to defunct industrial towns and many native-American reservations—indeed, in perhaps a quarter of the neighborhoods of our land—dignity and hope are threatened because of widespread unemployment, poorly paying jobs, lack of social services, and despair. What can we Americans do about such devastating problems?

Actually, we can do a lot of useful things. For one thing, we can take steps that are common in other Western countries to generate greater equity in incomes. Raising and extending the minimum wage is a good place to begin. The federal minimum wage is presently set at a very low figure and has never been applied to more than a portion of the jobs in the country, in part because investors are greedy for immediate profit, and in part because few voices are willing to speak up for poorly paid workers. But shouldn't responsible people be worrying about how long a consumer economy can last *without consumers*? It is the height of folly for our nation to be *reducing* the purchasing power of its less prosperous citizens, but that is exactly what we have been doing since the early 1980s. Not only does this mean that many of our citizens now cannot meet their basic needs, but it is a terribly shortsighted policy in an economy that demands consumer spending for its maintenance.

Other actions can also be taken that will help to improve job prospects for more Americans. As a rule, American industries choose to pay overtime wages instead of hiring more employees (who would require additional fringe benefits), but such policies are prohibited by law in many countries. Other industrialized countries require that full fringe benefits also be paid for part-time workers. Many other advanced countries require business and industries to pay for four weeks or more of vacation each year, to provide "refresher leave" programs, to fund the costs of retraining programs for workers whose jobs have been terminated, and to allow workers to retire with full benefits after a specific term of employment. Some countries have cut the work week to thirty-six or thirty-two hours, and others provide tax-funded employment programs for youth, workers in communities where industries have disappeared, and other population groups known to be "at risk" for unemployment. If we were to take steps such as these, *many* more Americans would be able to find full-time, secure jobs.

In addition, most advanced countries use various mechanisms to redistribute income from well-off to less well-off people. Many governments mandate that employers pay equal wages for jobs of comparable worth, regardless of who may be doing those jobs. Most industrialized countries employ a progressive income tax system that truly takes a larger tax bite from the best-paid workers in the land. Most advanced countries use their taxation systems to provide more social services to alleviate problems for poor citizens. For example, *all* other Western countries have national health-care systems that are at least partly financed through taxes; and, as a result, those countries pay a *lot* less for health care, have *lower* rates for many diseases, and, on average, live *longer* lives than do Americans. Most advanced countries also use taxes to finance fully paid maternity leave, free day-care centers for infants, community health and recreation facilities, and a guaranteed minimum income for all people who are unemployed. Most also provide better support for their colleges and universities through taxes; and many offer extensive, tax-supported, scholarship programs that pay the bulk of higher-education costs for talented but less well-off students. Clearly, services such as these could be provided in our country and would help to redistribute income and improve the lives of America's neediest citizens.

Here is one illustration of this effect. Several years ago one of us participated in research that compared the activities of inner-city youth in Australia and the United States who had dropped out of school. The values and interests of the two groups of young people were nearly identical, but the activities they reported doing were sharply different. Australia uses taxes to fund many recreational facilities in inner-city areas, and the Australian youngsters reported using those facilities regularly. America provides few such resources, of course, and the American kids (who said they *wanted* access to such facilities) reported much higher rates of boredom and illegal conduct. (All of which makes us wonder about the sanity of those in Congress who so vigorously opposed funding for "midnight basketball" and other recreation programs for inner-city youths in the recently passed national crime bill.)

It is not healthy for our nation to be so divided between haves and have-nots! The supposedly egalitarian United States of America is beginning to look more and more like the oligarchies of Central America and South America that we once derided. If concentrating the wealth among the few is allowed to continue, this nation will see the same kind of social unrest that has marked other nations for decades. Our country now has more private security guards than public safety officers, and this is just one of the inevitable outcomes of this kind of unequal distribution of wealth. In contrast, by redistributing income, increasing the number of job opportunities, and providing more social services, we could assure that more people in our country would experience or aspire to middle-class life styles; and this would accord more families the dignity and hope they need. Surely this would also mean greater student achievement, because children in the nation's poorer neighborhoods would then come to their schools with a sense of hope and a desire to learn. Schooling is, after all, about the future. To paraphrase the biblical quotation with which we opened this section, "When students have no vision, school achievements perish."

Prejudice, Dignity, and Hope

Although poverty, poor job prospects, and inadequate social services are prime reasons why families lose dignity and hope, other reasons why families lose dignity and hope, other reasons can also be cited—particularly the destructive influences of prejudice and discrimination. To illustrate, highly educated African Americans and Hispanic Americans regularly face outrageous indignities. An African American professor of religion at Princeton, Cornel West, recently described an experience he had in New York City:

[I] stood on the corner of 60th Street and Park Avenue to catch a taxi. I felt quite relaxed since I had an hour until my next engagement. . . . I waited and waited and waited. After the ninth taxi refused me my blood began to boil. The tenth taxi refused me and stopped for a kind, well-dressed smiling female fellow citizen of European descent. As she stepped in the cab, she said, "This is really ridiculous, is it not?"

Ugly racial memories of the past flashed through my mind. Years ago, while driving from New York to teach at Williams College, I was stopped on fake charges of trafficking cocaine. When I told the police officer I was a professor of religion, he replied "Yeh, and I'm the Flying Nun. Let's go nigger!" I was stopped three times in my first ten days in Princeton for driving too slowly on a residential street with a speed limit of twenty-five miles per hour. . . . The memories cut like a merciless knife at my soul as I waited on that godforsaken corner. Finally I decided to take the subway.[7]

Prejudice, stereotyping, racist jokes and the like rob even the most affluent minority family of dignity, and they keep less affluent minority families in castelike servitude and perpetual anger. The pervasive prejudice in our society against people of color engenders a kind of nihilism among them—feelings of hopelessness and that life is without meaning. Indeed, Cornel West continues.

The major enemy of black survival in America has been and is neither oppression nor exploitation but rather the nihilistic threat—that is, loss of hope and absence of meaning. For as long as hope remains and meaning is preserved, the possibility of overcoming oppression stays alive. The self-fulfilling prophecy of the nihilistic threat is that without hope there can be no future, that without meaning there can be no struggle.[8]

Ultimately, prejudice corrodes all Americans. It harms African Americans, Asian Americans, Hispanics, Native Americans, and other minority victims *directly* by robbing them of dignity and hope. In addition, it harms other Americans in *indirect* but serious ways. For example, it prevents many citizens from recognizing that the children of poverty—often of a different color and ethnicity—are *their* children too. Thus, prejudice prevents otherwise decent people from embracing a broader community, which hurts us all. Too often the children we ignore today—the "throwaway" children—become tomorrow's flotsam and jetsam, who can only command our attention when we have to spend precious resources imprisoning them or coping with the real threats they represent to our safety and economic welfare. But even if we are lucky, those same children will eventually become tomorrow's workers, part of the community on whom we must depend to help support us in our old age. Eventually, as Malcolm X once warned, "The chickens will come home to roost."[9]

Summary

It is clear, then, that the difficulties faced by many of our schools are closely tied to problems in their local communities—problems that are, in turn, a reflection of unwise social policies in the nation. Widespread poverty, inadequate job prospects, and lack of social services all contribute to loss of dignity in many families in the country and, therefore, to loss of hope among children. This is especially so for the most vulnerable of our citizens, those who must endure the additional burdens of prejudice. Given these facts, "school improvement" often really requires improvement in the overall quality of life of the members of the community. Unfortunately, many federal and state politicians seem disinterested in this message. They ignore it at our collective peril.

On Money and Equality in School Funding

Principle: *Schooling in America can be improved by making certain that all schools have funds needed to provide a decent education for their students. This will require more fairness in school funding.*

If the New York City schools were funded . . . at the level of the highest spending suburbs of Long Island, a fourth grade class of 36 children . . . would have had $200,000 *more* invested in their education during 1987. [This extra money] would have been enough to hire two extraordinary teachers at enticing salaries of $50,000 each, divide the class into *two classes* of some 18 children each, provide them with computers, carpets, air conditioning, new texts and reference books, and learning games—indeed with everything available today in the most affluent school districts—and also pay the costs of extra counseling to help those children cope with the dilemmas that they face at home. Even the most skeptical detractor of the "worth of spending further money in the public schools" would hesitate, I think, to face a grade-school teacher in the South Bronx and try to tell her that "this wouldn't make much difference."

—Jonathan Kozol (*Savage Inequalities*, 1991. pp. 123–124)

What the best and wisest parent wants for his own child, that must be what the community wants for all of its children. Any other ideal for our schools is narrow and unlovely; acted upon, it destroys our democracy.

—John Dewey (*The School and Society*, 1900, p. 3)

In addition to the serious problems that poor neighborhoods pose for their schools, those schools also face a huge additional burden. All too often in America they are funded at substandard levels. As we made clear earlier, our country now tolerates HUGE differences in levels of support for its public schools. In some states, schools in rich suburban districts may receive *five times* as much, or more, per-student funding than is provided to schools in poor, inner-city or rural, districts. Thus, our nation operates a viciously discriminatory system of public education that allows the sons and daughters of wealth to attend far better schools than those available for the children of poverty. This system reflects our custom of tying a good deal of school funding to local school taxes, and, as a result, school quality and student achievement are shortchanged for the poor. Such inequitable school funding normally does *not* exist in other advanced countries.

The Effects of Better School Funding:

Is it actually true that student achievement would rise if funding for schools in poor neighborhoods could be increased and those funds were used in appropriate ways? Good but indirect evidence supports this idea.

As we know from Chapter 3, recent studies now show that school funding affects student achievement in ways that are independent of the effects of parental and community affluence; but this does not mean that we yet know what would happen if a sample of impoverished schools were given reasonable financial support. If Jonathan Kozol is to be believed, that extra support would enable those schools to repair their dangerous buildings, buy long-needed equipment for instruction and recreation, build classrooms to relieve overcrowding, and hire enough teachers to cover core subjects. This would surely improve the morale and achievement of students in those schools. But alas, to the best of our knowledge, nobody seems yet to have funded the experiment that would confirm these ideas.

Mind you, the students in those hypothetical, experimental schools would still, on average, come from impoverished families, so most of them would not have the higher levels of home support for education that middle- and upper-class families can provide. Thus, one would predict only a modest rise in their achievement. This suggests that nontraditional, supplementary programs may be needed if schools that serve impoverished students are truly to help their youngsters "make it" into the mainstream of American life. Various efforts *have* appeared that explore this idea.

For example, in 1981 Eugene Lang, a self-made millionaire, came back to the New York City elementary school he had attended half a century earlier. He was there to give the sixth-grade commencement address. But now this East Harlem school was filled with extremely poor African American children. In an off-hand remark at the end of his talk, Lang promised the children that if they finished high school and got into college he would pay their tuition. One might think he was making an idle offer, but Lang became intrigued by the challenge his promise represented and decided to help the children take advantage of it. He also believed that these impoverished children needed tutoring, counseling, guidance, and friendship; so he set up an "I Have a Dream" Foundation, which provided these forms of supplementary help.

So what happened? The program has had effects that can only be described as amazing. As of March, 1993,

> Six students have bachelor's degrees, and 30 others are attending college. In all, at least 45 students graduated from high school or obtained equivalency diplomas. . . . For P.S. 121, one of the worst schools in a bad system, the record is stunning. School authorities [had] told Lang in 1981 that he would be lucky if two of his students graduated from high school.[10]

Why has the program had its amazing success? Eugene Lang has suggested that the college scholarship he offered was only part of the picture. Indeed, it may not have been as important as the personal involvement of mentors, himself included, who cared for the children over the next six years of their lives. Those six dangerous years on the streets of East Harlem were successfully negotiated by this group of young people because someone gave them and their families the hope and resources to help them realize their dreams. Moreover, Lang's efforts did not stop with this first demonstration project. He has also fostered and helped a number of other programs in which affluent Americans and their institutions have "adopted" groups of children from impoverished schools, pledging them future support, and providing them assistance, friendship, and help along the way.[11]

The Eugene Lang story suggests a moral. The scholarships he offered were a tangible and visible signal of opportunity, true; but hope for children arises out of everyday interactions with caring adults who provide them with reasons for believing in themselves and with tangible help. If children are lucky, they get this support from their families, but they might also receive this kind of emotional nourishment from teachers or other caring adults associated with their school.

This moral is very exciting, of course, and one test of it is being conducted by the Josiah Macy Foundation, which also developed an innovative program in the 1980s, now called Ventures for Education. This program provides supplementary support for high schools that have a history of poor student achievement.[12] The first group of schools in the program had large numbers of poor and minority children, many of whom spoke English as a second language. They were located in New York City; in New Haven, Connecticut; in Alabama; and near the Navajo Nation in Arizona. The program encourages more rigorous high school course work; provides college preparation experiences throughout high school; helps students prepare for SAT and ACT examinations; funds visits to universities, summer academic programs, and camps; and supports field trips involving hands-on research. But, perhaps most important, it provides counseling and guidance for students from caring adults as well as continuous support for teacher involvement with students and further development of the program.

So what has happened in the schools that were initially helped by the program? Evidence suggests that teacher expectations for both their own performance and for student achievement have risen, and the program has brought handsome dividends to students. In 1987 the high school graduation rate for the impoverished students in Ventures was 30 percentage points higher than the national average for all students. About 90 percent of the black, Hispanic, and white students in the program went on to college—a number far in excess of rates for these groups in the general population. (Many Native American students also went on to college, but the level of "success" for this group could not be assessed since comparable national data were missing.) Moreover, many students from the program chose to enter some of the most difficult and prestigious colleges in the nation—including Brown, Columbia, Cornell, Johns Hopkins, Vassar, and Yale.

In addition, the initial Ventures students have done well in college. Most report that they were well prepared for college classes and that they tended to earn high grade-point averages. When compared with other students, they also obtained scholarships and loans at a higher rate, despite working more hours while in college than did the general population. In sum, the first cohort through the program appears to have achieved marvelously. Caring, attention, and exposure to rigorous course work have helped these poor and minority students start productive lives that should eventually place them in the mainstream of American society.

Another way to provide supplementary services for the children of poor families is suggested by the work of Edward Zigler at Yale. Zigler has argued for years that local schools need to be active places for community renewal. They should be providing parent education, health care, job training, and high quality day care if they are to serve well the children and adults of the communities in which they are located.[13]

Yale is also the home of James Comer, whose model of school improvement is tied to family involvement. Comer's own family experience suggested that children from poor and minority families are more likely to achieve when their families have dignity and hope, and this means that involving those families in their neighborhood schools may be as important as providing a rigorous and well-taught curriculum.[14]

Schools hoping to fulfill the broad visions of Zigler and Comer are now being tried in four cities in Texas, with support from the Hogg Foundation.[15] It is still too early to know whether changing schools into providers of more comprehensive service will produce desired effects, but we are hopeful. In addition, other programs are being explored that could provide models for school districts truly interested in spending money to help impoverished students improve their lives through education.[16]

Is Equity Sufficient?

Although many recent critics of American schools may find this a surprising idea, it can be argued that the cheapest and most efficient way to raise the *average* achievement levels of American students is to provide additional dollars for our worst-funded schools! Thus, at a minimum, our country badly needs at least the same kind of equity in public school funding that is common in other Western countries. But is equity sufficient? Since children in poor neighborhoods usually do not come from families that can provide extensive support for education, their schools will need *extra* funds if America is to realize its long-cherished goal of providing equal opportunity for all students through public education.

Schools in poor neighborhoods need extra funds for several reasons. First, unlike suburban schools, they often have to erect barbed-wire fences, buy weapon-detectors, and hire armed guards in order to be secure. Second, they may need to hire additional school counselors merely to cope with the problems that impoverished and distressed students bring to the school. Third, these schools are often asked to provide outreach services to supplement social or recreational facilities missing in their neighborhoods. But, above all, supplemental programs that can generate dignity and hope, such as those we described above, require additional funds. Thus, instead of merely demanding strict equality in funding, Americans should spend *more* money on schools located in communities where the needs are greatest.

Perhaps you think this is a utopian ideal, unlikely ever to be realized. Think again. In some European countries, particularly in Scandinavia, whenever a school is having difficulty, that school can get extra money. For example, when a school must serve students who have language problems associated with immigration, or when parents become poor because a nearby factory has closed, that school can petition for and receive extra funding. This procedure sounds so fair and sane, and it so obviously would seem to reflect deeply felt American notions about equality of opportunity. Why didn't *we* think of it in *our* country?

In addition, some schools must serve children who have no place to go after school. It would be cheaper by far to fund recreational programs in those schools, to keep children off the streets, than to cope with the crime those children will commit—or at least the mischief they will create—if they are left unsupervised. Some impoverished communities would also benefit from school-based investments in parental education, outreach programs, or family health education. In other areas, such as in the cities of Los Angeles, Miami, and New York, schools serving new immigrants may want to fund bilingual classes for children, English-as-a-second-language classes for adults, and health care for everyone.

Yes, programs such as these will require extra funding for schools in impoverished neighborhoods. But what is the alternative? The problems of those neighborhoods will not go away, and the challenge they pose raises not only moral but very practical questions. Do Americans want to spend money now or later? Do they want to spend money now on education which offers constructive solutions to the needs of young people, or later on punitive actions to cope with problems they might have prevented?

Our own preference is, of course, to spend money now, to provide funds when local educators and their communities have devised plans that respond appropriately to clear needs. Critics suggest that "throwing money at problems" doesn't work, but that is *not* what we are recommending here. Instead, investing in school-based programs designed by local people in response to local needs makes both moral and economic sense—and such investments are clearly preferable to doing nothing.

Doing Something about It

How much funding should we then plan to provide for schools in poor neighborhoods? Our richest communities believe they know what constitutes good public education and are willing to spend ten to fifteen thousand dollars per child per year for it. Since some of the best schooled and most successful citizens in each state live in wealthy communities, we can reasonably assume that those communities provide guidelines for what good education should look like and cost elsewhere in their state. We should, then, use the per-pupil expenditures of those communities as guidelines that indicate the level of funding needed to support high quality education. Through the use of such guidelines, every district in each state would know what a high-quality educational program looked like and how much it cost. And if some communities have exceptional problems, they should be given *more* funds than those provided in wealthy communities.

Where will the money come from to provide equity and these extra resources? During the 1960s and 1970s, Americans turned largely to the federal government for funds that would help impoverished students, and by 1980 federal entitlement programs were generating nearly 10 percent of funds given to schools. However, federal support has proved to be weak. During the Reagan and Bush years, federal funds for education were slashed, and today only about 6 percent of the costs in primary and secondary education are covered by federal dollars.[17] Nor does it seem likely that this figure will rise in the near future. Demands for debt reduction and for funding medical and defense costs remain high at the federal level, and education (which Americans have traditionally conceived of as a local and state responsibility) will probably continue to receive short shrift.

Moreover, it does not seem likely that local school districts, which lacked resources for adequate school funding in the past, will magically acquire these resources in the near future.

This leaves the states as the most likely sources of additional revenue, and here one finds rays of hope. In fact, efforts to reform education funding have already appeared in about half the states, and some of these efforts have actually resulted in some equity. To date, most of these efforts have not involved legislative action. Rather, some citizens from poorer school districts have filed lawsuits demanding that state tax dollars be used to supplement local support. These lawsuits have not always succeeded, however, and even when they were successful, they have only partially solved the problem. Nevertheless, in some states it is now illegal to allow markedly unequal funding among school districts in the state, and one can hope that this principle will presently be applied to even more states across the nation.

But legal action alone will not correct these inequalities totally. Instead, well-meaning Americans must face up to a task they have long shunned, that of persuading their *state* legislators that it is in the public interest to fund schools equitably and to provide extra funding for schools that face special challenges. This will, of course, be a daunting task since most state legislators are successful, affluent people who do not normally think about the longterm advantages of investing tax dollars in ways that will benefit only poorer citizens now—but *all* citizens of their states down the road. In addition, we should remember that sharp differences also appear among the *states* in their present willingness to fund public education. It will eventually require *federal* legislative action to solve this problem.

Summary

Let it be clear—money matters in education; or, to be more precise, money spent *wisely* matters. Money can buy improvements in school buildings, more facilities, more textbooks and computers, smaller class sizes, and a better-paid, better-qualified, more numerous teaching staff—and these improvements will pay off in higher morale and higher achievement levels if applied to schools that are now badly underfunded. In addition, some schools will require extra funding if they are to establish programs needed to meet the needs of America's huge and growing numbers of students from impoverished families.

Plans for raising levels of funding for America's poorest schools *must* be devised. Well-functioning societies have always invested in resources for the common good—among them highway systems, the police, the armed forces, parks and libraries, medical research, public health, and the like. Public education is one of these common goods, and the fundamental goal of public education is defeated when its benefits are unfairly lavished on those who had the happy fate of being born to rich parents. High-quality public education and the opportunity to learn are *rights*, not privileges, in this democracy of ours. And if we do not uphold those rights for *all* our citizens, we can ultimately kiss our affluent democracy good-bye.

On School Size

Principle: *Schooling in America can be improved by reducing the size of our largest schools.*

The large school has authority: its grand exterior dimensions, its long halls and myriad rooms, and its tides of students all carry an implication of power and rightness. The small school lacks such certainty: its modest building, its short halls and few rooms, and its students, who move more in trickles than in tides, give an impression of a casual or not quite decisive educational environment.

These are outside views. They are illusions. Inside views reveal forces at work stimulating and compelling students to more active and responsible contributions to the enterprises of small than of large schools.

—Roger G. Barker and Paul V. Gump (*Big School, Small School,* 1964, p. 195)

Some primary schools in Finland are built to house only a few classrooms and are placed in local neighborhoods, right in the midst of residential areas. Why? Because the designers of those schools want children to be in small, close-to-home settings; to be in environments they know and in which they feel comfortable; to be close to their parents; and to feel that school and home are interwoven. That sounded good to us, so one of us suggested to a local school board that it buy a large house in each of the new housing tracts that were then under development in the community and use these houses for kindergarten and first-grade classrooms. That person was treated as if he was from Mars! It was unheard of! It couldn't be done! A big, anonymous elementary school was built instead. And the young students in these neighborhoods must now be bused to their school, away from their home neighborhoods, away from their nearest care givers and the environments in which they feel most comfortable. No money was saved, and the interests of the children were certainly not served.

Somehow Americans have come to believe that big schools are good and small schools are bad. This notion comes partly from the cult of efficiency that influenced industry early in the century.[18] In response to the efficiency ethic, schools are often designed to mimic production lines, where the economy of size takes precedence over human relationships. Also, Americans seem to be overly influenced by a form of civic boosterism that automatically equates bigger with better. Thus, we are all supposed to rejoice when our communities grow, when more highways are paved, when our industrial plants get bigger, when our population expands, and—by extension—when our schools increase in size.

Americans believe in the virtues of large schools also because of the writings of James Conant, a former president of Harvard and an influential educational theorist, who extolled the virtues of the large comprehensive high school a generation or more ago.[19] In the 1950s, in an era of cheap fuel for buses, the comprehensive high school was lauded for providing the variety of curricular offerings and extracurricular activities that a small rural school could never afford—advanced-placement courses, higher levels of mathematics and science, more foreign languages, sports and cultural clubs, and so forth. Thus, across the country the large regional school was promoted, and small, local high schools were abandoned.

Yet, a good deal of evidence has appeared indicating that large schools have many disadvantages. In pioneering research, completed decades ago, ecological psychologists Roger Barker and Paul Gump studied the activities of students in high schools of different sizes.[20] The authors indeed confirmed that the *very* small high school cannot provide the range of courses and extracurricular activities we have come to expect from the well-run high school in America. But when they compared a middle-sized high school with a large one, they discovered that students' lives were *very* different in these two settings. The two schools offered quite similar types of activities, but because the middle-sized high school had far fewer students, its typical activity tended to have too few participants. As a result, each activity constantly competed for more participants, and the average student participated in *many* more activities. In contrast, too many students in the large school were allowed to remain anonymous. More than enough students were available to fill each of the specialty classes (e.g., Conversational French), the varsity teams, the school clubs, the year-book staff, the cheerleading squad, and the like. This meant that in the large school many students did *not* take specialty classes and did *not* participate in extracurricular activities; worse, they were not missed. Those without marked skills or high status in favored cliques were simply left out of prestigious, events. Moreover, they often felt excluded, because, in fact, they *were* excluded.

Schools of modest size tend to have additional advantages. They promote community feeling and the ideal that students should be sharing ideas and experiences with each other. Affiliation, self-concept as a learner, and motivation to achieve all seem to be higher when a student is in a smaller, more intimate environment. This suggests that student achievement levels should be lower in truly large schools, and this effect has been confirmed by research evidence. Earlier, we mentioned the National Education Longitudinal Study (NELS), a major, ongoing research project that involves about 25,000 students across the nation. Another recent study of NELS data has examined the effects of school characteristics on student achievement. After controlling for other factors known to affect achievement, the authors found that achievement levels were substantially *lower* in large high school.[21]

In addition, smaller elementary schools and high schools can be run both *by* and *for* the teachers and the students. In contrast, the truly large schools too often are run by and for administrators and bureaucracies distant from the site. Control typically becomes more impersonal in large settings, and for this reason, some researchers have recommended that high schools serve no more than 250 students. In larger schools, these researchers claim, administrators become preoccupied with the problems of control and order; thus, teaching, learning, and *caring* are subordinated to those administrative concerns.[22]

Researchers have also put forth a persuasive theory about why students drop out of high school.[23] The theory suggests that dropping out is less likely when a student bonds with the school. Though not a profound insight, this idea summarizes various findings from the research literature and suggests that student attendance and graduation rates can be improved when schools find ways for students to bond with, identify with, and participate in the life of the school. Clearly, students are *far* more likely to bond with smaller schools than with very large ones. (Of course, keeping schools small is not the only way to foster bonding with the school. Later in the chapter we discuss cooperative learning and other strategies that can also help to promote students' bonding.)

All of this suggests that Americans should bend their efforts to prevent the construction of very large schools. But what should be done with very large school buildings that are already in place? Two solutions have been explored for this problem: a large school may be broken up into separate "schools-within-a-school"; or, distinct, specialized programs may be conducted on the site. Today, these specialized programs are commonly called magnet schools.

Schools-within-a-school recreate *some* of the advantages of the small school, albeit within the larger campus. For example, smaller school units might be formed to respond to themes of community service and might be "homes" for cohorts of junior and senior high school students. Each unit might develop a flexible class schedule so that students could work in the community on certain days, and parts of its curriculum could reflect the nature of the work students were doing. Or, a large, comprehensive high school of perhaps two thousand students could be divided into schools of, let's say, four hundred or so students each, in grades nine through twelve. In this model, the smaller school units share some services in common while also maintaining close relationships with students in their own unit. Each of the smaller units is administered by its own cohort of teachers so that every student is known personally to his or her team of teachers. This model fosters cooperative endeavors and high rates of participation within the smaller units and allows for rivalries between units for academic and athletic honors.

The magnet school concept offers another configuration that is useful at the high-school level. Magnet schools are smaller, special-purpose units that offer focused curricula (often leading to early career entry) in specific fields—for example, the performing arts, computer skills, foreign languages, or aerospace technology. Typically, these units are located physically within large, urban high schools or sit on their peripheries, sharing their campuses. They enroll a select group of students, who may take core courses from the larger school setting but who are also offered specialized courses in the magnet school proper. The magnet school keeps students focused and together as it promotes their special interests.

Magnet schools are also considered beneficial for promoting racial and ethnic integration and are sometimes used to bring talented and ambitious students to large, urban school buildings that had previously served only impoverished or minority students. For example, one of us recently helped to study an urban high school that enrolls large numbers of minority students. Five different magnet schools had been established in it to attract students from all over the district. Last year the graduation rate remained low among the school's two thousand regular students; but for the roughly two hundred students enrolled in each of the five magnet schools, the graduation rate was well above 90 percent.

The general moral of our argument should now be clear. Whether students are poor or rich, white or black, average or brilliant, it is easier to teach—and students have richer lives—in medium-sized schools. Large schools discourage high rates of student participation in school activities; students and teachers have difficulty identifying with the culture of the school; and students, bonding with classmates and with the school itself is reduced. As a result, student achievement suffers. Those who design schools for tomorrow need to consider this moral seriously and be prepared to resist arguments for larger and larger schools. And districts that are presently stuck with large school buildings should seriously consider plans for creating smaller units within those schools.

On the Aims of the School Curriculum

Principle: *Schooling in America can be improved by enlarging the goals of curricula. This will require developing thoughtful learning environments where the emphasis is on skills needed for membership in a democratic society.*

Most students, parents, teachers, civic leaders and other citizens have consistently made the cultivation of thoughtfulness a low priority among educational aims, in spite of paying lip service to the ideal for years. Why? [Because] higher-order thinking often calls for the resolution of conflicting views, tolerance for uncertainty and ambiguity, self-criticism, independence of judgment, and serious consideration of ideas that may challenge or undermine conventional wisdom.

Critical thinking also increases the probability of youth challenging adult authority and of citizens challenging economic and political centers of power. Thus, thinking can be considered subversive and socially dangerous by dominant interests whose legitimacy is questioned. Some would argue that the survival of certain social institutions (e.g., advertising, hierarchies of labor within corporations) depends on limiting the opportunity to think to a small segment of the population.

—Joseph Onosko and Fred Newmann (Creating more thoughtful learning environments, 1994, pp. 45–46)

We turn now to an issue that affects nearly all aspects of American education. Unfortunately, a great many Americans have traditionally held concrete and quite limited notions about the aims of school curricula. Worse, narrow and traditional ideas about curricula have been pushed strongly by critics of education during the past few years. We argue that these views are badly out of step with today's world. We need a broader, revised view of curricular aims if efforts to improve America's schools are to succeed.

Traditional Views

Let us assume that Americans were asked to explain what constitutes a good high school education. Many people might answer this question by citing a list of core courses that should be completed—English, mathematics, foreign languages, American history, and so forth. Others might stress knowledge units from those courses. They would argue that well-educated Americans should be able to appreciate literary works, write grammatically, solve compound-interest problems, read graphs, interpret menus in an Italian or a French restaurant, recognize quotations from Shakespeare, know about Franklin Delano Roosevelt, and so forth.

Such answers stress concrete accomplishments on the part of students. The first type of answer stresses specific, core courses that students should take while the second lists facts or skills that students should learn. Both approaches are backward looking and assign a passive role to the student. The aim of education, they assert, is to pump specific types of knowledge from the past into students, and if those students have passed core courses or are able to regurgitate information from those courses, they are—ipso facto—educated people.

One might assume that these traditional views about the aims of education are widely shared, and yet Americans have never actually agreed about them. Before World War II, high schools applied this traditional type of curriculum only to the small, select group of students who were planning to enter college. After the war, as high schools were asked to serve more and more students from different backgrounds, many high schools came to stress a broad range of curricula that focused more on specialized student interests and specific vocational needs. But more and more students were also becoming interested in college. As a result, the traditional curriculum was sometimes no longer required for young people who would eventually enroll in colleges, and traditionalists became worried about a putative "decline" in standards and to argue for a "return to the basics" in curricula.

Arguments for traditional curricula formed one important theme of the Manufactured Crisis, and these arguments have now become quite strident. A good illustration of them can be found in the recent writings of E. D. Hirsch, particularly in his book *Cultural Literacy*[24], and in a series of works setting forth what children at particular grades need to know to be culturally literate, Hirsch urges, for example, that children should know about James Monroe[25], DNA, tectonics, the Treaty of Versailles, Ichabod Crane, and so forth. These concrete bits of knowledge are to be learned by taking core courses in history, biology, earth science, literature, and the like; and high schools should encourage or require all students to take the courses that disseminate these "factoids."

This limited, traditional view of curricular aims was also pushed by leading educationists in the Bush administration and has since been endorsed by the Clinton White House. As we noted earlier, in 1992 the National Council for Education Standards and Testing recommended that concrete, nationwide standards be developed for five core subject areas—English, mathematics, science, history, and geography—"with other subjects to come."[26] These standards were to be backed up by a national system of assessments. Unfortunately, this approach to curricular reform has since been embraced by President Clinton and his supporters.

The New Curriculum: Skills for the Twenty-first Century

The traditional view suggests that schools are mechanisms for pumping bits of knowledge from the past into passive students. Such a view has always been questionable, but today it is truly archaic. Many thoughtful people have discussed problems in our society and the likely needs of the twenty-first century. Not only have vast changes taken place in our country in recent years, but the rate of those changes is clearly accelerating. Most Americans will now have to shift occupations at least once, perhaps many more times, during their lifetimes. Our work force now requires more and more people who can assume professional responsibilities, and this trend will surely continue. The problems of governing our nation become more complex each year, which means that if we are to understand and evaluate the performance of our government, Americans must develop more sophisticated understandings of those problems. And as our mechanical servants make more and more leisure time available, Americans must develop the ability to use their leisure time in independent and socially responsible ways.

All of these changes mean that America needs citizens who are flexible, who embrace new ideas, who can reason well when faced with complex ideas, and who are capable of self-directed learning. It is difficult to understand how citizens with these skills and interests are likely to develop if our high schools merely pump concrete bits of knowledge from the past into passive students. Americans need a broader, revised vision of curricular aims. Now is the time to reconceive the aims of high schools in ways that are more appropriate to the twenty-first century.

Not only is this possible, but various scholars have begun to take up the challenge. To illustrate, let's take economist and educational reformer Henry Levin's advice and list some of the goals of a good high school education in terms of attributes that will be needed in the work place of the next century.[28] According to Levin, the well-educated high school graduate should fit the following description:

- 🍎 Has initiative: possesses the drive and creative ability to think and work independently
- 🍎 Demonstrates cooperation: participates in constructive group activities that accomplish group goals
- 🍎 Can evaluate both self and others: has the ability to assess people or products; can determine their worth and merit
- 🍎 Can train others: has the ability to provide formal and informal instruction and advice to others; can mentor, coach, advise, tutor and train
- 🍎 Can obtain and use information: knows how to find things out and decide what is relevant for the particular purpose for which the information is needed
- 🍎 Can communicate effectively: can speak and write intelligibly and can listen and comprehend what others say or write
- 🍎 Can reason sensibly: can make and evaluate deductive and inductive logical arguments
- 🍎 Can plan: can order priorities so that reasonable schedules for accomplishing things are set and goals are met
- 🍎 Can solve problems: can identify problems, offer potential solutions from among alternatives, and implement actions that might reasonably be expected to solve the problems
- 🍎 Can engage in metacognition: can monitor his or her own activities while doing them
- 🍎 Can earn respect in multicultural settings: can work productively with people from other cultures who are likely to possess different communication styles and values as well as speak different languages

This list of skills is not definitive, of course, but it differs enormously from the concrete bits of knowledge listed by E. D. Hirsch and others who promote traditional curricular ideas. Moreover, the two approaches differ strikingly in their implications for classroom activities. To implement fully a traditional curriculum requires drill and practice, rote learning of facts and definitions, and tests of memory. In contrast, the skills we listed above suggest a curriculum that is more thoughtful, has less focus on rote memory, and allows more student involvement and problem solving. To implement it would require greater stress on teaching methods that feature student-initiated projects, cooperative-learning activities, self-evaluation, peer and cross-age tutoring, having students solve complex and ambiguous problems, self-aware thinking, and multicultural education.

These are radical ideas, far different from the stand-and-deliver classroom model that still dominates American high schools today. As a society, we need to decide which type of student would have an easier time of it and make a better citizen in the twenty-first century—one who knows hundreds of unintegrated facts, or one who can think independently, plan, cooperate with others, and solve complex problems.

Let there be no mistake. We are *not* arguing here that students should be ignorant of the knowledge base that constitutes our cultural heritage. On the contrary, our country badly needs a citizenry that shares such a heritage, but those who cannot think beyond the traditional image of a fact-oriented high school curriculum confuse the necessary with the sufficient. It is *necessary* that students have an appropriate knowledge base, but such a base is far from *sufficient* if students are to be well educated. To have well-educated students, we must greatly expand our view of curricular aims and recast learning activities.

Our argument applies to most, if not all, academic subjects that are now taught. Moreover, it is backed by arguments from experts in various subject fields. For example, leading science educators recommend that science lessons should open with questions about phenomena rather than answers to be committed to memory.[28] They argue that science should begin with discourse that builds on what students already know. Young people must be given opportunities to form hypotheses, collect data, analyze their findings, and talk about what they have learned. They must be allowed to design and carry out scientific projects that are intellectually challenging and require creativity. Alone, or more typically in small collaborative groups, with teacher guidance, young people should be asked to *do* science—not just to study it.[29]

The National Council for the Social Studies recommends that through a "process of active construction of knowledge" teachers and students should think reflectively and make informed decisions about real issues.[30] Teachers should reduce their direct instruction and find ways to help students become independent, self-regulated learners who can work collaboratively to solve authentic civic and community problems.[31]

Teachers of mathematics are also urged to encourage children to explore, develop, test, discuss, and apply mathematical ideas so that they can construct their own mathematical understandings.[32] Mathematics must not be about the teaching of algorithms for the solution of artificial problems. Rather, it should be an active and collaborative activity in which young people learn to uncover the underlying mathematical features of a topic, issue, or situation. "In contrast to current classroom practice in which much of the activity involves students practicing procedures that have been explained or modeled by the teacher, classrooms should provide ample opportunities for students to verbalize their thinking and to converse about mathematical ideas and procedures."[33] Thus, if leading mathematics educators have their way, the new mathematics curriculum will resemble social studies and literature curricula more than the old mathematics curriculum. Truly a revolution in pedagogy is being proposed.

Curriculum Aims and the Psychology of Learning

The types of curricular changes we are recommending also fit well with new understandings about the psychology of learning that have evolved over the past two decades.[34] Ideas psychologists held in the past were more compatible with the notion of a fragmented and decontextualized curriculum, which students were supposed to learn partly through drill and practice. Many psychologists once thought that it was sufficient to encourage individual students to learn through rewards and punishments and then to test them on their ability to reproduce what they had memorized, and this certainly fits with traditional ideas about curricula.

In contrast, psychologists now describe learning as more complex. This reflects greater understanding about the situational specificity of knowledge and how difficult it is for people to transfer knowledge from one realm to another. What students often learn by studying *Julius Caesar*, for example, are bits of knowledge about Rome, and perhaps something about the writing style that Shakespeare employed. It is often very difficult for students to take those knowledge bits and apply them to their own lives and to contemporary issues in city, state, and national politics—for example, to issues of power, political popularity, crowd manipulation, law, and the possibility of justifying political murder. If these kinds of transfer are to be promoted, teachers must lead students to explore how the themes of *Julius Caesar* relate to issues in their own lives or perhaps to create their own meanings from related reading or acting out bits of the play in contemporary settings.

In addition, psychologists are now more likely to view knowledge as something that is actively constructed by the individual.[35] Thus, meaningful knowledge is never really transmitted from an authority to a passive learner; instead, knowledge is created anew by learners as they struggle to integrate what they are learning with everything else they know. So teachers need to help students construct their own interpretations of ideas. But to do all this requires a good deal of time devoted to teacher-student interchange and discussion, and this may mean giving up extensive but superficial coverage of other matters. If we truly wanted students to have *broad* exposure to Shakespeare's tragedies, teachers could whip through *Julius Caesar* in ten days, give multiple-choice or short-answer tests, and then move on to *King Lear*. But the price of such process is that the students' knowledge remains inert, tied only to the ontexts in which it was learned, of little use or interest in the students' subsequent lives. Somehow, we doubt that most Americans would think that such an approach is appropriate for education in the twenty-first century.

Pyschologists are also now more aware of the social forces that encourage earning.[36] They now understand that learning and thinking often are collective as well as individual enterprises, that in the real world they often take place during group interactions. The distinguished Stanford psychologist James Greeno has recently provided a good example of this insight. We all know Rodin's great sculpture, *The Thinker*. This art work has become a widely accepted cultural icon for "Rational Man," for "Reflective Man," for a representation of thinking as a solitary task and the hard work entailed in thinking deep and long.

Now let us envision three girls and two boys, perhaps in the fifth grade, sitting around a computer and talking fast and with great animation to each other, trying to convince each other how they can estimate the world population in the year 2050 from data now available. Greeno rightly asks, why is *his* vision not our cultural representation of people thinking? Why did we choose a solitary, dour figure, possibly in some distress, to represent what can clearly be a joyful, social encounter? The students in the classroom are also thinking hard and for a lengthy period. They, too, are thinking deeply. Why should Rodin's model remain the icon?

If we assume that the small group of students around the computer are indeed learners and thinkers, then some of our old notions about learning and thinking must be expanded. Psychology offers new ideas that emphasize that knowledge is often constructed in group settings, among communities of learners; and in the classroom those communities will include both the teacher and the students. The goal in such settings, then, should be to construct jointly knowledge that is personally meaningful, and this calls for new and innovative types of pedagogy. (It also calls for new and different types of assessment, a matter to which we return later in the chapter.)

Summary

Traditional views of curricula have conceived the school as means for pouring discrete and relatively unintegrated ideas into passive students. These views have always been suspect, but they are now truly obsolete, given the type of citizens America needs for its evolving, postindustrial society. The new curricula we envision should be more concerned with developing thoughtfulness—and we make this recommendation regardless of subject-matter field and regardless of the students' socioeconomic backgrounds. The new curricula should also reflect current understanding of how learning takes place—about knowledge transfer and the social nature of knowledge acquisition. And such curricula will imply many changes in the ways in which Americans conceive of and conduct education in their schools.

On the Evaluation of Achievement

Principle: *Schooling in America can be improved by rethinking and redesigning the system for evaluating student achievement.*

Widely used standardized tests may be hampering efforts to improve math and science education, and they hurt minority students the most.

—Susan Chira (1992)

Let us take this statement from Susan Chira seriously. How can it be that traditional standardized tests might hurt students? One answer to this question was suggested earlier in the chapter. The typical standardized test is constructed of multiple-choice questions that assess students' recall of facts, definitions, and other bits of knowledge; and these tests encourage teachers to use teaching methods that stress little more than acquiring this concrete level of information. And, because teachers who instruct minorities are under the most pressure to produce gains on these tests, minority children often receive the most drill and practice. And in this way they often get the most boring curricula and are hurt the most.

In addition, standardized multiple-choice tests force teachers to focus on broad, superficial coverage. Teachers must maximize curriculum coverage because they do not know the exact test questions students will be asked each time the tests are given. This means that they must cover course content at a gallop, foreswearing the time that might be "wasted" on encouraging reasoning, student thoughtfulness, or applications of course content—which are, of course, the goals of education that most scholars now advocate. The lesson to be learned, then, is that *it is difficult to have both a new curriculum and traditional, multiple-choice tests*. The new curricula and traditional tests make poor bedfellows.

As we stressed in earlier chapters, standardized multiple-choice tests tend to drive the curriculum. If such tests feature no expository writing, expository writing drops out of our schools; and if those tests do not or cannot assess scientific reasoning, then such reasoning will not be taught in science classes.[54] In the end, fewer and fewer changes will appear in our curricula if current, standardized, multiple-choice tests continue to be the sole way we assess student achievement. Unfortunately, though the educational community knows full well how to build better tests, textbook and test publishers are making a lot of money from traditional testing methods. Thus, the testing industry is not keen on ideas that challenge traditional tests, since some of the newer forms of assessment may limit their profits.

What might more useful tests look like? The tests we have in mind should be more *authentic, performance oriented,* and *locally evaluated*. An authentic test confronts students with contextualized, complex, intellectually challenging tasks that represent knowledge in a given discipline. It often requires some form of performance assessment; therefore, authentic tests resemble more the dance recital or art show than they do the annual "herd 'em up, sit 'em down, get 'em going" ritual that accompanies standardized achievement tests.

It is odd that Americans readily accept performance tests as appropriate measures of achievement in the arts and athletics, or for school clubs, while we reject them for core academic subjects. The sports contest, the recital, the debate, the play, and the juried show have long been acknowledged as appropriate means for displaying skill and ability; but we rarely think about performance measures for English, mathematics, history, or physics. However, Grant Wiggins, a critic of traditional testing, has promoted a movement to do just that. He asks, do we truly want to find out whether our students are "deficient in writing, speaking, listening, artistic creation, finding and citing evidence, and problem solving? Then let the tests ask them to write, speak, listen, create, do original research, and solve problems."[55]

An authentic test, then, might ask students to demonstrate a law in physics to parents and other students. Or it might entail a group report for a biology class on the amount of *e. coli* and other bacteria in a stream that runs through the students' town: Or it could be the presentation of a year-long project in social studies on the oral histories of local female senior citizens as they reflect on the role of woman over the course of their lives.

The criteria for success on such authentic tests are designed to be transparent—to be known and understood by both the judges and those who are to be judged. Assessments for an art course or in ice skating provide good models. Generally, over a few months, students prepare their art work or their skating routine for a public exhibition. They prepare with help from parents, teachers, or coaches; and ultimately they are judged by competent individuals from the local community who have expert knowledge of the arts or of ice-skating techniques. The trick with performance assessments is, of course, to have tests worth preparing for and judges with appropriate vision of what constitutes good and bad performance on the tests. But these are not insurmountable problems. Moreover, many people will agree that when students actually demonstrate their literacy, numeracy, scientific thinking or research skills to panels of judges (classmates, other teachers, parents community members), their performances provide better indicators of knowledge than do 30-item, multiple-choice, end-of-the-semester examinations. And this seems to be true even with all the subjectivity and lack of standardization that may accompany performance assessments.

As in much of real life, authentic assessments allow people to get help preparing for the test over an extended period of time. Thus, preparing for an authentic performance test also becomes a major part of the new, integrated curriculum, which students often see as more intrinsically motivating than traditional curricula. Rather than cramming all night before the standardized test, students acquire knowledge of the subject over an extended period.

Moreover, if parents and others from the community act as judges, community understanding of what the schools are trying to accomplish will increase.

Results from performance tests and other records from the student's school work can also be stored in a portfolio, making it easier for teachers to understand a student's growth. Portfolio assessment can also help teachers explain to parents what the class has been doing and how their own child has been growing. (Compare this with the teacher's report of a standardized test result, which might be phrased, "Your child's raw score was 78, which means a grade equivalent of 6.3"; or ". . . a normal curve equivalent of 57." What can a typical parent make of such information?)

Given commitment, leadership, and support, many teachers are quite capable of designing creative, authentic assessment programs; and when such programs are explained to parents, many parents will choose them over standardized multiple-choice tests.[56] Traditional, standardized tests are clearly hampering efforts to improve the schools. If we are to hasten change we must develop and experiment with more performance tests. Performance and portfolio assessments are not yet in widespread use, largely because they are so different from past visions of what assessment ought to be. But they are surely an important part of the school-improvement effort. As our vision of curricular aims is expanded to promote greater thoughtfulness, self-awareness, and competence in students, we will also need a lot more testing procedures that are authentic, performance oriented, and locally evaluated?[57]

This does not mean that standardized multiple-choice tests should be done away with completely. On the contrary, such tests provide an effective means for assessing concrete information, and they will presumably be retained for their ability to evaluate students' command of basic skills, such as the elements of "reading, 'riting, and 'rithmetic." In addition, it is argued that scrupulously prepared, multiple-choice tests are able to tap into some aspects of higher-order skills—although performance assessments provide a more obvious, more integrated way to measure these complex outcomes. Standardized tests are useful tools, then, which have their own strengths and limitations. But we should give greater stress to other procedures, such as performance tests and portfolio assessments, for evaluating advanced levels of students' skills and knowledge.

Endnotes

1. Kozol (1991).
2. Bluestone & Harrison (1982).
3. See, for example, Thomas and Znaniecki (1918) who documented the cultural disintegration of the Polish immigrant families in America. The difficulties of the Puerto Rican immigration experience are described by Lewis. (1966)
4. Steinberg(1989).
5. Drazen (1994).
6. See Biddle et al. (1981).
7. West (1993, pp. x-xi).
8. West (1993, p. 15).
9. Malcolm X (1973).
10. Gugliotta (1993).
11. Hinds (1993).
12. Ventures in Education (1992).
13. Zigler (1989); Zigler & Lang (1 Comer (1988).
14. Comer (1988).

15. Holtzman (1992).
16. Natriello et al. (1990) provide a review of the efforts of schools serve at-risk students.
17. National Center for Education Statistics (1994).
18. Callahan (1962).
19. Conant (1959).
20. Barker & Gump (1964).
21. See Lee & Smith (1994).
22. Gregory & Smith (1987).
23. Finn (1989).
24. Hirsch (1987).
25. See, for example, Hirsch (1991) and Hirsch et al. (1993).
26. National Council on Education Standards and Testing (1992).
27. Adapted from Levin (1993) and Levin, Rumberger, & Finnan (1990).
28. Project 2061 (1989).
29. Project 2061 (1993).
30. National Council for the Social Studies (1994, p. 16).
31. National Council for the Social Studies (1993).
32. National Council of Teachers of Mathematics (1989).
33. Putnam, Lampert, & Peterson (1990, p. 138).
34. Presidential Task Force on Psychology in Education, American Psychological Association (1993).
35. See Driver et al. (1994).
36. See Cobb (1994).
37. Greeno (1994).
45. Cohen (1994a}; Educational Research Service (1990); Slavin (1990).
46. See Sapon-Shevin (1994, pp. 221ff).
47. Levin, Glass, & Meister (1984).
48. Blumenfeld et al. (1991).
49. Gardner (1963, pp. 21–22).
50. Newman (1988).
51. Newman (1988, p. 94).
52. Newman (1988, p. 240).
53. A good discussion of the way American industry has traditionally dealt with leisure may be found in Juliet Schor's *The Overworked American* (1991).
54. Smith (1991).
55. Wiggins (1989, p. 705).
56. Airasian (1991); Shepard & Bliem (1994).
57. Stiggins et al. (1985).
58. Good & Weinstein (1986); Good (1987); Haskins et al. (1983); Oakes (1985); Oakes et al. (1992); Peterson et al. (1994); Talbot (1990).
59. Useem (1992, p. 325).
60. See ASCD (1990). Mara Sapon-Shevin (1994, pp. 219ff) provides additional examples of responses to the threat of doing away with ability groups.
61. Oakes (1985, 1992, 1994); Wheelock (1992); Sapon-Shevin (1994).
62. Carroll (1963); Carroll (1985).
63. Holmes & Mathews (1984); Smith & Shepard (1988); Shepard & Smith (1989).
64. Oakes (1992); Wheelock (1992).
65. See Lareau (1989) and Epstein (1987).
66. Richardson et al. (1989).
67. Lareau (1989).
68. R. Clark (1983).
69. R. Clark (1983); Goldenberg (1985).
70. See Fruchter et al. (1993).
71. Moll & Greenberg (1990); Velez-Ibanez & Greenberg (1989).
72. This argument is made by Raywid (1989) and Nathan (1991). See also Harrington & Cookson (1992).

73. Driscoll (1993).
74. See particularly Cookson (1994, pp. 87ff).
75. Freedman (1993).
76. Heath (1994); Heath & McLoughlin (1994).
77. Holtzman (1992).
78. Popkewitz et al. (1982) provide an example and an analysis of why topdown reforms fail.
79. Giroux (1988, p. 9).
80. Good discussions of this principle may be found in various places, see, for example, Blase & Kirby (1992); Firestone & Bader (1992); and Romanish (1991).
81. Hollingsworth & Sockett (1994).
82. Little (1982).
83. Wasley (1991).
84. See Fantini (1986, Chapter 8).
85. Note particularly a (1985) speech by Albert Shanker, President of the American Federation of Teachers, before the National Press Club.
86. Schneider & Hood (1994).
87. Ashenden (1990, p. 11).
88. See, for example, Lane & Epps (1992).
89. Astuto & D. Clark (1992).
90. Sarason (1990, p. 7).
91. Astuto & D. Clark (1992, p. 99).
92. LeCompte & Dworkin (1991).

Note: For a complete list of references, see pages 363–391 in *The Manufactured Crisis* by Berliner and Biddle

🍎 Ideas for Discussion, Writing and Research

1. Review the findings reported in the selection from *A Nation at Risk* regarding course content, time, and expectations for high school students. With your classmates, develop survey questions focusing on one or more of these areas and survey other students about their related high school experiences. Share your findings in class and compare them to those reported in *A Nation at Risk* in 1983. How have students' experiences in these areas changed or remained the same?

2. Several authors in this chapter characterize the structure of courses in secondary schools as incoherent, fragmented, a kind of "cafeteria-style curriculum," and they suggest that this kind of structure impedes student learning and involvement. Using at least three selections from this chapter and your own experiences, explore the impact of this kind of curriculum on students and discuss how educators might address this problem. (For example, see the excerpt from Mike Rose's *Possible Lives* in Chapter Two for alternatives to the "cafeteria-style curriculum.")

3. According to several of the authors in this chapter, America's schools are expected to do too much, to solve too many of society's problems. Using *A Nation at Risk, America 2000*, and the pieces by Theodore Sizer and David Berliner and Bruce Biddle, discuss what Americans should and should not expect their schools to accomplish.

4. Several authors raise the issue of equality in school funding and increasing federal spending on education—in particular, Harold Howe II, David Berliner and Bruce Biddle, and the authors of *America 2000* and "A Crisis Created by Education Myths." Using information from these selections, explore this issue and formulate your own position.

5. According to Harold Howe II, author of "Sins of Omission in 'America 2000," the entire proposal lacks a sense of reality about the situation of children and youth in America. Their growing diversity is ignored, their growing poverty is not even mentioned, and muddled thinking about their motivation suggests that forcing them to fail tests will awaken a desire to learn." Drawing from other selections you've read in this and other chapters, respond to Howe's criticisms.

6. In "A Crisis Created by Education Myths," the authors discuss seven "myths about education" that have been "accepted by the public, political decision-makers, the media—and some educators." Discuss your reaction to these myths, particularly in light of what other authors in this chapter have to say about the problems facing America's schools.

7. The authors of "Equitable Treatment of Girls and Boys in the Classroom" examine possible reasons for the continuing gender differences in educational preparation and occupational choice among America's youth. They focus in particular on the "hidden curriculum" in many classrooms that "often create[s] an environment alien, if not hostile, to girls." With classmates, select and interview people from a variety of backgrounds about their views on and experiences with gender bias in education. For example, you might consider interviewing parents of elementary-school-aged children, teachers at all levels, and students and teachers in your college's education department. Synthesize and

discuss your findings in class. What conclusions can you draw about how different groups respond to the issue of gender equity in education?

8. David Berliner and Bruce Biddle in "Toward the Improvement of Education" offer "broad principles" and specific ideas for improving education in America. They cite research suggesting that the strongest factor related to student achievement is "hope": "when children have strong visions for their futures, they achieve more. . . . [H]ope is a major predictor of learning!" Drawing from your own experiences and from related pieces in other chapters, discuss the role of hope in educational achievement.

9. According to David Berliner and Bruce Biddle, prejudice and stereotyping are serious issues that need to be addressed in discussions of educational reform. They write:

Ultimately, prejudice corrodes all Americans. It harms African Americans, Asian Americans, Hispanics, Native Americans, and other minority victims *directly* by robbing them of dignity and hope. In addition, it harms other Americans in *indirect* but serious ways. For example it prevents many citizens from recognizing that the children of poverty —often of a different color and ethnicity—are *their* children too. Thus prejudice prevents otherwise decent people from embracing a broader community, which hurts us all.

Examine what other authors you have read have to say about how prejudice and stereotyping—whether based on race, religion, gender, nationality, or class—affect educational opportunities and achievement.

10. The selections in this chapter and others offer a variety of perspectives on what is wrong with America's schools and what needs to be done to improve them. Drawing from your own experiences as a student and/or parent and from information presented in several pieces you've read, discuss what you believe are the most important problems that need to be addressed in order to improve education. Compare your list of problems with those of your classmates and discuss why they are similar or different.